MASTERS OF P[

GW01045188

The Most Poignant and Powerful Homilists in Church History

Ray E. Atwood

Foreword by Jerome Hanus

Hamilton Books
A member of
The Rowman & Littlefield Publishing Group
Lanham · Boulder · New York · Toronto · Plymouth, UK

Copyright © 2012 by
Hamilton Books
First paperback edition 2013
4501 Forbes Boulevard
Suite 200
Lanham, Maryland 20706
UPA Acquisitions Department (301) 459-3366

10 Thornbury Road
Plymouth PL6 7PP
United Kingdom

The hardback edition of this book was previously cataloged by the Library of Congress as follows:

Library of Congress Control Number: 2011941314

ISBN: 978-0-7618-5780-8 (cloth : alk. paper)
ISBN: 978-0-7618-6161-4 (pbk : alk. paper)
eISBN: 978-0-7618-5781-5

Nihil Obstat:	Imprimateur:
Rev. Richard L. Schaefer	Most Rev. Jerome Hanus, O.S.B.
Censor Deputatus	Archbishop of Dubuque

The nihil obstat and imprimateur are official declarations that a book or pamphlet is free of doctrinal or moral error. No implication is contained herein that those who granted the nihil obstat and imprimateur agree with the contents, opinions, or statements expressed.

With gratitude to almighty God
for my parents Ron and Karen, my sisters Gail and Lin,
and my brother priests of the Archdiocese of Dubuque,
I dedicate this book to my family and friends.
Without your loving support, I would not be the priest I am today.
You are God's gift to me, and for you I will always be thankful.

The faith and the tradition of the churches founded in Germany are no different from those founded among the Spanish and the Celts, in the East, in Egypt, in Libya and elsewhere in the Mediterranean world. Just as God's creature, the sun, is one and the same the world over, so also does the Church's preaching shine everywhere to enlighten all men who want to come to a knowledge of the truth.

St. Irenaeus of Lyons
Against Heresies

Contents

Preface

History teaches many lessons, and the history of preaching is no exception. The history of preaching teaches us that divine grace and human will interact and intersect in the Church and the world. God's grace puts us here and calls us to help one another grow in Christ. That grace provides answers to our prayers, solutions to our problems, comfort in our afflictions, and afflictions in our comfort. God's grace inspires, directs, enlightens, and strengthens us. God always makes the first move on the chessboard of life.

But we are on the other side and we have a role to play as well. Human co-operation with God's grace is essential. God will not violate our free will. He wants us to utilize all the skills and resources at our disposal to deliver His Word to His people. One could say that masterful preachers called on God's grace, and utilized their skills, to produce theologically sound and spiritually uplifting messages that touched the lives of countless followers. It is up to us to learn that history as we walk through our time.

Writing a book on the history of preaching in the Catholic Church has been a wonderful but challenging experience. I first thought of writing this book while on retreat in the summer of 1996 at New Melleray Abbey, outside of Dubuque, Iowa. I was reading Paul Scott Wilson's fine work, *A Concise History of Preaching* (1992). While I enjoyed his book, it was obviously written from a Protestant perspective. I read about the fine preachers in Protestantism, but longed to read more about Catholic preachers. Wilson made the point that we will never be able to discuss a broad history of Christian preaching until a history of Catholic preaching is published. This I saw as a challenge for our Church generally, and for me in particular. As a homilist, I have a vested interest in studying the subject of preaching, and spreading that knowledge for the good of the Church.

There are many masterful homilists in our Church, for example, Saint Ambrose, Saint Leo the Great, Saint John Vianney, Archbishop Fulton J. Sheen, and Blessed John Paul II. I searched for a book that included these individuals and other Catholic homilists, but could find none. The desire for a good work on the history of preaching in the Catholic Church started me on a journey that has culminated in this book, which I offer to the Church I greatly love.

I am writing this book for three reasons: First, I love both history and preaching. They are fascinating subjects about which one can never learn enough. History is more than a cold presentation of facts. It is the story of peoples, nations, cultures, and civilizations. In the case of preaching, it is the story of the masterful proclamation of God's Word through the centuries, hence the title of this book. Preaching reveals much about Christian spirituality, challenges to the Faith, and various applications of the Gospel to daily living. Love of both subjects has been the principal motivation guiding me through this project.

Second, as I just mentioned, there is a great void in the literature on Catholic preaching. I have found few good books on the history of Catholic preaching or Catholic preachers. Most published writings focus on the great preachers of the early Church, and Protestant preachers of the sixteenth through the twentieth centuries. There are also numerous collections of homilies, both ancient and contemporary. The quality of these homilies varies greatly: some homilies are excellent, some are poor, and many are mediocre. Obviously much work in the area of homiletics must be done. Information on Catholic preachers themselves is scattered throughout many volumes. That is a void which needs to be filled, and this book is an attempt to fill it. If the void is left unfilled, the Church's rich homiletic heritage will remain unknown, which is both avoidable and unacceptable.

Third, I believe this book can be of great service to the Church. Priests, as well as theologians, seminarians, and historians need good resources, and I hope this will be one of them. Under one cover, this book combines material found in many sources, and succinctly outlines the history of Catholic preaching. This book is not intended only for the clergy. I hope lay people will benefit from it too. I hope they will find it useful for their personal meditation and spiritual growth. In addition, anyone interested in history will see Catholicism's rich history reflected in this book.

One problem in writing a book like this is the sheer number of fine preachers and sermons from which to choose. Determining an appropriate selection of preachers and homilies, while keeping the book to a reasonable length, requires careful thought and reflection, and the application of solid theological, historical, and spiritual principles. Many difficult choices had to be made in preparing this book. I have selected representatives of each historical period, as well as from both the Eastern and Western traditions of the Church. One gets a good sense of the development of preaching, along with the diversity of preaching styles, from this book. It also presents a brief overview of various historical periods in Church life, another subject of deep interest to me.

The purpose of this book is to assist bishops, priests, and deacons in their continuing education for preaching. Its methodology is biographical, and it puts today's preaching in the context of yesterday's preaching. The book is divided chronologically, beginning with the Old Testament period and ending with the Modern and Contemporary Era (which I define as the nineteenth century up to the present). I then present a brief biography of each homilist. The book provides a sample homily from each preacher to illustrate the style he presents, the insights he reveals, and the oratorical skills he practices. I do not expect the reader to use these homilies *verbatim*, but rather to see them as practical examples of the homilist's style and method. They also illustrate the spirituality, theological depth, and pastoral thrust of preaching ministry in each historical era.

The reader will notice several things as he or she goes through my book. First, the diversity of the homilies is great. One can see various pastoral approaches, theological perspectives, and spiritual insights developed by each homilist. The style and theology of the different homilists presented here reflects the diversity of spiritual, personal, and theological experiences of the homilists. It underscores the fact that "one size does not fit all" preachers. In other words, there is no one ideal way to preach. But there are common principles that all masterful preachers follow (e.g., sound theological training, continuing spiritual development, pastoral experience, well-crafted communication skills). These principles, applied to the lives of the homilists here, offer guidance for contemporary preachers of all backgrounds and theological perspectives.

Second, the reader will see history unfold through the centuries through the homilies. Homilies are a prism or lens through which to see our rich history. The reader will see, for example, how the early Christians interpreted Scripture, how the Scholastics supported arguments by using Scripture, and how modern homilists develop biblical themes based on the Scripture readings of the feast or occasion celebrated. Each historical period is different, and it shapes the application of biblical principles in different ways. The reader will see how ancient rhetorical skills are applied in modern circumstances. Clear transitions, a simple message, foreshadowing, referencing, and parallelism are among the skills this book highlights. The reader will walk through Church history with some of our finest preachers. He or she will read Saint Paul's address to the early Christians in Jerusalem, Chrysostom's homily to the Christians in Antioch, Venerable Bede's sermon in Wearmouth-Jarrow monastery, Saint John Vianney's inspiring words in the tiny French village of Ars, and Father Walter Burghardt's address at the John XXIII Pastoral Center in Charleston, West Virginia. You could call it the next best thing to being in the presence of the world's greatest orators. The reader will notice that a title has been inserted for each homilist. This title will help identify the homilist and provide some insight into his work.

Third, the reader should see the combination of scholarship with spirituality in the lives and homilies of our greatest preachers. For example, Saint Alphonsus Liguouri uses the image of fire when discussing the topic of anger, and Father Walter Burghardt illustrates the integration of faith and career in the life of Saint Thomas More, loyal servant of God and king. These men knew both the Scripture and Tradition of our Church, as well as contemporary literature, and developed effective means of illustrating biblical truths. Both scholarship and spirituality are essential for effective preaching. As theologian Karl Barth advised preachers: "Carry a Bible in one hand and a newspaper in the other."

Fourth, the reader will learn various literary genres of homiletics. Different homilists are featured in this book to illustrate these genres. It is up to the reader to decide how well they do this. I introduce the term *pastoral* or *homiletic integrity* in discussing the importance of utilizing the full range of biblical topics. I hope the reader finds this term useful.

In the interest of historical accuracy, I have retained the original spelling and references in some homilies. This explains the various inconsistencies in biblical citations, for example, "Mt.," "Mat.," and "Matt.," and early English usages such as "favour," "neighbour," and "colour."

Fifth, the reader will notice that the author uses numerous Protestant sources in presenting the history of preaching. The reason is simple: there is a dearth of Catholic sources on this topic. As mentioned above, there are many collections of homilies and biographies of homilists, but no Catholic history of preaching exists. I acknowledge the possibility of some distortion in the writing of this history, but one is shaped by one's sources. However, the author understands the Catholic theological perspective within which preaching occurs. Preaching the Word occurs within the context of the Church's sacramental economy. Therefore, Word and sacrament are closely linked. Word should not be emphasized at the expense of priesthood, sacrifice, altar, rituals, images, etc. The purpose of the preaching of the Word is to bring people to a deeper relationship with God, through participation in the sacraments. That participation, embracing Word and sacrament, is essential to Christian spiritual renewal.

Finally, Scripture quotations used herein are from the New American Bible, St. Joseph Edition (1986), with the exception of Our Lord's Sermon on the Mount in Chapter 3. There I have used the Confraternity Edition (1957) of the Challoner-Rheims Version, because its elegance and beauty is appropriate for the setting of that greatest of homilies.

While I have made every effort to ensure historical accuracy in this book, I have noticed discrepancies among various historians. Confusion sometimes multiplies with the abundance of Internet sources. Having said that, any errors contained herein are the responsibility of the author.

This book will have accomplished its goal if it stimulates further interest in preaching, and, more importantly, if it inspires homilists (whether they are Catholic or not) to further develop their preaching skills, so that God's People can be nourished by Spirit-inspired thoughts and reflections on God's revealed Word.

Rev. Ray E. Atwood
June 12, 2011
Pentecost Sunday

Foreword

Father Ray Atwood has served the Archdiocese of Dubuque for seventeen years. He has been an associate pastor in three city parishes and for the last six years has been pastor of five rural parishes called "Holy Rosary Cluster." It takes energy and time to shepherd a flock of more than seven hundred families in five parishes located in three different counties.

One of the duties of a pastor is preaching the Word of God. This is done in various settings, including weekday Mass, rest homes, care facilities, parish halls, schools, and cemeteries. Of course, the summit of weekly preaching occurs at Sunday Mass. Each Sunday the Catholic faithful gather for the celebration of Mass. The Holy Spirit calls God's people together to be nourished at the table of God's Word and the Eucharist. For most Catholics the Sunday homily is the only weekly catechesis and biblical exposition they experience.

There is little time in the busy lives of most people to reflect on Scripture and its application to their lives. Most lack the theological training and spiritual experience to delve deeply into God's Word. It is true that people pray and desire to know God's will. But, like the Ethiopian eunuch in the Acts of the Apostles, they need an interpreter. They require a shepherd to break open the Scripture passages they hear in the Lectionary readings.

That interpreter is usually their pastor. It is important that the priest or deacon who would preach well maintain a healthy prayer life and work to grow in union with Christ. In addition, a good library will feed one's intellectual curiosity and provide material for homiletic reflection. Prayer and study are the two wings that sustain a preacher's work.

In his book, *Masters of Preaching: The Most Poignant and Powerful Homilists in Church History*, Fr. Atwood breaks new ground in the literature of Catholic preaching. He presents a list of the finest homilists in our tradition. Reaching far back into history, he sheds light on each period of the Church's rich history, and reveals to the reader the names, biographies, key theological ideas, and a sample homily (or homily excerpts) of the Church's great orators. In the lives of these men, we see the keys to effective preaching. Those keys include deep spirituality, high intellectual interest, and a strong commitment to discipleship and evangelical zeal.

While different preachers possess various gifts, all preachers can learn from history how to improve their preaching style. Those who have gone before us leave a legacy of learning and practical experience that can enrich our lives and our ministry.

This book is a new resource for homilists and those interested in the field of preaching. I am pleased that a priest from the Archdiocese of Dubuque has taken the time to write it. I hope and pray that all who read Fr. Atwood's book will learn more about the important work of homiletics and be inspired to improve their own preaching.

Most Rev. Jerome Hanus, O.S.B.
Archbishop of Dubuque
June 11, 2011
Vigil of Pentecost

Acknowledgements

I am deeply grateful to those who have assisted me in various ways in this project: to my reviewers, Msgr. Neil Tobin (Archdiocese of Dubuque), deceased; Rev. Richard L. Schaefer, Censor deputatus of the Archdiocese of Dubuque, who made significant suggestions; and Dr. Allen Frantzen (Loyola University, Chicago); to the Sheen Archives in Rochester, New York and Peoria, Illinois; to the caretakers of St. Sixtus' Parish in Ars, France; to Msgr. Frank Chiodo (Diocese of Des Moines), who inspired me to become a priest and taught me the essentials of preaching; to Paul Scott Wilson, whose book inspired me to write my own book on the history of preaching; to my Josephinum Seminary Church History teacher, Msgr. Roger Cooney (Diocese of Covington, Kentucky), whose intelligence and academic curiosity have been an inspiration to me; to Mr. Sam Kramer, who spent many hours helping to prepare the final version of the text; to my able assistant Alix Paulus, whose patience and efforts were invaluable; to my editor, Laura Espinoza, whose advice and guidance were very helpful; to my father, Ron, who strongly encouraged me to write a book on a worthy topic, and who encouraged me throughout this project. I also wish to acknowledge the contributions of many others to this book. None of those who assisted me with this project bears any responsibility for its shortcomings.

Introduction

But how can they call on him in whom they have not believed?
And how can they believe in him of whom they have not heard?
And how can they hear without someone to preach?

Romans 10:14

THE SUBJECT OF PREACHING is an important one in the life of the Church. There is no doubt that good homilies touch and transform the lives of individuals and communities, and even impact civilizations. The homily usually occurs within the context of the sacred liturgy. The Church teaches that the homily is a liturgical act. Each Sunday, the faithful gather to sing the praises of God, to thank Him for the blessings of the past week, and to ask His help for the week ahead. In the course of the sacred liturgy, the faithful listen to God's Word as presented in the Church's three-year Sunday Lectionary cycle.

The homilist breaks open the Word that has been proclaimed. He may do this in several ways. Some homilists reflect on general themes in the Old and New Testament readings. Many direct their thoughts to a particular reading. Still others focus on a line or even a word in one reading. It all depends on how the Spirit moves a particular preacher.

The most effective preachers also tie their messages into contemporary events. For example, a recent book about heaven offers a fresh perspective on an eternal reality; an earthquake in Japan echoes the turmoil in the life of the Apostles; a local school shooting brings home the violence of a culture of death decried in a prophetic text; the recovery of a wounded congresswoman highlights the importance of faith and patience taught by Jesus; a World Series victory underscores the values of teamwork, cooperation, and skill found in a Pauline text about the Mystical Body of Christ. Real world stories, illustrations, images, and ideas can make the difference between abstract homilies that bore people to tears, and transformative homilies that inspire people to live their faith.

The homilist's prayerful reflections enable people to grow in their relationship with Christ as they better understand God's Word. In fact, they bring people into contact with Jesus Christ, who can change their lives in unimaginable ways. These reflections will also deepen their involvement in the Church, and thus continue building on the solid foundation which He laid.

Like other periods of history, our century contains tremendous opportunities for human growth and development, as well as the frightening possibility of world destruction. Science, technology, and ever-expanding knowledge are shaping peoples' lives in ways we could scarcely have imagined even twenty years ago. Whether we use the tools we have for good or evil depends on the degree to which we are in touch with God's saving grace. This was a point made in the Second Vatican Council's document *Gaudium et Spes* (The Pastoral Constitution on the Church in the Modern World), in December 1965. It is as true today as it was then.

The Word of God is here for our reading and reflection. That Word is not a letter on a page, but rather a dynamic reality that must be pondered, reflected upon, prayed on, and put into practice in order to have a positive impact on our world. That Word became flesh in the Person of Jesus Christ, who calls us to continue building the Church that He founded. Preaching is one of the ways we build our Church. Prayerful reflection is a key tool that all great homilists have employed in their sacred work. Daily time with the Lord in the quiet of one's room, church, or chapel gives the Lord time to speak to us. Hours spent before the Blessed Sacrament are indispensable homiletic aids. Prayer puts us in touch with the Holy Spirit, which is necessary if we want to be effective preachers. The saints stress the importance of Eucharistic adoration, especially for those in ministry. After all, how can we preach to others unless we allow the Lord to preach to us?

Intellectual curiosity and love of truth are two qualities of great homilists. The desire to learn results from love of truth, and love of truth leads one to desire to learn. It is false humility to claim that the Lord is the only actor in the drama of preaching. Of course, the Lord inspires, strengthens, and enlightens the homilist. He is indispensable to our work. But the Lord also gives us gifts and talents, in particular the gifts of our intellects. Not everyone is equally talented intellectually, but we can all read and learn at some level. With new technologies (e.g., the Internet, smartphones, iPads, Kindle readers, and computers), we have a world of information and ideas at our fingertips. These tools not only assist us in studying the Word of God as it is understood in and by the Church, they also connect us with the secular world in which our people live and work every day. Using the tools of solid theological research and biblical commentary, we can acquire and disseminate saving truth to our people. That truth is right in front of us. We just have to embrace it.

History demonstrates that various types of preachers exhibit various styles of preaching. The prophetic preacher uses one approach, and the evangelistic preacher uses another approach. Saint Paul, speaking of the Church as the Mystical Body of Christ, explained that each member of the body contributes to its overall function (just as in the physical body, the eye, the ear, and the foot each have a significant function). The same is true of preaching. God made us as unique individuals, and He gives various styles to enable us to approach the rich diversity of our congregations. In the end, these different styles are a tool for bringing the Word to each human heart.

The gift of the Holy Spirit is most important. It goes without saying that the Holy Spirit is the principal agent at work in the lives of preacher and listener alike. God, who inspired the biblical writers, continues to inspire biblical preachers. Without God, a preacher's words are meaningless, and can never touch hearts. In the end, the Lord will take our feeble words and transform them into a message that will touch the hearts of God's people.

Homilists put us in touch with God's grace and inspire us to call upon the Lord for help. They proclaim the saving truth of Christ in light of contemporary events, using clear language, in order to make the biblical message come alive in the hearts, minds, and lives of God's people. These people are the instruments God uses to touch the homes, workplaces, schools, hospitals, and other cultural centers of the world. The degree to which they change the world for good is the degree to which they themselves have been changed by the Word. If the Word touches a heart open to truth, that person can bring about enormous good. If the Word falls onto a closed heart, that person will make little positive difference in the world. The preaching moment is a key means of forming God's people so they can make that positive difference.

We humans have inherited a fallen nature. Darkness rather than light often dominates our lives. We do not "do the good we should do." Like the Ethiopian eunuch in the Acts of the Apostles, people need an interpreter. That eunuch was blessed to have the Word proclaimed to him by one of the first deacons of the Church (Acts 6:5-7; 8:26-40). Like him, we need an authentic teacher to guide us in the Christian life. Homilists too have a mandate from the Lord, and charismatic gifts which can help fulfill that mandate. The preacher is an interpreter of God's Word. Good preaching can shed light on our lives and guide us in the Lord's path, a path that can transform our Church and world.

Chapter 1
The Essence of Good Preaching

Presbyters who preside well deserve double honor,
especially those who toil in preaching and teaching.
1 Timothy 5:17

B EFORE DISCUSSING the Church's greatest preachers, it is essential to understand clearly what the Church means by preaching. What is the essence of
good preaching? In other words, what is a homily and how does it fulfill the
Lord's command to "make disciples of all nations" (Matt. 28:19)?

DEFINING THE HOMILY

It is easy to find a good definition of a homily. *The American Heritage Dictionary of the English Language* defines a *homily* (somewhat amusingly) as "a sermon, especially one intended to edify a congregation on some practical matter; a
tedious moralizing lecture or admonition."[1] A *sermon* is also defined as "a religious discourse delivered as part of a church service; any discourse or speech;
especially a lengthy and tedious reproof or exhortation."[2] (Of course, a good
homily or sermon is not tedious). The word *sermon* was used to describe homilies in the past. The words homily and sermon are used interchangeably today.

The *Modern Catholic Dictionary* defines a homily as

> a sermon or informal discourse on some part of the Sacred Scriptures. It aims to
> explain in an instructive commentary the literal meaning of the chosen text or
> subject and from this develop a practical application for the moral or spiritual
> life.[3]

It also indicates some methods of preaching:

> treating separately one or more parts of the biblical reading; combining the Scripture texts into a single idea; concentrating on some virtue or vice suggested by the Gospel text; paraphrasing a Bible passage as a basis for an exhortation to the people.[4]

The Catholic Source Book defines a homily as "a talk on a religious topic, usually at a worship service."[5] The homily is an explanation of a biblical text that contains a spiritual message. It is a living explanation of God's Word proclaimed in a liturgical setting. The homily is a liturgical act, part of the sacred liturgy itself.

The Jerome Biblical Commentary defines a biblical homily in two ways: "either (1) an explanation centered on the literal sense of a biblical passage, its setting, thought and import; or (2) an explanation and development of a biblical theme that runs through many passages."[6]

The U.S. Bishops' document *Fulfilled in Your Hearing* calls the homily

> a Scriptural interpretation of human existence which enables a community to recognize God's active presence, to respond to that presence in faith through liturgical word and gesture, and beyond the liturgical assembly, through a life lived in conformity with the Gospel.[7]

The goal of the homily is to effect concrete change in the listener's life.

LITERARY GENRES

A *genre* is a category of art or writing.. A *literary genre* refers to differing styles or approaches to writing. Preaching also can be analyzed by categories or styles. Hughes Oliphant Old discusses five major genres of preaching in his seven-volume work on the history of preaching.[8]

The first is *expository preaching*. This is a systematic explanation of Sacred Scripture done on a regular basis. This type of preaching goes back to the synagogue services when the Torah was read, Sabbath after Sabbath. Two examples are found in Moses' reading of the Torah from Mount Sinai and in Ezra's reading at the water gate (Exod. 19:20–24:17; Neh. 8:1–18). Thus the Word of God was unfolded before the Chosen People. Old cites Jesus Christ, Origen, Saint John Chrysostom, and Saint Bernard of Clairvaux as outstanding expository preachers.

Evangelistic preaching is a second preaching genre. It is the proclamation of the Christian message of repentance, discipleship, and obedience to Christ. "Evangelistic preaching in its more proper sense announces that the time is fulfilled; the time [for Christ] has come."[9] Evangelistic preaching involves baptizing, teaching, and making all people disciples of Jesus Christ. Jesus Christ, Saint

Paul, Origen, Saint Dominic, and Saint Francis are examples of this type of preaching.

Catechetical preaching is a third genre of preaching. Catechetical preaching expounds Christian beliefs by explaining the Creed, the Commandments, the Sacraments, and the Lord's Prayer in a systematic way. It assumes baptism and basic Christian belief and seeks to deepen that belief through a detailed presentation of the whole Christian message. Saints Gregory Nazianzus, Cyril of Jerusalem, Ambrose of Milan, and Augustine of Hippo exemplify catechetical preaching.

A fourth genre is *festal preaching*. Festal preaching describes and explains the significance of certain feast days in the Church's liturgical calendar. Its content is the feast day rather than the Scriptures. Peter's Pentecost sermon, in which he explains the unusual occurrences in Jerusalem, is a classic example of festal preaching (Acts 2:14–41). Melito of Sardis' Easter Sermon, preached in the middle of the second century, is another example. Saints Augustine, Gregory Nazianzus, Leo the Great, Venerable Bede, Saints Bernard of Clairvaux, and Anthony of Padua were festal preachers. They have left the Church a rich body of commentary and reflection on the feasts we celebrate each year.

A fifth kind of preaching is called *prophetic preaching*. Prophetic preaching is a message delivered to a specific place at a specific time. It is often outside the established religious order. The prophets Jeremiah, Isaiah, Elijah, Amos, Micah, and John the Baptist clearly fall into this category. Saints John Chrysostom and Bernardine of Siena are two Christian examples of prophetic preaching, delivering messages meant to encourage repentance and reflection.

There is another distinction the reader might find useful. It is the distinction between *ideal preaching* and *pragmatic preaching*. Ideal preaching challenges the listener to make a decision to move toward the ideals of a Christ-centered, Spirit-filled life. The ideal preacher takes the core message of the Scriptures as his starting point and develops it. He filters the message through the image or parable used by Jesus (e.g., weeds among the wheat) and reframes it using a contemporary image (e.g., family disintegration in our culture). He retranslates the message to help the listener grasp it. The retranslation or reconstruction of the message must be in an image that people can understand and to which they can relate. The preacher's goal is to move people to make a decision about the practice of their faith (e.g., go to Confession, forgive someone who has hurt you, read Scripture more often). A pragmatic preacher, on the other hand, simply restates the biblical message. He does not develop the message or use a contemporary image to illustrate it. My good friend, Monsignor Frank Chiodo, Pastor of Saint Anthony's Parish in Des Moines, Iowa, has employed the ideal preaching method with great effectiveness. The homilists in this book also employ elements of the ideal preaching method.

These provide a framework for understanding the preachers and homilies that follow. They are certainly not exhaustive but can be highly useful for the purposes of this book. Let us look now at the Church's official teachings on the role of homilies in Catholic liturgical tradition.

THE CATECHISM OF THE CATHOLIC CHURCH

The *Catechism of the Catholic Church* (hereafter cited as *CCC*) defines a homily as follows: "Preaching by an ordained minister to explain the Scriptures proclaimed in the liturgy and to exhort the people to accept them as the Word of God."[10] The *Catechism* refers to the homily in several sections. The homily is first mentioned explicitly in Part One, "The Profession of Faith," which talks about how we grow in our understanding of the gift of faith. We grow in part "from the preaching of those who have received, along with their right of succession in the episcopate, the sure charism of truth" (*CCC* 94). It later talks about the homily in "Sacred Scripture in the Life of the Church."

> The 'study of the sacred page' should be the very soul of sacred theology. The ministry of the Word, too—pastoral preaching, catechetics and all forms of Christian instruction, among which the liturgical homily should hold pride of place—is healthily nourished and thrives in holiness through the Word of Scripture (*CCC* 132).

In Part Two, "The Celebration of the Christian Mystery," the *Catechism* says, quoting Vatican Council II:

> In the celebration of the liturgy, Sacred Scripture is extremely important. From it come the lessons that are read and explained in the homily and the psalms that are sung. It is from the Scriptures that the prayers, collects, and hymns draw their inspiration and their force, and that actions and signs derive their meaning. (*CCC* 1100)

The fourth reference also is in Part Two, describing the Mass, when it says:

> The *Liturgy of the Word* includes 'the writings of the prophets,' that is, the Old Testament, and 'the memoirs of the apostles' (their letters and the Gospels). After the homily, which is an exhortation to accept this Word as what it truly is, the Word of God, and to put it into practice, come the intercessions for all men. (*CCC* 1349)

THE LECTIONARY

The Introduction to the *Lectionary* discusses the relationship between the homily and the rest of the Mass: "Through the readings and homily Christ's paschal mystery is proclaimed; through the sacrifice of the Mass it becomes present. Moreover Christ himself is always present and active in the preaching of his Church."[11] The homily leads the Catholic community to actively celebrate the Eucharist, so they will put into practice their baptismal faith.[12] It draws out the

implications of our Lord's suffering, death, and resurrection and gives the community spiritual nourishment before they partake of the sacrifice of the Mass.

The Church emphasizes the Lord's presence in the homily.[13] There are special graces that flow from preaching. Christ Himself is present in a unique and
special way when we preach. The effects can last for weeks, months, or years
after a homily is preached (Prov. 10:21; 12:19, 22; 15:2, 4, 7).

The *Lectionary* provides specific guidance on liturgical preaching.

> Through the course of the liturgical year the homily sets forth the mysteries of
> faith and the standards of the Christian life on the basis of the sacred text. Be-
> ginning with *The Constitution on the Sacred Liturgy* [*Sacrosanctum Concilium*,
> hereafter cited as *SC*], the homily as part of the liturgy of the word has been re-
> peatedly and strongly recommended and in some cases it is obligatory. As a
> rule it is to be given by the one presiding . . . From this living explanation, the
> word of God proclaimed in the readings and the Church's celebration of the
> day's Liturgy will have greater impact. But this demands that the homily be
> truly the fruit of meditation, carefully prepared, neither too long nor too short,
> and suited to all those present, even children and the uneducated.[14]

The *Lectionary* makes some excellent practical points for the homilist:

First, the homily must lead the community to a more active celebration of
the Eucharist. This means it must inspire people to sing and pray by touching
their hearts with God's Word. A good homily enhances the peoples' participation in the Eucharistic celebration.

Second, it must be the fruit of meditation. Prayer is the best preparation for
any homily. All the preachers featured in this book were men of prayer. They
spent hours before the Blessed Sacrament and in the quiet of their own rooms
praying and reflecting on the liturgical readings. Those holy hours bore fruit in
the words they spoke and the insights they provided to their listeners.

Third, the homily must be carefully prepared. Priests who "let the Spirit do
all the work" do a disservice to their people (and to the Holy Spirit, who gives
us the gift of our minds!). The preacher must prepare his homily well. This
means reading the sacred text carefully, pondering its meaning, doing some textual study from good Catholic biblical commentaries, and even writing it out. I
believe homilies should be written out for several reasons: They keep us focused
on our topic, they enable us to say what we need to say in a reasonable time, and
they are a journal of our spiritual lives. Looking back on past homilies can tell
us a lot about where we were in the past. Finally, they are useful in case we are
ever misquoted.

Fourth, it must be the right length. Generally, good homilies last eight to
twelve minutes. We will see that the great preachers spoke at length to their
congregations, but times have changed. Technology (television and the Internet,
in particular) has created a culture of short attention spans and the desire for
succinct messages. People don't have the patience they once did, so our homilies

should be of a reasonable length. In the secular world, television newscasts are made up of short segments meant to communicate clearly and concisely. We can learn from this fact. The Church lives within this context and should communicate in a similar fashion. Like it or not, we as clergy will accomplish more if we respect the people's sense of time.

Finally, the homily must be suitable to all. Everyone in the congregation should be able to understand it. The topic must be appropriate and take into account the various ages and backgrounds of the congregation. We should keep in mind that the Holy Spirit will touch different people in different ways through the homily, but we should do our best to create a suitable vehicle for Him to use.

BIBLICAL INJUNCTIONS

We preach in part because we are told to preach. Preaching is as old as the Scriptures themselves. God's Word was passed to His people through preaching. Throughout the Scriptures people are told to spread God's messages. In the Old Testament, the Hebrews were told through sermons how to keep the commandments and ordinances of the Lord. The prophets were told to call God's people to conversion and fidelity. The Wisdom books comprise mini-homilies.

The psalmist talks about the role of the Word in the universal reign of the Messiah: "I will proclaim the decree of the LORD, who said to me, 'You are my son; today I am your father'" (Ps. 2:7). He says that the Lord gives His Word to those who preach good tidings with great power. The prophet Isaiah spoke the words that were fulfilled eight hundred years later in the Person of Jesus Christ:

> The spirit of the Lord GOD is upon
>   me,
>   because the LORD has anointed me;
> He has sent me to bring glad tidings to
>   the lowly,
>   to heal the brokenhearted,
> To proclaim liberty to the captives
>   and release to the prisoners,
> To announce a year of favor from the
>   LORD
>   and a day of vindication by our God,
>   to comfort all who mourn. (Isa. 61:1–2)

Our Lord was found in the temple at the age of twelve, "sitting in the midst of the teachers, listening to them and asking them questions." He was following the Jewish tradition of gathering in the Temple to discuss the law. Jesus gave us his own example of preaching and teaching. Early in His ministry He went into a synagogue at Nazareth and explained the words of the prophet Isaiah. (Luke 4:14-21) After Easter, the Lord walked with two of the disciples to the village called Emmaus. He explained to them all that the prophets and psalms foretold of Him. Then He revealed Himself in the breaking of the bread,. The disciples later said to one another, "Were not our hearts burning [within us] while he spoke to us on the way and opened the scriptures to us? (Luke 24:32).

That is preaching at its best: setting the hearts of Christ's disciples on fire by explaining the Word of God to them. Good preachers not only inform, they inspire us to follow the Lord more closely. They touch the heart as well as the head. Before ascending to Heaven, Our Lord commanded His followers:

> Go, therefore, and make disciples of all nations, baptizing them in the name of the Father, and of the Son, and of the holy Spirit, teaching them to observe all that I have commanded you. And behold, I am with you always, until the end of the age." (Matt. 28:16–20)

He sent them out to win souls for the Kingdom. Preaching and teaching were part of this mission. Saints Peter and Paul preached and proclaimed the Word in the various Christian communities they established. Preaching was one means of calling people to discipleship and teaching them its implications.

ECCLESIAL DUTY

Henri Daniel-Rops points out that many breviary readings, which explain the Gospels from various Masses of the liturgical cycle, are taken from sermons actually preached: among the Latin Church Fathers, from Saints Augustine, Ambrose, Leo the Great, and Gregory the Great; from among the Greeks, Saints John Chrysostom, Gregory Nazianzen, and John of Damascus.[15] These readings are a source of grace and inspiration to priests, religious, and laity each day. The Church holds preaching to be an essential element of its public worship.[16] That is why the Councils of Trent and Vatican II stipulated that sermons be preached by clergy and listened to attentively by the faithful on Sundays and feasts. Pope Benedict XV once reminded bishops: "The duty of preaching, as the Council of Trent teaches, 'is the paramount duty of bishops.' And the Apostles, whose successors the bishops are, looked upon it as something peculiarly theirs."[17]

Preaching is a duty. Saint Lawrence of Brindisi described it as a duty that is "apostolic, angelic, Christian, divine."[18] But it is also a tremendously gratifying experience for the homilist, who looks forward to every weekend homily, thinks and prays about the readings for the coming week, and looks for ways to illustrate the message. And the illustrations are there too. As Pope Paul VI put it, "There are in fact innumerable events in life and circumstances in which men find themselves which furnish the occasion for preaching."[19] Many priests tell me how much they enjoy preaching (as opposed to attending pastoral council meetings, mediating staff disputes, and preparing parish financial reports!). Preaching is one of the most satisfying things priests do, in part because it was one of the central features of Our Lord's ministry and contains blessings for the preacher and the congregation. We preach because that's what God expects us to do, and we do it out of love for Him. Let us now look back at our rich history to learn more about preaching.

CHURCH HISTORY

Joseph Jungmann, the great liturgical scholar, provides some interesting history in his discussion of the homily in his magnum opus, *The Mass of the Roman Rite: Its Origins and Development.* "The sermon, which (together with its embellishments) is delivered in the vernacular after the Gospel, is currently regarded as an interpolation in the course of the liturgy rather than as a step forward in its progress," he wrote back in 1950.[20]

> As a matter of fact, however, it belongs to the earliest parts, linked to the pre-Christian elements of the liturgy. The Sabbath Bible reading in the synagogue, which according to rigid custom had to be followed by a clarifying explanation, was for our Lord the main opportunity for preaching the word of God to receptive hearers and to proclaim His Kingdom.[21]

In the early church, Saint Paul would preach at celebrations of the Holy Eucharist (Acts 20:7–11). At Antioch in Pisidia, "Paul and Barnabas, in similar circumstances, were ordered by the rulers of the synagogue to direct 'a word of encouragement' to the assembly," according to Jungmann.[22] (Acts 13:15).

In Christian worship, the homily was joined at the very start to the reading of the Sacred Scriptures. Saint Justin Martyr testifies to this in his *First Apology*: "When the reader has finished, the president in a discourse urges and invites us to the imitation of these noble things."[23] Indeed, the homily was considered to be an essential part of public worship, which took place on the Lord's Day.[24] The bishop who presided over the assembly would address the congregation after the Scripture readings. In his treatise *Against Heresies* (*Adversus Haeresus*), Irenaeus reminds us:

> The faith and the tradition of the churches founded in Germany are no different from those founded among the Spanish and the Celts, in the East, in Egypt, in Libya and elsewhere in the Mediterranean world. Just as God's creature, the sun, is one and the same the world over, so also does the Church's preaching shine everywhere to enlighten all men who want to come to a knowledge of the truth.[25]

Irenaeus talked about homilies in his *Demonstration of the Apostolic Preaching*. We also have extant homilies by Saint Clement, Origen, Saints Hippolytus of Rome, Jerome, Chryostom, Gregory the Great, Leo the Great, and others, which were delivered after the Scripture readings at Mass. In the fourth century, it became customary in the East, when several priests were present at the sacred liturgy, for each one to take his turn preaching after the reading.[26]

Saint Vincent Ferrer, a Spanish Dominican priest who lived in the fourteenth century, wrote a treatise on the spiritual life, in which he advised priests as follows:

> When you treat virtuous and sinful acts in your sermons and exhortations, use simple language and sensible idioms. Give apt and precise examples whenever you can. Each sinner in your congregation should feel moved as though you were preaching to him alone. Your words should sound as though they were coming, not from a proud or angry soul, but from a charitable and loving heart. Your tone of voice should be that of a father who suffers with his sinful children, as though they were seriously ill or were lying in a huge pit; and he struggles to free them, raise them up and cherish them like a mother, as one who is happy over their progress and the hope they have of heaven's glory. This way of preaching has proven profitable to congregations; for an abstract discourse on the virtues and vices hardly inspires those who listen.[27]

Adrian Fortescue, another prominent liturgical scholar, says the following about the homily:

> The priest who preaches to his people after the Gospel on Sunday morning follows the example of his predecessors in all ages back to the Apostles, and performs what is really an element of the liturgy itself—especially if his sermon explains the lessons, if he 'exhorts them to follow these glorious examples.'[28]

This idea that the homily is an element of the sacred liturgy is an ancient one.

In certain places, priests were actually banned from preaching due to various controversies and the defection from the Catholic Faith of many priests and bishops. Jungmann tells us that "after the fall of Arius, preaching was forbidden to priests at Alexandria [Egypt]."[29] He notes that "A similar practice [prevailed] for a long time in Italy and in Rome."[30] The ancient historian Sozomen claims that in his day no preaching was done in Rome. However, the homilies of Popes Leo I and Saint Gregory prove that this noted historian was exaggerating.[31] Church authorities did restrict preaching in some places, however, because of their lack of confidence in its orthodoxy. When faced with the possibility of false proclamation, restrictions on preaching were deemed the more prudent course of action.

Preaching was restored in the Middle Ages (e.g., in Germany and Northern Italy). The sermon then often followed the Creed, which was an expansion of the Gospel. Fortesque tells us that since about the ninth century, "a custom arose North of the Alps, of making a general confession and absolution [similar to the *Confiteor*] after the sermon."[32] This practice spread in Germany and Gaul, "and eventually found its way to Rome."[33] The Second Vatican Council restored the homily to its original place, and emphasized the importance of preaching, requiring it on Sundays and Holy Days of Obligation.

CANONICAL NORMS

The 1983 *Code of Canon Law* (CIC) devotes eleven canons to "The Preaching of the Word of God." A review of these canons will help us better understand the juridical dimensions of preaching. The *Code* deals primarily with the faculties for preaching. It tells us who can preach and provides some norms on preaching itself:

- Sacred ministers are to hold their preaching function in esteem, c. 762.
- Bishops have the right to preach everywhere, unless the local bishop forbids it for a particular reason, c. 763.
- Priests and deacons also have the right to preach everywhere unless the local ordinary forbids it, or their faculties are restricted or removed, c. 764.
- Only competent religious superiors can give permission for preaching to religious in their communities, c. 765.
- Lay persons may preach in churches or oratories *only in particular situations*, c. 766.
- The homily is one form of preaching. It is reserved to a priest or deacon. It explains the mysteries of faith and the norms of Christian life from a sacred text used throughout the liturgical year, c. 767, §1
- A homily is required at all Masses on Sundays and holy days of obligation, and can only be omitted for a grave cause, c. 767, §2.
- A homily is strongly recommended at daily Mass, especially during Advent, Lent, Feast Days, "or a sorrowful event," c. 767, §3.
- The pastor or rector of the Church is to observe these precepts "conscientiously," c. 767, §4.
- Preachers are to propose to the faithful those things which one must believe and do for the glory of God and the salvation of souls, c. 768, §1; c. 1752.
- Homilists also are to impart doctrine set forth by the Church's Magisterium concerning the dignity and freedom of the human person, the unity and stability of the human family and its duties, our social obligations, and "the ordering of temporal affairs according to the plan established by God," c. 768, §2.
- Christian doctrine is to be set forth in a way accommodated to the condition of the listeners and "in a manner adapted to the needs of the times," c. 769.
- At certain times (e.g., Lent, Forty Hours Devotions) pastors should arrange preaching for spiritual exercises and sacred missions, c. 770.
- Pastors of souls are to proclaim the Word of God to those who lack ordinary pastoral care, c. 771, §1.
- Pastors are to spread the Gospel to non-believers, since they are responsible for the care of their souls as well, c. 771, §2.
- In the exercise of preaching, the norms issued by the diocesan bishop are to be observed, c. 772, §1.

- In giving a radio or television talk on Christian doctrine, the prescripts of the Conference of Bishops are to be observed, c. 772, §2.

Canon Law deals with the legal dimensions of preaching (who can preach, when they should preach, and the basic content of preaching). The *Code* regulates the ministry of preaching and sets out broad guidelines for its content. The documents of the Second Vatican Council provide more insight into the Church's understanding of liturgical preaching.

VATICAN COUNCIL II

The Second Vatican Council was the most important ecclesial event of the twentieth century. The council, held from 1962 to 1965, set out to reinvigorate Catholic life through the reform of the Sacred Liturgy. The Church began implementing the council in Advent 1964, when the priest started facing the people at Mass. One improvement of the Church's liturgical celebration was the addition of the three-year Sunday reading cycle, which opened the treasury of the Bible to the faithful (*SC* 35, 51). Year A covers the Gospel of Saint Matthew, Year B covers the Gospel of Saint Mark, Year C covers the Gospel of Saint Luke, and Saint John is interspersed throughout all three years. *Sacrosanctum Concilium* emphasized the importance of preaching God's Word:

> By means of the homily the mysteries of the faith and the guiding principles of the Christian life are expounded from the sacred text during the course of the liturgical year. The homily, therefore, is to be highly esteemed as part of the liturgy itself. In fact at those Masses which are celebrated on Sundays and holy days of obligation, with the people assisting, it should not be omitted except for a serious reason."[34]

The Council makes the following points about the homily:
- The homily explains the Scripture readings of the day, and explains their implications for Catholic faith and morality.
- The homily has great value in the life of the Church. It is itself a liturgical act, rather than a talk or a speech inserted into the liturgy.
- The homily is a required part of liturgical worship. Thus, on Sundays and holy days of obligation, the celebrant should reflect on the biblical readings.

The *Dogmatic Constitution on Divine Revelation* (*Dei Verbum*) talks about the importance of spiritual preparation for preaching:

> All clerics, particularly priests of Christ and others who, as deacons or catechists, are officially engaged in the ministry of the Word, should immerse themselves in the Scriptures by constant sacred reading and diligent study. For it must not happen that anyone becomes 'an empty preacher of the Word of

God to others, not being a hearer of the Word of God in his own heart,' when he ought to be sharing the boundless riches of the divine Word with the faithful committed to his care, especially in the sacred liturgy.[35]

The *Decree on the Life and Ministry of Priests* (*Presbyterorum Ordinis*) says that the homily is a critical part of the spiritual formation of God's people:

The People of God is formed into one in the first place by the Word of the living God, which is quite rightly sought from the mouth of priests. For since nobody can be saved who has not first believed, it is the first task of priests as co-workers of the bishops to preach the Gospel of God to all men. In this way they carry out the Lord's command 'Go into all the world and preach the Gospel to every creature' (Mark 16:15), and thus set up and increase the People of God. [36]

The *Decree* goes on to say:

The priest's preaching, often very difficult in present-day conditions, if it is to become more effective in moving the minds of his hearers, must expound the Word of God not merely in a general and abstract way but by an application of the eternal truth of the Gospel to the concrete circumstances of life."[37]

This is a very important point. If we cannot relate the Gospel to people's everyday lives, we are not accomplishing much in the pulpit. Some preachers simply restate the readings and provide broad, "safe" messages each week. For instance, "Love your neighbor," "Do good deeds for others," and "Be nice to someone this week" are samples of the messages people sometimes hear. While these are not bad messages, they are very general and not particularly helpful. We can preach more effectively, and we owe it to our people to give them more than a watered down, politically correct version of the truth.

The Church does not need spineless, timid, or fainthearted preachers. Sometimes strong words and actions are needed. Speaking to the Roman Senate, the ancient writer Cicero once said, "I must remind you, Lords, Senators, that extreme patriotism in the defense of freedom is no crime, and let me respectfully remind you that pusillanimity in the pursuit of justice is no virtue in a Roman." These words were echoed more than two thousand years later by the great Barry Goldwater when he said, "Extremism in the defense of liberty is no vice, and moderation in the pursuit of justice is no virtue."

A gentleman once told me, "Priests need to be specific. For example, in talking about morality in daily life, use concrete examples like the example of a person who leaves Home Depot with more change than he should have because of a cashier's mistake. What should he do? That's a moral issue. We need guidance on specifics like that example."

Clear, specific examples facilitate the proclamation of God's Word. Remember the old saying, "If there's mist coming from the pulpit, there will be fog in the pews."

The *General Instruction on the Roman Missal* [hereafter cited as *GIRM*] said the following about the homily:

> The homily is part of the Liturgy and is strongly recommended, for it is necessary for the nurturing of the Christian life. It should be an explanation of some aspect of the readings from Sacred Scripture or of another text from the Ordinary or from the Proper of the Mass of the day and should take into account both the mystery being celebrated and the particular needs of the listeners."[38]

This document stresses the following aspects of the homily:
- The homily is necessary to nurture the spiritual life. It is *not* optional.
- The homily explains the Scripture readings or another text from the Ordinary (e.g., the Gloria, the Creed) or the Proper of the Mass (e.g., the Collect).
- The homily takes into account the feast day (e.g., Christ the King) and the congregation's needs (e.g., working class, rural, inner city).

The *GIRM* reminds us that the priest celebrant is the ordinary homilist, although he may entrust the homily to a concelebrant or a deacon, but "never to a lay person."[39] The instruction repeats the mandate that the homily is to be celebrated on Holy Days of Obligation and that it is recommended on weekdays.

The Third Instruction on the implementation of *Sacrosanctum Concilium* states: "The purpose of the homily is to explain the readings and make them relevant for the present day."[40] This task is accomplished in the same way Jesus did: through the use of stories, parables, illustrations, images, and symbols to which people can relate. The reason our Lord chose stories to illustrate His message is a basic one: Our lives are a story. They have a beginning, middle and an end, and are filled with interesting mini-stories and fascinating lessons. We can best relate to a story because of our nature as human beings. My friend Monsignor Frank Chiodo once said that the quality of preaching would improve greatly if every homilist could illustrate the weekend readings with a pertinent story.

The possibility of preaching on some ordinary part of the Mass, such as the Creed or the Lord's Prayer, leaves open the possibility of a homily series. Homily series were fairly common before the Council, but fell by the wayside in the 1960s. Given the lack of basic knowledge of the faith among Catholics today, it would seem opportune and appropriate to initiate a series of good homilies on pertinent topics. In Year B, for instance, there is a series of readings on the Bread of Life Discourse (John 6:1–52), which can be used to present a series on the Mass. On the seventeenth Sunday, for example, you could talk about the Gloria; on the eighteenth, speak on the Liturgy of the Word; on the nineteenth, discuss the Creed; on the twentieth, discuss the Eucharistic Prayer and Consecration; and on the twenty-first, talk about Holy Communion. You can remain faithful to the text and discuss one topic systematically.

I know of one pastor who preached a homily series on the Apostles (he took four the first weekend and two each for four more weekends, and in subsequent homilies talked about the development of the New Testament). While I wouldn't preach a homily series every year, a strong argument can be made for regular homily series on topics such as the Mass, the virtues, the Ten Commandments, or Christian prayer. A series is systematic, thematic, and easily remembered. In addition, it is a great teaching opportunity as well as a chance to show the continuity of Biblical texts in the *Lectionary* cycle.

In the Circular Letter on the Eucharistic Prayers, *Eucharisticae Participationem*, we are told: "In the homily the Word of God which has been proclaimed in the liturgical assembly is explained to the community present, taking into account its capacity and way of life, and in the context of the actual celebration."[41] *Context* is a very important word. Homilists must always consider the context, i.e. the needs and capacity of the community in which they preach. This does not mean they pander to or entertain the people, but rather understand them in order to communicate clearly and effectively.

SACRAMENTAL CELEBRATIONS

One of the goals of the Second Vatican Council was internal Church renewal. The key feature of this renewal was the full, conscious, and actual (internal and external) participation of the faithful in liturgical celebrations. This renewal required the revision of each of the seven sacraments. The revision simplified the rites and texts of each liturgy. Each book containing the sacramental liturgical ritual includes an introduction that discusses, among other things, the homily appropriate for that sacrament:

Baptism:

After the reading, the celebrant gives a short homily, explaining to those present the significance of what has been read. His purpose will be to lead them to a deeper understanding of the mystery of baptism and to encourage the parents and godparents to a ready acceptance of the responsibilities which arise from the sacrament."[42]

Confirmation:

The bishop [after the Presentation of the candidates] gives a brief homily. He should explain the readings and lead the candidates, their sponsors and parents, and the whole assembly to a deeper understanding of the mystery of confirmation.[43]

The ritual provides a sample homily:

"At Pentecost the apostles received the Holy Spirit as the Lord had promised. They also received the power of giving the Holy Spirit and so completing the work of baptism. This we read in the Acts of the Apostles. When Saint Paul placed his hands on those who had been baptized, the Holy Spirit came upon them, and they began to speak in other languages and prophetic words.

Bishops are successors of the apostles and have this power of giving the Holy Spirit to the baptized, either personally or through the priests they appoint.

In our day the coming of the Holy Spirit is not usually marked by the gift of tongues, but we know his coming by faith. He fills our hearts with the love of God, brings us together in one faith but in different vocations, and works within us to make the Church one and holy.

The gift of the Holy Spirit, which you are to receive, will be a spiritual sign and seal to make you more Christ-like and more perfect members of His Church. At his baptism by John, Christ was anointed by the Spirit and sent out on his public ministry to set the world on fire.

You have already been baptized into Christ and now you will receive the power of his Spirit and the sign of the cross on your forehead. You must be witnesses before all the world to his suffering, death and resurrection; your way of life should reflect the goodness of Christ. Christ gives varied gifts to his Church, and the Spirit distributes them among the members of Christ's body to build up the holy people of God in unity and love.

Be active members of the Church, alive in Christ Jesus. Under the guidance of the Holy Spirit give your lives completely in the service of all, as did Christ, who came not to be served but to serve.

Before you receive the Holy Spirit, renew the profession of faith you made in baptism or your parents and godparents made for you in union with the whole Church."[44]

Eucharist:

The homily is part of the liturgy and is strongly recommended. It is necessary for the nurturing of the Christian life. It should develop some point of the readings or another text from the Ordinary or from the Proper of the Mass of the day, and take into account the mystery being celebrated and the needs proper to the listeners.[45]

Marriage:

After the gospel, the priest gives a homily drawn from the sacred text. He speaks about the mystery of Christian marriage, the dignity of married love, the grace of the sacrament and the responsibilities of married people, keeping in mind the circumstances of this particular marriage.[46]

The rite also provides homiletic notes for the new readings with a classification of readings according to subject (e.g., Institution of Marriage, Accounts [Narratives] of Weddings, Sanctity of Marriage, Indissolubility of Marriage, Peace and Prosperity of Homes, Primacy of Love, and Christian Life). It is important to keep in mind (1) the centrality of Christ as proclaimed in Sacred

Scripture, (2) the presence of the couple exchanging vows, and (3) the community gathered to celebrate with them. Each of these elements is a critical component of effective wedding homilies.

Holy Orders:

Then all sit, and the bishop addresses the people and the candidate on the duties of a priest. He may use these or similar words:

"This man, your relative and friend, is now to be raised to the order of priests. Consider carefully the position to which he is to be promoted in the Church.

It is true that God has made his entire people a royal priesthood in Christ. But our High Priest, Jesus Christ, also chose some of his followers to carry out publicly in the Church a priestly ministry in his name on behalf of mankind. He was sent by the Father, and he in turn sent the apostles into the world; through them and their successors, the Bishops, he continues his work as Teacher, Priest and Shepherd. Priests are co-workers of the order of bishops. They are joined to the bishops in the priestly office and are called to serve God's people.

Our brother has seriously considered this step and is now to be ordained to priesthood in the presbyteral order. He is to serve Christ the Teacher, Priest and Shepherd in his ministry which is to make his own body, the Church, grow into the people of God, a holy temple.

He is called to share in the priesthood of the bishops and to be molded into the likeness of Christ, the supreme and eternal Priest. By consecration he will be made a true priest of the New Testament, to preach the Gospel, sustain God's people and celebrate the liturgy, above all, the Lord's sacrifice."

He then addresses the candidate:

"My son, you are now to be advanced to the order of the presbyterate. You must apply your energies to the duty of teaching in the name of Christ, the chief Teacher. Share with all mankind the word of God you have received with joy. Meditate on the law of God, believe what you read, teach what you believe, and put into practice what you teach.

Let the doctrine you teach be true nourishment for the People of God. Let the example of your life attract the followers of Christ, so that by word and action you may build up the house which is God's Church.

In the same way you must carry out your mission of sanctifying in the power of Christ. Your ministry will perfect the spiritual sacrifice of the faithful by uniting it to Christ's sacrifice, the sacrifice which is offered sacramentally through your hands. Know what you are doing and imitate the mystery you celebrate. In the memorial of the Lord's death and resurrection, make every effort to die to sin and walk in the new life of Christ.

When you baptize, you will bring men and women into the People of God. In the sacrament of penance, you will forgive sins in the name of Christ and the Church. With holy oil you will relieve and console the sick. You will celebrate the liturgy and offer thanks and praise to God throughout the day, praying not only for the People of God but for the whole world. Remember that you are chosen from among God's people and appointed to act for them in relation to God. Do your part in the work of Christ the Priest with genuine joy and love, and attend to the concerns of Christ before your own.

Finally, conscious of sharing in the work of Christ, the Head and Shepherd of the Church, and united with the bishop and subject to him, seek to bring the faithful together into a unified family and lead them effectively, through Christ and in the Holy Spirit, to God the Father. Always remember the example of the Good Shepherd who came not to be served but to serve, and to seek out and rescue those who are lost."[47]

Anointing of the Sick:

In the homily the celebrant should show how the sacred text speaks of the meaning of illness in the history of salvation and of the grace given by the sacrament of anointing.[48]

Reconciliation:

The homily, taking its theme from the Scriptural text, should lead the penitents to examine their consciences and to turn away from sin and toward God. It should remind the faithful that sin works against God, against the community, against one's neighbors, and against the sinner himself. Therefore it would be good to recall:

a) The infinite mercy of God, greater than all our sins, by which again and again he calls us back to himself.

b) The need for interior repentance, by which we are genuinely prepared to make reparation for sin.

c) The social aspect of grace and sin, by which the actions of individuals in some degree affect the whole body of the Church.

d) The duty to make satisfaction for sin, which is effective because of Christ's work of reparation and requires especially, in addition to works of penance, the exercise of true charity toward God and neighbor.[49]

Christian Funerals:

A brief homily based on the readings is always given after the gospel reading at the funeral liturgy and may also be given after the readings of the vigil service; but there is never to be a eulogy. Attentive to the grief of those present, the homilist should dwell on God's compassionate love and on the paschal mystery of the Lord, as proclaimed in the Scripture readings. The homilist should also help the members of the assembly to understand that the mystery of God's love and the mystery of Christ's victorious death and resurrection were present in the life and death of the deceased and that these mysteries are active in their own lives as well. Through the homily members of the family and community should receive consolation and strength to face the death of one of their members with a hope nourished by the saving word of God. Laypersons who preside at the funeral rites (in particular situations) give an instruction on the readings.[50]

The funeral homily should include three critical points: (1) the life, death, and resurrection of Jesus Christ as the reference point of the Christian life; (2) the life of the deceased; and (3) the life of the Christian community that gathers to say a final farewell to the deceased and comfort his or her family. Each point should be properly addressed in every funeral homily.

PAPAL TEACHINGS

Popes throughout the twentieth century have stressed in their encyclicals and other messages the importance of preaching. They speak of the preaching ministry within the context of the Sacred Liturgy, and discuss its value for the people homilists serve. Pope Benedict XV makes some excellent points about preaching in his encyclical The Redemption of the Human Race (*Humani Generis Redemptionem*). Benedict describes homilists as "ambassadors for Christ" (2 Cor. 5:20). He discusses the goal of preaching, as reflected in Christ's mission of testifying to the truth and giving life:

> [Preachers] must diffuse the light of truth made known by God, and in those who hear them they must quicken and nourish the supernatural life. In a word, by seeking the salvation of souls they are to promote the glory of God.[51]

He goes on to compare the preaching ministry to secular professions:

> As it would, therefore, be wrong to call anyone a doctor who does not practice medicine, or to style anyone a professor of some art who does not teach that art, he who in his preaching neglects to lead men to a fuller knowledge of God and on the way of eternal salvation may be called an idle declaimer, but not a preacher of the Gospel. And would there were no such declaimers![52]

The pope criticizes those preachers who seek fame, or attempt to entertain people. "How sadly are those preachers deceived!" he writes.

> Granted that they receive the applause of the uneducated, which they seek with such great favor and not without sacrilege, is it really worthwhile when we consider that they are condemned by every prudent man, and, what is worse, have reason to fear the stern judgment of Christ?[53]

Benedict pulled no punches when talking about the sacred preaching ministry.

He talked about the value of three types of knowledge needed for effective preaching: *self-knowledge*, which leads a priest to renounce his own advantage, *knowledge of God*, which leads him to know and love God, and *knowledge of his office*, which leads him to discharge his duties well and teach others to do the same.[54] "If he lacks these three kinds of knowledge, whatever other learning he has, will only puff him up and will be useless," he wrote.[55] The pope points out:

The priest who discharges the office of preaching should cause showers of heavenly wisdom to fall from his lips, and from his life rays of piety to shine out, just as the angel in telling the shepherds of Our Lord's birth, both shone with great splendor and expressed in words the tidings he had come to announce.[56] (*see* Luke 2:9–10)

The Second Vatican Council stressed the need for good preaching, especially in *Presbyterorum Ordinis.*. Pope Paul VI wrote an encyclical on evangelization called *Evangelization in the Modern World* (*Evangelii Nuntiandi*), issued on the Feast of Saint Ambrose, Dec. 8, 1975. He opens the document with these words:

The preaching of the Gospel to the men of our times, full as they are of hope, but harassed by fear and anxiety, must undoubtedly be regarded as a duty which will redound to the benefit, not only of the Christian community, but of the whole human race.[57]

The pope then discusses the various means of evangelization (e.g., witness of life, catechetical instruction, the mass media, person-to-person contact). The homily is one of those means. It is an opportunity to share the Good News of salvation offered by Christ's death on Calvary. The pope talks about the material for the homily in these words:

There are in fact innumerable events in life and circumstances in which men find themselves which furnish the occasion for preaching, prudently but clearly, those truths which the Lord would wish to impart, given the suitable opportunity. It suffices for each man to have that spiritual sense which can detect the expression of God's message in the course of events.[58]

He calls the homily "a powerful and most suitable instrument of evangelization."[59] He then lays out the qualities or characteristics of a fruitful homily:

[It must be] simple, clear, straightforward, well adapted to the hearers and firmly rooted in the teaching of the Gospel. It must faithfully follow the magisterium and should be inspired and guided by that apostolic zeal which is inherent in it. It must be full of salutary hope, and foster peace and unity. When it possesses these qualities the Sunday homily is a source of life and strength to many parish and other communities.[60]

Let's look at each of these qualities:
- The homily should be simple. Complex ideas confuse people and make it difficult for them to take a message home with them.
- The homily should be clear. It should avoid fuzzy, vague, nebulous or theological language that people must decipher and interpret.

- The homily should be straightforward. It should be presented in a direct way. It shouldn't be too subtle (although it can and sometimes should have subtleties).
- The homily should be well adapted to the hearers. This is important. Our Lord used images like the Good Shepherd because He lived in a rural, agricultural part of the world. Shepherds and sheep are a common sight in the Holy Land. The image was something to which His listeners could relate. So, too, the preacher today must adapt his message to his listeners. Good homilists create a bond between themselves and their listeners. Disjointed, fuzzy, ambiguous, irrelevant images and illustrations don't facilitate the creation of such a bond. Clear, colorful, pertinent images help create such a bond. All good communicators connect with their audience. Our Lord connected well because of the way He adapted His message to His audience. Homilists should do the same.
- The homily should be firmly rooted in the Gospel. The Gospel is the heart of Sacred Scripture. The homily should be based on a Gospel or other Lectionary text or Ordinary or Proper part of the Mass (*GIRM*, 65).
- The homily should faithfully follow the Church's teaching authority. Homilies are not outlets for personal opinions or political exhortations. They must adhere to and reinforce the Church's teachings. The *Catechism of the Catholic Church* and the *Compendium of the Catechism of the Catholic Church* are excellent references for the Church's official teachings and should be used often in homily preparation.
- The homily should be guided by apostolic zeal. Zeal comes from a heart filled with faith and love. Our Lord showed zeal in learning the Jewish religion and in cleansing the Temple (Luke 2:41–52, 19:45–48). Bishops, priests and deacons should show that same zealous spirit when preaching and proclaiming God's Word today. That spirit is one fruit of a life of prayer.
- The homily should be full of hope, and foster peace and unity. Hope is a great virtue badly needed today. The world is a dark place, and Christianity is seen as increasingly irrelevant or even hostile to American culture. As official representatives of the Church, we must be agents of peace and unity. The homilist should radiate hope and love in his words and actions.

Jesus was called "the Prince of Peace" (Isa. 9:5). He came to bring peace (Luke 2:14), and to render it effective by reconciling humanity to God (John 14:27; Eph. 2:14–17). The Kingdom of peace is extended throughout the world when we love each other and spread the gift of God's peace and love. In the Mass, before the Sign of Peace, we pray: "Lord Jesus Christ, you said to your apostles: I leave you peace, my peace I give you. Look not on our sins, but on the faith of your Church, and grant us the peace and unity of your Kingdom where you live forever and ever."[61] This should be the homilist's goal as well.

Blessed John Paul II's first letter on catechesis, *Catechesis in Our Time* (*Catechesi Tradendae*), following the 1975 synod on the topic, addressed the homily as a means of instructing people on the Christian life. He writes:

> The homily takes up again the journey of faith put forward by catechesis, and brings it to its natural fulfillment. At the same time it encourages the Lord's disciples to begin anew each day their spiritual journey in truth, adoration and thanksgiving. Preaching, centered upon the Bible texts, must then in its own way make it possible to familiarize the faithful with the whole of the mysteries of the faith and with the norms of Christian living.[62]

He then lists the qualities of good preaching:

> Much attention must be given to the homily: it should be neither too long nor too short; it should always be carefully prepared, rich in substance and adapted to the hearers, and reserved to ordained ministers. The homily should have its place not only in every Sunday and feast day Eucharist, but also in the celebration of baptisms, penitential liturgies, marriages and funerals.[63]

Once again the pope lists criteria for good homilies:
- The fruit of attention.
- Appropriate length.
- Carefully prepared.
- Rich in substance.
- Adapted to the hearers.
- Reserved to ordained ministers.

The homily is not *per se* an instruction or discourse, but there is plenty of room for good catechesis.

Blessed John Paul's first letter on the Eucharist, *The Supper of the Lord* (*Dominicae Cenae*), issued Feb. 24, 1980, makes this point about the homily:

> The homily is supremely suitable for the use of [scriptural texts], provided that their content corresponds to the required conditions, since it is one of the tasks that belong to the nature of the homily to show the points of convergence between revealed divine wisdom and noble human thought seeking the truth by various paths.[64]

The pope is telling us two important things: First, the homily must be based on the Scripture readings heard at Mass. Second, the homily must connect those readings to human thoughts and ideas. The homily is a bridge between God and humanity. Biblical truth and human truth are connected.

Popular culture, as well as the writings of Church scholars, can be used to illustrate homily points. For example, Saint Luke tells us: "You also must be prepared, for at an hour you do not expect, the Son of Man will come" (Luke

12:40). In the movie *The Bells of St. Mary's* (1945), Bing Crosby quotes an old saying to a wealthy old developer: "I shall pass this way but once. If there is any good, let me do it now, for I shall not pass this way again." He reminds the old man that time is passing and we have only a limited opportunity to do good works, and we should do so while on this earth. Here a biblical text and a classic movie convey a similar truth. Citing this movie in a homily is an excellent way to convey a spiritual message. Movies, books, magazines, and the Internet are vast resource for the homilist. He should tap into that resource.

The homily must touch the heart and not simply the head. In his Apostolic Letter, *The Day of the Lord* (*Dies Domini*), Blessed John Paul puts it this way:

> The liturgical proclamation of the Word of God, especially in the Eucharistic assembly, is not so much a time for meditation and catechesis as a dialogue between God and his people, a dialogue in which the wonders of salvation are proclaimed and the demands of the covenant are restated.[65]

This is a powerful statement. The Mass is not a setting for doctrinal instruction and quiet meditation *per se*, although both can and should happen at Mass. It is essentially a time for the worship of almighty God in which He speaks to us through the preached and proclaimed Word. The homily is the Word of God broken open for us. It is a practical and living commentary on the Scripture readings or other parts of the Mass. We may not break out our blackboard and chalk at Mass, but we can provide sacred instruction on the mysteries we celebrate and bring God's people to a deeper level of participation in those mysteries.

In a message to the Congregation for Divine Worship and Sacraments, Blessed John Paul II praised the council members for devoting special attention to the homily at their March 2005 meeting. He noted that the homily is different from catechesis. He said the priest or deacon giving the homily has a "double responsibility," (1) ensuring his reflections are based on the day's Scripture readings, and (2) ensuring that the congregation understands them. "The homily must promote the most intimate and advantageous encounter between God, who speaks, and the community, which listens," he said.[66] The pope said the Second Vatican Council "produced great fruits in the area of liturgy, but it was time "to pass from renewal to thorough understanding."[67]

Pope Benedict XVI's first Post-Synodal Apostolic Exhortation is titled *The Sacrament of Charity* (*Sacramentum Caritatis*). In the document, released in March 2007, he discusses the value and importance of the Eucharist. In a section on preaching he writes:

> Given the importance of the word of God, the quality of homilies needs to be improved. The homily is 'part of the liturgical action,' and is meant to foster a deeper understanding of the word of God, so it can bear fruit in the lives of the faithful. Hence ordained ministers must 'prepare the homily carefully based on adequate knowledge of Sacred Scripture.' Generic and abstract homilies are to be avoided. In particular, I ask these ministers to preach in such a way that the

homily closely relates the proclamation of the Word of God to the sacramental celebration and the life of the community, so that the Word of God truly becomes the Church's vital nourishment and support.[68]

The pope recommends homilists deliver "thematic homilies" on the "great themes of the Christian faith," the Creed, the Ten Commandments, the seven sacraments and the Lord's Prayer, based on the Catechism and the Compendium of the Catechism of the Catholic Church.

In his 2010 Post-Apostolic Exhortation *The Word of God* (*Verbum Domini*), Pope Benedict stresses the importance of the homily as a means of bringing the biblical message to bear on the everyday lives of the faithful. He talks about its functions of leading the faithful to a deeper understanding of the mysteries of salvation, preparing the assembly to profess their faith in the Creed and participate fully in the Eucharistic sacrifice. He urges homilists to remain in close contact with the Scriptures and requests the publication of a Directory on homiletics (*VD* 60).

The homily enhances our participation in the sacred liturgy. A good homily is something we anticipate when we go to Mass and in a sense carries us through the rest of Mass and out into the secular world. Now let us look at some documents of the Magisterium for instruction on the nature and purpose of homilies.

MAGISTERIAL DOCUMENTS

The Church's Magisterium provides guidance and directives for the homilist. The *Instruction on the Eucharistic Mystery* (*Inaestimabile Donum*) tells us: "The purpose of the homily is to explain to the faithful the Word of God proclaimed in the readings, and to apply its message to the present. Accordingly the homily is to be given by the priest or the deacon."[69]

The Vatican *Instruction on the Collaboration of the Non-Ordained Faithful I the Sacred Ministry of Priest*, issued in 1997, says:

> The homily, being an eminent form of preaching . . . also forms part of the liturgy. The homily, therefore, during the celebration of the Holy Eucharist, must be reserved to the sacred minister, priest or deacon, to the exclusion of the non-ordained faithful, even if these should have responsibilities as 'pastoral assistants' or catechists in whatever type of community or group. This exclusion is not based on the preaching ability of sacred ministers nor their theological preparation, but *on the function which is reserved to them in virtue of having received the Sacrament of Holy Orders* [emphasis mine]. For the same reason the diocesan bishop cannot validly dispense from the canonical norm since this is not merely a disciplinary law but one which touches upon the closely connected functions of teaching and sanctifying. For the same reason, the practice, on some occasions, of entrusting the preaching of the homily to seminarians or theology students who are not clerics, is not permitted. Indeed, the homily should not be regarded as a training for some future ministry.[70]

These statements say as much about holy orders as they do about preaching itself. Part of the three-fold *munera* of holy orders is preaching and proclaiming the Word of God. Preaching is a sacred function and flows from the character we receive at ordination. Therefore it is not something we can ordinarily delegate to lay people.

In 1994, the Congregation for Clergy published a *Directory for the Life and Ministry of Priests*. In it the Congregation talks about preaching the Word of God: "Christ entrusted to the Apostles and to the Church the mission of preaching the Good News to all men."[71] It says preaching the Word must be connected to the life of the people. Preaching must be "carried out with extreme responsibility" for the welfare of God's people. The document calls on priests to be witnesses, heralds, and transmitters of the faith.[72] As it is an essential part of the formation of the People of God, preaching must "manifest with frankness the truth before God," and therefore, the *Directory* states,

> [Preaching] cannot be reduced to the presentation of one's own thought, to the manifestation of a personal experience, to simple explanations of a psychological, sociological or humanitarian nature; nor can it excessively concentrate on rhetoric, so often found in mass-communication. It concerns proclaiming a Word which cannot be altered, because it has been entrusted to the Church in order to protect, penetrate and faithfully transmit it.[73]

The Congregation calls preaching "the preferred channel for the transmission of the faith and for the mission of evangelization."[74] It calls on priests to cultivate knowledge of Sacred Scripture, study patristic and other exegesis on the Word, meditate and develop their manner of teaching, and respect the dignity of the message and the hearers of the message.

Five years later, the same Congregation put out a document titled *The Priest and the Third Millennium: Teacher of the Word, Minister of the Sacraments, and Leader of the Community*. In it, the Congregation stresses the importance of remote and proximate preparation for preaching. *Remote preparation* involves studying contemporary problems and their possible solutions. It requires priests to be well versed in the documents of the Church's Magisterium, especially ecumenical councils and popes. "Efforts in this regard will always reap a rich harvest," it says.[75] *Proximate preparation* involves studying Sacred Scripture, personal prayer, and study of suitable books. "The Fathers of the Church and the other great writers of the Catholic tradition teach us how to penetrate the meaning of the revealed Word and communicate it to others," writes the Congregation.[76] It also suggests the lives of the saints can help preachers:

> The lives of the saints, their struggles and heroism, have always produced positive effects in the hearts of the Christian faithful who, today, have special need of the heroic example of the saints in their self-dedication to the love of God and, through God, to others.[77]

The document then talks about the "formal aspects of preaching." In an age of rapid communication, the message of salvation must be presented in an attractive manner. "[The homilist's] apostolic spirit should move him to acquire competence in the use of the 'new pulpits' provided by modern communications and ensure that his preaching is always of a standard congruent with the preached Word."[78] Priests should develop their presentation of the message. "Like that of Christ, priestly preaching should be positive, stimulating and draw men and women to the goodness, beauty and truth of God," it says.[79]

> Elegant, accurate language, comprehensible to contemporary men and women of all social backgrounds, is always useful for preaching. Banal commonplace language should be eschewed . . . The human 'key' to effective preaching of the Word is to be found in the professionalism of the preacher who knows what he wants to say and who is always backed up by serious remote and proximate preparation. This is far removed from the improvisation of the dilettante. Attempts to obscure the entire force of truth are insidious forms of irenicism. Care should therefore be taken with the meaning of words, style and diction. Important themes should be highlighted without ostentation, after careful reflection. A pleasant speaking voice should be cultivated. Priests should know their objectives and have a good understanding of the existential and cultural reality of their congregation. Theories and abstract generalizations must always be avoided. Hence every preacher should know his own flock well and use an attractive style which, rather than wounding people, strikes the conscience and is not afraid to call things for what they really are.[80]

The Congregation suggests priests help each other with such things as the theological content of preaching, the length of homilies, the proper use of the ambo, and the development of voice tone and inflection. Finally, it says that humility is a virtue for effective preaching.

The 2004 document titled *The Sacrament of Redemption* (*Redemptionis Sacramentum*) reiterates these norms and adds:

> Particular care is to be taken so that the homily is based upon the mysteries of salvation, expounding the mysteries of the faith and the norms of the Christian life from the biblical readings and liturgical texts throughout the course of the liturgical year and providing a commentary on the texts of the Ordinary or the Proper of the Mass or of some other rite of the Church. It is clear that all interpretations of Sacred Scripture are to be referred back to Christ himself as the one upon whom the entire economy of salvation hinges, though this should be done in light of the specific context of the liturgical celebration. In the homily to be given, care is to be taken so that the light of Christ may shine upon life's events. Even so, this is to be done so as not to obscure the true and unadulterated Word of God; for instance, treating only of politics or profane subjects or drawing upon notions derived from contemporary pseudo-religious currents as a source.[81]

The working paper (called a *Lineamenta*) for the October 2005 Synod on the Eucharist, talked about two kinds of homilies. The first is a *mystagogical homily*:

> Homilies of this kind, based on the proclaimed texts and avoiding any inappropriate or profane references, allow the faithful to grow in their knowledge of the sacred mysteries they are celebrating so that the light of Jesus Christ might shine on their lives.[82]

The other kind is a *thematic homily*, which "in the course of the liturgical year can treat the great tracts of the Christian faith: the Creed, the Our Father, the parts of the Mass, the Ten Commandments and other subjects."[83]

BISHOPS' PASTORAL STATEMENT

The United States Conference of Catholic Bishops (USCCB) provides norms and directives for Catholic preaching. Their Priestly Life and Ministry Committee released a document titled *Fulfilled in Your Hearing: The Homily in the Sunday Assembly* in 1982 (reprinted in 1999). This document makes some important points about the homily (and its very existence indicates the importance of the topic). It calls the preacher a *mediator of meaning*. "The person who preaches in the context of the liturgical assembly is thus a mediator, representing both the community and the Lord," it says.[84]

> The preacher acts as a mediator, making connections between the real lives of people who believe in Jesus Christ but are not always sure what difference faith can make in their lives, and God who calls us into ever deeper communion with himself and with one another.[85]

The image of a mediator is appropriate. It is both biblical and spiritual, and reminds us of the encyclical *Mediator Dei*, written in 1947 by Pope Pius XII on Christ the Mediator. In it, he developed the image of the priest as *channel* of God's grace through the celebration of the sacred liturgy. In the homily, the priest announces the good news of salvation, and brings God's Word to the faithful, as a channel delivers water to a well.

Another closely related image for the preacher is a *bridge-builder*. A preacher creates spiritual bridges of communion between God and His people.

Fulfilled in Your Hearing recommends the following tools in a preacher's toolbox:

1. A good dictionary for help in forming sentences and phrases;
2. A Catholic Concordance to help locate related Biblical passages;
3. A "theological" dictionary of Scripture to trace ideas in the Old and New Testaments;
4. Gospel parallels;
5. Standard commentaries—the *Jerome Biblical Commentary* is standard;

6. Exegetical commentaries—the *Navarre Bible* series is excellent; and
7. Newspapers, magazines, Internet sites, and books on a wide range of topics.

What do all these documents teach us about preaching homilies? The Church's official documents have much to say about the nature and importance of preaching. The reader will notice they say many of the same things. First, a homily is a proclamation and explanation of the Scripture readings or other parts of the Mass. Second, the homily deals with faith and morals. Third, the homily is a sacred act carried out within the context of the Church's liturgy. Fourth, the homily is ordinarily carried out by those in holy orders. Fifth, the homily is to relate the Gospel message to the daily lives of God's people. Finally, the homily must be carefully prepared, elegant in style, and rich in substance.

PASTORAL OR HOMILETIC INTEGRITY

"And so I solemnly declare to you this day that I am not responsible for the blood of any of you, for I did not shrink from proclaiming to you the entire plan of God" (Acts 20:26–27). Saint Paul understood the importance of announcing the fullness of the message of salvation, and that quality is as important today as it was in Paul's time. I call that quality *homiletic* or *pastoral integrity*. This means that homilists must present the full range of topics contained in the Scriptures for the benefit of God's people. They exclude no topic in their proclamation of Christ to the world.

As the liturgical year unfolds, so too should our presentation of the message of salvation in Christ. The Christian message should touch a wide range of topics and situations in which homilist and congregation find themselves. Unfortunately, too many preachers present the saving message of Christ in a narrow and shallow way. They talk about "soft" subjects like love, joy, and peace, but fail to talk about "hard" subjects such as abortion, human cloning, and hell. This omission is a disservice to God's people.

One objection priests and others have to this idea is that some of the most controversial topics are not found in the Scriptures, and they do not wish to impose a topic on the text. I agree with those concerned with fidelity to Sacred Scripture, but it is possible to discuss a wide range of theological and spiritual topics in the *Lectionary* while remaining faithful to the sacred text.

It is essential to be open to the promptings of the Holy Spirit in preparing one's homily, and never to exclude any topic because of its apparent lack of relevance to the *Lectionary*. The virtue of prudence demands that preachers keep in mind the importance of proclaiming the *entire* message of Christ. The presentation of the message of salvation in all its aspects throughout the course of the liturgical year should be a goal all homilists seek to attain. In seeking this goal, homilists remain faithful to the example of Christ and fulfill their God-given responsibilities, which brings a profound sense of satisfaction and joy.

Table 1.1 Possible homily topics

Topic	Biblical Text	Sunday Reading
Abortion	Jeremiah 1:5	4th Ordinary Time (C)
Birth Control	Genesis 15:5–12	2nd Lent (C)
Capital Punishment	Sirach 27:30–28:9	24th Ordinary Time (A)
Humility	Luke 18:9–14	30th Ordinary Time (C)
Immigration	Exodus 22:20–26	30th Ordinary Time (A)
Lust	Matthew 5:17–37	6th Ordinary Time (A)
Mercy	John 8:1–11	5th Lent (C)
Real Presence	John 6:51–58	20th Ordinary Time (B)
Temptation	Matthew 4:1–11	1st Lent (A)

The above table of possible homily topics are not "proof texts" as much as legitimate opportunities to address a wide range of issues relevant to the people of today. I am not suggesting that the homilist should begin with a preconceived idea, and search for biblical support in the Sunday readings. I do suggest, however, that the Sunday readings provide many occasions to preach on a wide variety of important topics and themes.

Many priests say, for example, "I won't preach on birth control because no one will believe me or live what I preach." Topics like this one are unpopular and sensitive, but they must be preached. Saint Paul reminds Timothy

> proclaim the word, be persistent whether it is convenient or inconvenient; convince, reprimand, encourage through all patience and teaching. For the time will come when people will not tolerate sound doctrine but, following their own desires and insatiable curiosity, will accumulate teachers and will stop listening to the truth and will be diverted to myths. But you, be self-possessed in all circumstances; put up with hardship; perform the work of an evangelist; fulfill your ministry. (2 Tim. 4:2–5)

We need to tell our people things they don't want to hear because we care about the salvation of their souls.

I remember the time when I was preaching at a small church in northeast Iowa shortly after my ordination. It was a warm summer day, and in the back of this small church a woman was sitting with her little girl. Right in the middle of my homily, the little girl said, "Mom, when's he gonna shut up?" The surprised mother whispered something in the little girl's ear, and the girl sat still for a minute or so. Then she said, "Mom, you said he was gonna shut up in a minute or so, but he's still talking." I had a hard time containing my laughter, and decided to wrap up the homily quickly.

The world is in many ways like that little girl. It wants us to shut up about topics like abortion, birth control, human cloning, and embryonic stem-cell research. But the Church can't shut up. She must speak clearly, correctly, and consistently. When priests tell me they won't preach on sensitive topics, I respond by saying that preaching on difficult topics is part of our vocation, and we have to leave the rest up to God and His people. We are not in control—and should not be—of the reception of the message. But we are in control of sending the message. The question for us as homilists is not "Will the people live the message I present?" Rather, the question is "Do I have the courage to preach the fullness of truth out of love for Christ?" Hopefully, we have that courage. Let us remember Saint Paul's question, "And how can they hear without someone to preach?" (Rom. 10:14).

People are formed by the culture in which we live. Their opinions, viewpoints, and ideas are shaped by television, radio, the Internet, newspapers, newsmagazines, and their friends, co-workers, and neighbors. The Church has a golden opportunity each week to form them spiritually and intellectually. If we forfeit that opportunity, we are doing them a tremendous disservice.

Pastoral or homiletic integrity can come with a price tag. One example is the indictment, conviction, and sentencing of a Pentecostal pastor for preaching against homosexual behavior. One Sunday in the summer of 2003, the Reverend Ake Green stepped into the pulpit of his small church in the southern Swedish village of Borgholm and delivered a stinging sermon: "Our country is facing a disaster of great proportions," he told the seventy-five parishioners at the service. "Sexually twisted people will rape animals," Green declared, and homosexuals "open the door to forbidden areas," such as pedophilia.[86]

Green's words were interpreted as being counter to Swedish laws against hate speech. The conviction, which was eventually overturned, sparked a sharp debate about the balance between free speech and minority rights. Politicians and gay rights advocates denounced Green as intolerant, homophobic, and crazy. But others, including the Christian Democratic Party, expressed deep concern for the assault on freedom of religion and speech represented by the pastor's prosecution. If similar restrictions against freedom of religion and speech continue, we could see Catholic and other pastors arrested for preaching the Gospel. It is therefore more necessary than ever to form our people well, so such laws are not enacted, and free speech, including religious speech, is protected.

Another example of the need for good preaching is found in Chicago. In the spring of 2005, the Illinois legislature passed a "gay rights" anti-discrimination measure, one step in a larger effort to normalize so-called "gay marriage." In response, Mary Anne Hackett, president of Catholic Citizens of Illinois, wrote the following in her organization's popular newsletter *The Catholic Citizen*:

> [The Illinois bishops and priests] could have taught the truth and prepared the Catholic laity to mount a massive opposition to this bill and they could have motivated the legislators to vote against it once and for all. But instead, there have not been sermons from the pulpits of the Catholic Church to educate the people in the pews on the moral issues involved. There has only been a resounding silence."[87]

Catholic legislators and other cultural figures are going to act based on *some* worldview. Should it not be a Catholic worldview formed by the Church's solid teachings found in the Catechism, and proclaimed from the pulpit? The consequences of failing to fulfill our ministry as clergy are serious, and they are becoming more evident all the time.

Bishop Sheen, in his penetrating work *Peace of Soul*, commented on the anxiety of modern man:

> Since the basic cause of man's anxiety is the possibility of being either a saint or a sinner, it follows that there are only two alternatives for him. Man can either mount upward to the peak of eternity or else slip backward to the chasms of despair and frustration. Yet there are many who think there is yet another alternative, namely, that of indifference. They think that, just as bears hibernate for a season in a state of suspended animation, so they, too, can sleep through life without choosing to live for God or against Him. But hibernation is no escape, winter ends, and one is then forced to make a decision—indeed, the very choice of indifference itself is a decision. White fences do not remain white fences by having nothing done to them; they soon become black fences. Since there is a tendency in us that pulls us back to the animal, the mere fact that we do not resist it operates to our own destruction. Just as life is the sum of the forces that resist death, so, too, man's will must be the sum of the forces that resist frustration. A man who has taken poison into his system can ignore the antidote, or he can throw it out of the window; it makes no difference which he does, for death is already on the march. St. Paul warns us, "How shall we escape if we neglect. . ." (Heb. 2:3). By the mere fact that we do not go forward, we go backward. There are no plains in the spiritual life; we are either going uphill or coming down. Furthermore the pose of indifference is only intellectual. The will must choose. And even though an "indifferent" soul does not positively reject the infinite, the infinite rejects it. The talents that are unused are taken away, and the Scriptures tell us that, "But because thou art lukewarm, and neither cold nor hot, I will begin to vomit thee out of my mouth" (Apoc. 3:16).[88]

People have good reason to be anxious these days. However, we can help ease the anxiety of our people, and equip them to face the world's disorder and hostility in part through good preaching.

SUMMARY

The purpose of a homily is to nourish the faith of God's people. Homilies are a liturgical act that proclaims Christ to the listener. There are various styles of homilies and different approaches to effective preaching. In her catechism, papal and episcopal letters, and code of law, the Church provides clear guidance for preachers in terms of preparation, delivery, style, and content of homilies.

We have seen how homilies can be developed and adapted to the needs and concerns of the listener. As we proceed through this historical survey of preaching, it will be important to keep in mind the principles outlined in this chapter. My approach follows the guidelines set by the Second Vatican Council:

> The following order should be observed in the treatment of dogmatic theology: biblical themes should have first place; then students should be shown what the Fathers of the Church, both of the East and West, have contributed toward the faithful transmission and elucidation of each of the revealed truths; then the later history of dogma, including its relation to the general history of the Church.[89]

Beginning, then, with the Old Testament, we will follow the development of preaching through the centuries within the social and ecclesial contexts in which it occurred.

NOTES

1. *The American Heritage Dictionary of the English Language*, s.v. "homily."
2. Ibid., s.v. "sermon."
3. John Hardon, S.J., *Modern Catholic Dictionary* (Bardstown, KY: Eternal Life Publications, 1999), s.v. "homily."
4. Ibid.
5. Rev. Peter Klein, ed., *The Catholic Source Book* (Dubuque, IA: Brown-ROA Publishing Media, 2000), 292.
6. Raymond E. Brown, Joseph A. Fitzmeyer, and Roland E. Murphy, eds., *Jerome Biblical Commentary* (Englewood, NJ: Prentice-Hills, 1968), 621–22.
7. The Bishops' Committee on Priestly Life and the Ministry—National Conference of Catholic Bishops, *Fulfilled in Your Hearing: The Homily in the Sunday Assembly* (Washington, DC: USCC, 1999), 29.
8. Hughes Oliphant Old, *The Reading And Preaching Of The Scriptures in the Worship of the Christian Church* (Grand Rapids, MI: Eerdmans, 1998), 1:8–16.
9. Ibid., 1:11.
10. *Catechism of the Catholic Church,* 2nd ed. (Vatican City: Libreria Editrice Vaticana, 1997), nn. 132, 1100, 1349; glossary, s.v. "homily.".
11. United States Catholic Conference. Introduction to *Lectionary for Mass, Second Typical Edition*. Liturgy Documentary Series 1. (Washington, DC: United States Catholic Conference, 1998), 16; Second Vatican Council, Constitution on the Sacred Liturgy *Sacrosanctum Concilium* (December 4, 1963), nn. 6, 47, 52, in *The Conciliar and Post-*

Conciliar Documents, vol. 1 of *The Vatican Collection: Vatican Council II*, ed. Austin Flannery (Northport, NY: Catholic Publishing, 1998), 4, 16.

12. *Lectionary*, 18; *SC*, no. 10.

13. *Lectionary*, 18; Paul VI, Encyclical on the Mystery of Faith *Mysterium Fidei* (September 3, 1965), no. 36, *Acta Apostolicae Sedis* 57 (1965), 753–74; Paul VI, Apostolic Exhortation on Proclaiming the Gospel *Evangelii Nuntiandi* [hereafter cited as EN] (December 8, 1975), no. 43 in *More Post-Conciliar Documents*, vol. 2 of *The Vatican Collection: Vatican Council II*, ed. Austin Flannery (Northport, NY: Catholic Publishing, 1998), 728–29.

14. *Lectionary*, 18, no.24.

15. Henri Daniel-Rops, *This is the Mass: New and Revised* (New York: Hawthorn Books, 1965), 78.

16. Ibid., 81.

17. Benedict XV, Encyclical of Pope Benedict XV on preaching the Word of God *Humani Generis Redemptionem* (June 15, 1917), no. 5, http://www.vatican.va

18. International Commission on English in the Liturgy [ICEL], *Liturgy of the Hours* (New York: Catholic Book Publishing, 1975), 3:1542.

19. Paul VI, *EN*, no. 43.

20. Joseph A. Jungmann, *The Mass of the Roman Rite: Its Origin and Development* (Westminster, MD: Christian Classics, 1950), 1:456.

21. Ibid.

22. Ibid.

23. Cyril C. Richardson, *Early Christian Fathers* (New York: Macmillan, 1970), 287.

24. Jungmann, *Mass of the Roman Rite*, 1:456.

25. ICEL, *Liturgy of the Hours*, Lenten-Easter Season, 2:1785.

26. Jungmann, *Mass of the Roman Rite*, 1:456–57.

27. ICEL, *Liturgy of the Hours*, Lenten-Easter Season, 2:1763.

28. Adrian Fortesque, *The Mass: A Study of the Roman Liturgy* (Albany: Preserving Christian Publications, Inc., 1999), 285.

29. Jungmann, 1:457.

30. Ibid.

31. Ibid.

32. Fortesque, 285.

33. Ibid.

34. Second Vatican Council, *Sacrosanctum Concilium*, no. 52.

35. *St. Augustine's Sermon* 179: PL 38, 166; see Second Vatican Council, Dogmatic Constitution on Divine Revelation *Dei Verbum* (November 18, 1965), no. 25, in Flannery, *Conciliar and Post-Conciliar Documents*, 764–65.

36. Second Vatican Council, Decree on the Ministry and Life of Priests *Presbyterorum Ordinis* (December 7, 1965), no. 4, in Flannery, *Conciliar and Post-Conciliar Documents*, 868–69.

37. Ibid., 869.

38. United States Conference of Catholic Bishops, *General Instruction on the Roman Missal*, Liturgy Document Series 14 (Washington, DC: USCC, 2011), no. 65.

39. Ibid., no. 66.

40. Second Vatican Council, Third Instruction on the Correct Implementation of the Constitution on the Sacred Liturgy *Liturgiae Instaurationes* (September 5, 1970), 2(a), in Flannery, *Conciliar and Post-Conciliar Documents*, 212–213.

41. Sacred Congregation for Divine Worship, Circular Letter on the Eucharistic Prayers *Eucharisticae Participationem* (27 April 1973), no. 15, in Flannery, *Conciliar and Post-Conciliar Documents*, 239..

42. *The Rite of Baptism for Children* (NJ: Catholic Book Publishing, 2004), no. 45.

43. Committee on the Liturgy, NCCB, *The Rites* (Collegeville, MN: Liturgical Press, 1991), no. 39, 1:487–88, 497–98.

44. Ibid.

45. *GIRM*, no. 65.

46. Committee on the Liturgy, NCCB, introduction to *The Rites,* 1:725.

47. *The Rites,* 2:14, 62–63.

48. ICEL, *Pastoral Care of the Sick, The Roman Ritual* (NJ: Catholic Book Publishing, 1983), no.137.

49. ICEL, *Rite of Penance*, The Roman Ritual (NJ: Catholic Book Publishing, 2009) 25.

50. ICEL, *Order of Christian Funerals with Cremation Rite*, The Roman Ritual (NJ: Catholic Book Publishing, 1998), no. 27.

51. *Humani Generis Redemptionem*, no.10.

52. Ibid.

53. Ibid.

54. Ibid., no. 14.

55. Ibid.

56. Ibid., no. 18

57. *EN*, no. 1.

58. Ibid., no. 43.

59. Ibid.

60. Ibid.

61. ICEL, *The Roman Missal (*New York: Catholic Book Publishing, 1985), 562.

62. John Paul II, Apostolic Exhortation on Catechesis in our Time *Catechesi Tradendae* (October 16, 1979), no. 48 (Boston: Daughters of St. Paul, n.d.), 39–40.

63. Ibid.

64. John Paul II, Letter on the Mystery and Worship of the Eucharist *Dominicae Cenae* (February 24, 1980), no. 10 (Boston: Pauline Books & Media, 1980).

65. John Paul II, Apostolic Letter on Keeping the Lord's Day Holy *Dies Domini* (May 31, 1998), no. 41, *Origins* 28, no. 9 (1998), 142.

66. Catholic News Service, March 11, 2005.

67. Ibid.

68. Benedict XVI, Apostolic Exhortation on The Eucharist as the Source and Summit of the Church's Life and Mission *Sacramentum Caritatis* (February 22, 2007), no. 46. http://www.vatican.va

69. John Paul II, Instruction concerning Worship of the Eucharistic Mystery *Inaestimabile Donum* (April 17, 1980), no. 3 (Boston: St. Paul Books & Media, 1980), 6.

70. John Paul II and Eight Vatican Dicasteries, *Instruction on Certain Questions Regarding the Collaboration of the Non-Ordained Faithful in the Sacred Ministry of Priest* (Nov. 13, 1997), art. 3, no. 1. http://www.vatican.va

71. Congregation for the Clergy, *Directory for the Life and Ministry of Priests* (Rome: Libreria Editrice Vaticana, 1994), no. 45.

72. Ibid.

73. Ibid.

74. Ibid., no. 46.

75. Congregation for the Clergy, *The Priest and the Third Millennium: Teacher of the Word, Minister of the Sacraments & Leader of the Community* (Washington, DC: USCC, 1999), 18.

76. Ibid., 19.

77. Ibid.

78. Ibid.

79. Ibid., 20.

80. Ibid.

81. John Paul II, Instruction on certain matters to be observed or to be avoided regarding the Most Holy Eucharist *Redemptionis Sacramentum* (March 19, 2004), no. 67, Liturgy Documentary Series 15 (Washington, DC: USCCB, 2004), 34–35.

82. Vatican Synod Secretariat, "Working Paper for 2005 Synod on the Eucharist, (July 21, 2005), no. 47, *Origins* 35, no. 9 (2005).

83. Ibid.

84. *Fulfilled in your hearing*, 7.

85. Ibid., 8.

86. *Washington Post*, January 29, 2005, A01.

87. *The Wanderer* (St. Paul, MN), March 17, 2005.

88. Fulton J. Sheen, *Peace of Soul* (Garden City, NY: Doubleday, 1954), 18–19.

89. Second Vatican Council, Decree on The Training of Priests *Optatam totius* (October 28, 1965), no. 16, in Flannery, *Conciliar and Post-Conciliar Documents*, 719–21.

Chapter 2
Preaching in the Old Testament
as a Prelude to Christian Preaching

You, son of man, I have appointed watchman for the house of Israel;
when you hear me say anything, you shall warn them for me.
Ezekiel 33:7

T HE OLD TESTAMENT is an indispensable part of Sacred Scripture. Its books are divinely inspired and retain a permanent value, for the Old Covenant has never been revoked," says the *Catechism of the Catholic Church*, quoting Vatican II's Constitution *The Word of God* (*Dei Verbum*) (CCC 121). Pope Pius XII made this observation about the spiritual value of the Old Testament in his encyclical *Divino Afflante Spiritu*: "For what was said and done in the Old Testament was ordained and disposed by God with such consummate wisdom, that things past prefigured in a spiritual way those that were to come under the new dispensation of grace."[1] The *Catechism* teaches that "the economy of the Old Testament was deliberately so oriented that it should prepare for and declare in prophecy the coming of Christ, the redeemer of all men."[2]

The Old Testament begins with the Book of Genesis and ends with the Book of Malachi (forty-five or forty-six books, depending on how one counts them). It is the story of Israel's relationship with God. It covers more than five thousand years and many historical periods. There is a great variety of literature contained in these books: historical narrative, poetry, biography, wisdom sayings, genealogy, and "a storehouse of sublime teaching on God and of sound wisdom on human life, as well as a wonderful treasury of prayers; in them, too, the mystery of our salvation is present in a hidden way," says the *Catechism*.[3]

The Old Testament Canon can be divided up into three major sections: Histories, Wisdom, and Prophets. The primary preachers in the Old Testament were the prophets. One purpose of the structure of the Old Testament "is to prepare for and declare in prophecy the coming of Christ, Redeemer of all men, and of His Messianic Kingdom."[4] Our Lord explains: "These are my words that I spoke to you while I was still with you, that everything written about me in the law of Moses and in the prophets and psalms must be fulfilled" (Luke 24:44). The Church Fathers spoke of the Old Testament prefigurements of New Testament ideas (for example, the Ark of the Covenant prefigures Mary, the manna in the desert prefigures the Eucharist). *Dei Verbum* explains:

> For in the context of the human situation before the era of salvation established by Christ, the books of the Old Testament provide an understanding of God and man and make clear to all men how a just and merciful God deals with mankind. These books, even though they contain matters imperfect and provisional, nevertheless show us authentic divine teaching."[5]

It goes on to note that "God, the inspirer and author of the books of both Testaments, in his wisdom has so brought it about that the New should be hidden in the Old and the Old should be manifest in the New."[6] Saint Paul points to this unfolding in his doxology to the Romans:

> Now to him who can strengthen you, according to my gospel and the proclamation of Jesus Christ, according to the revelation of the mystery kept secret for long ages but now manifested through the prophetic writings and, according to the command of the eternal God, made known to all nations to bring about the obedience of faith, to the only wise God, through Jesus Christ be glory forever and ever. Amen. (Rom. 16:25–27)

The Old Testament is best read in light of the Lord's death and resurrection, and in the context of the Church. The Church, under the inspiration of the Holy Spirit, decided which books were canonical and which were not. The Scriptures cannot be fully understood apart from or outside of the Catholic Church. Saint Augustine declared: "For my part, I should not believe the gospel except as moved by the authority of the Catholic Church."[7]

Preaching in the Old Testament was part of the preparation for the events of the New Testament, although preaching had its own value in the time and place in which it originally occurred. It typically took shape in the revelation of the Law and the proclamation of prophecies. It consisted of moral exhortations and the communication of God's will through the Mosaic Law. Old Testament preaching was tied into Israel's history. Through sermons, the Hebrew people were exhorted to follow the commandments, statutes, and decrees God set forth. The prophet Isaiah announced that the Lord's Word would be sent from His very mouth. It would not return "void," but instead would accomplish a special mission for God (Isa. 55:11). The Hebrew term for "word" is *dabar*, which means "event" or "occurrence" in many contexts. The *Word* going forth from the preacher's heart and lips had an impact on his listeners, but that impact is neither totally measurable nor totally comprehensible. Before discussing our first Old Testament homilist, it is useful to briefly discuss the context of his preaching, which is found in the Pentateuch.

THE PENTATEUCH

The Pentateuch (from the Greek *Pentateuchos*, meaning "a book composed of five scrolls") consists of the books of Genesis, Exodus, Leviticus, Numbers, and Deuteronomy. It is the proximate context for Moses' preaching (the remote being the Old Testament itself, and the immediate being the Book of Exodus, which describes the setting and content of Moses' preaching). The content of the Pentateuch is as follows: *Genesis* describes God's creation of the earth, the human race, and the Chosen People; *Exodus*, the Israelites' escape from captivity in Egypt with the help of Moses; *Leviticus*, the laws on holiness and worship prescribed for priests of the tribe of Levi; *Numbers*, the account of two censuses and lists of the Hebrew people taken at the beginning and toward the end of their journey from Egypt to the Promised Land; and *Deuteronomy*, the Last Will and Testament of Moses before Israel's entrance into the Promised Land.[8]

Scripture scholars tell us the Pentateuch in its current form dates to the time of Israel's return from the Babylonian exile (sixth–fifth centuries BC).[9] Recent research shows that the writings attributed to Moses, known as the Torah or Pentateuch, came from numerous sources, and were rearranged and rewritten by the sacred writers. These five books came to the Jewish people, and through them, to the Church.[10]

Moses: Covenant Preacher

Moses (ca. 1571–1406 BC) was the "founder and lawgiver" of Israel.[11] Moses is one of the central figures in the Old Testament. Pope Benedict, in an audience given in early June 2011, described Moses as

> the great prophet and leader during the time of the Exodus, [who] carried out his role as mediator between God and Israel by becoming, among the people, the bearer of the divine words and commandments, by guiding them toward the freedom of the Promised land, and by teaching the Israelites to live in obedience and trust toward God during their long sojourn in the desert; but also, and I would say especially, by praying (General Audience, June 1, 2011). [See, e.g., Ex. 8:10; Num. 12:9–13; 14:1–19; 21:4–9].

After the death of Joseph in Egypt, a new king arose there, who enslaved the Hebrews because he feared their potential power in a war. Moses was born in Egypt at a time when Pharaoh had ordered that all new-born male Hebrew children should be killed (Exod. 1:6–16). Moses' mother hid him in a basket and floated him down a river, where he was found and adopted by Pharaoh's daughter. Hence his name, which in Hebrew means "I drew him out of the water."

Moses received a "divine commission" to return to Egypt and rescue the Hebrews from bondage (Exod. 3).[12] After much opposition from Pharaoh, which was met by the infliction of ten plagues on the Egyptians, Moses led his people out of Egypt on the night of the Passover (Exod. 7–13). A dramatic chase followed. God manifested His glory when He led Israel across the Red Sea and Pharaoh and his armies drowned there. This remarkable event is recounted at the Easter Vigil Mass, and linked to the sacrament of Baptism.

Moses shepherded his people through the desert and to the holy mountain of Sinai. There he received the Ten Commandments. Saint Irenaeus, in his famous work *Against Heresies*, describes that time: "For forty days Moses was engaged in remembering the words of God, the heavenly patterns, the spiritual images, the foreshadowings of what was to come."[13] God's people continued their journey across the desert (the Sinai), where they frequently complained and rebelled against Moses. God provided them with manna for their physical nourishment and a Law to teach them. Saint Irenaeus comments: "The Law was therefore a school of instruction for them, and a prophecy of what was to come."[14]

On reaching the desert of Paran, Moses dispatched spies to the Promised Land. When the spies brought back exaggerated reports of the strength of its inhabitants, the Israelites turned against Moses, and "incurred the Divine sentence that they should wander in the desert for forty years."[15] Later, Moses and Aaron, "because of their unbelief," were told they would not enter the Promised Land (Num. 20:12). However, God allowed Moses to view it "from Mt. Pisgah."[16] Shortly afterwards, he blessed the tribes of Israel (Deut. 33), and died on Mt. Nebo in Moab at the age of 120 (Deut. 34:5–7).

Moses has a prominent place in Christian tradition. He appears in the Synoptic Gospels in the Transfiguration scene as the representative of the Law (Matt. 17:3; Mark 9:4; Luke 9:30). In the Letter to the Hebrews (3:1–6), the author compares his mission with that of Christ.

> Therefore, holy "brothers," sharing in a heavenly calling, reflect on Jesus, the apostle and high priest of our confession, who was faithful to the one who appointed him, just as Moses was "faithful in [all] his house." But he is worthy of more "glory" than Moses, as the founder of a house has more "honor" than the house itself. Every house is founded by someone, but the founder of all is God. Moses was "faithful in all his house" as a "servant" to testify to what would be spoken, but Christ was faithful as a son placed over his house. We are his house, if [only] we hold fast to our confidence and pride in our hope.

"In later tradition, he became the subject of many, often extravagant, legends."[17]

The Preaching of Moses

The Book of Exodus presents Moses in three important roles: as "leader and guide," as "prophet and teacher," and as "model and prototype" of the Chosen People.[18] As leader, Moses overcame many obstacles—"firstly, the opposition of the Israelites themselves, and then the stubbornness of the Pharaoh, and, later still, the forces of nature."[19] He lifted his people's spirits and shored up their weak faith.[20] When the people grumbled, Moses took their complaints to God, who punished them for their lack of faith.

As prophet and teacher, Moses brought God's Holy Law to the Israelites. The Book of Deuteronomy puts it this way: "I will raise up for them a prophet like you from among their kinsmen, and will put my words into his mouth; he shall tell them all that I command him" (18:18). The prophet Hosea says, "By a prophet the LORD brought Israel out of Egypt, and by a prophet they were protected" (12:14). The sacred writers placed on Moses' lips all the rules and regulations to do with the moral, religious and social life of the people. In the Book of Exodus, three codes or groups of important laws were included. They are the Moral Decalogue or Ten Commandments (20:1–17), the Code of the Covenant (20:22–23:33), and the Ritual Code (34:14–26). The Books of Numbers and Leviticus "attributed to Moses the laws that they contain," and Deuteronomy "takes the form of a long discourse spoken by Moses."[21] Finally, Moses is "regarded and projected as a model for his people."[22] His life is an image of the life of Israel; his remarkable birth "prefigures the birth of the people in the waters of the Red Sea";[23] his pleasant childhood in Pharaoh's court (Exod. 2:10) is "like the easy years the sons of Israel spent in Egypt" (1:6); his flight, which brought him to live as a stranger in Midian (2:11–22) is also "an image of the persecution of the people."[24] In the end, Moses' faith in the Divine plan (4:1–17) will serve as "the basis of the faith of the entire people."[25]

God chose Israel to be His own special people by means of a covenant. A covenant (in Hebrew *berit*, meaning "between two") was an agreement initiated by God with His people. It was more than an imposition of certain rules designed to regulate the people's moral and religious life; it was more than a commitment "to put certain basic laws into practice";[26] and it was more than a mutually beneficial arrangement. The covenant was an event that regulated the people's moral and religious activities. But it was also a bond between God and His people. He would protect them and they would follow His lead.

Moses is the mediator between God and the people. He was a preacher and promoter of the covenant. He brought the Ten Commandments down from Mount Sinai and explained the details to them. Herein lies the essence of the preaching of Moses. Moses' preaching is closely tied to the giving of the Law to the Hebrew people. He explains the Law to them and exhorts them to follow it closely. We find classic examples of covenant preaching and theology in Exodus, Numbers, and Deuteronomy.

The Mosaic code dealt first of all with the worship of God. The Jewish faith is a monotheistic faith. It requires the commitment of God's people to worship the one true God. The body of Hebrew legislation in the Pentateuch developed through many centuries and constituted a single body.[27] But it also dealt with political, social, and family affairs in "a progressive spirit" ahead of its time.[28] For example, unlike other Near Eastern societies, even a Hebrew king must fear God and obey the law, so that his heart will not become estranged from his brothers, and that he will not turn aside from the commandment, either to the right or to the left (Deut. 17:20).

Starting with chapter 20, the Book of Exodus outlines various details contained in the Book of the Covenant. There are laws concerning worship, slaves, homicide, violence, restitution, social relations, justice, the sabbath and great feasts, concluding with a series of warnings and promises (23:20–33). These binding laws are a guide and a protection for God's people. They enable the people to live as He intends.

The preaching of Moses took place for the first time on Mount Sinai, in the midst of God communicating the Ten Commandments to His People. Moses ascended the mountain, brought down the tablets, and conducted a sacred ritual. It is within this ritual that Moses' preaching first occurs. This service is found within the Sinai narrative (Exod. 19:1–24:11). "God's deliverance of Israel from slavery in Egypt, the revelation of the Law, and Israel's entering into a covenantal fellowship with God in worship became the theological foundation of the faith of Israel," says Hughes Old.[29] These events were reinterpreted and applied to peoples' lives throughout the rest of Scripture.

Exodus 24 describes the liturgical setting for the earliest reading of Scripture. Moses came to the people, related the word of God, to which they responded, "We will do everything that the LORD has told us" (24:3). He then wrote down the words, erected an altar and twelve pillars (representing the twelve tribes) at the foot of the mountain. Then he sent young men to offer sacrifices, took half of the blood, put it in large bowels (the other half splashed on the altar), and read from the Book of the Covenant. After the people vowed to do all the Lord commanded, he splashed the people with the blood, an act symbolizing the sealing of the covenant. He and his sons and seventy elders then ascended Mount Sinai, where they ate, drank and beheld the glory of God.

Nothing is said here about preaching the Word of God. But Old suggests that preaching did occur. He gives two principal reasons.

First, the Book of the Covenant found in Exodus 21–23 (which contains laws regarding the treatment of slaves, personal injury, property damage, social and religious laws) is an interpretation of the Ten Commandments. "Indeed, even in these earliest records one finds that the reading of the Scriptures entails their preaching," he writes.[30] The purpose of covenant preaching was to help God's people understand the Decalogue and apply it to their lives. This would better enable them to assume the obligations set forth on Mount Sinai.

Second, Old contends that preaching was a means of creating and maintaining communion with God, as we see in the incident of the Golden Calf. "For Moses himself on the top of Mount Sinai, it was not the sight of God that was the means of experiencing God's presence, but rather hearing his Word."[31] I disagree with Old on this point. Scripture does not say that Moses' primary experience of God was through the Word. The Burning Bush, the revelations on Mount Sinai and God's "passing by" are *visual* as well as *verbal* encounters, as this passage from Exodus 34:5–8 illustrates:

> Having come down in a cloud, the LORD stood with him there and proclaimed his name, "LORD." Thus the LORD passed before him and cried out, "The LORD, the LORD, a merciful and gracious God, slow to anger and rich in kindness and fidelity, continuing his kindness for a thousand generations, and forgiving wickedness and crime and sin; yet not declaring the guilty guiltless, but punishing children and grandchildren to the third and fourth generation for their fathers' wickedness!" Moses at once bowed down to the ground in worship.

I agree with Old that worship itself is an act of grace that transforms the worshiper through prayer, word, and ritual. God is a "holy fire," and to come near to him is to catch fire and glory with the same holy radiance. It is through entering into that covenant that we experience the glory of His presence, and through living in His presence, that we become holy.[32]

Finally, Old points out that the establishment of the Sabbath required preaching because the Sabbath was a day of religious memorial. The people were to imitate God, who rested from His work on the seventh day (Gen. 2:2). But they would also attend to the worship of God. This worship occurred in a memorial service, at which God's mighty works of creation and redemption were recounted. This requires an explanation and application of those works to contemporary Jewish life. This is the essence of Old Testament preaching.

Old tells us, "the sermonic material in Deuteronomy portrays Moses as the first great preacher and the founder of the long tradition of biblical preaching."[33]

With von Rad's understanding of Deuteronomy as background, Old makes five interesting observations about the preaching in Deuteronomy:

1. *Preaching activity was a ministry fulfilled by the Levitical priesthood.* Old quotes from Moses' words to the Levites in 33:10, in which the Levites promulgated decisions and communicated the Law to the Jews. It was they who brought the sacrifices and burnt offerings to the Lord. The tribe of Levi was responsible for the proclamation of God's Word as well as service at the altar of sacrifice. The Deuteronomist may have been trying to resist the Canaanite theology in regard to "cult, sacrifice, and priesthood," which led to the neglect of the teaching of the Law and the recounting of the Sinai traditions.[34] The ministry of the Word was an essential component of the Levitical priesthood.

2. *Deuteronomy contains covenantal theology, which has implications for preaching.* God and His Chosen People were bound in a covenantal relationship.

Therefore, the details of the covenant had to be read and preached to Israel. In Deuteronomy, as in Exodus, the covenant is the basis for Israel's worship and communion with God. Moses' reading and explaining the Law on the Plains of Moab (1:5) was "inherent in the whole nature of the covenant and a covenantal relationship."[35] In order to maintain the covenant relationship, the people had to understand its requirements and implications for their daily lives. These requirements and implications were brought out in covenant preaching.

3. *God reveals Himself in Deuteronomy through His Word.* The Hebrew word *dabar* refers to "a spoken utterance" (Deut. 4:10–13).[36] The words God spoke were commandments, decrees, and laws. *Dabar* refers to the Word of God revealed to Moses "as well as the word Moses preached to all Israel."[37] The clouds, thunder, and lightning on Mount Sinai were signs of the awesome power and mighty presence of God. These signs and God's Word constituted the communication with Moses. Preaching was a means of manifesting God's mighty presence and teaching people what He required of them.

4. *In Deuteronomy, we see the first evidence of the practice of a regular reading of Scripture in public worship.*[38] Chapter 31 describes Moses' final preparations to leave Israel to "the care of his successor, Joshua."[39] Moses then commanded that the Law "be read in the hearing of the people" every seven years.[40] In addition, the Shema (Deut. 6) is a traditional interpretation of the Commandments. The Shema was recited in the Jewish liturgy of morning and evening prayer.[41] Jewish scholars say it was originally recited with the Ten Commandments. It was considered vitally important for Israel to learn and live the covenant. The reading and preaching of Sacred Scripture in a proper liturgical setting was part of the covenant. The Third Commandment requires a regular gathering of the people to observe the Sabbath.

5. *Deuteronomy reveals much about the components of preaching.* Old cites the author Gerhard von Rad, who identifies three components of covenant preaching in Deuteronomy. These components are a useful way of understanding covenant preaching.

a. *Remembrance* is retelling the story of God's saving works (Deut. 4:9–14; 7:18; 8:2). The story of the victory at the Red Sea, as well as the story of the victory over the kings of Bashan, illustrate God's power and fidelity to His people. Remembering "leads to thanksgiving, and thanksgiving leads to faithfulness."[42]

b. *Interpretation* is the application of the Law to the concrete events of daily life (Deut. 1:5). Samuel Driver, a nineteenth century Old Testament scholar, tells us that the phrase "undertook to explain" suggests that the purpose of Deuteronomic preaching was to expound the Law of Moses.[43] For example, in chapter 4 of Deuteronomy we hear the prohibition of idol worship. God was not to be represented by human forms, and even solar, lunar, or astral divinities were not to be adored as gods. The reason was that the sun, moon, and stars are known to all people; the true God is the God who has revealed Himself to Israel alone.

c. *Exhortation* is the urging of Israel to keep the faith, obey the Law, and
    love the Lord their God. Old explains:

> The Levitical preachers whose work we come to know in Deuteron-
> omy understood the need for exhortation. They knew that human
> minds forget and human hearts can harden. They understood well that
> again and again the faithful must be exhorted to faith and the saints
> must be inspired to holiness . . . [Studying] the book of Deuteronomy
> one recognizes that it is the work of a very conscientious priesthood,
> a priesthood ministering to God's people in days of apostasy.[44]

Having examined the features of covenant preaching, it is now time to look
an example of it. The following excerpt is from the Book of Deuteronomy,
which is Moses' last will and testament. It develops the Covenant theme, and its
implications for the Chosen people. This passage captures the wonder and awe
of the Divine Election.

In this example, we have an excellent homily on the election of Israel, one
of the stylistic and theological high points of the Book of Deuteronomy. It may
come from the exilic period. The Exodus theme in relation to God's creation of
the world is a basic motif in this passage. The polemic against idolatry acknowledges Yahweh as the one true God (Isa. 45:5–6, 18, 22), and Israel as His own
unique People. This passage is found in the weekday Lectionary, on Friday of
the Eighteenth Week in Ordinary Time, Year I.

Homily: Israel's unique vocation

> "Ask now of the days of old, before your time, ever since God created man
> upon the earth; ask from one end of the sky to the other: Did anything so great
> ever happen before? Was it ever heard of? Did a people ever hear the voice of
> God speaking from the midst of fire, as you did, and live? Or did any god ven-
> ture to go and take a nation for himself from the midst of another nation, by
> testings, by signs and wonders, by war, with his strong hand and outstretched
> arm, and by great terrors, all of which the LORD, your God, did for you in
> Egypt before your very eyes? All this you were allowed to see that you might
> know the LORD is God and there is no other. Out of the heavens he let you hear
> his voice to discipline you; on earth he let you see his great fire, and you heard
> him speaking out of the fire. For love of your fathers he chose their descendants
> and personally led you out of Egypt by his great power, driving out of your way
> nations greater and mightier than you, so as to bring you in and to make their
> land your heritage as it is today. This is why you must now know, and fix in
> your heart, that the LORD is God in the heavens above and on earth below, and
> that there is no other. You must keep his statutes and commandments which I
> enjoin on you today, that you and your children after you may prosper, and that
> you may have long life on the land which the LORD, your God, is giving you
> forever." (Deut. 4:32–40)

THE MAJOR PROPHETS

The prophets were God's spokesmen. They proclaimed the message given to them by the Lord in the particular circumstances in which they lived. There were major prophets and minor prophets. The term *major prophets* refers to the length of their books. Jeremiah, Isaiah, Daniel, and Ezekiel are considered to be the major prophets because their books are the longest in the Old Testament prophetic corpus. Their mission was to bring comfort to those who heard and accepted the Word, and to warn Israel to repent and to return to God.

Roland de Vaux, in his monumental work on the institutions of ancient Israel, sums up the difference between the ministry of the Word as it was exercised by the priests, and the ministry of the Word as it was exercised by the prophets: the *priests* were concerned with the interpretation and application of God's Word as revealed in the Law of Moses, whereas the *prophets* were concerned with proclaiming God's Word as revealed directly to them.[45]

The prophets never claimed to be men of profound human wisdom, to have a deep knowledge of history, or to be shapers of culture. Rather they were convinced that God spoke directly to them, and that their mission was to communicate God's Word to His people. When the prophets pronounced God's Word, they had something dynamic in mind. They understood that Word to be a powerful force, "an *authoritative word* by which God ruled his kingdom, a *creative word* by which the heavens and earth came into existence, a *word of judgment* that made the crooked straight and the rough places smooth, a *redemptive word* by which God's ultimate purposes were brought to fulfillment," says Old.[46]

The prophets had two essential tasks: to denounce evil, injustice, and infidelity, in other words, *to condemn*; and to inspire God's people to holiness, fidelity, and love, in other words, *to uplift*. The prophet offered a message of hope and healing. His words were anointed to bring comfort to the hearts of God's people. He also challenged them to live out their covenant commitments.

The prophet offered a vision that would encourage people to live as He taught. On the one hand, the prophet Amos was adept at denouncing the infidelity of Israel. The prophet Isaiah, on the other hand, painted a beautiful picture of an ideal society in chapter seven of his book.

We will examine three prophets in order to understand the proclamation of the Word. Two, Jeremiah and Isaiah, are major prophets and one, Jonah, is a minor prophet. Each provides good insights into the proclamation of the Word.

Jeremiah: Preaching Prophet[47]

The prophet Jeremiah (ca. 650–570 BC) was from the land of Judah, and belonged to the family of Abiathar, the high priest whom King Solomon had deprived of his priestly functions. Jeremiah received his vocation to the prophetic office in 626 BC (Jer. 1:1–19).

His ministry coincided with the reign of King Josiah (640–608). Jeremiah was caught up in the religious, political and military events of that time, as Israel wavered between fidelity to the Lord on one hand and surrender to the surrounding culture on the other. Although he was not involved in civic affairs during the first years of his ministry, he probably "approved of King Josiah's religious reform (2 Kings 22:1–23:30) without [participating] in it."[48] Josiah died at a place called Megiddo (608), and the people and its leaders under King Jehoiakim (607–597) relapsed into idolatry. Jeremiah's reaction was swift and strong. From then on, Jeremiah proclaimed "the destruction of Jerusalem and the Temple."[49]

After the fall of Nineveh (606) Jeremiah counseled submission to the Babylonians, but the king resisted, and Judah did not surrender until after Jehoiakim's death in 597 BC. Under the new king, Zedekiah, Judah continued to side with Egypt against Babylon, rejecting the warnings of the prophet, who again counseled both submission to Babylon and trust in the Lord. During the siege of Jerusalem, he was first imprisoned, and then "thrown into a pit from which he was later rescued."[50] In Jerusalem's final destruction in 586 BC, Jeremiah was released and returned to Judah. But after the assassination of the governor Gedaliah, the Jews took him with them into Egypt, where he continued to reproach his countrymen for their idolatry (Jer. 44). There is no record of his death. The ancient writer Tertullian claims that Jeremiah was stoned to death by the Jews. The author of the Letter to the Hebrews must have had Jeremiah, among others, in mind when he wrote:

> [The prophets] were stoned, sawed in two, put to death at sword's point; they went about in skins of sheep or goats, needy, afflicted, tormented. The world was not worthy of them. They wandered about in deserts and on mountains, in caves and in crevices in the earth. (Heb. 11:37–38)

The Preaching of Jeremiah

Jeremiah was one of the greatest preachers in the Old Testament. His public ministry had a profound effect on his people and changed the course of his own life. Jeremiah is the most passionate Old Testament prophet, conscious throughout of his closeness to God, and of the dignity and responsibility of the individual toward his Creator. His prophetic vocation, which entailed the denunciation of the sins of Judah and the proclamation of their punishment, conflicted tragically with his love for his people, which led him to intercede on their behalf.

Jeremiah's intercession was a sign of his concern for a people who had sinned, and who were now being called to account for their sins. God told Jeremiah that if Israel refused to repent of its idolatry, He would destroy the Temple, the central focus of divine worship. On the other hand, if they repented, He would save them (7:5–7). Their destiny was in their hands.

The prophet's sufferings, caused by the ingratitude and misunderstanding of his people, his prophecy of the destruction of Jerusalem, and his weeping over the doomed city, have traditionally been interpreted as figures of the life of Christ (Luke 19:41). The Church has used this Book, together with the Book of Lamentations ascribed to him, in her offices at the end of Lent (Passiontide).[51]

The preaching of Jeremiah must be understood in the context of his prophetic mission to a people who had fallen away from the worship of the one true God. Israel's infidelity led to Jeremiah's warnings and denunciations. Unfortunately his warnings fell on deaf ears.

Although the personalism of Jeremiah was different from the collectivism of the apocalyptists, one feature of his preaching may have indirectly but profoundly affected the latter. His recognition of the individual's worth and responsibility underscores that it is not enough to be an Israelite; implicit in this belief is the recognition that Gentiles can be absorbed into the kingdom of God.[52]

Hughes Old notes that Jeremiah's sermons are often sealed with a sign. For example, in chapter nineteen, God tells Jeremiah to purchase a *potter's flask* and then preach to the priests and the elders of Israel. He is then to smash the flask in the sight of those he brought with him as a sign that God will "break this people and this city" so that "it cannot be repaired" (19:11). Another prophetic sign appears in chapter twenty-seven. In this case, it is a *yoke*. Jeremiah entered the courts of the Temple with a yoke around his neck, and there delivered a message regarding the breaking of the yoke of Nebuchadnezzar, and the return of subject peoples to Israel. A third prophetic sign is found in chapter thirty-two. This is a sign of restoration. God tells Jeremiah that before long some of his relatives from Anathoth will come to him and offer to sell him *a field* that was apparently part of the family patrimony.[53] Jeremiah had the right to the property, but he had to buy it if he wanted to keep it within the family. God told Jeremiah to buy the property as a sign that the time would finally come when God's people would be reestablished in their own land.[54] Old concludes that these prophetic signs do more than illustrate the Word; they "confirm and seal" it.[55]

The Temple in Israel was the place where God resided. It was an appropriate physical and symbolic setting for Jeremiah's famous sermon (the Temple Sermon). As a physical location, it was the appropriate place in which to exhort the people, as the Word was broken open there. As a spiritual location, it was equally appropriate, because Jeremiah denounced the spiritual infidelity of the people and defilement of the Temple. You could call the Temple Sermon "Jeremiah's theological debut."

The Temple Sermon pointed out the errors held by God's people: a false confidence in the power of Jerusalem, false behavior among believers, false worship, false expectations. The peoples' confidence was misplaced because the Temple would not serve as a refuge for the Jews against their enemies as long as they refused to thoroughly reform their ways. This sermon gets to the heart of repentance. Excerpts from this homily are found on Thursday of the third week of Lent, and Saturday of the sixteenth week in Ordinary Time, Year II.

Homily: The Temple Sermon

The following message came to Jeremiah from the LORD: Stand at the gate of
the house of the LORD, and there proclaim this message: Hear the word of the
LORD, all you of Judah who enter these gates to worship the LORD! Thus says
the LORD of hosts, the God of Israel: Reform your ways and your deeds, so that
I may remain with you in this place. Put not your trust in the deceitful words:
"This is the temple of the LORD! The temple of the LORD! The temple of the
LORD!" Only if you thoroughly reform your ways and your deeds; if each of
you deals justly with his neighbor; if you no longer oppress the resident alien,
the orphan, and the widow; if you no longer shed innocent blood in this place,
or follow strange gods to your own harm, will I remain with you in this place,
in the land which I gave your fathers long ago and forever.

But here you are, putting your trust in deceitful words to your own loss!
Are you to steal and murder, commit adultery and perjury, burn incense to
Baal, go after strange gods that you know not, and yet come to stand before me
in this house which bears my name, and say: "We are safe; we can commit all
these abominations again"? Has this house which bears my name become in
your eyes a den of thieves? I too see what is being done, says the LORD. You
may go to Shiloh, which I made the dwelling place of my name in the beginning. See what I did to it because of the wickedness of my people Israel. And
now, because you have committed all these misdeeds, says the LORD, because
you did not listen, though I spoke to you untiringly; because you did not answer, though I called you, I will do to this house named after me, in which you
trust, and to this place which I gave to you and your fathers, just as I did to Shiloh. I will cast you away from me, as I cast away all your brethren, all the off-
spring of Ephraim.

You, now, do not intercede for this people; raise not in their behalf a
pleading prayer! Do not urge me, for I will not listen to you. Do you not see
what they are doing in the cities of Judah, in the streets of Jerusalem? The children gather wood, their fathers light the fire, and the women knead dough to
make cakes for the queen of heaven, while libations are poured out to strange
gods in order to hurt me. Is it I whom they hurt, says the LORD; is it not rather
themselves, to their own confusion? See now, says the Lord GOD, my anger
and my wrath will pour out upon this place, upon man and beast, upon the trees
of the field and the fruits of the earth; it will burn without being quenched.

Thus says the LORD of hosts, the God of Israel: Heap your holocausts
upon your sacrifices; eat up the flesh! In speaking to your fathers on the day I
brought them out of the land of Egypt, I gave them no command concerning
holocaust or sacrifice. This rather is what I commanded them: Listen to my
voice; then I will be your God and you shall be my people. Walk in all the ways
that I command you, so that you may prosper.

But they obeyed not, nor did they pay heed. They walked in the hardness
of their evil hearts and turned their backs, not their faces, to me. From the day
that your fathers left the land of Egypt even to this day, I have sent you untiringly all my servants the prophets. Yet they have not obeyed me nor paid heed;
they have stiffened their necks and done worse than their fathers. When you
speak all these words to them, they will not listen to you either; when you call

to them, they will not answer you. Say to them: This is the nation which does not listen to the voice of the LORD, its God, or take correction. Faithfulness has disappeared; the word itself is banished from their speech.

> Cut off your dedicated hair and throw
> it away!
> on the heights intone an elegy;
> For the LORD has rejected and cast off
> the generation that draws down his
> wrath.

The people of Judah have done what is evil in my eyes, says the LORD. They have defiled the house which bears my name by setting up in it their abominable idols. In the Valley of Ben-hinnom they have built the high place of Topheth to immolate in fire their sons and their daughters, such a thing as I never commanded or had in mind. Therefore, beware! days will come, says the LORD, when Topheth and the Valley of Ben-hinnom will no longer be called such, but rather the Valley of Slaughter. For lack of space, Topheth will be a burial place. The corpses of this people will be food for the birds of the sky and for the beasts of the field, which no one will drive away. In the cities of Judah and in the streets of Jerusalem I will silence the cry of joy, the cry of gladness, the voice of the bridegroom and the voice of the bride; for the land will be turned to rubble. (Jer. 7:1–34)

Ezekiel: Exilic Preacher

The prophet Ezekiel (ca. seventh century BC) was one of the great figures in ancient Israel. Like Jeremiah, he was a priest as well as a prophet. His complex character also makes him one of the most interesting figures in Israel's history. Ezekiel's prophecy focused on the Temple and the liturgy. This made him unique among prophets. His influence on the post-exilic Jewish religion led to his being called "The Father of Judaism." Ezekiel was the son of a priest named Buzi. He was educated as a young man in preparation for priestly ministry. Though no biography of Buzi survives, he was probably a man of great importance in priestly circles.

Ezekiel was born around 623 BC, probably in Jerusalem where his father served in the great Temple. He grew up in the waning years of the independence of Judah, which was constantly threatened with military subjugation by the superpower of that time, the Babylonian Empire.[56] When Ezekiel was around twenty-six years old, his native city of Jerusalem was attacked and quickly defeated by the powerful armies of the Babylonian Emperor Nebuchadnessar. The state of Judah survived this time, but ten years later it was attacked again, and many of Jerusalem's ruling citizens, Ezekiel included, were carried off as exiles to Babylon.

Ezekiel belonged to a community established at a place called Tel Abib, by the river Chebar, which was actually "an irrigation canal, drawing waters from the Euphrates River near Babylon itself."[57] The exiles built mud brick homes, planted gardens, and settled near the capital city. In the fifth year of his exile, Ezekiel had a profound religious experience. He was called to be a prophet, and fulfilled that call for the next twenty years.

Ezekiel was "an astute observer of political events, possessing an extensive knowledge of geography, human commerce, priestly lore, foreign literature, and mythology."[58] Ezekiel was the first prophet to receive the call to prophesy outside the Holy Land. His first task as an exile was to prepare his fellow countrymen for the destruction of Jerusalem, which they believed was inviolable. Therefore, the first part of his book dealt with Israel's present sins and predictions of the future. The prophet wrote as one overawed by the mystery, majesty, and holiness of God.[59] His own experience, shared by his fellow exiles, had convinced him of the universality of the rule of God, who must be worshiped in Babylon as well as in Palestine. Like Jeremiah, he stressed the responsibility of the individual in the sight of God, but he also had a deep respect for the corporate nature of the religious community, as is shown "by his careful provisions for the future well being of the restored state."[60] His famous vision of the dry bones in chapter thirty-seven expresses his firm belief in a forthcoming restoration, Israel rising to new life from the graveyard of Babylon. But Ezekiel's "new covenant" would see its fulfillment with the coming of Jesus in the New Testament. The last of his prophecies can be dated with certainty in 571 BC. The date and location of his death are uncertain.

The Preaching Of Ezekiel

Ezekiel is one of the most fascinating preachers in the Old Testament. In many ways, he resembles prophets of old like Elijah and Elisha. He clearly depends on his predecessors, and his teaching is a development of theirs. Like Elijah and Elisha, Ezekiel was not afraid to challenge the sins of Israel, and warn his people of the consequences. His visions cannot be fully comprehended apart from a priestly mentality. He was an exilic prophet whose writings profoundly influenced the Jewish community. His message was two-fold: warning and promise.

As one of the first Jews captured after the 597 BC Babylonian invasion, Ezekiel's focused on preparing his fellow countrymen in Babylon for the destruction of Jerusalem. He reproached Israel for her past and present sins, and warned of further destruction if the people failed to repent. When the people rejected or ignored his message, God punished Israel through Nebuchadnezzar, king of Babylon. In 587 BC, the armies of Nebuchadnezzar returned to Jerusalem, killed many of its citizens, and took many captives. This terrible atrocity completed the destruction of Jerusalem, and the lives and fortunes of its inhabitants changed dramatically. In response, Ezekiel's message shifted in tone and content. A bright ray of sunshine was cast upon Israel as he now spoke of a new covenant, and announced the dawn of a new age when Israel would be restored and live under the rule of the Lord. Perhaps no other prophet stressed the absolute majesty of God the way Ezekiel did. He was in awe of the God of Israel and used various images to bring that message out. While sections of his book are clearly the work of redactors, the substance of it belongs to the prophet.

Certainly Ezekiel employed speech, but his words were rarely simple sermons. He recounted "visions, expounded allegories, and propounded parables."[61] His words, both prosaic and poetic, were "penetrated with symbolism and hidden meanings lying beneath the surface of the words themselves."[62] Ezekiel's actions are also heavily laden with symbolism. For example, during a period of dumbness, the prophet's silence spoke as eloquently as anything he said (Ezek. 3:22–27). The vision of his eating a scroll was an effective means of communication (Ezek. 3:1–3). The prophet's message cannot be summed up in a single sentence, but perhaps its most distinctive characteristic is "the awareness expressed throughout the book of God's holiness."[63] God was "other," vastly different from mortals in His power and purity (Ezek. 1:1–3).[64] Nevertheless, there was a close relationship between God and human beings. Ezekiel believed people to be sinful, irresponsible, weak, and in desperate need of God's mercy.

Israel's identity had been founded on "its unique calling as God's *chosen people*, and the possession of the Promised Land."[65] Now that their land was gone, many Jews asked themselves if God had abandoned them, and if so, what would they do? Ezekiel spent much time talking about judgment and doom for God's people, yet he also stressed God's mercy and the hope He offered. God would put a new heart and a new spirit into His people, and rescue them from the dark valley of their exilic existence. Somehow the disasters happening to them were part of His plan, and Israel was called to put its trust in Him. In the end, the hope expressed in this book triumphs over the doom he foretells. One partial realization of the hope Ezekiel offered was in the restoration of the Temple in Jerusalem. Nehemiah and Ezra were in the spirit of Ezekiel in their emphasis on Jerusalem, the restored Temple, the Law, and the priesthood.

In the interest of brevity, I chose one passage from the Book of Ezekiel, chapter seventeen, to illustrate the importance of the use of images in preaching. This passage is a great piece of literary art. Ezekiel uses clear and powerful images to make his points. Keeping in mind that allegory is "an extended metaphor in which one series of events or persons represents another series of events or persons," let us pay attention to the prophet's style and method.[66] Excerpts from this passage are found on the Eleventh Sunday in Ordinary Time, Year B.

Homily: The Eagles and the Vine

Thus the word of the LORD came to me: Son of man, propose a riddle, and speak this proverb to the house of Israel: Thus speaks the Lord GOD:

The great eagle, with great wings, with
   long pinions,
with thick plumage, many-hued,

came to Lebanon.
He took the crest of the cedar,
   tearing off its topmost branch,
And brought it to a land of tradesmen,
   set it in a city of merchants.
Then he took some seed of the land,
   and planted it in a seedbed;
A shoot by plentiful waters,
   like a willow he placed it,
To sprout and grow up a vine,
   dense and low-lying,
Its branches turned toward him,
   its roots lying under him.
Thus it became a vine, produced
     branches
   and put forth shoots.
But there was another great eagle,
   great of wing, rich in plumage;
To him this vine bent its roots,
sent out its branches,
That he might water it more freely
   than the bed where it was planted.
In a fertile field by plentiful waters it
     was planted,
   to grow branches, bear fruit,
   and become a majestic vine.

Say: Thus says the Lord GOD: Can it prosper? Will he not rather tear it out by the roots and strip off its fruit, so that all its green growth will wither when he pulls it up by the roots? [No need of a mighty arm or many people to do this.] True, it is planted, but will it prosper? Will it not rather wither, when touched by the east wind, in the bed where it grew?

Thus the word of the LORD came to me: Son of man, say now to the rebellious house: Do you not understand what this means? It is this: The king of Babylon came to Jerusalem and took away its king and princes with him to Babylon. Then he selected a man of the royal line with whom he made a covenant, binding him under oath, while removing the nobles of the land, so that the kingdom would remain a modest one, without aspirations, and would keep his covenant and obey him. But this man rebelled against him, sending envoys to Egypt to obtain horses and a great army. Can he prosper? Can he who does such things escape? Can he break a covenant and still go free? As I live, says the Lord GOD, in the home of the king who set him up to rule, whose oath he spurned, whose covenant with him he broke, there in Babylon I swear he shall die! When ramps are cast up and siege towers are built for the destruction of many lives, he shall not be saved in the conflict by Pharaoh with a great army and numerous troops. He spurned his oath, breaking his covenant. Though he gave his hand in pledge, he did all these things. He shall not escape!

Therefore say: Thus says the Lord GOD: As I live, my oath which he spurned, my covenant which he broke, I swear to bring down upon his head. I will spread my net over him, and he shall be taken in my snare. I will bring him to Babylon and enter into judgment with him there over his breaking faith with me. All the crack troops among his forces shall fall by the sword, and the survivors shall be scattered in every direction. Thus you shall know that I, the LORD, have spoken.

Therefore say: Thus says the Lord GOD:

> I, too, will take from the crest of the
>   cedar,
>   from its topmost branches tear off a
>   tender shoot,
> And plant it on a high and lofty moun-
>   tain;
>   on the mountain heights of Israel I
>   will plant it.
> It shall put forth branches and bear
>   fruit,
>   and become a majestic cedar.
> Birds of every kind shall dwell beneath
>   it,
>   every winged thing in the shade of its
>   boughs.
> And all the trees of the field shall know
>   that I, the LORD,
> Bring low the high tree,
>   lift high the lowly tree,
> Wither up the green tree,
>   and make the withered tree bloom.

As I, the LORD, have spoken, so will I do. (Ezek. 17:1–24)

THE MINOR PROPHETS

The term *minor prophets* refers to the length of the books by several prophets. The books are short, only a few chapters in each. But these short books contain powerful messages. Among them are Micah, Hosea, Amos, and Jonah. For the purpose of this book, we select the most popular of the minor prophets: Jonah.

Jonah: Reluctant Preacher

The Book of Jonah (ca. sixth century BC) is the story of a prophet who struggles with his divine commission. On the one hand, he knows that God has called him to preach repentance to his hated enemy. On the other hand, he prefers his enemy to be destroyed by God, and so he tries to escape his prophetic responsibilities. The book was written during the fifth or sixth century BC, when Jews were struggling to adjust to the Babylonian Exile. It is the common view of scholars that Jonah did not exist. In addition, the Book of Jonah is considered by many to be a work of didactic fiction, an extended parable, or a humorous tale, intended to undermine the exclusiveness of some prophets upon the return of the Jews from exile. The book has been called "a literary masterpiece that has captivated its readers and stirred artistic imaginations from the Midrash to Melville—long after the particular issues faced by the post-exilic community had been resolved."[67] "Jonah, son of Amittai" (1:1) probably refers to the eighth-century Northern Kingdom prophet briefly described in 2 Kings 14:25 as a popular prophet who proclaims divine mercy and support for that kingdom. Jonah means "Dove son of truth." The dove has two major characteristics in the Hebrew Bible: it is easily put to flight and seeks secure refuge in the mountains (Ezek. 7:16; Ps. 55:6–8), and it moans and laments when in distress (Isa. 38:14).[68]

Jonah is commanded to enter the foreign city of Nineveh and pronounce divine judgment. Nineveh is the later capital of Assyria, the very nation that in sixty years would destroy and exile Jonah's countrymen—the ten tribes of the Northern Kingdom. Nineveh, "whose evil is antithetical to God's will, is therefore a threat to Israel's very existence."[69] Jonah's response is an unexpected one for a prophet. He flees to the city of Tarshish to the far west, probably because he thought it was beyond God's presence (Isa. 66:19). The author depicts Jonah's flight from YHWH's presence as a series of "descents"—into Joppa, into the ship, into the bowels of the ship.[70] Jonah then lies down and falls into a deep sleep. The Lord hurls a violent tempest at the ship as a sign of His divine displeasure and as part of the divine plan. The ship's captain and crew pray to their gods, jettison their cargo, and cast lots. They know that their destiny is in the hands of a higher power (Jon. 1:14). The sailors' frantic activity is contrasted with Jonah's inactivity. Unlike Jesus (Mark 4:35–41), "his sleeping suggests paralysis rather than faith."[71] Ironically, Jonah's flight from his divine commission leads the sailors to worship the Lord.

Jonah is cast into the sea, swallowed by a large fish, where he spends three days and three nights, and then is spewed out on shore. He then proceeds to preach to the citizens of Nineveh. He announces God's word of judgment and a remarkable thing occurs. The Ninevites turn from their evil ways, put on sackcloth and ashes, and fast. Surprisingly, Jonah's response is anger, frustration, and rebellion. He camps out east of the city, probably in the hope that Nineveh will falter, builds a booth for himself (perhaps a reflection of the Temple), and waits. He takes shelter under a tree, which is attacked by a worm (perhaps an allusion to the tree of life in Eden attacked by Satan (Gen. 3:1–2). Throughout the story, Jonah has sought shelter in various places (Tarshish, a ship, a large fish, a tree) and each shelter passes away. Perhaps the message is that in a world that offers no eternally secure shelters, Jonah is "encouraged to understand and even emulate the divine pity shown to the Ninevites."[72]

Jonah is more than an ancient preacher. He is a symbol of those who struggle with preaching the Word of God. Jonah did not desire the conversion of Nineveh. In fact, he wanted its utter destruction at the hand of God. And he knew that God's Word would convert them if preached. Therefore, he fled. But God caught up with him, and gave him time and space to reflect on the error of his ways. God refuses to take "no" for an answer. In the end, God's will prevailed, and both Jonah and the citizens of Nineveh were better as a result.

The Preaching Of Jonah

Jonah's homily teaches us that an abundance of words, ideas and facts does not necessarily make effective preaching. As a parishioner often reminds me: "Less is more, Father." In other words, you can say much in few words. Jonah's preaching centers around one theme: *Reform*. Reform means changing one's ways and breaking with one's sinful past attitudes and behavior. It means changing the direction of one's spiritual life in the hope of growing in union with God. Jonah, inspired by the Spirit of God, successfully carried this message to Nineveh, and, ironically, was upset when it worked because he preferred Nineveh's destruction. The justice and graciousness of God are evident throughout this short book. God treats Nineveh justly when it repents. He reproves Jonah in a gentle, almost playful way. But the real message is the function of judgment and the power of the message to reform individuals and even whole communities.

Among the characteristics of Jonah's preaching, we can identify the following: clarity, brevity, effectiveness, and divine origin. His message was *clear*. He understood what God wanted him to say but, as we have seen, resisted God's call to say it. *Brevity* was another characteristic. His message was for Nineveh to repent of its sins. They were to express sorrow for their behavior and turn away from their former sins. That simple message, which the Church has echoed ever since, had a profound impact on the Ninevites. This brings us to the third characteristic of his preaching: *effectiveness*. When the Ninevites heard the message, they repented of their sins, put on sackcloth, sat in ashes, and fasted from food and water. Fourth, the message was effective because it came *from God*. God, who in various ways encouraged Jonah, filled the message with His grace and changed the hearts of the Ninevites. These four characteristics, common to many preachers, constitute powerful homilies.

The theme of reform in this passage is an excellent one for Advent or Lent, a season of reconciliation and repentance. Here we see the election of Jonah as prophet, his reluctance to accept this Divine mandate, and his final fulfillment of it. It is found on Tuesday of the 27th Week in Ordinary Time, Year 1.

Homily: Repent and Reform!

The word of the LORD came to Jonah a second time: "Set out for the great city of Nineveh, and announce to it the message that I will tell you." So Jonah made ready and went to Nineveh, according to the LORD's bidding. Now Nineveh was an enormously large city; it took three days to go through it. Jonah began his journey through the city, and had gone but a single day's walk announcing,

"Forty days more and Nineveh shall be destroyed," when the people of Nineveh believed God; they proclaimed a fast and all of them, great and small, put on sackcloth.

When the news reached the king of Nineveh, he rose from his throne, laid aside his robe, covered himself with sackcloth, and sat in the ashes. Then he had this proclaimed throughout Nineveh, by decree of the king and his nobles: "Neither man nor beast, neither cattle nor sheep, shall taste anything; they shall not eat, nor shall they drink water. Man and beast shall be covered with sackcloth and call loudly to God; every man shall turn from his evil way and from the violence he has in hand. Who knows, God may relent and forgive, and withhold his blazing wrath, so that we shall not perish." When God saw by their actions how they turned from their evil way, he repented of the evil that he had threatened to do to them; he did not carry it out. (Jon. 3:1–10)

Pre-Christian Homiletic History

Prophetism was silent until 460 BC, when Malachi appeared, leveling sharp reproaches against the priests and rulers of the people. The severity of his reproaches may help explain the anonymous name he used (Malachi means "My Messenger"). This criticism of the abuses of priests and religious indifference in the community may have prepared the way for the reform measures of Ezra and Nehemiah (who arrived in Jerusalem around 445 BC). Nehemiah, a governor/king, and Ezra, a priest, did carry out the wishes of the prophet Malachi by recommitting the people to the Law and the Temple.

There was a decisive shift after the Babylonian exile. As Caroll Stuhlmueller puts it: "In the post-exilic age, preaching no longer strove primarily to instill personal goodness and social justice; its goal was the careful functioning of the liturgy."[73] This is an important development. The previous prophets were focused on delivering oracles and other messages from God to His people. Unlike Moses, their focus was on communicating a message which was mediated through their cultural, social, and personal experiences. Now preaching centered around the Temple and liturgical celebrations.

As we will see, Jesus was the fulfillment of the prophets and psalms (Luke 24:27). All that was said in the Old Testament foreshadowed and prepared the people for the coming of the Messiah. Jesus the Messiah is the greatest preacher in history, not only because of His style and message, but also because He perfectly embodied the message He proclaimed, namely, that He is the Chosen One who came to redeem the world. He teaches us how to preach, as well as serving as the content of the preached message itself.

Before delving into the New Testament period, it would be helpful to briefly examine the development of preaching in the centuries before Christ. Several developments in Judaism influenced the shape and course of preaching history in Christianity.

First, the Wisdom Tradition contains important contributions to the history of preaching. The Wisdom School goes back at least to the time of Solomon, the son of David and the king of Israel. This school flourished later than either the priestly or prophetic schools, and reached its zenith in the post-exilic period. *Priests* were concerned with "preserving the oral tradition," while *prophets* were concerned with "uttering the oracles of God in a living voice," and the *wisdom teachers* were concerned with "the written word."[74] In the post-exilic community, the written word became more important, so memorizing, copying and interpreting the Word of God became a highly refined process. Scribes were devoted to learning the Word of God. In fact, this learning process was seen as an act of worship. The devout Jew loved and lived the Word of God. The Wisdom School sought to instill "the fear of the LORD," in other words holy awe and reverence. The fear of the Lord was called "the beginning of wisdom," and knowledge of the Holy One was called "understanding" (Prov. 9:10). The Wisdom School taught high moral and ethical values. It sought to promote justice and right living. Wisdom was a spiritual and practical art. This theology of the Wisdom School taught that the opening of scrolls, reading and scholarly devotion to a text, and sacred studies glorified God. A highly specialized training in biblical interpretation also developed.

This school had a profound impact on preaching as well. This was the time "when the expository sermon came into its own."[75] "Preaching was not simply a matter of moral or theological training, merely inculcating moral principles into the community, or telling again the old traditions of the community." Expository preaching "was the presentation of the Scriptures in which these traditions and principles had received their canonical form."[76] Sermons at this time focused on the biblical text—its structure, grammar, and literary form. Preachers were not simply historians, but rather contemporary interpreters of divine revelation.

Second, the synagogue services shaped the ministry of the Word in several ways. "It is most often suggested that the synagogue originated during the Babylonian exile, when the Jerusalem Temple had been destroyed and the Jews needed a place to worship."[77] The account of the reading of the Law in chapter 8 of Nehemiah is the oldest description of a Liturgy of the Word.[78] This service was the basic form that has been handed down through the centuries in Jewish worship. The service involved the systematic reading and reflection on the Law as an essential feature of the worship of a restored Israel. In the Book of Nehemiah, Ezra the scribe stands on a platform, surrounded by community leaders, and reads from the Book of the Law. The people respond by lifting their hands and bowing their heads.

Several developments that influenced the history of Christian preaching took place at this time (post-428 BC). One was a systematic reading of the Scripture lessons. Early on in this development, a Scripture passage was read each Sabbath, beginning with Genesis and ending with Deuteronomy. This ensured that the community heard the entire Word in the course of one to four years. It also provided a systematic basis for preaching the Word. This is what we now call the *lectio continua*. The *lectio selecta*, that is, special lessons for certain feast days, was also part of the Sabbath proclamation. Cycles for the reading of the Law and Prophets were eventually developed. By the beginning of the Christian era, preaching was an important part of the worship in the synagogue. The goal of preaching was to interpret and apply the lessons read in worship to the daily lives of the congregation.[79] Preaching would do various things, including teach, admonish, inspire, and comfort the people.

Several different sermon methods were used. These included explaining a passage from the Law phrase by phrase; bringing in several secondary texts that dealt with a subject in a principal text; or beginning with a text in the lesson and adding to it text after text on the same topic. The rabbis preferred using parables in their preaching. "The homiletic parable took the central teaching of the text and illustrated it by means of an imaginative story that made the same point as the text." Homilists also elaborated and even exaggerated biblical stories (such as the victory at the Red Sea) to enlighten and inspire their congregations.[80]

Finally, a word on the rabbinical schools, which played an important role in the history of preaching, is in order. The rabbinical schools came from the courts of the Temple, where rabbis taught. The story of Jesus in the Jerusalem Temple (Luke 2:41–51) is a classic example of a rabbinical method in operation. The oral tradition of these schools was divided up into two kinds: "(1) *Midrash*, that is, a commentary on Scripture; and (2) *Mishnah*, the systematic interpretation of the Law that proceeds from one subject to another."[81] The rabbis proposed a discussion of certain subjects, questions were asked, students gave certain answers and the rabbi guided the discussion by questions and comments. He gave his solution and concluding comments at the end of the session. Hughes Old calls the study of Scripture a "sacred duty" and a "heavenly delight." It was both, as the ministry of the Word was an act of worship. The history we have been discussing is the necessary backdrop for our discussion of the preacher *par excellence* and His impact on the history of this subject. We are now ready to delve into the topic of preaching in the New Testament period.

SUMMARY

Preaching in the Old Testament was rooted in the Word of God as revealed to the patriarchs and prophets. This preaching was shaped by the events of the day, especially the Hebrews' liberation from Egypt and later the Babylonian Exile. The Word of God was applied to contemporary life by means of the Sabbath homily. Understanding the Word of God was not only a duty imposed on priests and rabbis. It was the duty of every Jew to know and live that Word. Through preaching, the Jews better understood how to apply that Word to their lives. The preaching of the Word also laid the groundwork for preaching in the time of Jesus and the early Church. As we move into the New Testament, we remain conscious of the events that shaped and guided Old Testament proclamation of the Word of God.

NOTES

1. Pius XII, Encyclical on Promoting Biblical Studies *Divino Afflante Spiritu* (September 30, 1943), no. 26, *Acta Apostolicae Sedis* 35 (1943): 290–345.

2. *Catechism of the Catholic Church,* 2nd ed. (Vatican City: Libreria Editrice Vaticana, 1997), 122.

3. Ibid.

4. *Dei Verbum*, no. 15.

5. Ibid.

6. Ibid., no. 16.

7. Augustine, *Against the Fundamental Epistle of Manichaeus*, no. 6, at New Advent, http://www.newadvent.org/fathers/1405.htm

8. *The Navarre Bible: Pentateuch,* Readers ed. (Princeton, NJ: Scepter, 2002), 17.

9. Ibid., 19.

10. Ibid.

11. *Oxford Dictionary of the Christian Church,* rev ed. (Oxford: Oxford University Press, 1983), s.v. "Moses."

12. Ibid.

13. *Liturgy of the Hours*, (Lent-Easter Season), 2:178.

14. Ibid.

15. *Oxford Dictionary of the Christian Church*, s.v. "Moses."

16. Ibid.

17. *Oxford Dictionary of the Christian Church*, s.v. "Moses."

18. *Navarre Bible: Pentateuch*, 239.

19. Ibid.

20. Ibid.

21. Ibid., 240.

22. Ibid.

23. Ibid.

24. Ibid.

25. Ibid.

26. Ibid., 242.

27. Joan Comay and Ronald Brownrigg, *Who's Who in the Bible*, 2 vol. (New York: Random House, 1971), s.v. "Moses."

28. Ibid., 279.

29. Old, *Reading and Preaching of the Scriptures*, 1:22.

30. Ibid., 24.

31. Ibid., 25.

32. Ibid.

33. Ibid., 28.

34. Ibid., 31.

35. Ibid., 33.

36. Ibid., 34.

37. Ibid.

38. Ibid.

39. Ibid.

40. Ibid.

41. Ibid.

42. Ibid., 38.
43. Ibid., 39.
44. Ibid., 41.
45. Ibid.; Roland de Vaux, *Ancient Israel: Its Life and Institutions* (Grand Rapids: Eerdmans, 1961), 2:354.
46. Old, *Reading and Preaching of the Scriptures*, 1:42.
47. Ibid., 1:74.
48. *Oxford Dictionary of the Christian Church*, s.v. "Jeremiah."
49. Ibid.
50. Ibid.
51. Ibid.
52. Raymond E. Brown, Joseph A. Fitzmyer, and Roland E. Murphy, ed., *The Jerome Biblical Commentary: Old Testament* (Englewood, NJ: Prentice-Hills, 1968), 1:338, no. 7.
53. Old, *Reading and Preaching of the Scriptures*, 1:83–84.
54. Ibid.
55. Ibid.
56. Peter C. Cragie, *Ezekiel*, Daily Study Bible Series (Philadelphia: Westminster, 1983), 3.
57. Ibid.
58. Robert Alter and Frank Kermode, ed., *The Literary Guide to the Bible* (Cambridge, MA: Belknap Press of Harvard University Press, 1987), 195.
59. *Oxford Dictionary of the Christian Church*, s.v. "Ezekiel."
60. Ibid.
61. Cragie, *Ezekiel*, 4.
62. Ibid.
63. Ibid., 5.
64. Ibid.
65. Ibid., 6.
66. *Jerome Biblical Commentary*, 354.
67. Alter, *Literary Guide*, 234.
68. Ibid.
69. Ibid., 235.
70. Ibid.
71. Ibid., 236.
72. Ibid.
73. *Jerome Biblical Commentary*, 341.
74. Old, *Reading and Preaching of the Scriptures*, 1:87.
75. Ibid., 93.
76. Ibid.
77. Ibid., 94.
78. Ibid., 95–96.
79. Ibid., 103.
80. Ibid., 105.
81. Ibid., 107.

Chapter 3
Preaching in the New Testament

When he saw the crowds, he went up the mountain,
and after he had sat down, his disciples came to him.
He began to teach them.

Matthew 5:1–2

JESUS CHRIST IS THE FOCUS and center of New Testament preaching. The New Testament encompasses the birth, life, and death of Jesus of Nazareth, and the early years of the Church He established (Matt. 16:16–19). John the Baptist, the first of the New Testament preachers, exhorted his followers to prepare for the Lord's coming through preaching and a baptism of repentance. Jesus Himself preached the Gospel of the Kingdom through word and deed. Saints Peter and Paul preached on various aspects of Christ's teaching (e.g., Resurrection). They established churches and strengthened the communities they served. The Church was loosely structured in its first century, but its foundation was solidly laid by its Master.

The preachers of the New Testament era began to bring out the implications of our Lord's teachings. Philip, after converting and baptizing the Ethiopian eunuch, "came to Azotus, and went about proclaiming the good news to all the towns until he reached Caesarea" (Acts 8:40). After his conversion, Paul "stayed some days with the disciples in Damascus, and he began at once to proclaim Jesus in the synagogues, that he is the Son of God" (Acts 9:20). Preaching the Word of God reflected the zeal in the hearts of the Lord's followers.

The Word was preached and proclaimed orally at this time. To the early Christians, it was not a series of letters on a page but rather a living Word of truth, life, and love, inspired by the Holy Spirit, touching the heart of the preacher, and flowing forth from his mouth to the ears and hearts of his listeners. Jesus, the Word made Flesh, preached and proclaimed the Kingdom of Heaven. After He returned to the Father, His mission on earth continued in His Mystical Body, the Church, and His Apostles extended His preaching to the ends of the earth (Mark 16:15; John 5:20).

THE KINGDOM PREPARED

John the Baptist was a man inspired by God to speak the truth of salvation. From his early years, John followed the path God laid out for him. That path took him into the desert, where he bore witness to the coming of Christ by word, deed and example. Unhindered by material possessions and unafraid to challenge the religious authorities of his day, John proclaimed a difficult but saving message: that God would not take second place in the lives of men. Men's hearts had to be prepared to receive the Christ and John would help prepare those hearts. Loved and accepted by many, he would also be rejected by some, and ultimately killed by a few who refused to open their hearts to his message. But even death could not silence his eloquent voice, which continues to bear witness in our day.

Saint John the Baptist: Preparatory Preacher

Saint John the Baptist (ca. AD 29) was the last and greatest of the prophets. He was a contemporary of Jesus who preached in the desert in preparation for the coming of the Messiah. John was an interesting character. He lived in the desert, wore garments made of camel's hair, and survived on locusts and wild honey. His preaching ministry focused on preparing the way for the Messiah. Many of John's listeners mistook him for the Messiah. Partly in response, John spent his time doing three things: (*a*) baptizing and preaching repentance for the forgiveness of sins in preparation for the coming of the Messiah and God's Kingdom, (b) denying that he was the Messiah, and (c) pointing to Jesus as the Messiah and explaining his own limited role. John was loyal to the Word of God and died at the hands of Herod at the request of Salome, because he denounced as unlawful Herod's marriage to his own sister-in-law, the mother of Salome.

In Eastern art, John the Baptist is sometimes portrayed with wings. The reason is twofold: (1) Wings are a reminder of his role as messenger of the Messiah. The prophet Malachi tells us: "Lo, I am sending my messenger to prepare the way before me" (3:1). The word "messenger" in Greek is *angelos*. Like the angel, John carried a message of reform into the desert. (2) Wings represent John's ascetical lifestyle. In the desert, John lived, dressed and ate simply. That lifestyle would become a model for men and women in the centuries to come. You could call John "the prototype of Eastern Monasticism." He lived an "angelic" life and inspires us to direct our lives "upward."

John's feast days are June 24 (his birth), and August 29 (his martyrdom).

The Preaching of Saint John the Baptist

John's preaching centered around three themes: *repentance, renewal,* and *expectation*. First, he stressed the need to repent or turn away from sin. "Reform your lives!" he said more than once. To *repent* means to change the course or direction of one's life. Repentance clears away the obstacles of sin and redirects us to the life of grace. John preached the message of repentance with fervor, faith, and conviction. He was unrelenting in holding people accountable for their sins, including King Herod, who unlawfully married his half-brother's wife (Mark 6:18). His unorthodox methods sparked a spiritual revival that prepared Israel for Jesus. Jesus would later use the image of fresh wineskins to illustrate the idea that peoples' hearts must be open and ready to receive the "wine" of the Gospel message He proclaimed.

John preached *renewal* as well as repentance. The baptism of repentance reminded people of the need for inner cleansing of their lives in order to receive the Messiah. The popularity of John the Baptist is explained in part by the message of renewal he preached. His words and example reinforced the message in his heart. He lived a simple life which reflected devotion to his God-given mission. John had first-hand knowledge of the renewal coming from a close relationship with God. Like prophets before him and saints after him, John's heart burned to share that life with others.

Finally, *expectation* was a key theme in his preaching ministry. He pointed out the Messiah, whom people were told to expect in the future. He cultivated that expectation by his message. He remained faithful to God and paid the ultimate price for his fidelity to the truth. The Preface for the Feast of Saint John the Baptist expresses it well: "You [God] found John worthy of a martyr's death, his last and greatest act of witness to your Son."[1] The shedding of his blood was his most eloquent homily.

I offer one scripture passage in particular on John, because it is brief and gives the reader a fuller sense of his preaching ministry. It is found on the Second Sunday of Advent, Year A.

Homily: Reform your lives!

> In those days John the Baptist appeared, preaching in the desert of Judea [and] saying, "Repent, for the kingdom of heaven is at hand!" It was of him that the prophet Isaiah had spoken when he said:
> "A voice of one crying out in the des-
> ert,
> 'Prepare the way of the Lord,
> make straight his paths.'"
> John wore clothing made of camel's hair and had a leather belt around his waist. His food was locusts and wild honey. At that time Jerusalem, all Judea, and the whole region around the Jordan were going out to him and were being baptized by him in the Jordan River as they acknowledged their sins.

When he saw many of the Pharisees and Sadducees coming to his baptism, he said to them, "You brood of vipers! Who warned you to flee from the coming wrath? Produce good fruit as evidence of your repentance. And do not presume to say to yourselves, 'We have Abraham as our father.' For I tell you, God can raise up children to Abraham from these stones. Even now the ax lies at the root of the trees. Therefore every tree that does not bear good fruit will be cut down and thrown into the fire. I am baptizing you with water, for repentance, but the one who is coming after me is mightier than I. I am not worthy to carry his sandals. He will baptize you with the holy Spirit and fire. His winnowing fan is in his hand. He will clear his threshing floor and gather his wheat into his barn, but the chaff he will burn with unquenchable fire." (Matt. 3:1–12)

John the Baptist prepared the way for the coming of Jesus by his preaching and example. As John "decreased," so Jesus "increased" in salvation history (John 3:30). We now look at the perfect model of preaching, Jesus Himself.

THE KINGDOM FULFILLED

To sum up the life and teachings of Jesus is a tremendous challenge. He has the distinction of being the only preacher who is also the object of all Christian preaching. Jesus is both the ideal of preaching, and the reason for preaching.

Jesus Christ: The Perfect Preacher

Jesus Christ (ca. AD 1–33) is the Son of God, the Word who became flesh and made His dwelling among us (John 1:14). He is also the son of Mary, the Virgin Mother of God. Saint Joseph was His foster father and looked after His human needs. Our Lord's earthly life began in Bethlehem, where he was born. He grew up in Nazareth, was baptized by John the Baptist, and ministered throughout Galilee and Judea. He was betrayed by Judas Iscariot, and was tried and sent to be crucified under Pontius Pilate. He died after three hours of agony and pain on a cross outside Jerusalem. He was buried, rose from the dead three days later, returned to His Apostles, and after forty days ascended into Heaven. The Mystical Body of Christ, the Church, is His living presence on earth extended through space and time. We await His Second Coming in glory at the end of time.

> Their faces were like this: each of the four had the face of a man, but on the right side was the face of a lion, and on the left side, the face of an ox, and finally each had the face of an eagle. . . . [wherever the spirit wished to go, there they went; they did not turn when they moved.] (Ezek. 1:10, 12)

Saint Irenaeus of Lyons likened these four creatures in Ezekiel's vision to the four evangelists: the man represented Matthew; the lion, Mark; the ox, Luke; and the eagle, John. Our primary source for understanding the life and teachings of Jesus is the New Testament, in particular the Gospels of Matthew, Mark,

Luke, and John. These are "synoptic" gospels (meaning they contain similar stories and wording). Each Gospel was written for a particular audience and focused on specific dimensions of Christ's life, using various strands of tradition passed on through the Church. Let us examine each Gospel in order to understand some aspects of Our Lord's earthly life and preaching ministry.

The Gospel of Saint Matthew presents Jesus as the preacher who perfectly fulfills the Mosaic Law and the prophetic writings. He teaches the Law and applies it to the circumstances of His day, and explains how prophecy is completed in Himself. Matthew opens his Gospel with an Infancy Narrative (1:1–2:23), the first part of which is a genealogy of Jesus that begins with Abraham, the father of Israel (1:1–17). Jesus here is called "the son of David, the son of Abraham" (1:1). In the first of the episodes of the Infancy Narrative that follows the genealogy, the mystery of Our Lord's Person is proclaimed. By the power of the Holy Spirit, He is conceived of a virgin (1:18–25). Matthew quotes Scripture to demonstrate that Jesus fulfills the writings of both the Law and the Prophets. (1:23). He will be named Emmanuel, a name meaning "God is with us." The announcement of our Lord's birth disturbs King Herod and his cohorts (2:1–3), yet the Gentile Magi are overjoyed, and bring the Christ-Child treasures of gold, frankincense, and myrrh (2:10–14). His rejection by the Jews and acceptance by the Gentiles is foreshadowed early in the Gospel. Warned in a dream that Herod seeks the Child's life, Joseph flees with Mary and Jesus into Egypt. By His time there and return after Herod's death, Jesus embodies the Exodus story. He is the One who will lead the "new Israel" out of the slavery of sin and into the promised land of Heaven. After the Holy Family returns, Jesus is taken to Nazareth in Galilee because the threat to his life remains in Judea, where Herod's wicked son Archelaus now reigns (2:22–23). The Lord's sufferings in the Infancy Narrative foreshadow those of His Blessed Passion, but His life is spared at the moment so He can later offer it on the cross "as a ransom for many" (20:28).

Matthew's account of Christ's ministry is recorded in chapter 4. There he introduces Christ's ministry with the preaching of John the Baptist (3:1–12), the Baptism of Jesus, in which the Father declares Jesus His "beloved Son" (3:13–17). We read of the triple temptations by which Jesus triumphs over the devil's attempts to keep Him from following the will of His Father (4:1–11). The focus of Christ's preaching is the reality of the Kingdom of Heaven, and the need for repentance for those desiring this special gift (4:17). While most of His ministry occurs in Galilee, He does travel to Judea (19:1), and, in Matthew's account, spends only a few days in Jerusalem (21:1–25:46).

Matthew's Gospel is structured in a series of narrative-discourses. The discourses are the Sermon on the Mount (5:3–7:27), the Missionary Discourse (10:5–42), the Parable Discourse (13:3–52), the Church Discipline Discourse (18:1–35), and the Eschatological Discourse (24:4–25:46). The Sermon on the Mount deals with *righteousness or holiness*. The righteousness of our Lord's disciples is expected to exceed that of the scribes and elders. *Righteousness* is to do the will of the "Father in Heaven" (7:21). The narrative section following the

Sermon is composed of accounts of His miraculous deeds. It also shows the nature of the unique community that He will establish. At the end of the Missionary Discourse, Jesus sends His disciples out to proclaim the Kingdom of God. The increasing opposition to Jesus is addressed in the Parable Discourse. Jesus laments the lack of faith in His disciples, and reproaches the towns for their failure to accept His call to repentance. In chapter 16, Jesus establishes His Church on the "rock of Peter" and promises to remain with His Church. The Transfiguration account in chapter 17:1-8 best illustrates Our Lord as preacher in relation to Moses and the prophets. Chapters 19:1–23:39 recount the journey of Jesus and His disciples from Galilee Jerusalem, where He will undergo His crucifixion and death. The Gospel concludes with a "great commissioning" of the Apostles.

The Gospel of Saint Mark presents Jesus as a traveling preacher who proclaims good news. Like John the Baptist, Our Lord preached outdoors and presented various implications of prophetic writings. Mark highlights the identity of Jesus and His message about the Kingdom of Heaven entering the human condition (1:14–15). Jesus is the Son of God sent to rescue man by serving the poor and by giving His life (10:45). Jesus calls twelve Apostles (3:13-19), and goes forth to teach (1:21, 22, 27), to heal the sick (1:29–31, 34, 40–45), to preach (1:38-39), and to exorcise demons (1:22–27, 34, 39). Mark presents Jesus as a popular preacher in Galilee (2:2; 3:7; 4:1). He chooses disciples to aid Him in preaching and driving out demons (3:13–19). Chapter 8 is a pivotal chapter in Mark's Gospel. Here Peter confesses Jesus as "the Christ" (8:27–30). Jesus emphasizes His coming Passion and Death (8:31; 9:31; 10:33–34). His Transfiguration gives Peter, James, and John a close look at His divine glory (9:2–8). The rest of the Gospel presents Jesus making His way to Jerusalem, where He will die ignominiously on the cross. The Gospel ends with the women at the tomb, which they find empty (16:1–8). The angel tells them He is risen, and directs them to remind the disciples that Jesus will precede them into Galilee.

The Gospel of Saint Luke presents Jesus as the preacher who addresses the Gentiles. The accounts of the Boy Jesus at the Temple (2:41-52), the rejection at the synagogue of Nazareth (4:16-30), and the appearance on the road to Emmaus (24: 13-35) illustrate Jesus as the perfect embodiment of law and prophecy. Luke shows how God's promises to Israel have been fulfilled in the Person of Jesus, and how the salvation promised to Israel and accomplished in Jesus is now extended to Gentiles around the world. Luke the physician reveals Christ's concern for the sick, women, and the poor in His words and actions. Luke notes at the beginning of his Gospel that his purpose is to bring Theophilus to "realize the certainty of the teachings" he has received (1:4). He relates the Acts of the Apostles back to his Gospel to demonstrate how the preaching and teaching of the early Church flows from the preaching and teaching of its Founder.

The Gospel of Saint John presents Jesus the preacher as the Word made Flesh who dwells among men. From the Prologue at the beginning, through the various "I AM" statements throughout, to the post-Resurrection appearances at the end, John offers well-developed theological reflections which grew out of a unique social milieu and theological tradition. John's Gospel illuminates the book of Genesis, and offers profound insights into many themes in salvation history (e.g., Gen. 1:12 and John 1:1–3; see also Gen. 3:21–24 and John 19:41).

There are two parts of this Gospel. The first part of the Gospel is the *Book of Signs*, or wondrous deeds of Jesus. The first of these signs is the changing of water into wine at Cana (2:1–12). The second sign is the cure of the royal official's son (4:46–54). The third sign is the cure of the paralytic at the pool of Bethesda (5:1–18). Chapter 6 contains two signs: the multiplication of loaves, and walking on the Sea of Galilee. They symbolize a new exodus or departure from sin to salvation. The sixth sign is the curing of the blind man in chapter 9, which concludes with a discussion of spiritual blindness and which reveals the symbolic meaning of the cure. The seventh sign is the raising of Lazarus in chapter 11. Lazarus is presented as a foreshadowing of the kind of life that Jesus Christ will provide to those who believe in Him after He has been raised from the dead.

The second half of John's Gospel contains the *Book of Glory*, in which Our Lord's rejection by the Jewish leaders, and ultimately His crucifixion, are presented in glorious terms. Here the discourses precede the traditional narrative of the Passion (chapters 14–17). John presents details of Our Lord's life not found in the synoptic accounts. Examples include Jesus Himself baptizing (3:22), the acknowledgement of the divine name *I am* during Our Lord's arrest at Gethsemane (18:6), and, finally, Jesus being put to death on the day before Passover (18:28).

The Preaching of Jesus

Author Hughes Old has called Jesus "the fulfillment of generations of preaching and teaching that went before him, and . . . the type or perhaps prototype, of generations of preaching that have followed him."[2] Our Lord Himself is the model and content of Christian preaching. He came to bring glad tidings to the lowly and proclaim liberty to captives (Luke 4:18). He has been described as an "itinerant preacher of the Gospel."[3] His Apostles continued His ministry, as recorded in the Acts of the Apostles and the New Testament Epistles. The early Church's life and worship were characterized by preaching (*kerygma*) as well as teaching (*didache*).

Jesus devoted much of His three-year public life to preaching and proclaiming the Word of God. His preaching ministry prepared and inspired His followers to continue after He died. Eventually, through them, His saving message reached the ends of the earth. Our Lord refers to this when He tells His disciples: "Amen, amen, I say to you, whoever believes in me will do the works that I do, and will do greater ones than these, because I am going to the Father" (John 14:12). The word *greater* here refers to geographical influence rather than theological significance.

There are several important characteristics of Our Lord's preaching. One is the use of concrete images. Jesus knew His listeners better than they knew themselves. He also knew how to connect with them, which is a critical part of effective preaching. He preached in concrete terms and touched hearts. Jesus often used natural settings for His preaching (e.g., lakes, shores, and mountains). His parables and imagery were simple and easily understood (e.g., birds, flowers, shepherds, fishermen, mustard seed, a falling tower, and whitened sepulchres). Christ taught by means of parables, an effective vehicle for delivering God's saving truth.

Jesus also preached effectively by miracles, and especially by miraculous healings. For example, His first sign in John's Gospel was the water made wine at Cana (John 2:1–11). He showed his disciples that the Kingdom excludes Satan by driving out demons (Mark 1:23–28; Luke 4:33–37); He calmed a storm and thus taught the value of trust in the midst of the "storms" of life (Matt. 8:5–13; Mark 4:35–41; Luke 8:22–25); He cured two blind men just as He offers light for the spiritually blind (Matt. 9:27–31); He foretold His own rising from the dead by raising Lazarus (John 11:1–44); He showed by a catch of fish his power to bring in a "great haul" (John 21:1–14). He healed the crippled, blind, and mute (Matt.15:29). By the use of images and stories and by His own actions, Jesus illustrated important aspects of the Kingdom of God.

There are many excellent examples of Christ's preaching. The most obvious is the incident of Our Lord in the synagogue, as recorded in chapter 4 of Luke. Jesus reads from the scroll and declares "Today this scripture passage is fulfilled in your hearing" (4:13). Another example is John chapter 6, the Bread of Life Discourse, in which Jesus lays out His teaching on Himself and on the Eucharist. These are literary and theological masterpieces. But time and space require a narrow and careful selection of Our Lord's preaching material.

I have chosen the Lord's *Sermon on the Mount* for my example. This sermon, presented in Matthew chapters 5–7, is an elaboration of the Decalogue. In it, Jesus makes the point that the Law is written on human hearts. It deals with the roots of sin in the heart of man. Jesus internalizes the external requirements of the Jewish Law. It is a masterful piece of preaching: concrete, specific, colorful, insightful, and clear. It is our Lord's teaching at its best.

In order to properly understand this sermon, it is useful to examine Our Lord's preaching as recorded in Saint Matthew's Gospel. This provides the immediate context for the message we will present later. Saint Matthew proclaims Jesus as the preacher who fulfills "the *priestly* role of teaching the Law of Moses, and the *prophetic* role of proclaiming the Word of God."[4] We see this clearly in the account of the Transfiguration (Matt. 17:1–8), where Moses and Elijah, representing the Law and the Prophets, appear conversing with Him. At the end of the account, the two Old Testament figures disappear and the Apostles see only Jesus. The message is that Jesus fulfills and completes the Law and the Prophets in His Person.

Matthew sets forth a multi-faceted account of Our Lord's preaching ministry. Jesus preaches on mountains and by seashores, in synagogues and houses, in towns and countrysides. He preaches privately and publicly. He preaches to the rich and the poor. He preaches by word and by deed. Matthew's Gospel is structured in a narrative-discourse fashion, where homilies are interspersed with miracle narratives.

Matthew's account teaches us several things about Christ's preaching:

1. *Preaching is a divinely inspired and mandated mission, and preachers are God's instruments of that mission.* As a result, they rely on Divine Providence for their survival. They need not worry about food or shelter—God will provide for their material needs. They need not worry about persecution—God will provide them with strength and inspiration. Jesus, the Anointed One, would anoint their words too—"When they hand you over, do not be anxious about what you are to say; for you will be told what to say at that hour, for it will not be you who speak but the Father speaking in you" (Matt. 10:19–20). The Lord's disciples were sent "as sheep in the midst of wolves" (10:16). They would meet with persecution, resistance and even death. Because of the danger involved, trust in God is critical.

2. *Parables are a key tool Jesus uses in His ministry of the Word.* Parables were ancient forms of discourse. Rabbis employed them long before Jesus came on the scene. Our Lord used parables to illustrate various facets of the Kingdom of God. For example, the parable of the sower illustrates the fruitfulness of the Word; the parable of the weeds and wheat assures us that the Gospel will bear fruit "even if competing gospels are proclaimed."[5] Hughes Old summarizes the meaning of parables in Our Lord's preaching ministry:

> The literary form of the biblical parable is not quite the same thing as the literary form of the parable in the classical literature of ancient Greece and Rome. . . . Although it functioned as a sermon illustration, a parable as it was used by Jesus is more than an illustration . . . As it was developed in the biblical tradition, a parable was a device used by preachers to epitomize a sermon. A whole sermon could be packed up into a parable, put away in the memory and then later brought out again when the occasion arose and unpacked by a process of explanation and elaboration.[6]

Jesus' use of parables is classic. Although they were used in other parts of the ancient world, Jesus perfected and popularized them in a way never done before. By comparing the Kingdom of God to seeds, trees, treasures and pearls, He brought extraordinary truths down to ordinary levels. Old reminds us that

> preaching in its very nature is parabolic just as life in its very nature is parabolic. Life is filled with signs and intimations of a higher unseen reality. The sowing of seed, its growth, fruition and harvest is one of these signs, as is the beauty of a pearl. The sharing of a meal is a powerful sign. The relation of sheep to a shepherd, the relation between mother and child, the marriage relationship, and by all means the marriage feast—all are signs of the fundamental realities of existence.[7]

Jesus was not diminishing or trivializing the power or value of the Kingdom in His approach. Instead, He was presenting it in a way people could easily grasp, and the fact that we can relate to them today is a sign of their enduring value.

Table 3.1 Some Parables Used in Christ's Preaching

TOPIC	IMAGE/PARABLE	BIBLE PASSAGE
The Church	The Vine and the Branches	John 15:1–17
Complacency	The Rich Man and Lazarus	Luke 16:19–31
Forgiveness	The Two Debtors	Luke 7:41–42
God's Care and Compassion	The Lost Sheep	Matt. 18:12–14
Humility	The Pharisee and the Tax Collector	Luke 18:9–14
The Kingdom of Heaven	Weeds among the Wheat	Matt. 13:24–30
Prudence	The Clever Steward	Luke 16:1–13
The Second Coming of Jesus	The Wedding Banquet	Matt. 22:1–14
Vigilance	A Thief in the Night	Matt. 24:43–44

3. *Jesus preached in continuity with the Jewish tradition.* Saint Matthew's Gospel is called "The Gospel of Fulfillment" for a good reason. In it, Jesus comes to fulfill in His Person the teachings in the Law and Prophets. We have already seen this in the Transfiguration. In fact, Our Lord's entire preaching ministry was the fulfillment of the preaching ministry of the Old Testament. Jesus, in the parable of the vineyard owner, portrays Himself as the culmination of the prophetic ministry. Jesus fully reveals and fulfills God's will.

With this said, let us proceed to the Sermon on the Mount, the greatest sermon ever preached. This sermon illustrates Our Lord's style and content. A word about the actual setting is useful. Matthew tells us that the Lord went up a mountain and sat down.

A preacher or teacher in the ancient Orient sat to teach; the disciples stood to listen. It was a matter of honor being given to the preacher, and for that reason Matthew makes this clear. But Matthew wants to say more by using this setting. The sermon is given on a mountain and somehow, as more than one New Testament scholar has pointed out, one sees in this mountain a reference to Mount Sinai.[8]

Jesus preached good news on the mountain. That good news was proclaimed in a particular way to the neediest and most vulnerable members of society.

The Beatitudes are addressed to those to whom Jesus will preach throughout Matthew's Gospel: the poor, those who mourn, the meek, the merciful, the clean of heart, peacemakers, and the persecuted. "The sermon moves on to a series of interpretations of Scripture, which again underlines the importance Jesus gave in His preaching to the Bible."[9] He internalizes the Commandments against killing, divorce, swearing falsely, retaliation, and coveting. He also interprets laws regarding prayer, fasting and almsgiving.[10] Finally, He urges His followers to "turn away from concerns of the Gentiles—food, clothing, etc.—and to seek the Kingdom of God."[11] We are to "enter by the narrow gate and build our house on the rock. While the Sermon on the Mount may not be a report of a particular sermon, it contains a good digest of the material Jesus typically taught in His preaching."[12] It is found in the 4th Sunday in Ordinary Time, Year A.

Homily: The Sermon on the Mount

And seeing the crowds, he went up the mountain. And when he was seated, his disciples came to him. And opening his mouth he taught them, saying:
"Blessed are the poor in spirit, for theirs is the kingdom of heaven.
Blessed are the meek, for they shall possess the earth.
Blessed are they who mourn, for they shall be comforted.
Blessed are they who hunger and thirst for justice, for they shall be satisfied.
Blessed are the merciful, for they shall obtain mercy.
Blessed are the clean of heart, for they shall see God.
Blessed are the peacemakers, for they shall be called children of God.
Blessed are they who suffer persecution for justice' sake, for theirs is the kingdom of heaven.
Blessed are you when men reproach you, and persecute you, and, speaking falsely, say all manner of evil against you, for my sake.
Rejoice and exult, because your reward is great in heaven; for so did they persecute the prophets who were before you.
"You are the salt of the earth; but if the salt loses its strength, what shall it be salted with? It is no longer of any use but to be thrown out and trodden underfoot by men.
"You are the light of the world. A city set on a mountain cannot be hidden. Neither do men light a lamp and put it under the measure, but upon the lampstand, so as to give light to all in the house. Even so let your light shine before men, in order that they may see your good works and give glory to your Father in heaven.
"Do not think that I have come to destroy the Law or the Prophets. I have not come to destroy, but to fulfill. For amen I say to you, till heaven and earth pass away, not one jot or one tittle shall be lost from the Law till all things have been accomplished. Therefore whoever does away with one of these least commandments, and so teaches men, shall be called least in the kingdom of heaven; but whoever carries them out and teaches them, he shall be called great

in the kingdom of heaven. For I say to you that unless your justice exceeds that of the Scribes and Pharisees, you shall not enter the kingdom of heaven.

"You have heard that it was said to the ancients, 'Thou shalt not kill'; and that whoever shall kill shall be liable to judgment. But I say to you that everyone who is angry with his brother shall be liable to judgment; and whoever says to his brother, 'Raca,' shall be liable to the Sanhedrin; and whoever says, 'Thou fool!', shall be liable to the fire of Gehenna. Therefore, if thou art offering thy gift at the altar, and there rememberest that thy brother has anything against thee, leave thy gift before the altar and go first to be reconciled with thy brother, and then come and offer thy gift. Come to terms with thy opponent quickly while thou art with him on the way; lest thy opponent deliver thee to the judge, and the judge to the officer, and thou be cast into prison. Amen, I say to thee, thou wilt not come out from it until thou hast paid the last penny.

"You have heard that it was said to the ancients, 'Thou shall not commit adultery.' But I say to you that anyone who so much as looks with lust at a woman has already committed adultery with her in his heart.

"So if thy right eye is an occasion of sin to thee, pluck it out and cast it from thee; for it is better for thee that one of thy members should perish than that thy whole body should be thrown into hell. And if thy right hand is an occasion of sin to thee, cut if off and cast it from thee; for it is better for thee that one of thy members should be lost than that thy whole body should go into hell.

"It was said, moreover, 'Whoever puts away his wife, let him give her a written notice of dismissal.' But I say to you that everyone who puts away his wife, save on account of immorality, causes her to commit adultery; and he who marries a woman who has been put away commits adultery.

"Again you have heard that it was said to the ancients, 'Thou shalt not swear falsely, but fulfill thy oaths to the Lord.' But I say to you not to swear at all: neither by heaven, for it is the throne of God; nor by the earth, for it is his footstool; nor by Jerusalem, for it is the city of the great King. Neither do thou swear by thy head, for thou canst not make one hair white or black. But let your speech be 'Yes, yes'; 'No, no'; and whatever is beyond these comes from the evil one.

"You have heard that it was said, 'An eye for an eye,' and 'A tooth for a tooth.' But I say to you not to resist the evildoer; on the contrary, if someone strike thee on the right cheek, turn to him the other also; and if anyone would go to law with thee and take thy tunic, let him take thy cloak as well; and whoever forces thee to go for one mile, go with him for two. To him who asks of thee, give; and from him who would borrow of thee, do not turn away.

"You have heard that it was said, 'Thou shalt love thy neighbor, and shalt hate thy enemy.' But I say to you, love your enemies, do good to those who hate you, and pray for those who persecute and calumniate you, so that you may be children of your Father in heaven, who makes his sun to rise on the good and the evil, and sends rain on the just and the unjust. For if you love those that love you, what reward shall you have? Do not even the publicans do that? And if you salute your brethren only, what are you doing more than others? Do not even the Gentiles do that? "You therefore are to be perfect, even as your heavenly Father is perfect.

"Take heed not to do your good before men, in order to be seen by them; otherwise you shall have no reward with your Father in heaven.

"Therefore when thou givest alms, do not sound a trumpet before thee, as the hypocrites do in the synagogues and streets, in order that they may be honoured by men. Amen I say to you, they have received their reward. But when thou givest alms, do not let thy left hand know what thy right hand is doing, so that thy alms may be given in secret; and thy Father, who sees in secret, will reward thee.

"Again, when you pray, you shall not be like the hypocrites, who love to pray standing in the synagogues and at the street corners, in order that they may be seen by men. Amen I say to you, they have received their reward. But when thou prayest, go to thy room, and closing thy door, pray to thy Father in secret; and thy Father, who sees in secret, will reward thee.

"But in praying, do not multiply words, as the Gentiles do; for they think that by saying a great deal, they will be heard. So do not be like them; for your Father knows what you need before you ask him. In this manner therefore you shall pray:
'Our Father who art in heaven,
   hallowed be thy name.
Thy kingdom come,
   thy will be done
   on earth, as it is in heaven.
Give us this day our daily
   bread.
And forgive us our debts, as
   we also forgive our debtors.
And lead us not into temptation, but deliver us from
   evil.'
For if you forgive men their offenses, your heavenly Father will also forgive you your offenses. But if you do not forgive men, neither will your Father forgive you your offenses.

"And when you fast do not look gloomy like the hypocrites, who disfigure their faces in order to appear to men as fasting. Amen I say to you, they have received their reward. But thou, when thou dost fast, anoint thy head and wash thy face, so that thou mayest not be seen fasting by men, but by thy Father, who is in secret; and thy Father, who sees in secret, will reward thee.

"Do not lay up for yourselves treasures on earth, where rust and moth consume, and where thieves break in and steal; but lay up for yourselves treasures in heaven, where neither rust nor moth consumes, nor thieves break in and steal. For where thy treasure is, there also will thy heart be.

"The lamp of the body is the eye. If thy eye be sound, thy whole body will be full of light. But if thy eye be evil, thy whole body will be full of darkness. Therefore if the light that is in thee is darkness, how great is the darkness itself!

"No man can serve two masters; for either he will hate the one and love the other, or else he will stand by the one and despise the other. You cannot serve God and mammon.

"Therefore I say to you, do be not anxious for your life, what you shall eat; nor yet for your body, what you shall put on. Is not the life a greater thing than the food, and the body than the clothing? Look at the birds of the air: they do not sow, or reap, or gather into barns; yet your heavenly Father feeds them.

Are not you of much more value than they? But which of you by being anxious about it can add to his stature a single cubit?

"And as for clothing, why are you anxious? Consider how the lilies of the field grow; they neither toil nor spin, yet I say to you that not even Solomon in all his glory was arrayed like one of these. But if God so clothes the grass of the field, which flourishes today but tomorrow is thrown into the oven, how much more you, O you of little faith!

"Therefore do not be anxious, saying, 'What shall we eat?' or, 'What shall we drink?' or, 'What are we to put on?' (for after all these things the Gentiles seek); for your Father knows that you need all these things. But seek first the kingdom of God and his justice, and all these things shall be given you besides. Therefore do not be anxious about tomorrow; for tomorrow will have anxieties of its own. Sufficient for the day is its own trouble.

"Do not judge, that you may not be judged. For with what judgment you judge, you shall be judged; and with what measure you measure, it shall be measured to you. But why dost thou see the speck in thy brother's eye; and yet dost not consider the beam in thy own eye? Or how canst thou say to thy brother, 'Let me cast out the speck from thy eye'; and behold, there is a beam in thy own eye? Thou hypocrite, first cast out the beam in thy own eye, and then thou wilt see clearly to cast out the speck from thy brother's eye.

"Do not give to dogs what is holy, neither cast your pearls before swine, or they will trample them under their feet and turn and tear you.

"Ask, and it shall be given you; seek, and you shall find; knock, and it shall be opened to you. For everyone who asks, receives; and he who seeks, finds; and to him who knocks, it shall be opened. Or what man is there among you, who, if his son asks for a loaf, will hand him a stone; or if he asks for a fish, will hand him a serpent? Therefore, if you, evil as you are, know how to give good gifts to your children, how much more will your Father in heaven give good things to those who ask him!

"Therefore all that you wish men to do to you, even so do you also to them; for this is the Law and the Prophets.

"Enter by the narrow gate. For wide is the gate and broad is the way that leads to destruction, and many there are who enter that way. How narrow the gate and close the way that leads to life! And few there are who find it.

"Beware of false prophets, who come to you in sheep's clothing, but inwardly are ravenous wolves. By their fruits you will know them. Do men gather grapes from thorns, or figs from thistles? Even so, every good tree bears good fruit, but the bad tree bears bad fruit. A good tree cannot bear bad fruit, nor can a bad tree bear good fruit. Every tree that does not bear good fruit is cut down and thrown into the fire. Therefore, by their fruits you will know them.

"Not everyone who says to me, 'Lord, Lord,' shall enter into the kingdom of heaven; but he who does the will of my Father in heaven shall enter the kingdom of heaven. Many will say to me in that day, 'Lord, Lord, did we not prophesy in thy name, and cast out devils in thy name, and work many miracles in thy name?' And then I will declare to them, 'I never knew you. Depart from me, you workers of iniquity!'

"Everyone therefore who hears these my words and acts upon them, shall be likened to a wise man who built his house on rock. And the rain fell, and the floods came, and the winds blew and beat against that house, but it did not fall, because it was founded on rock. And everyone who hears these my words and does not act upon them, shall be likened to a foolish man who built his house on sand. And the rain fell, and the floods came, and the winds blew and beat against that house, and it fell, and was utterly ruined" (Matt. 5:1–7:27)

Our Lord was the greatest preacher because He embodied in the perfect way the message He proclaimed. We now turn to the man Jesus chose to lead the Church He established. As we will see, Saint Peter's preaching was critical to the growth of the early Church.

THE KINGDOM EXPANDED

Saints Peter and Paul were apostolic partners in the proclamation of the Gospel, serving the Lord in unique but complementary ways. Different in personality, background and temperament, each man was transformed by the love of God and committed to proclaiming the message of Christ. Peter was a man of great faith and charity, but he was also impulsive and weak. Paul was brilliant and dedicated, but he was also irascible and quarrelsome. Peter was an Apostle to the Jews, and Paul was an Apostle to the Gentiles. The Church is blessed to possess the writings of both men. Peter's letters deal with the call of Baptism, the hostility of the world, Christian living, and the Parousia. Paul's letters deal with salvation, the Eucharist, the Resurrection, and various pastoral matters. Both sets of letters provide valuable insights into the lives, teachings and theological emphases of these men. Both struggled with pastoral issues surrounding the Christian faith. Through them, the Church grew and expanded its horizons.

Saint Peter: Preacher to the Jews

Saint Peter (ca. 1 BC–AD 64) was the chief Apostle and the *rock* on which Jesus Christ built His Church (Matt. 16:16–19). He was a spokesman for the Twelve apostles, and became known as "Prince of the Apostles." He first appears in the New Testament as a fisherman named Simon, making his living from the Sea of Galilee. His brother Andrew introduced him to Jesus, who declared that He would make them both "fishers of men."

In the New Testament, Peter is always listed first among the disciples and he witnessed the most important events of Jesus' ministry—sometimes with only a few disciples present (e.g., the Transfiguration, the raising of Jairus' daughter). Although he denied Jesus at the Passion, Jesus appeared to him at the Resurrection, and instructed him to preach, teach, and spread the Kingdom. Peter became the first bishop of Antioch in Syria. The New Testament throws no light on the ancient tradition that Peter ministered in Rome, where he was martyred during the reign of Nero. Peter is the patron of fishermen. Two epistles are ascribed to him. There are two feast days of Saint Peter—The feast of the Chair of Peter (February 22) and the Solemnity of Saints Peter and Paul (June 29).

Saint Ephrem of Syria extolled the primacy of Peter in these words:

Hail, light of the world . . . Christ is the light and the lamp stand is Peter; the oil, however, is the activity of the Holy Spirit . . . Hail, O Peter, gate of sinners, tongue of the disciples, voice of preachers, eye of the Apostles, guardian of heaven, the first-born of the keepers of the keys.[13]

Elsewhere Saint Ephrem says,

Blessed are you, O Peter, the head and tongue of the body of your brothers, the body which is joined together with the disciples, in which both sons of Zebedi are the eyes. They indeed are blessed, who contemplating the throne of the Master, seek a throne for themselves. The true revelation of the Father singles out Peter, who becomes the firm rock."[14]

In another hymn Saint Ephrem presents our Lord addressing Peter:

Simon, my disciple, I have made you the foundation of the holy Church. I called you 'rock' that you might sustain my entire building. You are the overseer of those who built a Church for me on earth. If they should wish to build something forbidden, prevent them, for you are the foundation. You are the head of the fountain from which my doctrine is drawn. You are the head of my disciples. Through you all nations shall drink. Yours is that vivifying sweetness that I bestow. I have chosen you to be as a firstborn in my institution and heir to all my treasures. The keys of the kingdom I have given to you, and behold, I make you prince over all my treasures."[15]

The Preaching of Saint Peter

Peter's preaching, as we read in the Gospels, Acts and his own Letters, reflects his concern for the Jewish people, to whom he preached six sermons. He wants them to recognize Jesus as the Messiah and accept baptism in His name. Peter struggles with unbelievers and those Jews who want to hold on to the old law as the means of salvation while awaiting the Messiah. His dramatic vision of the animals in the canvas in the sky illustrates the fact that the ancient distinction between clean and unclean animals and humans is not part of Christian discipleship (Acts 10:9–23). He focused on spiritual discipline and the expectation of the Lord's coming. Peter utilizes his experience with Our Lord as well as his knowledge of Judaism to construct effective arguments for the Christian way.

Peter preached two sermons in Jerusalem. The first occurred on the feast of Pentecost. We don't know exactly where the sermon was preached, but we do know that he preached to a crowd, and that some three thousand were converted and entered the Church (Acts 2:14–40).[16] The event reversed the sin of Babel. "Whereas once the peoples of the earth were all divided against each other by different languages, now there were brought together by the Holy Spirit and the proclamation of the gospel of the resurrection of Christ."[17] Peter's first sermon occurred in the context of the first public worship of the Christian Church.[18] The prophetic sign at this event was the outpouring of the Holy Spirit in the form of "[fiery] tongues and ecstatic language."[19] The essence of Peter's proclamation was that "God has made him both Lord and Christ, this Jesus whom you crucified" (Acts 2:36). With this, the proclamation of the Resurrection of Christ is publicly made in Israel, and would soon reach beyond Israel's borders.[20]

The second sermon occurred after the healing of the lame beggar at the Beautiful Gate (Acts 3:1–24). Peter spoke about the healing which took place by the power of God. It was the Suffering Servant spoken of by Isaiah, "by whose wounds we are healed," who healed this man.[21] He expands on the exaltation of the Christ, and called for repentance and faith. He shows the necessity of Christ's suffering and the fulfillment in His life of the Law and Prophets.

Peter preached to a largely Jewish audience and stressed the value of the new way. From our study of the New Testament and other early Christian texts, we can conclude the following:

- Peter preached largely to Jews (Acts 2:14–36; 3:12–26; 4:8–12; 5:29–32; 10:34–43; 13:16–41).
- Peter preached what he personally witnessed (e.g., the Resurrection).
- Peter preached the first Gospel message and was instrumental in the formation of the Church in Rome.
- Peter used his authority to correct faulty practices and beliefs, to commend, and to rebuke churches.
- Peter bore witness to the truth of his teachings by shedding his blood on the same instrument as his Savior.

The following homily was given after the Apostles received the Holy Spirit at Pentecost. It is found in the Acts of the Apostles, chapter 2. Here we see Peter explaining the remarkable coming of the Holy Spirit. He talks about Jesus as the fulfillment of all prophecy and about the essential demands of His coming.

Homily: The Pentecost Sermon

Then Peter stood up with the Eleven, raised his voice, and proclaimed to them: "You who are Jews, indeed all of you staying in Jerusalem. Let this be known to you, and listen to my words. These people are not drunk, as you suppose, for it is only nine o'clock in the morning. No, this is what was spoken through the prophet Joel:

'It will come to pass in the last days,'
God says,
'that I will pour out a portion of my
Spirit
upon all flesh.
Your sons and your daughters shall

> prophesy,
>> your young men shall see visions,
>> your old men shall dream dreams.
> Indeed, upon my servants and my
>> handmaids
>> I will pour out a portion of my spirit
>>> in those days,
>>> and they shall prophesy.
> And I will work wonders in the heavens
>> above
>> and signs on the earth below:
>>> blood, fire, and a cloud of smoke.
> The sun shall be turned to darkness,
>> and the moon to blood,
>>> before the coming of the great and
>>> splendid day of the Lord,
> and it shall be that everyone shall be
>> saved who calls on the name of
>> the Lord.'

You who are Israelites, hear these words. Jesus the Nazorean was a man commended to you by God with mighty deeds, wonders, and signs, which God worked through him in your midst, as you yourselves know. This man, delivered up by the set plan and foreknowledge of God, you killed, using lawless men to crucify him. But God raised him up, releasing him from the throes of death, because it was impossible for him to be held by it.

For David says of him:

> 'I saw the Lord ever before me,
>> with him at my right hand I shall not
>> be disturbed.
> Therefore my heart has been glad and
>> my tongue has exulted;
>> my flesh, too, will dwell in hope,
> because you will not abandon my soul
>> to the nether world,
>> nor will you suffer your holy one to
>> see corruption.
> You have made known to me the paths
>> of life;
>> you will fill me with joy in your pres-
>> ence.'

My brothers, one can confidently say to you about the patriarch David that he died and was buried, and his tomb is in our midst to this day. But since he was a prophet and knew that God had sworn an oath to him that he would set one of his descendants upon his throne, he foresaw and spoke of the resurrection of the Messiah, that neither was he abandoned to the netherworld nor did his flesh see corruption. God raised this Jesus; of this we are all witnesses. Exalted at the right hand of God, he received the promise of the holy Spirit from the Father and poured it forth, as you [both] see and hear. For David did not go up into heaven, but he himself said:

'The Lord said to my Lord,
"Sit at my right hand
until I make your enemies your footstool."'

Therefore, let the whole house of Israel known for certain that God has made him both Lord and Messiah, this Jesus whom you crucified."

Now when they heard this, they were cut to the heart, and they asked Peter and the other apostles, "What are we to do, my brothers?" Peter [said] to them, "Repent and be baptized, every one of you, in the name of Jesus Christ for the forgiveness of your sins; and you will receive the gift of the holy Spirit. For the promise is made to you and to your children and to all those far off, whomever the Lord our God will call." He testified with many other arguments, and was exhorting them, "Save yourselves from this corrupt generation." Those who accepted his message were baptized, and about three thousand persons were added that day. (Acts 2:14–41)

Saint Paul: Preacher to the Gentiles

Saint Paul (ca. AD 67) was a tentmaker from Tarsus in present-day Turkey (Acts 18:3). He was a Pharisee who became the "Apostle to the Gentiles" (Rom. 15:14-33). Paul describes himself as a faithful Jew who lived according to Pharisaic law and persecuted the followers of Jesus, until a revelatory experience brought him into the Christian camp as an Apostle commissioned directly by God and by Jesus (Gal. 1:12–17; 1 Cor. 9:1, 15:9; 2 Cor. 5:20). His miraculous conversion, described, for instance, by Saint Luke in Acts chapter 9, was the beginning of a life-long ministry to the Gentiles. He established churches, made repeated visits and preached in various countries (modern-day Syria, Turkey, Greece, Malta, and Italy). His letters may be dated around AD 50–65. Saint Paul was martyred in Rome (by the sword) about AD 67 at the Tre Fontani in Rome. He is the patron of the lay apostolate, the Cursillo Movement, Catholic Action, and the countries of Malta and Greece (Acts 20:1; 28:1). The Church celebrates the conversion of Saint Paul on January 25 and the feast of Saints Peter and Paul on June 29.

The Preaching of Saint Paul

After his miraculous conversion, Saint Paul traveled the world spreading the Good News that Jesus Christ was the Messiah, and that in Him all people find salvation. Paul taught that Jesus was the perfect fulfillment of all the promises God had made to Israel. Paul at all times presupposed the authority of the Jewish Scriptures (Old Testament) in the Gentile churches. Paul often alluded to the Scriptures instead of extensively quoting them.

Paul kept the Word alive by establishing churches, preaching in synagogues, and writing to the communities he founded. The central theme of Paul's preaching was the risen crucified Christ (1 Cor. 1:23; 2:2; Gal. 3:1) and the Gospel (1 Thess. 2:9; Gal. 2:2; Col. 1:4–6). Paul rejoices at the thriving of Christianity even though at times Christ is preached from impure motives. His preaching focused on the central tenets of the Christian faith: the cross, faith, humility, self-denial, chastity, obedience, forgiveness, the resurrection of the body, the Resurrection of Jesus, the divinity of Jesus, justification. He preached faithfully and fearlessly until the end of his life.

Paul preached in a variety of cities (e.g., Athens, Corinth, Ephesus). His favorite homiletic setting was in a Jewish synagogue, although he also spoke at Christian gatherings, and probably in market squares. He preached in a synagogue at Antioch about the history of Israel, the judges, John the Baptist's preparation for the Lord's coming and God's fulfillment of His promises (Acts 13:16–43).

Saint Luke tells us that Barnabas, a close associate of Paul, is one of the hidden heroes of Scripture. He and Paul worked together in their mission of spreading the Gospel (Acts 11:19–26). They worked side by side for years spreading Christ's message and building up the early Church. This is well known. What is less well-known, however, was that during their time together, Barnabas was considered the leader of the two men. It was only after spending time with Barnabas and learning from him that Paul went on to become a more effective speaker. In Iconium, Paul and Barnabas

> spoke in such a way that a great number of both Jews and Greeks came to believe. . . . So they stayed for a considerable period, speaking out boldly for the Lord, who confirmed the word about his grace by granting signs and wonders to occur through their hands. (Acts 14:1–3)

They also preached in Lystra and Derbe (14:6). Saint Luke relates that "when Silas and Timothy came down from Macedonia, Paul was absorbed in preaching and giving evidence to the Jews that Jesus was the Messiah" (18:5). Paul used his God-given authority to address concerns and strengthen the faith of the infant communities he established.

The words *paraklesis* and *parakaleo* (meaning "protector" or "advocate") are characteristic descriptions of early Christian preaching (2 Cor. 5:20; Acts 2:40, 13:15; Phil. 2:1; Isa. 40:1). Homilists were ambassadors or advocates for Christ. Paul did not preach in error or act out of impure motives or resort to trickery to spread the Word of God. These three vices (error, impure motives, trickery) characterized many itinerant rhetoricians, philosophers, and charlatans of religious mysteries in the Church's early history. Paul was responsible only to God who had chosen and approved him for this task (1 Cor. 4:1–5; Gal. 1:10, 15–16).[22] Preaching was the instrument through which the call of God was made known (Rom. 8:30; 10:14–17).

Paul's ministry was difficult for him. He encountered hardship and hostility in his itinerant evangelization journeys. He also had a personal handicap (2 Cor. 12:7), which he called a "thorn in the flesh." We don't know what that "thorn" was exactly, but it may have involved eye trouble because he speaks in at least one of his letters of writing in his "own hand" with "large letters." (Gal. 6:11). When Paul met King Agrippa, he preached and taught just as he had done on other occasions. When Paul finished his discourse, Agrippa exclaimed in almost exasperating terms, "You will soon persuade me to play the Christian." (Acts 26:28). The king resisted the grace of the Holy Spirit, but Paul did his part, and God was with him.

Paul had God-given assistants in his ministry. Jesus sent the disciples out two by two (Mark 6:7), and Paul himself regularly associated with a fellow worker from the beginning of his letters: Sosthenes, Barnabas, Silas, Silvanus, Timothy, and Erastus. Paul often did the pioneering work of establishing churches, and men like Apollos nurtured the faith of the churches Paul established (1 Cor. 3:6).

Pope Benedict XV spoke of the lessons and qualities of Saint Paul's preaching. First, he noted that Paul was well prepared for preaching. This meant primarily "the knowledge poured into his soul by revelation."[23] Secondly, it meant the learned studies Paul pursued under Gamaliel (Acts 22:3).

He also observed Paul's spiritual preparation for preaching. First, he fully submitted to God's will (Acts 9:6). "There can be no doubt that he made such progress in his apostolate because he conformed with such perfect submission to the will of God," the Pope explained. Paul always sought the glory of God in his ministry. Second, he showed zeal for God's service and a willingness to suffer in that service. "I exceedingly abound with joy in all our tribulations" (2 Cor. 7:4). Third, he was a man of prayer (Acts 9:11). "What gives a man's words life and vigor and makes them promote wonderfully the salvation of souls is Divine grace: 'God gave the increase' (1 Cor. 3:6). But the grace of God is not gained by study and practice; it is won by prayer," Benedict remarked.[24]

He spoke by way of letters to the Christian communities in Corinth, Ephesus, Galatia, Philippi, Rome, and other places. Messengers carried the letters and delivered them to the proper authorities. In sending his message to the communities, Paul claims the same authority as if he were actually present.[25] "As for me, though absent in body I am present in spirit," he wrote the Corinthians (1 Cor. 5:3).

Paul Scott Wilson makes the following observations about Paul's letters:

If we understand Paul's letters in various ways as his sermons we discover a number of things. Foremost among these is that Paul's preaching differs radically from the pre-gospel preaching of his contemporaries in the Jerusalem-centered church. It is primarily centered in conceptual argument [rather than] narratives which dominate the Jesus traditions . . . Paul uses Scripture with great frequency, though not in detailed fashion. He often appeals to texts as simple proofs of arguments and will follow a brief explanation of a text with an application. He sees Adam as a "type" of Christ (Rom. 5:14). He finds in Hagar and Sarah an "allegory" concerning the two covenants (Gal. 4:24). His uses of Scripture, particularly the types and allegories, will be expanded and developed by later preachers, largely due to precedent.[26]

Paul preached in order to win converts to Christ and to convince the Jewish people that Jesus was their Savior. His preaching ministry focused its attention on those two goals. We can conclude the following about Paul's preaching:

- He preached to Jews and Gentiles alike.
- He stressed Jesus as the fulfillment of the promises of the Old Testament.
- His message was received and rejected by many. He made converts and enemies at the same time.
- He relied on the Holy Spirit for strength and inspiration.
- His preaching caused his expulsion from more than one community.

The following example is taken from Saint Luke's account in Acts, and illustrates the style and content of the Apostle to the Gentiles. This passage discusses God's promises to Israel. Paul is addressing a mixed audience ("Fellow Israelites and others who are God-fearing"). He describes various blessings conferred on God's People through the centuries and demonstrates how Christ fulfilled ancient prophetic utterances. He concludes with a warning to avoid the mistake of rejecting Christ. It is found on Thursday and Friday of the Fourth Week of Easter. The dynamics of this incident are repeated in Acts 28:24-29.

Homily: The Synagogue Sermon

So Paul got up, motioned with his hand, and said, "Fellow Israelites and you others who are God-fearing, listen. The God of this people Israel chose our ancestors and exalted the people during their sojourn in the land of Egypt. With uplifted arms he led them out of it and for about forty years he put up with them in the desert. When he had destroyed seven nations in the land of Canaan, he gave them their land as an inheritance at the end of about four hundred and fifty years. After these things he provided judges up to Samuel [the] prophet. Then they asked for a king. God gave them Saul, son of Kish, a man from the tribe of Benjamin, for forty years. Then he removed him and raised up David as their king; of him he testified, 'I have found David, son of Jesse, a man after my own heart; he will carry out my every wish.' From this man's descendants God, according to his promise, has brought to Israel a savior, Jesus. John heralded his coming by proclaiming a baptism of repentance to all the people of Israel; and as John was completing his course, he would say, 'What do you suppose that I am? I am not he. Behold, one is coming after me; I am not worthy to unfasten the sandals of his feet.'

"My brothers, children of the family of Abraham, and those others among you who are God-fearing, to us this world of salvation has been sent. The in-

habitants of Jerusalem and their leaders failed to recognize him, and by con-
· demning him they fulfilled the oracles of the prophets that are read sabbath after sabbath. For even though they found no grounds for a death sentence, they
asked Pilate to have him put to death, and when they had accomplished all that
was written about him, they took him down from the tree and placed him in a
tomb. But God raised him from the dead, and for many days he appeared to
those who had come up with him from Galilee to Jerusalem. These are [now]
his witnesses before the people. We ourselves are proclaiming this good news
to you that what God promised our ancestors he has brought to fulfillment for
us, [their] children, by raising up Jesus, as it is written in the second psalm,
'You are my son; this day I have begotten you.' And that he raised him from
the dead never to return to corruption he declared in this way, 'I shall give you
the benefits assured to David.' That is why he also says in another psalm, 'You
will not suffer your holy one to see corruption.' Now David, after he had served
the will of God in his lifetime, fell asleep, was gathered to his ancestors, and
did see corruption. But the one whom God raised up did not see corruption.
You must know, my brothers, that through him forgiveness of sins is being
proclaimed to you, [and] in regard to everything from which you could not be
justified under the law of Moses, in him every believer is justified. Be careful,
then, that what was said in the prophets not come about:

'Look on, you scoffers,
    be amazed and disappear.
For I am doing a work in your days,
    a work that you will never believe
        even if someone tells you.'"

As they were leaving, they invited them to speak on these subjects the following sabbath. After the congregation had dispersed, many Jews and worship-
ers who were converts to Judaism followed Paul and Barnabas, who spoke to
them and urged them to remain faithful to the grace of God. (Acts 13:16–43)

SUMMARY

Preaching in the New Testament begins with John the Baptist, who lays the
foundation for the preaching ministry of Christ. John, the forerunner of the Messiah, preached repentance and renewal to those awaiting the coming of Christ.
By word and example, he prepared hearts for the One who would save all people. In addition, John baptized Jesus and introduced him to the world. The lives
of Jesus and John are intertwined in the early part of Our Lord's ministry.

The Gospels tell the story of the life and ministry of Jesus Christ. The Lord
Jesus was the greatest preacher who ever lived. He was the Word made Flesh,
the One who perfectly embodied the message He proclaimed. His sermons are
the great model for Christian preaching. No book on the history of Christian
preaching would be complete without a discussion of the Lord's preaching. The
style and structure of His homilies are clear. Our Lord would illustrate a point
using a familiar image (sheepfold, vine, net, salt and light), or He would tell a

story or a parable to highlight His teaching. His sermons would then rapidly conclude. He used His homilies to challenge some of His contemporaries and comfort those who were open to His words. We can see this preaching was the model for His twelve Apostles and later Saint Paul.

Peter and Paul carried the message of the Gospel beyond the borders of Israel. Their direct experience with the Master was the best preparation for their preaching. Both men followed in the footsteps of the Master, including offering their lives for Him. The Church is blessed with their letters as well as accounts of their lives. The presence of two major basilicas in Rome dedicated to Peter and Paul attest to the Church's devotion to these great evangelists. As we conclude the New Testament, we realize how the early Church learned from and built on the foundation Christ laid by His preaching style and content.

NOTES

1. Preface of St. John the Baptist, *The Roman Missal,* 495.

2. Old, *Reading and Preaching of the Scriptures*, 1:8.

3. Ibid., 1:111.

4. Ibid., 1:137.

5. Ibid., 1:143.

6. Ibid., 1:145.

7. Ibid.

8. Ibid., 1:138–39.

9. Ibid.

10. Ibid.

11. Ibid.

12. Ibid.

13. Benedict XV, Encyclical on St. Ephrem the Syrian *Principi Apostolorum Petro* (October 5, 1920), no. 20. http://www.vatican.va/holy_father/benedict_xv/encyclicals /documents/hf_ben-xv_enc_05101920_principi-apostolorum-petro_en.html.

14. Ibid.

15. Stephen K. Ray, *Upon This Rock: St. Peter and the Primacy of Rome in Scripture and the Early Church*, Modern Apologetics Library (San Francisco: Ignatius Press, 1999), 194–95.

16. Old, *Reading and Preaching of the Scriptures*, 1:167.

17. Ibid.

18. Ibid.

19. Ibid.

20. Ibid.

21. Ibid., 1:169.

22. *Jerome Biblical Commentary: New Testament*, 2:230, no. 16.

23. *Humani Generis Redemptionem*, no. 14.

24. Ibid., nn. 15–17.

25. Paul Scott Wilson, *A Short History of Preaching*, 24.

26. Ibid., 25.

Chapter 4
Preaching in the Post-Apostolic Church

If I preach the gospel, this is no reason for me to boast,
for an obligation has been imposed on me,
and woe to me if I do not preach it!
1 Corinthians 9:16

A S THE CHURCH ENTERED THE POST-APOSTOLIC PERIOD, preaching developed along sundry paths. Preaching addressed various topics: the end
times, Christian morality, steadfast witness during persecution. The Post-
Apostolic Church further clarified and expounded Christian doctrine and morals.
It built on the solid foundation laid by Christ and the Apostles. The writings of
the Apostolic Fathers are of a pastoral character. They are closely related to the
writings of the New Testament in style and content. You could call them living
bridges between the teaching of Apostles and the teaching of early Church Fathers, and they are important witnesses to the Christian faith.

The authors come from very different regions of the Roman Empire (Rome,
Egypt, Syria). The eschatological character, with its tension between the "already" and "not yet", is evident in the writings of this period. On the one hand,
the Second Coming of Christ was regarded as imminent. On the other hand, the
Person of Christ was still vividly remembered on account of the direct relation
of these authors to the Apostles. The writings of the Post-Apostolic Fathers reveal a deep longing for Christ, the departed and expected Savior. This longing
often took a mystical form, as in the case of St. Ignatius of Antioch. In general
the Post-Apostolic Fathers present a uniform Christological doctrine: Christ is
the Son of God, who pre-existed and collaborated in the creation of the world,

and His Second Coming was eagerly anticipated. The expectation of that coming shaped the attitudes and actions of early Christians.

One of the challenges in the study of the early Church is the limited amount of literature in comparison with other centuries covered in this work. The paucity of documentary material makes study of the early Church difficult. The culture of the Church's early centuries was primarily an oral culture. Information and ideas were passed on by word of mouth. For Christians, there was little distinction between reading and preaching the Word. Ancient rules of rhetoric guided preachers. Because of the advanced state of oral presentation, we have few written sources for preaching. While we do have important sources for liturgy (e.g., the New Testament, *the Didache*, Justin Martyr's description of the early liturgy, Hippolytus' *Apostolic Tradition*), they are the exception to the norm. Fortunately, images, inscriptions, architecture, and extra-biblical sources can help fill in the gaps with regard to the culture in which preaching occurred. These sources are no substitute for ecclesial sources, but they help us better understand the context of post-Apostolic homiletics.

THE FOUNDATIONS FOR POST-APOSTOLIC PREACHING

The Apostolic Fathers were Christian writers of the first and early second centuries, whose teachings were a fairly immediate echo of the preaching of the Apostles. They were either in personal contact with the Apostles, or received instruction from their disciples. Scholars in general agree that Barnabas, Clement of Rome, Ignatius of Antioch, Polycarp of Smyrna, and Hermas are part of the group called "The Apostolic Fathers." Later, it became customary to extend the category of Apostolic Father to include Papias of Hieropolis, and the unknown author of the Epistle to Diognetus.

The writings of the Apostolic Fathers are pastoral in character. They closely resemble the New Testament in style and content. Consequently, they may be regarded as connecting links between the time of revelation and the time of tradition, and as important witnesses to the Christian Faith. The writings of the Apostolic Fathers reveal a deep longing for Christ, the departed and expected Savior.

In their preaching, the post-Apostolic Fathers built on the foundation laid by Christ and the Apostles. They sought to aid Christians, especially converts, in living out the faith handed on by the Apostles. They dealt with issues such as state persecution, the challenge of a pagan culture, the date of Easter, and the heresy of Gnosticism, as they built up the Church founded by Jesus Christ. Their faith, nourished by prayer and the sacraments, strengthened them in living their lives by Christian standards. The Church was blessed with the patronage and teaching of Saints Peter and Paul in the city of Rome, and Saint Irenaeus of Lyons, France, who was the most important theologian of the second century. Clement and Origen are featured in this section. Clement is an obvious choice because he is widely regarded as an Apostolic Father. I include Origen here because he is a bridge to the critical period of the Church Fathers, which is the fourth century.

Clement of Rome: Papal Preacher

Clement (ca. AD 30–100) was the fourth bishop of Rome (after Peter, Linus, and Cletus). The ancient writer Tertullian claims that Clement was ordained by St. Peter. Clement wrote a famous letter to the Church at Corinth, and died under the Emperor Trajan. His feast day is November 23.

The Second Letter of Clement

The document ascribed to Clement is an anonymous Christian sermon—the earliest sermon that we possess.[1] The name "Clement's Homily" is misleading because there is no evidence that Clement actually wrote it. It was written "around the middle of the second century," probably in Egypt. It was read to a congregation "immediately after the [biblical] lessons."[2] It is "simple, direct," and free of a particular style or clear organization.[3] The preacher reflects on the prophetic lesson in an effort to promote moral purity, and steadfastness in persecution, emphasizing the need to repent "in the light of the coming Judgment."[4]

The author is addressing Gentile converts who are in danger of "falling prey to Gnostic teachings."[5] Therefore, he stresses the divinity of Christ, the resurrection of the body, and the way in which the Church "is the continuity of the Incarnation."[6] These themes emphasize Christ as the Mediator between God and man. Gnostics, on the other hand, held that the material world was the creation of an evil god, and therefore rejected the doctrine of the Incarnation. The Gnostic heresy is critical to a proper understanding of this homily. Gnosticism denied the divine origin of creation. It attributed spiritual reality to a "good God" and the material world to an "evil god." Clement was among those Christians who opposed this heresy, in part through his preaching.

We do not know exactly how this homily, dubbed "The Second Letter," came to be associated with Clement. The historian Eusebius rejects it as unauthentic because it is not cited by earlier writers.[7] However, the vast majority of early Church scholars believe it to be authentic. The author is unknown. He was most likely an elder of the Church of Corinth, but could be from Alexandria or even Rome. The author obviously lived the faith about which he preached. As Hughes Old puts it, "One gets the impression that the life that stood behind the sermon was its greatest eloquence."[8]

Old describes it as "well organized and carefully thought out. It is a direct and clear presentation of the Christian faith and worthy of our most careful attention."[9] He later comments:

This sermon is an expository sermon in the classic sense of the term. It is an exposition and application of a passage of Scripture. It is the same sort of preaching that was done in the synagogue. One notices one significant variation. Instead of the primary text being taken from the Law, it is taken from the prophets, and instead of the secondary text being taken from the prophets, it is taken from the Gospels.[10]

The purpose of the homily is to call the congregation to repent, to encourage steadfastness in persecution, to challenge basic Gnostic notions, and to promote Christian purity.[11] It stresses Christ's divinity and the resurrection of the body. It discusses morality and the need to keep the seal of baptism from defilement, to confess Christ by our actions, and to engage in acts of charity. These good works lighten the burden of sin.[12] They also glorify God. Repentance and meritorious deeds are important threads running throughout the fabric of this work. The most noteworthy theological idea in the sermon is the doctrine of the Church.[13] The author tells us the Church is the continuation of the Incarnation. The Church is a spiritual reality manifested in the Incarnation and in the bodies of true Christians. This idea has important implications for Christian behavior: to "respect the flesh" means to keep the Church from defilement; to "abuse the flesh" is to defile the spiritual reality of the Church. This document is the earliest extra-biblical Christian sermon that has been preserved.

The following homily is based on Isaiah 54:1. It develops a Pauline interpretation of this prophetic text, especially as in Galatians 4, where Paul takes up the subject of the "spiritual Church," the heavenly Jerusalem (4:25).[14] It urges the congregation to pray, bear witness to Christ, gather frequently, and praise God in their works. The reading is found on Thursday of the Third Week of Advent.

Homily: Rejoice in the Lord always!

Brothers, we ought to think of Jesus Christ as we do of God—as the "judge of the living and the dead." And we ought not to belittle our salvation. For when we belittle him, we hope to get but little; and they that listen as to a trifling matter, do wrong. And we too do wrong when we fail to realize whence and by whom and into what circumstances we were called and how much suffering Jesus Christ endured for us. How, then, shall we repay him, or what return is worthy of his gift to us? How many blessings we owe to him! For he has given us light; as a Father he has called us sons; he has rescued us when we were perishing. How, then, shall we praise him, or how repay him for what we have received? Our minds were impaired; we worshiped stone and wood and gold and silver and brass, the works of men; and our whole life was nothing else but death. So when we were wrapped in darkness and our eyes were full of such mist, by his will we recovered our sight and put off the cloud which enfolded us. For he took pity on us and in his tenderness saved us, since he saw our great error and ruin, and that we had no hope of salvation unless it came from him. For he called us when we were nothing, and willed our existence from nothing.

"Rejoice, you who are barren and childless; cry out and shout, you who were never in labor; for the desolate woman has many more children than the one with a husband." When he says, "Rejoice, you who are barren and childless," he refers to us; for our Church was barren before it was given children. And when he says, "Shout, you who were never in labor," this is what he means: we should offer our prayers to God with sincerity, and not lose heart like women in labor. And he says, "The desolate woman has many more children than the one with the husband," because our people seemed to be abandoned by God. But now that we believe, we have become more numerous than those who seemed to have God. And another Scripture says, "I did not come to call the righteous, but sinners." This means that those perishing must be saved. Yes, a great and wonderful thing it is to support, not things which are standing, but those which are collapsing. Thus it was that the Christ willed to save what was perishing; and he saved many when he came and called us who were actually perishing.

Seeing, then, that he has had such pity on us, firstly, in that we who are alive do not sacrifice to dead gods or worship them, but through him have come to know the Father of truth—what is knowledge in reference to him, save refusing to deny him through whom we came to know the Father? He himself says, "He who acknowledges me before men, I will acknowledge before my Father." This, then, is our reward, if we acknowledge him through whom we are saved. But how do we acknowledge him? By doing what he says and not disobeying his commands; by honoring him not only with our lips, but with all our heart and mind. And he says in Isaiah as well, "This people honors me with their lips but their heart is far from me."

Let us not merely call him Lord, for that will not save us. For he says, "Not everyone who says to me, Lord, Lord, will be saved, but he who does what is right." Thus, brothers, let us acknowledge him by our actions, by loving one another, by refraining from adultery, backbiting, and jealousy, and by being self-controlled, compassionate, kind. We ought to have sympathy for one another and not be avaricious. Let us acknowledge him by acting in this way and not by doing the opposite. We ought not to have greater fear of men than of God. That is why, if you act in this way, the Lord said, "If you are gathered with me in my bosom and do not keep my commands, I will cast you out and will say to you, 'Depart from me. I do not know whence you come, you workers of iniquity.'"

Therefore, brothers, ceasing to tarry in this world, let us do the will of Him who called us, and let us not be afraid to leave this world. For the Lord said, "You will be like lambs among wolves." But Peter replied by saying, "What if the wolves tear the lambs to pieces?" Jesus said to Peter: "After their death the lambs should not fear the wolves, nor should you fear those who kill you and can do nothing more to you. But fear him who, when you are dead, has power over soul and body to cast them into the flames of hell." You must realize, brothers, that our stay in this world of the flesh is slight and short, but Christ's promise is great and wonderful, and means rest in the coming Kingdom and in eternal life. What, then, must we do to get these things, except to lead a holy and upright life and to regard these things of the world as alien to us and not to desire them? For in wanting to obtain these things we fall from the right way.

The Lord says, "No servant can serve two masters." If we want to serve both God and money, it will do us no good. "For what good does it do a man to gain the whole world and forfeit his life?" This world and the world to come are two enemies. This one means adultery, corruption, avarice, and deceit, while the other gives them up. We cannot, then, be friends of both. To get the one, we must give the other up. We think that it is better to hate what is here, for it is trifling, transitory, and perishable, and to value what is there—things good and imperishable. Yes, if we do the will of Christ, we shall find rest, but if not, nothing will save us from eternal punishment, if we fail to heed his commands. Furthermore, the Scripture also says in Ezekiel, "Though Noah and Job and Daniel should rise, they shall not save their children in captivity." If even such upright men as these cannot save their children by their uprightness, what assurance have we that we shall enter God's Kingdom if we fail to keep our baptism pure and undefiled? Or who will plead for us if we are not found to have holy and upright deeds?

So, my brothers, let us enter the contest, recognizing that it is at hand and that, while many come by sea to corruptible contests, not all win laurels, but only those who have struggled hard and competed well. Let us, then, compete so that we may all be crowned. Let us run the straight race, the incorruptible contest; and let many of us sail to it and enter it, so that we too may be crowned. And if we cannot all be crowned, let us at least come close to it. We must realize that if a contestant in a corruptible contest is caught cheating, he is flogged, removed, and driven from the course. What do you think? What shall be done with the man who cheats in the contest for the incorruptible? For in reference to those who have not guarded the seal, it says, "Their worm shall not die and their fire shall not be quenched, and they shall be a spectacle to all flesh."

So while we are on earth, let us repent. For we are like clay in a workman's hands. If a potter makes a vessel and it gets out of shape or breaks in his hands, he molds it over again; but if has once thrown it into the flames of the furnace, he can do nothing more with it. Similarly, while we are in this world, let us too repent with our whole heart of the evil we have done in the flesh, so that we may be saved by the Lord while we have a chance to repent. For once we have departed this world we can no longer confess there or repent any more. Thus, brothers, by doing the Father's will and by keeping the flesh pure and by abiding by the Lord's commands, we shall obtain eternal life. For the Lord says in the Gospel: "If you fail to guard what is small, who will give you what is great? For I tell you that he who is faithful in a very little, is faithful also in much." This, then, is what he means: keep the flesh pure and the seal undefiled, so that we may obtain eternal life.

Moreover, let none of you say that this flesh will not be judged or rise again. Consider this: In what state were you saved? In what state did you regain your sight, if it was not while you were in this flesh? Therefore we should guard the flesh as God's temple. For just as you were called in the flesh, you will come in the flesh. If Christ the Lord who saved us was made flesh though he was at first spirit, and called us in this way, in the same way we too in this very flesh will receive our reward. Let us, then, love one another, so that we may all come to God's Kingdom. While we have an opportunity to be healed, let us give ourselves over to God, the physician, and pay him in return. How?

By repenting with a sincere heart. For he foreknows everything, and realizes what is in our hearts. Let us then praise him, not with the mouth only, but from the heart, so that he may accept us as sons. For the Lord said, "My brothers are those who do the will of my Father."

So, my brothers, let us do the will of the Father who called us, so that we may have life; and let our preference be the pursuit of virtue. Let us give up vice as the forerunner of our sins, and let us flee impiety, lest evils overtake us. For if we are eager to do good, peace will pursue us. This is the reason men cannot find peace. They give way to human fears and prefer the pleasures of the present to the promises of the future. For they do not realize what great torment the pleasures of the present bring, and what delight attaches to the promises of the future. If they did these things by themselves, it might be tolerable. But they persist in teaching evil to innocent souls, and do not realize that they and their followers will have their sentence doubled.

Let us therefore serve God with a pure heart and we shall be upright. But if, by not believing in God's promises, we do not serve him, we shall be wretched. For the word of the prophet says, "Wretched are the double-minded, those who doubt in their soul and say, 'We have heard these things long ago, even in our fathers' times, and day after day we have waited and have seen none of them.' You fools! Compare yourselves to a tree. Take a vine: first it sheds its leaves, then comes a bud, and after this a sour grape, then a ripe bunch. So my people too has had turmoils and troubles; but after that it will receive good things." So, my brothers, we must not be double-minded. Rather must we patiently hold out in hope so that we may also gain our reward. For "he can be trusted who promised" to pay each one the wages due for his work. If, then, we have done what is right in God's eyes, we shall enter his Kingdom and receive the promises "which ear has not heard or eye seen, or which man's heart has not entertained."

Loving and doing what is right, we must be on the watch for God's Kingdom hour by hour, since we do not know the day when God will appear. For when someone asked the Lord when his Kingdom was going to come, he said, "when the two shall be one, and the outside like the inside, and the male with the female, neither male nor female." Now "the two" are "one" when we tell each other the truth and two bodies harbor a single mind with no deception. "The outside like the inside" means this: "the inside" means the soul and "the outside" means the body. Just as your body is visible, so make your soul evident by your good deeds. Furthermore "the male with the female, neither male nor female," means this: that when a brother sees a sister he should not think of her sex, any more than she should think of his. When you do these things, he says, my Father's Kingdom will come.

Right now, my brothers, we must repent, and be alert for the good, for we are full of much stupidity and wickedness. We must wipe off from us our former sins and by heartfelt repentance be saved. And we must not seek to please men or desire to please only ourselves, but by doing what is right to please even outsiders, so that the Name may not be scoffed at on our account. For the Lord says, "My name is continually scoffed at by all peoples;" and again, "Alas for him through whom my name is scoffed at!" How is it scoffed at? By your failing to do what I want. For when the heathen hear God's oracles on our lips they marvel at their beauty and greatness. But afterwards, when they mark that our

deeds are unworthy of the words we utter, they turn from this to scoffing, and
say that it is a myth and a delusion. When, for instance, they hear from us that
God says, "It is no credit to you if you love those who love you, but it is to your
credit if you love your enemies and those who hate you," when they hear these
things, they are amazed at such surpassing goodness. But when they see that we
fail to love not only those who hate us, but even those who love us, then they
mock at us and scoff at the Name.

So, my brothers, by doing the will of God our Father we shall belong to
the first Church, the spiritual one, which was created before the sun and the
moon. But if we fail to do the Lord's will, that passage of Scripture will apply
to us which says, "My house has become a robber's den." So, then, we must
choose to belong to the Church of life in order to be saved. I do not suppose
that you are ignorant that the living "Church is the body of Christ." For Scripture says, "God made man male and female." The male is Christ; the female is
the Church. The Bible, moreover, and the Apostles say that the Church is not
limited to the present, but existed from the beginning. For it was spiritual, as
was our Jesus, and was made manifest in the last days to save us. Indeed, the
Church which is spiritual was made manifest in the flesh of Christ, and so indicates to us that if any of us guard it in the flesh and do not corrupt it, he will get
it in return by the Holy Spirit. For this flesh is the antitype of the spirit. Consequently, no one who has corrupted the antitype will share in the reality. This,
then, is what it means, brothers: Guard the flesh so that you may share in the
spirit. Now, if we say that the Church is the flesh and the Christ is the spirit,
then he who does violence to the flesh, does violence to the Church. Such a
person, then, will not share in the spirit, which is Christ. This flesh is able to
share in so great a life and immortality, because the Holy Spirit cleaves to it.
Nor can one express or tell "what things the Lord has prepared" for his chosen
ones.

The advice I have given about continence is not, I think, unimportant; and
if a man acts on it, he will not regret it, but will save himself as well as me who
advised him. For no small reward attaches to converting an errant and perishing
soul, so that it may be saved. For this is how we can pay back God who created
us, if the one who speaks and the one who hears do so with faith and love. Consequently, we must remain true to our faith and upright and holy, so that we
may petition God in confidence, who says, "Even while you are speaking, I will
say, 'See, here I am.'" Surely this saying betokens a great promise; for the Lord
says of himself that he is more ready to give than we to ask. Let us, then, take
our share of such great kindness and not begrudge ourselves the obtaining of
such great blessings. For these sayings hold as much pleasure in store for those
who act on them, as they do condemnation for those who disregard them.

So, brothers, since we have been given no small opportunity to repent, let
us take the occasion to turn to God who has called us, while we still have One
to accept us. For if we renounce these pleasures and master our souls by avoid-
ing their evil lusts, we shall share in Jesus' mercy. Understand that "the day" of
judgment is already "on its way like a furnace ablaze," and "the powers of
heaven will dissolve" and the whole earth will be like lead melting in fire. Then
men's secret and overt actions will be made clear. Charity, then, like repentance from sin, is a good thing. But fasting is better than prayer, and charity
than both. "Love covers a multitude of sins," and prayer, arising from a good

conscience, "rescues from death." Blessed is everyone who abounds in these things, for charity lightens sin.

Let us, then, repent with our whole heart, so that none of us will be lost. For if we have been commanded to do this too—to draw men away from idols and instruct them—how much more is it wrong for the soul which already knows God to perish? Consequently we must help one another and bring back those weak in goodness, so that we may all be saved; and convert and admonish one another.

Not only at this moment, while the presbyters are preaching to us, should we appear believing and attentive. But when we have gone home, we should bear in mind the Lord's commands and not be diverted by worldly passions. Rather should we strive to come here more often and advance in the Lord's commands, so that "with a common mind" we may all be gathered together to gain life. For the Lord said, "I am coming to gather together all peoples, clans, and tongues." This refers to the day of his appearing, when he will come to redeem us, each according to his deeds. And "unbelievers will see his glory" and power, and they will be surprised to see the sovereignty of the world given to Jesus, and they will say, "Alas for us, for you really existed, and we neither recognized it nor believed, and we did not obey the presbyters who preached to us our salvation." And "their worm will not die and their fire will not be quenched, and they will be a spectacle to all flesh." He refers to that day of judgment when men will see those who were ungodly among us and who perverted the commands of Jesus Christ. But the upright who have done good and patiently endured tortures and hated the pleasures of the soul, when they see those who have done amiss and denied Jesus in word and act being punished with dreadful torments and undying fire, will give "glory to their God" and say, "There is hope for him who has served God with his whole heart."

Consequently we too must be of the number of those who give thanks and have served God, and not of the ungodly who are sentenced. For myself, I too am a grave sinner, and have not yet escaped temptation. I am still surrounded by the devil's devices, though I am anxious to pursue righteousness. My aim is to manage at least to approach it, for I am afraid of the judgment to come.

So, my brothers and sisters, after God's truth I am reading you an exhortation to heed what was there written, so that you may save yourselves and your reader. For compensation I beg you to repent with all your heart, granting yourselves salvation and life. By doing this we will set a goal for all the young who want to be active in the cause of religion and of God's goodness. We should not, moreover, be so stupid as to be displeased and vexed when anyone admonishes us and converts us from wickedness to righteousness. There are times when we do wrong unconsciously because of the double-mindedness and unbelief in our hearts, and "our understanding is darkened" by empty desires. Let us, then, do what is right so that we may finally be saved. Blessed are they who observe these injunctions; though they suffer briefly in this world, they will gather the immortal fruit of the resurrection. A religious man must not be downcast if he is miserable in the present. A time of blessedness awaits him. He will live again in heaven with his forefathers, and will rejoice in an eternity that knows no sorrow.

But you must not be troubled in mind by the fact that we see the wicked in affluence while God's slaves are in straitened circumstances. Brothers and sis-

ters, we must have faith. We are engaged in the contest of the living God and
are being trained by the present life in order to win laurels in the life to come.
None of the upright has obtained his reward quickly, but he waits for it. For
were God to give the righteous their reward at once, our training would
straightway be in commerce and not in piety, since we would give an appearance of uprightness, when pursuing, not religion, but gain. That is why the divine judgment punishes a spirit which is not upright, and loads it with chains.

"To the only invisible God," the Father of truth, who dispatched to us the
Saviour and prince of immortality, through whom he also disclosed to us the
truth and the heavenly life—to him be glory forever and ever. Amen. (*Early
Christian Fathers*, 193–202)

Origen: Allegorical Preacher

Origen (AD 185—254) was a Christian theologian, ascetic, and writer who lived
in the third century. Jean Cardinal Danielou once called him "the genius of the
ancient Christian Church." Hughes Old calls him "a saintly genius. He was an
exciting intellect, a poet of theological insight, one of the most imaginative
thinkers who ever lived," and "totally devoted to the cause of Christ."[15] He grew
up in Alexandria, Egypt, a large Mediterranean port city on the western end of
the Nile Delta. Egypt is a land of contrasts. It contains an ascetical simplicity in
its vast desert and a worldly sophistication in its great cities. Alexandria was the
capital of ancient Egypt. It is famous for its lighthouse (one of the seven ancient
wonders of the world) and library. It is also the place where seventy-two scholars are said to have translated the Jewish Scriptures into Greek (the *Septuagint*).
It is where Saint Mark founded a church, where Philo (ca. 50 BC) taught a
method of harmonizing Jewish thought and Greek philosophy, and where Clement of Alexandria taught at a famous catechetical school attached to the cathedral. Alexandria, with its great scientific tradition, and the interest generally
shown by its educated upper classes in religious and philosophical questions,
was fertile soil for the development of Christian theology on a solid intellectual
basis.

Origen was the greatest of Alexandria's teachers, and one of the most important theologians of Eastern Christianity. Danielou proclaimed him "the most
eminent theologian of the early Church." Origen mastered the Hebrew language,
and was well read in philosophy and ancient literature, as well as Sacred Scripture. He studied under the philosopher Ammonius Saccas. His philosophical
training enabled him to express the faith clearly and correctly. He sought to
bridge the religious and secular cultures of his day.

With Romans 1:20 as a base text, Origen taught that "even as all things visible are related to the invisible and all actual things teach us of things unseen, so
also events recorded in Scripture symbolize unseen things."[16] Origen subscribed
to a four-fold sense of Scripture: there was the *literal* meaning, a *moral* meaning, a *spiritual* meaning, and an *allegorical* meaning of each passage. He saw
the Spirit at work in every passage and found hidden meanings and insights

throughout the Bible. In the year 231, he moved to Caesarea and became the most famous and respected preacher in Palestine. His homilies urged people to listen carefully to, and obey, the Word of God. Origen is the author of the oldest extant collection of Christian homilies.[17] He wrote commentaries on almost every book of the Bible and is known in particular for the *Hexapla*, a massive comparison of different Old Testament texts.[18] Origen saw the close connection between the Old and New Testaments, and spoke often of the relationship between them. He barely escaped arrest and execution during a persecution, and was made head of the catechetical school after his teacher Clement was forced to flee. Origen took the meaning of Sacred Scripture literally. After reading in Matthew 10:10 that Jesus said not to have a change of clothes or to wear sandals, he gave up wearing shoes.[19] And he followed the Scripture literally, in other ways. He was ordained a priest, and was considered a man of wisdom and honor. He traveled widely and preached throughout Caesarea, Jerusalem, and the Near East. He suffered under the Decian persecution (249–51), and died in the year 254. Even though he was never canonized, the value of his work is reflected in the Church's inclusion of his writings in *The Liturgy of the Hours*.

The Preaching of Origen

The preaching style and content of the great Origen were shaped largely by his experience at the Alexandrian school. The Alexandrian school was characterized by the use of allegory. *Allegory* is a literary, pictorial, or dramatic representation that parallels and illustrates a deeper spiritual meaning of a Biblical passage. For instance, the crossing of the Red Sea is viewed allegorically as Christ's victory over sin, and the victory over evil in Christian Baptism (CCC 117). Origen was well read in secular as well as religious literature. Eusebius tells us that Origen

> associated himself at all times with Plato, and was at home among the writings of Numenius and Cronius, Apollophanes, Longinus and Moderatus, Nichoma-chus and the more eminent followers of Pythagoras. He made use of the books of Chaeremon the Stoic and Cornutus, which taught him the allegorical method of interpreting the Greek mysteries, a method he applied to the Jewish Scriptures."[20]

Paul Scott Wilson summarizes the influence of Alexandrian biblical exegesis on Origen's thought. Wilson finds several ideas in Book Four of Origen's *On First Principles*, which he believes shaped Alexandrian homiletics. Among the points he makes are the following:
- The Old Testament reveals Christ via types or models. For example, "Joshua becomes a type of his namesake Jesus Christ, and Joshua's life is a commentary on our life."
- Revelation is hidden in Sacred Scripture. "We progress from knowledge of the small and visible [realities] to knowledge of the great and invisible . . ."

- "The word is the unit of meaning. It both discloses meaning to the discerner and hides meaning from those unable to interpret it correctly." This assertion demonstrates the need for an authentic interpreter of Scripture, which is within the competence of the Church.
- Scripture is "more like poetry than prose. It is like a coded message from God." Using tools such as Greek philosophy, arithmetic, etymology, parables, typology, and allegory, we are able to discern their meaning.
- The individual word is "free-floating," by which Origen means "freed from history and the restrictions of adjacent sentences and paragraphs." Instead, "allegory functions as the word's context." Origen uses allegory to rebuff charges that certain passages are "amoral, trivial, or absurd."
- The Scriptures have three senses: literal, moral, spiritual or mystical. *Literal* refers to the word itself. *Spiritual* or *mystical* refers to the allegorical interpretation of the word. *Moral* refers to the application of the word in the Christian life. Origen could bring out all three senses in a single sermon. Thus, concerning Noah and the great Flood, he talks about the composition of the ark itself; then he develops the allegorical or spiritual meaning, with the flood as a figure of the Last Judgment; finally, he speaks of the moral interpretation, which deals with how one lives the Christian life.
- When problems arise in understanding the literal sense of a Scripture passage, "it is a signal of a spiritual meaning to be discovered."
- "The key to a correct interpretation of Scripture lies in the spirituality and knowledge of the interpreter." (Wilson, *A Concise History of Preaching*, 36–38)

The bulk of Origen's literary product derived from his concern for better understanding of Scripture and true piety in life. Hughes Old reminds us that Origen was the first biblical scholar in the Church. He knew Greek and some Hebrew. He was also in contact with Jewish scholars in Alexandria and Caesaria. Therefore he read, memorized, studied, and reflected upon the Bible at length. His work in biblical studies was truly groundbreaking. It took the form of critical and philological work on the scriptural text, scientific commentaries on individual books, and abundant discourses on Scripture, which were recorded by stenographers and later published. Origen approached Scripture with an attitude of deep reverence and profound awe. The understanding of scripture was for him "the art of arts" and "the science of sciences." Scripture was full of mysteries that unveiled themselves only to those who prayed and reflected on them. Origen frequently implored the Lord to unlock for him the mysteries of Christ in the Bible. He likened the letter of Scripture to a hidden treasure in a field, which could be discovered with the help of scholars like himself (Matt. 13:44, 52).

The allegorical method of interpreting Scripture was not merely a traditional and easily applied exegetical method, but also a compelling necessity for him in order to transcend the text's literal meaning. Origen was fully aware that allegory had its limits. It certainly could lead to erroneous interpretations of Scripture, and could mislead people about the true meaning of the literal text. At times, Origen confused biblical allegory with Greek allegory and Hebrew typology. The presence of types or models of Jesus in Scripture (e.g., Abraham, Noah, Joseph, and Joshua) were an integral part of Scripture itself; but at times he took allegory too far, as Old points out in an excellent analysis of Origen's use of this device.[21] Nevertheless, in the hands of a master, allegory could get to the heart of Scripture, revealing religious insight and knowledge.

The daily reading of Scripture, to which Origen exhorted people, became for him a wellspring of his spiritual life and made him a teacher of the Christian ideal of striving after perfection (Matt. 5:48). The ultimate goal of the spiritual life was one's resemblance to God, to which a person was called when God created man in his own image and likeness (Gen. 1:27). The surest way to reach this goal was to imitate Christ, and so focusing on Christ was the characteristic attitude of Origen's piety. A man who imitated Christ chose the path of light and life. Correct self-knowledge brought awareness of one's sinfulness, which imposed an obligation to do penance and repent of one's sins. Fasting and vigils were as important as prayer and reflection in Origen's spirituality. The ascent to mystical union with the Logos took place by degrees, a progress Origen saw prefigured in the journey of the Hebrew people to the Promised Land. The profound yearning for Christ was fulfilled in a union with Him accomplished in the form of a "mystical marriage." Christ became the Bridegroom of the soul, and in turn, the individual soul and the Church become His bride. Origen was therefore the first representative of a profound devotion to Jesus (which was expressed in later centuries by St. Margaret Mary's Devotion to the Sacred Heart), and the founder and developer of a deep Christocentric and bridal mysticism. Saint Bernard of Clairvaux (among others) would follow in Origen's footsteps, and develop this mysticism in his writings in the Middle Ages.

The greater part of his writings perished in the violent quarrels that broke out concerning his orthodoxy. The conflict eventually led to his condemnation by the Synod of Constantinople in 553. As a result, Origen's theological reputation suffered for a time, and the reading of his works was forbidden. Few of his works survive, and the greater part of his biblical homilies has survived only in Latin translations, particularly those done by Jerome and Rufinus. Hughes Old compares Origen's surviving corpus to the ruins of a classical monument, pieces of which survive here and there.[22] Yet enough homilies remain to enable us to imagine the grandeur of his complete works. "Jerome lists for Origen 444 Old Testament sermons, and 130 New, a third of which have survived. Of these, only 21 (primarily his series on Jeremiah) survive in the Greek; they are an accurate reflection of both his content and style."[23] Hughes Old tells us there are sixteen sermons on Genesis, thirteen on Exodus, sixteen on Leviticus, twenty-eight on Numbers, twenty-six on Joshua, nine on Judges, nine on Isaiah, twenty on Jeremiah, fourteen on Ezekiel, and thirty-nine on Luke.[24] Old notes that Origen's homiletic approach was representative of that used from the time of the Apostles until the time of Constantine.[25]

Origen's homilies on the Book of Joshua were, for the most part, preserved in Rufinus' Latin translations. These homilies reveal Origen's concern about the erosion of faith in his listeners. In the *Homilies on Joshua*, Origen "unfolds the story of the Christian life from baptism to resurrection and the heavenly rewards, basing his exposition on the death of Moses, the crossing of the Jordan, and the conquest of Palestine."[26] The death of Moses becomes the death of the Law; and the destruction of the Temple and its sacrifices reveals their natures as "shadows and types" that fade away when the Morning Sun arises.[27]

The following homily is based on Joshua chapter 3. You will notice how Origen portrays the Jordan River as being almost a servant of God, helping the Chosen People. You will also notice the clear connection to baptism. This homily is based on a biblical text found on Thursday of the nineteenth week in Ordinary Time, Year I.

Homily: The crossing of the Jordan River

> To a sinner, all creation is an enemy, just as it is written concerning the Egyptians: The land fought them, the river fought them, the air itself and the heavens fought them. But to the just person, even things that seem inaccessible are made plain and easy. The just person crosses the Red Sea as though on dry land, but if an Egyptian wishes to cross, he is overwhelmed, and no wall of water will be made for him on the right and on the left. Even if the just person enters a dreadful wilderness and wasteland, food is provided from the heavens.
>
> Thus in the Jordan, the ark of the covenant was the leader for the People of God. The order of priests and the Levites stand together, and the waters, as though signifying a certain respect, hold back their course for the ministers of God and are heaped up together into a mass, yielding a harmless journey for the People of God.
>
> Lest you marvel when these deeds concerning the former people are applied to you, O Christian, the divine word promises much greater and loftier things for you who, through the sacrament of baptism, have parted the waters of the Jordan. It promises a way and a passage for you through the air itself. Indeed, hear what Paul says concerning just persons: "We," he says, "shall be seized up into the clouds to meet Christ in the air and thus shall always be with the Lord." There is nothing at all that the just one should fear. All creation waits upon that person. Hear, finally, how God makes this promise even through the prophet, saying to him, "If you pass through the fire, the flame will not hurt you, because I am the Lord your God." Therefore each place receives the just one, and all creation renders a servitude it owes.
>
> And do not imagine that these deeds are only in former times and nothing so great as this is brought forth in you who are now the hearer of them. For all things are fulfilled in you, according to a mystical reckoning. Indeed you who long to draw near to the hearing of the divine law have recently forsaken the darkness of idolatry and are now for the first time forsaking Egypt. When you

are reckoned among the number of catechumens and have undertaken to submit to the precepts of the Church, you have parted the Red Sea and, placed in the stations of the desert, you daily devote yourself to hearing the Law of God and to looking upon the face of Moses, through which the glory of the Lord is revealed. But if you also have entered the mystic font of baptism and in the presence of the priestly and Levitical order have been instructed by those venerable and magnificent sacraments, which are known to those who are permitted to know those things, then, with the Jordan parted, you will enter the land of promise by the services of the priests. In this land, Jesus receives you after Moses, and becomes for you the leader of a new way.

Mindful of such great and excellent powers of God—that the sea was divided for you and that the river's water stood upright—you will turn around and say to it, "Why is it, O Sea, that you fled? And you, Jordan, that you turned backwards? Mountains, why did you skip about like rams, and the hills like lambs of the flock?" But the divine word will respond to you and say, "By the face of the Lord is the land aroused, by the face of the God of Jacob who turns the rock into a pool of water and the cliff into springs of waters."

2. What great things were manifested before! The Red Sea was crossed on foot, manna was given from heaven, springs were burst open in the wilderness, the Law was given through Moses. Many signs and marvels were performed in the wilderness, but nowhere is it said that Jesus was "exalted." But where the Jordan is crossed, there it is said to Jesus, "In this day I am beginning to exalt you in the sight of the people." Indeed, Jesus is not exalted before the mystery of baptism. But his exaltation, even his exaltation in the sight of the people, assumes a beginning from then on. If "all who are baptized [into Christ Jesus] are baptized into his death," and the death of Jesus is made complete by the exaltation of the cross, deservedly then, Jesus is first exalted for each of the faithful when that person arrives at the mystery of baptism. Because thus it is written that "God exalted him, and gave him a name that is above every name, that at the name of Jesus every knee should bend, in heaven and on earth, and below the earth."

Nevertheless, the people are led by the priests and make the journey to the land of promise by the teaching of those priests. And who today is so great and so excellent among priests as to deserve to be added to that rank? For if anyone be so excellent, the waters of the Jordan will yield to that one, and the elements themselves will show their respect. Part of the waters of the river will leap backwards and be restrained behind his back, but the other part will disappear into the salty sea in a rapid glide.

Still I believe it was not without reference to a mystery that this was written, that part of the waters of the Jordan plunges into the sea and flows into bitterness, while the other part continues on in sweetness. For if all who are baptized maintained the sweetness of the heavenly grace they received and no one were changed into the bitterness of sins, it would never have been written that part of the river was plunged into the abyss of the salty sea. Therefore, it seems to me that the variety of those baptized is designated in these words, a variety we ourselves—I remember with grief—often see occur. When some who receive holy baptism surrender themselves again to the affairs of the world and to the lures of pleasure, and when they drink the salty cup of avarice, they are symbolized by that part of the waters that flows into the sea and perishes in salty billows. But the part that continues steadfast and protects its own sweetness stands for those who unchangeably hold the gift of God they have received. And suitably, there is one part of them who are saved, because there is also one bread "who descends from heaven and gives life to the world" and "there is one faith and one baptism and one spirit," from which all are caused to drink in baptism, and "one God the Father of all."

Meanwhile, it is the priestly and Levitical order that shows the way to the people of God who have gone forth from Egypt. For they themselves are those who instruct the people to go forth from Egypt, that is, from the delusions of the world; and to cross through the desolate wilderness, that is, to hasten past diverse kinds of temptations; and not to be harmed by the serpents, which are bites of demons; and to escape the venom of evil suggestions. Wherefore, if by chance anyone should be struck by a serpent in the wilderness, the priests show him a bronze serpent, suspended on a cross. The person who sees it, that is, the one who believes in him whose figure that serpent was meant to represent, will be able to disperse the diabolical venom.

It is the priestly and Levitical order that stands by the ark of the covenant of the Lord in which the Law of God is carried, doubtless, so that they may enlighten the people concerning the commandments of God. As the prophet says, "Your word is a lamp for my feet, Lord, and a light for my paths." This light is kindled by the priests and Levites. Wherefore, if by chance anyone from this order "puts the kindled lamp under a peck" and not "upon a lampstand so that it may shine forth for all who are in the house," let him see what he must do when he begins to render an account of the light to the Lord for those who, receiving no illumination from the priests, walk in shadows and are blinded by the darkness of their sins.

3. Finally, see what is said: "Let the people be at a distance from the ark of the covenant," it says, "by two thousand cubits." The priests and the Levites, however, are very near, and near enough so that the ark of the Lord and the divine Law are carried on their own shoulders. Blessed are those who deserve to be very close to God." But remember that it is written, "Those who draw near to me, draw near to fire." If you are gold and silver and have drawn near to the fire, you will shine forth more splendid and glowing because of the fire. But if you are conscious of building "wood, hay, and stubble" upon the foundation of your faith, and you approach the fire with such building, you will be consumed. Blessed, therefore, are those who are very near, who are so very near that the fire illumines and does not burn them. Nevertheless, even Israel will be saved; but it will be saved from far away, and it makes its journey, not by its own power but by the support and foresight of the priests.

4. And when do they come to the crossing of the Jordan? For I have noted that this also has been indicated, so that even the time might be distinguished, and with good reason. "On the tenth," it says, "of the first month." That is also the day on which the mystery of the lamb was prefigured in Egypt. On the tenth of the first month, these things were celebrated in Egypt; on the tenth of the first month, they go into the land of promise. This seems to me exceedingly fortunate, that on the very same day in which someone has escaped the errors of the world, that person may also be worthy to enter the land of promise, that is, on this day in which we live in this age. For all our present life is designated as one day. Therefore we are instructed through that mystery not to put off our

acts and works of righteousness until tomorrow, but rather "today"—that is, while we are living, while we are lingering in this world—to make haste to accomplish all things that pertain to perfection, so that on the tenth day of the first month, we shall be able to enter the land of promise, that is, the blessedness of perfection.

But, if you observe carefully, you will notice that many other things are brought together on this day in the narration of the Scriptures. Concerning those individual things—lest the discourse from us be extended now more than we wish—we must understand this thing: the day is repeated so often because, even if in general we think there is one perfection, still, each one of the virtues that we undertake to unfold has its own perfection, if we can complete it wholly and perfectly. For example, if he who is prone to anger desires to acquire the virtue of gentleness, undoubtedly he at first offends in many ways, until by long meditation he can change a longstanding practice into something natural. And when he obtains what he proposed, he acquires a certain perfection of meekness, though he will not possess the perfection of all virtue from this. Thus, therefore, by means of individual virtues, many perfections are found. But perfection in general is that which contains in itself the summation of all perfections. Because of that, therefore, many deeds are brought together on this day so that they may signify that many perfections proceed to one end, just as the prophet says, "Much has my soul wandered about"; and again, "When they say to me day after day, Where is your God? I remembered these things and poured out my soul within me, for I am going into the place of the wonderful tabernacle, even to the house of God, with a voice of exultation and confession, sounds of those who keep a festival."

For after the labors and temptations that we shall have borne in the wilderness of this world, after the crossing of the Red Sea, after the waves of the Jordan, if we shall have been worthy to enter the land of promise, we shall arrive with gladness and exultation, following the priests of the Lord, our Christ and Savior, to whom is "the glory and power forever and ever. Amen!"[28]

SUMMARY

The post-Apostolic Church was beset by persecutions, heresies, and confusion, amidst the growth in faith. Walking in the footsteps of the Master, early Christian writers and preachers sought to reconcile biblical truth with pagan thought and philosophy. In addition, they had to meet the objections of the Jews and pagans who lived around them. Their ultimate goal was not a kind of uncritical synthesis, or syncretism, of Christian and pagan ideas. They recognized the superiority of Christian thinking and spirituality. Their goal was to bring the world they encountered to Christ.

Preaching in the post-Apostolic Church was guided by the life and example of Jesus Christ. The early Christian homilists used rich imagery, allegory, and personal experience to enlighten the faithful on the mysteries of salvation. These preachers kept the Faith alive, and moved the hearts of the early Christians to good works. Christian preaching would develop in fervor and mystical depth as the Age of the Fathers began.

NOTES

1. Cyril C. Richardson, ed., *Early Christian Fathers* (New York: Macmillan, 1970), 183.

2. Ibid.

3. Ibid.

4. Ibid.

5. Ibid.

6. Ibid.

7. Eusebius, *Ecclesiastical History*, trans. C. F. Cruse, bk. 3, ch. 38, no. 4 (Peabody, MA: Hendrickson, 1998) reprint, 103.

8. Old, *Reading and Preaching of the Scriptures*, 1:283.

9. Ibid., 279.

10. Ibid., 284.

11. Richardson, *Early Christian Fathers*, 187.

12. Ibid.

13. Ibid., 188.

14. Old, *Reading and Preaching of the Scriptures*, 280–81.

15. Ibid., 306.

16. Origen, *Homilies on Joshua*, ed. Cynthia White, The Fathers of the Church (Washington, DC: Catholic University Press, 2002), 7.

17. Ibid., 5n10.

18. Ibid.

19. Eusebius, *Ecclesiastical History*, bk. 6, ch. 3, no.12., p.195.

20. Ibid., bk. 6, ch.19, no. 8, p. 209.

21. Old, *Reading and Preaching of the Scriptures*, 1:333–41.

22. Ibid., 1:322.

23. Wilson, 36.

24. Old, *Reading and Preaching of the Scriptures*, 1:312–13.

25. Ibid., 313.

26. Origen, *Homilies on Joshua*, 20.

27. Ibid.

28. Origen, *Homilies on Joshua*, 51–8.

Chapter 5
Preaching in the Age of the Fathers

There were some Cypriots and Cyrenians among them, however,
who came to Antioch and began to speak to the Greeks as well,
proclaiming the Lord Jesus.

Acts 11:20

THE FATHERS OF THE CHURCH were a group of men who had a formidable
influence on the early Church. Boniface Ramsey lists four criteria for determining who is a *Father of the Church*: antiquity, holiness of life, orthodox
teaching, and ecclesiastical approval.[1] He dates the patristic period from the first
century to the middle of the eighth century.[2]

The Patristic or Church Fathers were consummate preachers. Their insights
into Sacred Scripture were profound. The Fathers taught that there were several
senses or layers of Scripture. The first was the *literal*, which referred to the literal meaning of the biblical text. The second sense or layer was *spiritual*. This
was a deeper level, and itself was divided into the moral, allegorical, and anagogical meanings. The *moral* sense focuses on how to live uprightly; the *allegorical* sense focuses on recognizing the significance of ancient events in their
relation to Christ (e.g., the victory of Moses at the Red Sea is a type of Christ's
victory over sin at the Cross); and the *anagogical* sense deals with the eternal
significance of current events (e.g., the Church as a sign of the heavenly Jerusalem) (CCC 117).

One central feature of patristic preaching was *typology*, which was the use
of images or types in the Old Testament that pointed to realities in the New Testament, thus connecting the two. Moses, Jacob, and Joseph were types of Christ.
Mary was the New Eve. Christ was the New Adam. The Fathers often detached,
from their original context, the passages of Scripture on which they preached

and taught, believing that every passage had special grace and wisdom.[3] This opened them up to the criticism of distorting our understanding of Scripture. After Vatican II, the Church Fathers and their biblical interpretations were criticized, and their status was downplayed by some teachers. But they are making a comeback now, as we regain an appreciation of their contributions to biblical study and ecclesiastical life.

PREACHING IN THE EAST

The theology of Eastern churches is rich in expression and content. Eastern theology has ancient roots and unique characteristics, including an appreciation of icons, an emphasis on the Holy Spirit, and an emphasis on the theme of light. Blessed John Paul II underscored the importance of this Eastern theology of light when he presented the Luminous Mysteries of the Rosary (The Baptism in the Jordan, the Wedding Feast of Cana, the Proclamation of the Kingdom, the Transfiguration, the Institution of the Eucharist) for the Church's reflection.

The Eastern Church was blessed with a rich liturgical heritage (which is a feast for the senses, with smells [incense], images [icons], and sound [chant] playing important roles in liturgical life); theological schools in Alexandria and Antioch; a great monastic tradition; and various early Christian documents, such as the *Didache* and the *Apostolic Constitutions*, which were originally written in Greek. Eastern churches use leavened bread, and baptize by immersion. In the Eastern rite, married men may become priests, but bishops are chosen solely from the ranks of the celibate clergy (CCC 1580). There is no tradition for marriage *after* ordination.

Eastern culture tends to be contemplative and mystical. It is shaped by encounters with the Islamic faith. Preachers from the East reflected the theological, spiritual, and historical forces which shaped Eastern Church history.

Saint John Chrysostom: The Golden Tongue

John Chrysostom (ca. 347– 407) was born the son of noble and wealthy parents, and was raised in the Church by his widowed mother. After her death in 375, he became an ascetic, and lived under the direction of an old monk.

Chrysostom received a classic education from a famous pagan scholar who admired his talents. John enjoyed the courts, theaters, and other cultural venues of Antioch, but gave them up when he joined a monastic order. From this point on, John dedicated his life to prayer and study. He became part of a community of ascetics. He authored many ascetical, apologetic, and polemical treatises and letters. He wrote works in the defense of monasticism, lives of various saints, and six treatises on the priesthood. When his own health declined, Chrysostom returned to Antioch. He was ordained a deacon in 381, a priest five years later, and in 398, he was named bishop of Constantinople in present-day Turkey.

John was an outstanding preacher (Chrysostom means "golden-mouth" or "golden-tongue"). His homilies on Saint Paul's Letters, and on Lazarus and the Rich Man in Luke's Gospel, are particularly noteworthy. By word and example, he taught that people of various backgrounds and lifestyles can live in intimate union with the Savior. His promotion of saints' feasts, all-night vigils, and processions to the tombs of various martyrs underscored his love of the liturgy. He was a defender of the faith and reformer of the clergy. He stressed that preachers should teach first by example and later by words. He did this in his own life in outstanding ways, especially by his charity.

The arrival of the emperor Arkadios and his wife Eudoxia ushered in a difficult period in John's life. Ironically, these two individuals would be the instruments for his rise to ecclesiastical power and his exile from his see. The emperor and his wife brought Chrysostom to Constantinople where he was ordained a bishop. Arkadios and Eudoxia thought that their capital should have the finest orator in the land. However, they underestimated the "Golden Tongue." He condemned clergy engaged in sex scandals, decried those who stole from the poor, deposed bishops who were convicted of financial irregularities, and spoke out against vanity, particularly the extravagance of women's fashions. The empress became offended when John once compared her to Queen Jezebel in the Old Testament (1 Kings 21).

Together with disgruntled clerics and the Archbishop of Alexandria, whom John chastised for abusing his office, Eudoxia had him deposed from office and exiled. He returned, but another dispute arose, and he left Constantinople voluntarily. A long and painful journey took John from one frontier outpost to another, and his health deteriorated. He died on September 14, 407, at a remote location on the Black Sea.

John was vindicated some thirty years after his death, when the heir of Arkadios and Eudoxia had Chrysostom's relics returned to the capital, and publicly asked God to forgive his parents' sins. John Chrysostom is a Doctor of the Church, a great Eastern Father of the Church, and the patron saint of preachers, and the present city of Istanbul (Constantinople). His feast is September 13.

The Preaching of Saint John Chrysostom

Saint John Chrysostom has been called "the crowning example of how the faithful preaching of the Word of God ever purifies and enlightens the Church so that the Lord of the Church is glorified."[4] Hughes Old says that Chrysostom left the Church "impressive examples of several genres of Christian preaching."[5] First he was an expository preacher, leaving us an vast series of sermons on Old and New Testament books.[6] He was also a catechetical and prophetic preacher (the latter directed toward the wealthy and powerful persons of Constantinople).[7] Some five hundred sermons are extant, including sixty-seven sermons on Genesis, fifty-eight on selected psalms, ninety on Saint Matthew's Gospel, eighty-eight on John's Gospel, fifty-five on the Acts of the Apostles, and thirty-four on the Letter to the Hebrews.[8] Like the great Origen, Chrysostom's sermons were preached at liturgical services daily and were recorded by stenographers, to whom contemporary scholars owe a debt of gratitude.

John Chrysostom's life and work were shaped by the theological school at Antioch, the ancient capital of Syria. Antioch is a Syrian city on a strip of land between the Orontes River and a chain of mountains, twenty miles from the Mediterranean Sea.[9] Saint Luke reminds us that "it was in Antioch that the disciples were first called Christians" (Acts 11:26). Antioch was therefore "an important center of Christian faith."[10] The emperor Constantine built a huge church there, and the Christian community thrived in it. Tradition unanimously names Lucian as the founder of the theological school at Antioch.

Antioch was also the center of Hellenistic civilization and culture, and a gateway to the Orient, "where Romans, Greeks, Jews, and Syrians were in constant contact."[11] Many Jews came to hear Chrysostom's sermons, which led to lively discussions about various interpretations of the Old Testament. Good oratory was a popular attraction in the early Christian centuries.

Alexandrian and Antiochene exegesis did not rise in tandem. Hughes Old tells us that the Antiochene school "came as a reaction" to the Alexandrian school of biblical interpretation.[12] From the middle of the third century until almost the end of the fourth century, Christian preaching in the East had been "strongly influenced by Alexandrian exegesis."[13] Origen popularized this approach, and Eusebius of Caesarea, Cyril of Jerusalem, and Hesychius of Jerusalem followed in his footsteps. Diodore, "the outstanding biblical scholar of Antioch," systematized the Antiochene approach.[14]

Born in Tarsus, Diodore (died ca. 390) studied in Athens, and received a fine literary education. He studied theology carefully, and maintained his orthodoxy in the face of the abominable Arian heresy. His steadfast loyalty to the Faith earned him exile to Armenia, but he was later brought back and made bishop of Paul's native city of Tarsus. His opponents were able to obtain his "official condemnation," but the Antiochene school is widely respected today.[15]

Antioch was a major center of learning and thought in the East. It had several distinguishing characteristics. Antiochene scholars taught that God, as the author of Scripture, revealed Himself in its history, and the biblical text had a specific original meaning. The interpreter's job was to establish the historical context and sense of the biblical passage through a careful study of the language, grammar, rhetoric, and literary form of the text. This produced a great emphasis on the historical and literal understanding of Scripture, emphasizing reason in interpreting the Bible. Antiochene exegetes followed Jewish principles of interpreting the law, including analysis, induction, deduction, and analogy, with "consideration of the surrounding context."[16]

As noted earlier, the historical approach to biblical interpretation came about for two principal reasons. The first was the reaction to the allegorical approach practiced in Alexandria. Chrysostom and other adherents to the historical approach believed that biblical typology was confused with Greek allegory, and thus led to inaccurate or misleading interpretations of Scripture passages. They thought a grammatical-historical approach was more sound. The other reason was the concern for heresy. Chrysostom's sermons on Genesis, for example, stress the goodness of creation. These sermons were presented to catechumens in a culture often infected with the heresies of Marcion, Manichaeus, and others with Gnostic tendencies, which devalued the created order in general, and human nature in particular. Homilists wanted to make sure that converts to the Faith understood clearly and correctly the essentials of Christianity.

An image is useful. If the Bible was a plant, the Antiochene scholar would be concerned with the quality of the soil, rainfall amounts, exposure to sunlight, and surrounding plant life. The Alexandrian scholar, on the other hand, would be concerned with the roots and nutrients deep in the soil.

The form and structure of Chrysostom's homilies range "from non-biblical narrative about contemporary life to a form of exegetical preaching, in which he moves from one verse to another, or from one text to another."[17] His training was in rhetoric, but he is not concerned with sticking to a precise theme or text. Chrysostom helps us appreciate the historical dimension of Sacred Scripture.

Chrysostom mastered the art of rhetoric and oratory. A famous example is found in his "Sermons on the Statues." Some background is in order: In 386, a riot occurred in Antioch over a new tax imposed by the Emperor Theodosius. At its height, the rioters toppled the statues of the emperor and imperial family. This in turn led to reprisals by officials, who arrested and executed citizens from all walks of life. This was the setting when Chrysostom entered his pulpit, to begin preaching as the congregation began "a forty-day fast."[18]

In twenty-one sermons during the fast, the "Golden Tongue" lamented the sins of the city, and urged the people to fast and pray in atonement. Not only that, but they were encouraged to repent of such sins as cursing and swearing. He spoke of the crisis as a warning to turn away from sin, and believe in the Gospel. "Instead of trusting in riches, influence, and honor, the wise Christian should trust in God, and cultivate a simple and sober life."[19] Fame, wealth, power, and political connections did no good for a populace facing severe retribution for their excesses. Chrysostom was a calming influence on the community, many of whom had fled earlier. In the end, Bishop Flavian of Antioch reached Constantinople, and persuaded the emperor to grant the city clemency. Chrysostom had the joy of announcing the good news. The Sermons on the Statues are regarded as "outstanding monuments of Christian oratory."[20] They are among the important homiletic materials of the early Church.

Following are several examples[21] of Chrysostom's masterful eloquence. In the first example, our preacher opens with a lament:

> What shall I say, or what shall I speak of? The present season is one for tears, and not for words; for lamentation, not for discourse; for prayer, not for preaching. Such is the magnitude of the deeds daringly done; so incurable is the wound, so deep the blow, even beyond the power of all treatment.

In the second example, he exclaims the difficulty of expressing his grief:

"Scarcely am I able to open my mouth, to part my lips, to move my tongue, or to utter a syllable! So, even like a curb, the weight of grief checks my tongue, and keeps back what I would say."

The third example depicts Antioch gripped by fear and anxiety:

We live in constant terror . . . every one is pent up within the walls of his own house! And as it is not safe for those who are besieged to go beyond the walls, while the enemy without is encamped around; so neither, to many of those who inhabit this city, is it safe to go out of doors, or to appear openly; on account of those who are everywhere hunting for the innocent as well as the guilty; and seizing them even in the midst of the forum, and dragging them to the court of justice, without ceremony, and just as chance directs. For this reason, freemen sit in doors shackled up with their domestics; anxiously and minutely enquiring of those to whom they may safely put the question, "Who has been seized to-day; who carried off; or punished? How was it? And in what manner?"

In the fourth example, he compares his own preaching to the sun blocked by dark clouds of gloom:

And as when some dense cloud has formed, and flying under the solar rays, re-turns back to him all his splendor again, so indeed does the cloud of sadness, when it stands before our souls, refuse to admit an easy passage for the word, but chokes it and restrains it forcibly within. And this is the case not only with those who speak but with those who hear; for as it does not suffer the word to burst forth freely from the soul of the speaker, so neither does it suffer it to sink into the mind of those who listen with its natural power."

In the final example, Chrysostom uses a clever metaphor to discuss the illu-sory and fleeting nature of wealth:

For nothing is so faithless as wealth; of which I have often said, and will not cease to say, that it is a runaway, thankless servant, having no fidelity; and should you throw over him ten thousand chains, he will make off dragging his chains after him. Frequently, indeed, have those who possessed him shut him up with bars and doors, placing their slaves round about for guards. But he has over-persuaded these very servants, and has fled away together with his guards; dragging his keepers after him like a chain, so little security was there in this custody. What then can be more faithless than this?"

In the last century or so, a number of John Chrysostom's catechetical ser-mons have been discovered. Father Auguste Piedagnel published an analysis of John's catechetical sermons, as did Byzantine scholar A. Papadopulos in St. Petersburg just before World War I.[22] These sermons were preached to the catechúmens when they were enrolled, after their baptism "very early on Easter morning," and again during Easter week.[23] Unlike Cyril of Jerusalem, whose sermons were mystagogical, catechetical, or doctrinal instructions, Chrysostom focused on moral instruction and exhortation. He was inspired by Saint Paul, who wrote to the Romans,

> Or are you unaware that we who were baptized into Christ Jesus were baptized into his death? We were indeed buried with him through baptism into death, so that, just as Christ was raised from the dead by the glory of the Father, we too might live in newness of life. (6:3–4)

Chrysostom's method was an exposition of Scripture, followed by an exhortation to Christian morality. Baptism was the beginning of a covenant relationship between God and His people. When one received this holy sacrament, he or she was obliged to live in a certain way. The preacher's duty was to lay out this lifestyle and the moral obligations comprising the new life of baptism. As he put it to the newly baptized, "The promises which you have exchanged with the Master, written not with ink on paper, but by faith and the profession of that faith, hold firm and uncompromised."[24] The baptismal covenant obliges us to live as Christ taught. He stressed the need to keep one's baptismal garment pure and undefiled by living chastely, soberly, and honestly one's relationship with God and neighbor.

The following homily was delivered on the Fifth Sunday after the Epiphany of the Lord. It is based on Matthew 13:24–30. Chrysostom discusses the ancient battle between God and Satan using the parable of the weeds among the wheat. The Scripture passage is found on the 16th Sunday in Ordinary Time, Year A.

Homily: The Weeds and the Wheat

Synopsis:
    I. The difference between the two parables concerning the good seed.
    II. The artifice of the devil in leading men into error.
    III. Heretics should not be put to death.

I. What is the difference between this and the preceding parable. In the first He speaks of those who hearkened not to Him, turning away, and rejecting the good seed. Here He speaks of heretics. He foretold this also lest later His Disciples might be troubled regarding this very matter. The parable that precedes this refers to those who did not receive His Word. This speaks of those who receive the corruptors of His Word. For it is the guile of the spirit of evil to commingle his own errors with the sowing of the truth, so that they have the shape and colour of truth, and so deceive the trusting. He then here speaks not of any seed, but only of tares, which resemble wheat.

Then He speaks of the manner of this guile, *while men are asleep*. Here lies no small danger of headlong disaster for the rulers of the Church, to whom has been confided the care of the field; and not only to the rulers, but to the subjects as well. He shows here very clearly that wherever the seed of truth has been sown, error follows after, as events have truly confirmed. For after the Prophets have come the pseudo-prophets; after the apostles the pseudo-apostles; and after Christ anti-Christ. For the devil, except he sees what he can imitate, or against whom he may plot, knows not what to do, and neither does he attempt anything. But since he has learned that of the seed that was sown some brought fruit a hundredfold, some sixty, and some thirty, he tries yet another stratagem. Not being able to carry off what has taken firm root, nor choke it, nor wither it, he conspires against it by oversowing it with his own evil seed.

But what difference, you may ask, is there between those that sleep, and those who are signified by the wayside? There is this. That in the latter case the devil immediately snatched away the seed, not permitting it to take root. But in this case he has need of greater cunning. And Christ tells us this in order to teach us of the need for unsleeping vigilance. For though, He says, you escape these snares, you are not yet safe and secure; yet others remain. For as in the preceding parable disaster came to some by the wayside, to others because of stony ground, to others through being smothered by thorns, so here it came because of sleep. There is need therefore for continual watchfulness. Because of this He has said: *he that shall persevere unto the end, he shall be saved* (Matt. x. 22).

Something of this evil happened in the beginning of the Church. For many among the bishops, not being vigilant, received into the Church men who were evil and unworthy, secretly heretics, and gave them authority and opportunity to lay snares of this kind. The devil has no further need to labour after he has planted in our midst such men as these. But, you may ask, how is it possible we are never to sleep? As to natural sleep, it is indeed impossible; but it is otherwise with the sleep of the will. So Paul has said: *watch ye, stand fast* (1 Cor. xvi. 13).

He shows that this artifice of the devil is not alone injurious, but wanton. For when the tilling of the field is completed, and no more toil remains, then last of all he sows his seed, which also the heretics do, who for no other cause than vain glory scatter abroad their poison. That this the manner of their acting appears not alone from His words, but also from what follows. *And when the blade was sprung up,* He says, *and had brought forth fruit, then appeared also the cockle.* This undoubtedly is the method of the heretics; at first concealing their true selves, then, having acquired boldness, and after being entrusted with the teaching of the word, they boldly pour out their poison.

But why does He here bring in the servants, hastening to tell what has happened? That He may thus have an opportunity of declaring that such heretics are not to be killed. He calls the devil an enemy because of the injuries he ever strives to inflict on all men. Though the ill-will of the devil is directed against us, in its beginning it was not directed against us, but against the divine majesty. Hence it is apparent that we are loved more by God than we are loved by ourselves. See likewise the craft of the devil. For he did not sow his seed before, when there was nothing he could destroy, but only when he saw that the work of the sowing was completed, so as the more thoroughly to undo the work of the Husbandman. And with such malevolence of mind has he ever worked against Him.

Note in the parable also the zeal and affection of the servants. They are eager to root out the tares, though in this they are not wise, yet their concern for the good seed is very manifest, and they have thought only for this, not that someone be punished, but that the seed that was sown be not lost. And so they hasten to find out how the evil may be undone. Neither do they themselves decide what to do, but they look to the word of the Lord, asking: *Wilt Thou that we go and gather it up?* But the Lord forbids them, *lest you root up the wheat also*; which He also said in order to forbid wars and slaughters. For if men were to be killed for heresy it would lead to interminable war throughout the world.

II. How we are to act regarding heretics—*The Forbearance of Christ*. The Lord forbade this for two reasons. First, lest the wheat be injured; second, because whoever has a disease that is not cured, will not escape punishment. Therefore if you desire to see them punished without injury to the wheat, then you must wait for the due time. What else does He mean when He says *lest you root up the wheat also together with it*, unless that if you take up arms, and kill heretics, it must also follow that many of the sanctified will fall with them. And even of many from among the tares it is likely that they will be converted into wheat. If therefore you now uproot them, you will also destroy the wheat they would become, should they be converted. He did not however forbid us to reprove heretics, to silence their mouths, to restrict their liberty of speech, to scatter their assemblies; but He forbade that they should be killed.

But observe His gentleness and forbearance. He not alone forbids, but He also gives His reasons. What if the tares continue til the end? Then He says *I will say to the reapers, gather up first the cockle, and bind it into bundles to burn*. He recalls to their minds the words of John speaking of Him as the Judge (Mt. iii. 10), and says: we must spare the tares as long as they stand close to the wheat in the field, for it is possible that they too may become wheat. But when they have been cut down, and have not profited from the forbearance of the Lord, then they must receive their inevitable chastisement. *For I will say to the reapers*, He says, *gather up first the cockle*. Why first? Lest the good be anxious, fearing that the wheat will be carried off with the cockle. Let the cockle first be burned, He says, and then let the wheat be gathered into my barn.

Amen. (*Sunday Sermons of the Great Fathers*, 1:334–37)

Saint Ephrem the Deacon: Shakespeare of Syriac Literature

Saint Ephrem (ca. 306–373) has been called by some "The Shakespeare of Syriac literature, the incomparable poet of the language."[25] But he was also a theologian and a saint. Ephrem was born of a Christian family at Nisibis or Edessa (modern-day Iraq) around the year 306. The city of Nisibis was a major commercial and political center in northeastern Mesopotamia. Situated on a fertile plain adjacent to the River Mygdonius, the city was an urban center for more than a thousand years before Ephrem's time.[26] Its population included Arameans, Arabs, Greeks, Jews, Parthians, Romans, and Persians. The culture, and consequently the pre-Christian religion, consisted of a complex mixture of elements distilled from several civilizations that had remained there through the centuries. The pagan deities still worshipped in the fourth-century Mesopotamian cities included Babylonian gods such as Bel and Nebo, and Aramean *baalim* and their consorts, more remotely derived from Phoenician religion.[27] The language spoken there by Christians was Syrian, an East Aramean dialect. Nisibis was a frontier city that changed hands between the Roman and Persian Empires throughout the fourth century. The Persians were particularly brutal overlords. The city's Christians were once massacred after they were unable to pay a "double tax" to the Persian Emperor Shapur.[28] Syrian authors ascribe the deliverance of Nisibis from the Persian armies in 338 to Ephrem's prayers.

Ephrem was raised as Christian. As a young boy he was quick-tempered, quarrelsome, and imprudent. His imprisonment on a false charge led him to serious reflection on his life, and to a change of heart. He began to see the emptiness of worldly things and decided to embrace the consecrated life. After his release, he put on the monk's habit and devoted himself to exercises of piety and the study of Sacred Scripture. He was later ordained a deacon by Saint Basil the Great (St. Amphilocus, *Vitae St. Basil*), and exercised his sacred office throughout the country and in Edessa. Ephrem established a school of biblical and theological studies at Edessa. He was a great theologian and poet who authored biblical commentaries and homilies, and composed various hymns. He devoted his time to teaching Scripture, preaching, and instructing nuns in sacred psalmody. His interest and work with music earned him the title "Harp of the Holy Spirit." Kathleen McVey notes that "Although study of the nature and extent of his influence on later Western Christianity is still in a rudimentary stage, it is clear that he played a significant role in the development of both Byzantine hymnography and Western medieval religious drama."[29] In one hymn on virginity, for example, he compares the Hebrew Scriptures to their realities in the New Testament:

> [Christ's] power perfected the types,
> and His truth the mysteries,
> His interpretation the similes,
> His explanations the sayings,
> and His assurances the difficulties.
>
> By His sacrifice He abolished sacrifices,
> and libations by His incense,
> and the [passover] lambs by His slaughter,
> the unleavened bread by His bread,
> and the bitter [herbs] by His Passion.
>
> By His healthy meal
> He weaned [and] took away the milk.
> By His baptism were abolished
> the bathing and sprinkling
> that the elders of the People taught.
> (*Hymn to Virgins* 8, 8–10)[30]

Saint Ephrem wrote commentaries on Scripture to strengthen the orthodox faith.[31] His learning and insight also earned him the title "Doctor of the Syrians." St. Gregory of Nyssa once compared Ephrem to the River Euphrates because he "irrigated by his waters the Christian community to bring forth fruits of a faith a hundred-fold."[32] Pope Benedict XV lists his various types of writings:

> He is said to have written three thousand myriad poems if one counts them altogether. His writings cover most ecclesiastical doctrines. There are extant commentaries on Sacred Scripture and the mysteries of the faith: sermons on obligations and the interior life; studies on the sacred liturgy; hymns for the feast days of our Lord and the Blessed Virgin and the saints, for the processions of prayers and penitential days, for the funerals of the departed.[33]

Ephrem lived the faith he taught. He showed active charity during times of famine, but castigated those who were hoarding grain. He nursed the sick, and met pilgrims who came to Edessa looking for bread. Before he died, he exhorted his followers to maintain the Church's precepts and doctrines, and to guard against adversaries—"evildoers, boasters, and tempters to sin."[34] In the course of caring for the sick during an outbreak of the plague, he died on June 9, 373.

Saint John Chrysostom called Ephrem the "scourge of the slothful, consoler of the afflicted, educator, instructor and exhorter of youth, mirror of monks, leader of penitents, goad and sting of heretics, reservoir of virtues, and the home and lodging of the Holy Spirit."[35] The value of his works is reflected in part in the fact that from the very beginning, the neighboring Chaldeans, Armenians, Maronites, and Greeks translated the writings of the deacon of Edessa into their languages, and eagerly read them in their liturgical celebrations. Even today his songs can be found among the Slavs, Copts, Ethiopians, Jacobites, and Nestorians.[36] Pope Benedict XV declared the Syrian exegete and theologian a Doctor of the Universal Church on Oct. 5, 1920. His feast day is June 9.

The Preaching of St. Ephrem the Deacon

Ephrem's homilies are characterized by precise language, and were the fruit of deep meditation. He was a careful thinker and powerful presenter. Ephrem was concerned with promoting devotion and asceticism, and correcting the errors of his day. His homilies defended the dogmas of the faith from growing heresies. His favorite preaching subjects were the Last Judgment, the Blessed Virgin Mary, and the saints. His preaching reflected his philosophy of biblical interpretation. Ephrem was heavily influenced by the Antiochene School, given his proximity to Antioch. He accepted biblical typology, but not allegory. He believed that Scripture could be best understood by those living in the world of Scripture.[37]

"The most remarkable series of sermons which has come down to us from Ephrem is the *Hymns on Paradise*."[38] Comprising fifteen *madrashe* or metrical sermons, the series discusses the creation of Adam and Eve in the garden.

> 1. Moses, who instructs all men with his celestial writings,
> He, the master of the Hebrews,
> Has instructed us in his teaching—
> The Law, which constitutes a very treasure house of revelations,
> Wherein is revealed the tale of the Garden—
> Described by things visible, but glorious for what lies hidden,
> Spoken of in few words,
> Yet wondrous with its many plants.
>
> Response: Praise to your righteousness which exalts those who prove
>   victorious.
>
> 2. I took my stand halfway between awe and love;
> a yearning for Paradise, invited me to explore it, but awe at its
> majesty restrained me from my search.
> With wisdom, however, I reconciled the two;
> I revered what lay hidden and meditated on what was revealed.
> The aim of my search was to gain profit,
> The aim of my silence was to find succor.[39]

Ephrem communicated the Gospel through poetry, which intimates more than what is explicitly stated.

There are several characteristics of Ephrem's approach to Scripture and preaching:

First, he believed Scripture is the revealed Word of God, a Word of life and love that brings vitality and spiritual refreshment. In the ministry of the Word, Wisdom flows from God to the listener. This basic idea was fundamental to Ephrem's approach.

Second, Scripture moves from "promise to fulfillment."[40] To understand Scripture is to see the movement from the "promise of redemption made to the patriarchs all the way to its fulfillment in Christ."[41] There are hints and premonitions of the fulfillment of the promise throughout the Bible. For instance, the Tabernacle was a type of the heavenly Dwelling, reminding us of the place being prepared for those who love God. The ascent of Mount Sinai and the descent of the Holy Spirit on Pentecost beckon the faithful toward the Promised Land. The manna in the desert foreshadows the Eucharist given to hungry hearts by Christ Himself.

Third, Ephrem subscribes to the literal and spiritual interpretations of Scripture. Scripture has an outward and inward meaning. Origen, and later Augustine, developed the theology of these two meanings, although in very different ways. For Ephrem, Scriptural interpretation was an act of worship. "It is to stand be-

fore the presence of God in wonder and awe, and, hearing His Word, to be transfigured by that Word into the image of the Son of God."[42]

As with many preachers of the patristic period, Ephrem's theology of
preaching is closely related to the Wisdom theology of that period. "The Christian is nourished by divine Wisdom."[43] Discipline removes the spiritual scales
from our eyes, and the reading of Sacred Scripture nourishes the soul with divine teaching. As a result, the Syrian Church put great emphasis on the reading
of Scripture in the sacred liturgy.

Ephrem delivered *homiletical poetry*. Homiletical poetry is a sermon
preached in metrical lines arranged in stanzas. The congregation responded to
this line by singing a refrain. This genre of poetry was familiar to Semites generally, and Syrians in particular. The prophets Amos, Micah, Isaiah, and
Jeremiah spoke in poetic verse centuries before Christ. And Mohammed composed the Koran in extemporized verse six centuries after Christ.[44] Ephrem also
used "alliterations, word plays, rhymes, and antitheses similar to poetry of other
times and places."[45] Some illustrations follow.

In speaking of the rock in the desert pouring out water as a "type" of Christ
(1 Cor. 10:4), he developed the idea by showing that the rock of Christ is also a
type of Christ as the Word of the Creator.

I considered the Word of the Creator,
and likened it to the rock
that marched with the People of Israel
in the wilderness.[46]

A beautiful example of thought rhyme is found in a hymn where Ephrem
speaks of the saints being clothed in light. These garments of light have taken
the place of the fig leaves Adam and Eve wore after the Fall:

Both men and women
are clothed in raiment of light;
the garments provided to cover
their nakedness are swallowed
up in glory.[47]

Ephrem's verse offers a unique contribution to the history of preaching. He
used poetry as an effective vehicle for communicating the truth that is the Word
of God. His technique reflects not only his scholarship, but also a profound
spirituality linked to the Catholic tradition in which he ministered to the People
of God.

The following homily is from the Transfiguration, which the Church celebrates on August 6th, and reflects on during the Second Sunday of Lent. He discusses the reasons for the Transfiguration and carefully unfolds the biblical text
for the listener.

Homily: On the Transfiguration of Our Lord and God and
            Saviour Jesus Christ

The harvest comes joyfully from the fields, and a yield that is rich and pleasant from the vine; and from the Scriptures teaching that is life giving and salutary. The fields have but one season of harvest; but from the Scripture there gushes forth a stream of saving doctrine. The field, when reaped, lies idle and at rest, and the branches when the vine is stripped lie withered and dead. The Scriptures are garnered each day, yet the years of its interpreters never come to an end; and the clusters of its vines, which in it are those of hope, though also gathered each day, are likewise without end. Let us therefore come to this field, and take our delight of its life-giving furrows; and let us reap there the wheat of life, that is, the words of Our Lord Jesus Christ.

And after six days Jesus taketh unto Him Peter and James, and John his brother, and bringeth them up into a high mountain apart; and He was transfigured before them. And His face did shine as the sun: and His garments became white as snow. For the men whom He had said would not taste death until they should see the form and the foreshadowing of His Coming are these three Apostles, whom having taken with Him He brought to a mountain, and showed them in what manner He was to come on the last day: in the glory of His Divinity, and in the Body of His Humanity.

He led them up to the mountain that He might also reveal to them Who this Son is, and Whose Son is He. For when He asked them: *Whom do men say the Son of man is,* they said to Him: *Some Elias; some others Jeremias, or one of the prophets.* And so He led them up into a high mountain, and showed them that He was not Elias, but the God of Elias; that neither was He Jeremias, but He that had sanctified Jeremias in his mother's womb; that neither was He one of the prophets, but the Lord of the prophets, and He that had sent them.

And He showed them also that He was the Creator of heaven and earth, and the Lord of the living and the dead; for He spoke to the heavens, and they sent down Elias; He made a sign to the earth, and raised Moses to life again. And He brought them to Sinai, that He might show them He was the Son of God, and begotten of the Father before all ages, and last of all taking flesh from the Virgin Mary and, in a manner which He knows, was born without seed in an ineffable manner, without stain whatsoever of her virginity. For where God wills it, the order of nature is superseded. For God the Word dwelt in the womb of the Virgin: and the fire of His Divinity consumed not the members of the virginal body; and in that dwelling place she kept watch over him for the space of nine months. He dwelt in the womb of the Virgin, not despising our nature; and from it God came forth clothed in human flesh, that He might redeem us.

He took them up into a high mountain apart, that He might also show them the glory of His Divinity, and that He might declare Himself the Redeemer of Israel, as He had foretold by the prophets, and so that they would not be scandalized in Him when they would see Him in the Passion He had taken upon Himself; and which for our sakes He was about to suffer in His human nature. For they knew that He was man; but they knew not that He was God. They knew Him as the Son of Mary, and as a man sharing their daily life in the world. On the mountain He revealed to them that He was the Son of God, and

Himself God. For they knew that He hungered and that He ate; that He thirsted and that He drank; that He laboured and that He took rest, that He felt need of sleep and that He slept, that He feared and that He sweated. And all this belonged not to His divine nature, but only to His humanity; and therefore He led them to the mountain, so that the Father may with His own voice call Him Son, and that He may show that He is in truth His Son, and God.

He took them therefore up to the mountain, that He might show them His Kingdom, before they witnessed His suffering and death; and His glory before His ignominy: so that when He was made a prisoner, and condemned by the Jews, they might understand that He was not crucified by them because of His own powerlessness, but because it had pleased Him of His goodness to suffer, for the salvation of the world.

He brought them up to the mountain that He might also show them, before His Resurrection, the glory of His Divinity, so that when He had risen from the dead they might then know that He had not received this glory as the reward of His labour, and as one who had it not; but that He had had it from all eternity, together with the Father and the Holy Spirit; as He had already said when He came of His own will to suffer: *Now glorify me, O Father, with thyself, with the glory which I had, before the world was, with thee* (Jn. xvii. 9). It was therefore this glory of His Divinity, which was hidden and veiled to humanity, that He revealed to the Apostles on the mountain. For they beheld His Face shining as the sun, and His garments white as snow.

The Disciples upon the mountain beheld two suns, one, to which they were accustomed, shining in the sky, and Another, to which they were unaccustomed; one which shown down on them, and from the firmament gave light to the whole world, and One which then shone for them alone, which was the Face of Jesus *before them*. And His garments appeared to them white as light: for the glory of His Divinity poured forth from His whole body, and all His members radiated light. His Face shone, not as the face of Moses, from without; from His Face the glory of His Divinity poured forth, yet remained with Him. From Himself came His own light, and was contained within Him. For it did not spread out from elsewhere, and fall on Him; it did not come slantwise to adorn Him. Neither did He receive it, to use for a while, nor did He reveal to them the unfathomable depths of his glory, but only as much as the pupils of their eyes could take in and distinguish.

And there appeared to them Moses and Elias talking with him. And this was the manner of their speech with Him. They gave thanks to Him that their own words had been fulfilled, and together with them the words of all the prophets. They adored Him for the salvation He had wrought in the world for mankind, and because He had in truth fulfilled the mystery which they had themselves foretold. The Prophets therefore were filled with joy, and the Apostles likewise, in their ascent of the mountain. The Prophets rejoiced because they had seen His Humanity, which they had not known. And the Apostles rejoiced because they had seen the glory of the Divinity, which they had not known.

And when they heard the voice of the Father, giving testimony of the Son, they learnt through this that which till now had been obscure to them: that humanity had been assumed by Him. And together with His Father's Voice the glory of His own Body gave testimony to Him, shining resplendent because of

That within Him which partakes of the Divinity, unchangeably and without confusion. And this was confirmed by three witnesses: by the Voice of the Father, and by the presences of Moses and Elias, who stood by Him as servants. And they looked, the one upon the other, the Prophets upon the Apostles, the Apostles upon the Prophets. They looked upon each other, the Princes of the Old and the Princes of the New Testament. Moses the holy man looks upon Simon the Sanctified. The servant of the Father looks upon the vicar of the Son. The one had divided the sea, so that the people might walk in the midst of the waves (Ex. xiv). The other made a tabernacle, that he might build a church.

The virgin of the old Testament looks upon the virgin of the New: Elias looks upon John. He who had ascended into heaven in a fiery chariot looks upon him who had rested his head upon a Burning Breast (IV Kings ii; Jn. xiii. 21). His mountain became a figure of the Church; and in Himself Jesus has united the Two Testaments, which the Church receives, revealing to us that He is the Giver of both. The one received His divine secrets; the other has proclaimed the visible glory of His works.

And so Simon says: *Lord, it is good for us to be here.* What is it you say, O Simon? If we should remain here, who would fulfill the words of the Prophets? Who confirm the tidings of the Heralds? Who accomplish the mysteries of the Just? If we should remain here, then that prophecy: *They have pierced my hands and my feet* (Ps. xxi. 17), in whom would it be fulfilled? Or that other: *They parted my garments among them, and upon my vesture they cast lots* (Ps. xxi. 19), to whom would it then pertain? *And they gave me gall for my food, and in my thirst they gave me vinegar to drink* (Ps. lxviii. 22), to whom would these words apply? And the words: *Free among the dead,* who would make them true? (Ps. lxxxvii. 6).

If we should remain here who would tear up the writ against Adam, and who would pay his debt? And who would give him back his garment of glory? If we should remain here how would the things I have told you be fulfilled? How would the Church be built upon you, Peter? And the Keys of the Kingdom of Heaven, how would you receive them from Me? Whom would you bind? Whom would you loose? If we should remain here all these things will remain unfulfilled which were spoken of by the Prophets.

Then he said: *Let us make here three dwelling-places, one for thee, and one for Moses, and one for Elias.* Simon was sent to build the Church in the world, and he wishes to build three dwellings upon a mountain: for he still continues to speak with Christ as one speaks with a man, placing Him on a level with Moses and Elias. But immediately the Lord shows him that He has no need of dwelling-places. For He it was who concealed His dwelling-place in a cloud among their forefathers in the wilderness throughout forty years (ix. 10). For as He was speaking to them *a bright cloud* overshadowed them. Behold, O Simon, a dwelling-place made without hands; a dwelling-place that protects you from the heat, and that is without any darkness; a dwelling place that shines as the sun. And to the great wonder of the Disciples, behold a voice, which proceeds from the Father, is heard from the cloud saying: *This is my beloved Son, in whom I am well pleased; hear ye Him.*

The Father having spoken Moses returns to his own place and Elias to his fatherland; and the Apostles fall down with their faces to the earth; and Jesus stands alone, since only in Him were these words fulfilled. The Prophets are gone, and the Apostles lie prone upon the earth, for it is not in any of these that the words are fulfilled which the Father spoke: *This is my beloved Son in whom I am well pleased. Hear ye him.*

The Father teaches them that the Dispensation of Moses had been fulfilled; and now they must hearken to the voice of His Son. For the former, as a servant, had spoken that which he was commanded; and that which was told him he had made known; and in like manner all the Prophets, until He had come in place of them, namely, Jesus, Who is the Son, not a servant of His household, the Lord, not a slave, the Ruler, not one subject to rule, the Lawgiver, not one subject to the law; His Son by nature, not by adoption.

Accordingly, the Father makes manifest upon the mountain what was yet obscure to the Apostles regarding the divinity of His Son. He Who is signifies to them *Who* He is. The Father by His voice gives testimony to His Son; and at the sound of His voice the Apostles fall prone upon the ground. Since it was awesome as the thunder, and as the earth trembled at His voice, so likewise they sink down upon the earth. It told them that the Father had come nigh them, and had called Him Son Who by His voice had comforted them. For as that dread voice of the Father cast them prone upon the earth, so the voice of the Son caused them to rise up again by the power of His divinity. Which, since It dwells in His flesh, is united unchangeably to Him: Both dwell within the one hypostasis, and in the one Person abide without separation and without commingling.

Nor did He appear as Moses, outwardly beautiful, but shone as God; for it was from the light of the glory of His countenance that the face of Moses was clothed with beauty. But Jesus shone forth in His own Body, as the sun in the midst of its rays; from the glory of His divinity. The Father indeed cried out: *This is My beloved Son, in whom I am well pleased, Hear ye Him.* He is not separate from the glory of the divinity of His Son. For One is the Nature of the Father, and of the Son, together with the Holy Ghost: One is the Power, One the Essence, One the Kingdom, and it calls Him with one voice, by a name that is simple, but of a glory that is fearful.

And Mary called Him her Son, Who was undivided by His human body from the glory of His Divinity: since One is God, seen in this world in our body. His glory reveals His divine nature, which is from the Father; and His body reveals his human nature, which is from Mary. Both natures have united, and, without change and without commingling, have been joined together in one hypostasis or person. The Same is the Only-begotten of the Father who is the Only-begotten of Mary. And he who separates them is himself separated from His Kingdom; and he who commingles His natures into one will have no part in His life. He that denies that Mary gave birth to God shall not see the glory of His divinity; and whosoever denies that He was clothed in flesh Who was free from the stain of every sin shall be shut out from salvation, and from the life which is given by His Body.

The events of His life, and His own divine powers, teach those who can learn that He is true God and His sufferings openly proclaim Him true man. And if this does not convince those who are weak and foolish of mind, they shall suffer punishment on the day of His dread judgement.

For if He were not flesh, for what reason did Mary bring Him forth? And if He was not God, who then did Gabriel call Lord?

If He was not flesh, who then lay in the manger? If He was not God, to whom did the angels coming on earth give glory?

If He was not man, who was wrapped in swaddling clothes? If He was not God, whom then did the Shepherds adore?

If He was not man, whom did Joseph circumcize? And if He was not God, in whose honour did a new star appear in the heavens?

If He was not man, whom did Mary nourish at the breast? And if He were not God, to whom did the Magi offer gifts?

If He was not man, whom did Simeon take in His arms? And if He was not God, to whom did Simeon say: *Dismiss me in peace?*

If He was not man, whom did Joseph take and fly with him into Egypt? And if He was not God, in whom was the prophecy fulfilled: *Out of Egypt have I called my son?* (Mt. ii. 15; Os. xi. 1)

If He was not man, whom did John baptize? And if He was not God, of whom did the Father from heaven say: *This is my beloved Son, in whom I am well pleased?* (Mt. iii. 17).

If He was not man, who fasted and hungered in the desert? And if He was not God, to whom did the descending angels minister?

If He was not man, who was invited to the wedding feast at Cana of Galilee? And if He was not God, who changed the water into wine?

If He was not man, in whose hands were the loaves of bread placed? And if He were not God, who fed and filled from five barley loaves and two fishes the multitude in the desert, five thousand men, not counting the women and children?

If He was not man, who slept in the boat? And if He were not God, who was it rebuked the winds and the sea?

If He was not man, who was it ate with Simon the Pharisee? And if He were not God, who forgave the woman her sins?

If He was not a man, who sat by the well weary from the journey? And if He was not God, who gave the Samaritan woman the water of life; and who rebuked her, she that had already five husbands?

If He was not of our flesh, who wore the garments of a man? And if He were not God, who then was it that wrought signs and wonders?

If He was not a man, who spat upon the earth, and made mud from the clay? And if He were not God, who caused eyes to see because of the clay? (Jn. ix).

If He was not man, who wept at the tomb of Lazarus? And if He were not God, who by His command alone called forth the four days dead?

If He was not a man, who was it sat upon an ass's colt? And if He were not God, before whom did the crowd march to give Him glory?

If He was not a man, whom did the Jews make prisoner? And if He were not God, who commanded the earth, and it threw them flat to the ground?

If He was not a man, who was beaten with blows? And if He were not God, who healed the ear which Peter had cut off, and who restored it to its place?

If He was not a man, whose face was spat upon? And if He were not God, who breathed the Holy Spirit upon the faces of the Apostles? (Jn. xx. 22).

If He was not a man, who was it stood before Pilate at the judgement seat? And if He were not God, who caused the wife of Pilate to suffer many things in a dream?

If He was not a man, upon whose garments did the soldiers cast lots, dividing them amongst them? And if He were not God, for what reason did the sun grow dark above the Cross?

If He was not a man, who was it hung upon a cross? And if He were not God, who moved the earth from its foundations?

If He was not a man, whose hands were pierced by the nails? And if He were not God, how was the veil of the temple rent in two, and the rocks split asunder, and the graves opened?

If He was not a man, who cried out: *My God, My God, why hast Thou abandoned me?* And if He were not God, who then hath said: *Father, forgive them, for they know not what they do?*

If He was not man, who hung with thieves upon a cross? And if He were not God, for what cause did He say: *This day thou shalt be with me in paradise?*

If He was not man, to whom did they offer gall and vinegar? And if He were not God, at whose voice did they shake and tremble? (Ps. lxxvi. 19).

If He was not a man, whose side was opened by a lance, *and there came out blood and water?* (Jn. xix. 34). And if He were not God, *who hath broken the gates of hell, and burst the iron bars?* (Ps. cvi. 16). And by whose command did the dead that slept in their graves come forth?

If He was not a man, whom did the Apostles behold in the Upper Room? And if He were not God, in what manner did He enter, *the doors being closed?*

If He was not a man, in whose hand did Thomas feel the wounds of the nails and the lance? And if He was not God, to whom did Thomas cry out saying: *My Lord and My God?*

If He was not a man, who ate food by the Sea of Tiberiades? And if He were not God, at whose command was the net filled with fishes?

If He was not man, whom did the Apostles and the Angels see received into the heavens? If He was not God, to whom were the heavens opened, whom did the powers adore in fear and trembling, and to whom had the Father said: *Sit thou on my right hand*, and the rest which follows? (*Ps. cix.* 1).

If He were not both God and man, then is our salvation a false thing; and false likewise the voices of the prophets. But the prophets have spoken what is true, and their testimonies are far from falsehood of any kind. For they spoke that which they were bidden to speak, and through them the Holy Spirit spoke. For which reason the chaste John, who leaned upon the burning Breast, confirming the voices of the prophets, and discoursing of the divinity, teaches us in His Gospel, saying: *In the beginning was the Word, and the Word was with God, and the Word was God. All things were made by Him; and without Him was made nothing that was made. And the Word was made flesh, and dwelt among us*; who is God the Word from God, and the Only-begotten Son of the Father, Who is consubstantial with the Father, Who is, from Him Who is: the Word before all ages: ineffably and before all ages Begotten of the Father without a mother; the Same in these last days is born without a father, God Incarnate, from a daughter of men, from the Virgin Mary; taking flesh from Her, and from Her made man, which He was not, remaining God, which He was, that He might redeem the world.

And He is Christ the Son of God: the Only-begotten of the Father, the Only-begotten of His Mother. And I confess that the Same is perfect God and perfect man, Who in His two natures is acknowledged to be indivisibly, unchangeably, and without confusion, united in the *one hypostasis* or person; clothed in living flesh, and having a soul that is endowed with reason and understanding, subject in all things to the same afflictions as ourselves, sin alone excepted.

The same is of both earth and heaven: of time and eternity; Who began, and is without beginning; free of time, yet subject to time; created and uncreated; impassible, and capable of suffering; God and man; perfect as either one or the other; One sharing two natures, and in two natures One. One the Person of the Father, and one the Person of the Son, and one the Person of the Holy Ghost. One the Godhead, one the Majesty, one the Kingdom in three Persons or Hypostases.

So let us give glory to the Holy Unity in Trinity, and to the Holy Trinity in Unity! In Which the Father has declared from heaven: *This is My beloved Son, in whom I am well pleased: Hear ye Him.* This the Most Holy Catholic Church professes. In this same Holy Trinity She baptizes into eternal life. She venerates the same with equality of honour; and confesses the Same without division, and without separation; and without superstition adores, proclaims, and glorifies the same Holy Trinity.

To that Unity in three Persons, to the Father, Son, and Holy Ghost, glory, thanksgiving, honour, power, and glory, now and for ever. Amen. (*Sunday Sermons*, 2:44–51)

Saint Basil: Prince of the Patristic Pulpit

Saint Basil the Great (ca. 330–379), called a "Prince of the Patristic Pulpit," was one of the Fathers of the Eastern Church. He was born around 330 in Caesarea, Cappadocia (modern day Turkey), one of ten children. His family was renowned for its Christian spirit, as well as its wealth and nobility. He received his elementary training from his father, Basil the Elder, the famous rhetorician in Cappadocia (now known as Kayseri, Turkey). His mother Emmelia, the daughter of a martyr, gave birth to ten children, three of whom became bishops: Basil, Gregory of Nyssa, and Peter of Sebaste, while her oldest daughter was well known as Saint Macrina the Younger, a model of the ascetic life.

The talented youth attended to his higher education in the schools of rhetoric at his native Caesarea, at Constantinople, and finally, after 351, at Athens. While a student in Constantinople and Athens, he began a life-long friendship with Gregory Nazianzus. He also befriended the Emperor Julian the Apostate (ca. 361–363). He returned to his native city around 356 and began his career as a rhetorician, which he quickly renounced to embrace a life entirely devoted to God. Saints Basil, Gregory of Nyssa, and Gregory of Nazianzus are sometimes called "the three great Cappadocians."

After his baptism, he toured Palestine, Syria, and Egypt, where he met famous ascetics and established a hermitage on the Iris River (the modern Black Sea region). When Gregory of Nazianzus visited him in 358, they prepared together the *Philokalia*, an anthology of Origen's works, and the two *Rules. The Rules* had a decisive influence in the expansion of cloistered life in common, and earned Basil the nickname "The Lawgiver of Greek Monasticism." Basil was ordained a priest in 365 in Caesarea, and returned to Pontus on the Iris River. He later was ordained a bishop in Caesarea when Eusebius died in 370. He soon won the hearts of his people. He established hospitals for the sick and victims of contagious diseases, homes for the poor, and hospices for travelers and strangers. He remained faithful to the Christian religion despite fierce persecution from state-supported Arian adherents. Basil was a courageous defender of orthodoxy, as well as an outstanding ecclesiastical statesman and organizer, a great exponent of Christian doctrine, a Father of Eastern Monasticism, and a reformer of the sacred liturgy. He was deeply concerned for the terrible condition of the churches in the East, and wrote Pope Damasus begging him to visit them. He was convinced that orthodoxy could succeed if there were no dissension, and no waste of time and energy among believers. It was not to be. The rift between East and West continued, although he lived to see at least the dawning of better days, when the Arian Emperor Valens died on August 9, 378. External conditions then permitted the restoration of peace.

Basil was a man of deep holiness, profound learning, and great scholarly ability. His most famous work is *On the Holy Spirit*. He also wrote books against Eunomius, an Arian bishop who taught that a single supreme Substance exists, whose simplicity is opposed to all distinctions, even virtual, whether of properties or absolutes. Eunomius regarded the Son of God as being immediately produced by the Father, and said the Holy Ghost was a created being. Basil's constitutions or directions for monks were influential and far-reaching. They are mentioned by Gregory of Tours and in the great *Concordia* of Benedict of Aniane in the ninth century. Basil died on January 1, 379. His feast day is January 2.

The Preaching of St. Basil the Great

His sermons are a small part of Basil's rich literary legacy.[48] We have nine sermons on the six days of creation, eighteen sermons on the Psalms, and various sermons on the feast of the Epiphany, martyrs' feasts, and sermons on piety and vice. Basil emphasized the importance of the Christian life. He was a masterful expository preacher, commenting on the biblical text one line at a time.

Basil was always well prepared to preach, although he didn't write out his sermons (that task was left to stenographers). After a period of prayer, he carefully studied the text, thought out his interpretation, and consulted commentaries.[49] He would put his homilies together in his head as he entered church (a practice I would not recommend!).

The striking characteristic of Basil's homilies on the psalms is that he stresses their pastoral nature. He says they are at one and the same time hymns of praise to God and instructions on how to live the Christian life.[50] The psalms have a healing quality to them. Basil noted:

> The delight of the melody He mingled with the doctrines so that the pleasantness and softness of the sound we might receive without perceiving it the benefit of the words, just as wise physicians who, when giving the fastidious rather bitter drugs to drink, frequently smear the cup with honey.[51]

The therapeutic quality of the psalms goes back centuries before Christ (1 Sam. 16:23). Basil says in another sermon, "A psalm implies serenity of soul; it is the author of peace, which calms bewildering and seething thoughts." He goes on to ask, "Can you learn the grandeur of courage? The exactness of justice? The nobility of self-control? The perfection of prudence? A manner of penance? The measure of patience? And whatever other good things you might mention?"[52]

Hughes Old describes Basil as not only "the master of classical rhetoric as it had been taught by the intellectuals of ancient Greece and Rome, he was as well the fulfillment of what the philosophers taught about virtue."[53] Basil taught that true Christian living glorifies God. It is a form of worship. He uses allegory in making his point. He compares the human body to a harp and the body's actions to a psalm. True virtuous living is like playing a beautiful psalm on the living harp of our lives. It is pleasing to the ears when one lives out God's Commandments.

Basil's *Hexaemeron* (a series of nine sermons preached in the course of several days at Lauds and Vespers) is a classic piece of work. It shows a re-emphasis on the literal interpretation of Scripture. While it is true that Basil grew up in the Alexandrian School, it is also true that he felt more secure in the Antiochene tradition. He felt better able to defend the Christian faith against Arians, Gnostics, and other heresies by using a historical approach to Sacred Scripture.

Basil loved nature, and his homilies rejoice in the goodness of creation. Basil is a preacher who shows how knowledge of the natural world can lead the Christian to a deeper understanding of Scripture.[54] God reveals Himself through creation, and creation itself points to the beauty, power, knowledge, and plan of God.

Saint Basil, his brother Gregory of Nyssa, and his friend Gregory of Nazianzus were well schooled in the literary arts. They had mastered the rhetorical forms of classical antiquity, in order to present their message in a clear and convincing way. They saw Greek learning as a means of advancing the Kingdom of Heaven and the cause of truth, and they succeeded in convincing the Church of the wisdom of orthodoxy, through their brilliant literary activities.[55]

Basil had a deep appreciation for ancient Greek and Roman rhetoric. Examples of the various techniques he employed in preaching are:

- *Parallelism*: a sense of balance and symmetry in writing; proportion.
    > As the beginning of the road is not yet the road, and the beginning of the house, not yet the house, so also, the beginning of time is not yet time. (*Hexaemenon*, 1.6)
- *Antithesis*: the clarification of ideas by setting them off against their opposites; antithesis can involve whole paragraphs or be contained within a single compound sentence.[56]
    > But the marvel is that you may find in plants the characteristics closely resembling those of human youth and old age. Around the young and thriving plants the bark is stretched smooth, but around the old it is as if wrinkled and rough. (*Hexaemeron*, 5.7)
- *Metaphor*: the use of visible images to describe invisible realities.
    > Truly, it is a spider's web that these writers weave, who suggest such weak and unsubstantial beginnings of the heavens and earth and sea. (*Hexaemeron*, 1.2)
- *Simile*: simple comparisons or likenesses.
    > In fact, as the potter, although he has formed innumerable vessels by the same art, has exhausted neither his art nor his power, so also the Creator of the Universe, possessing creative power not commensurate with one world, but infinitely greater, by the weight of His will alone, brought the mighty creatures of the visible world into existence. (*Hexaemeron*, 1.2)

"Basil's concept of the Word of God is dynamic. It is a word of creation, a word of redemption and a word of revelation. It is that word which rhetoric serves and in so doing, achieves its telos [or end]," Old writes.[57]

For Basil, God's Word revealed truth, and the preacher's job of rhetoric was to explain and describe it. Unlike some ancient Greek preachers, who drew attention to *themselves* in debates and discussions, Christian preachers called attention to *the Word*. They were God's servants or messengers. Through His servant, God fed His people with spiritual food and drink. Basil believed that forgetting this basic point was a serious mistake.

Basil the Great brilliantly put his rhetorical skills at the service of the Gospel, and has left the Church with a rich spiritual and literary legacy. His homily on the creation of the world is based on Genesis 1:2 ("The earth was a formless void"). The reading is proclaimed at the Easter Vigil.

Homily: The Creation of the World

> In the few words which have occupied us this morning we have found such a depth of thought that we despair of penetrating farther. If such is the forecourt of the sanctuary, if the portico of the temple is so grand and magnificent, if the splendor of its beauty thus dazzles the eyes of the soul, what will be the holy of holies? Who will dare to try to gain access to the innermost shrine? Who will look into its secrets? To gaze into it is indeed forbidden us, and language is powerless to express what the mind conceives.

However, since there are rewards, and most desirable ones, reserved by the just Judge for the intention alone of doing good, do not let us hesitate to continue our researches. Altho we may not attain to the truth, if, with the help of the Spirit, we do not fall away from the meaning of Holy Scripture, we shall not deserve to be rejected, and with the help of grace, we shall contribute to the edification of the Church of God.

"The earth," says Holy Scripture, "was without form and void"—i.e., invisible and unfinished. The heavens and the earth were created together. How, then, is it that the heavens are perfect whilst the earth is still unformed and incomplete? In one word, what was the unfinished condition of the earth and for what reason was it invisible? The fertility of the earth is its perfect finishing; growth of all kinds of plants, the up-springing of tall trees, both productive and unfruitful, flowers' sweet scents and fair colors, and all that which, a little later, at the voice of God came forth from the earth to beautify her, their universal mother.

As nothing of all this yet existed, Scripture is right in calling the earth "without form." We could also say of the heavens that they were still imperfect and had not received their natural adornment, since at that time they did not shine with the glory of the sun and of the moon, and were not crowned by the choirs of the stars. These bodies were not yet created. Thus you will not diverge from the truth in saying that the heavens also were "without form." The earth was invisible for two reasons: it may be because man, the spectator, did not yet exist, or because, being submerged under the waters which overflowed the surface, it could not be seen, since the waters had not yet been gathered together into their own places, where God, afterward, collected them and gave them the name of sea.

What is invisible? First of all, that which our fleshly eye can not perceive—our mind, for example; then that which, visible in its nature, is hidden by some body which conceals it, like iron in the depths of the earth. It is in this sense that the earth, in that it was hidden under the waters, was still invisible. However, as light did not yet exist, and as the earth lay in darkness because of the obscurity of the air above it, it should not astonish us that for this reason Scripture calls is "invisible."

But the corrupters of the truth, who, incapable of submitting their reason to Holy Scripture, distort at will the meaning of the Holy Scriptures, pretend that these words mean matter. For it is matter, they say, which from its nature is without form and invisible—being by the conditions of its existence without quality and without form and figure. The Artificer submitting it to the working of His wisdom clothed it with a form, organized it, and thus gave being to the visible world.

If the matter is uncreated, it has a claim to the same honors as God, since it must be of equal rank with Him. Is this not the summit of wickedness that utter chaos, without quality, without form or shape, ugliness without configuration, to use their own expression, should enjoy the same prerogatives as He who is wisdom, power, and beauty itself, the Creator and the Demiurge of the universe enjoys? This is not all. If the matter is so great as to be capable of being acted on by the whole wisdom of God, it would in a way raise its hypostasis to an equality with the inaccessible power of God, since it would be able to measure by itself all the extent of the divine intelligence.

If it is insufficient for the operations of God, then we fall into a more absurd blasphemy, since we condemn God for not being able, on account of the want of matter, to finish His own works. The resourcelessness of human nature has deceived these reasoners. Each of our crafts is exercised upon some special matter—the art of the smith upon iron, that of the carpenter on wood. In all there is the subject, the form and the work which results from the form. Matter is taken from without—art gives the form—and the work is composed at the same time of form and of matter.

Such is the idea that they make for themselves of the divine work. The form of the world is due to the wisdom of the supreme Artificer; matter came to the Creator from without; and thus the world results from a double origin. It has received from outside its matter and its essence, and from God its form and figure. They thus come to deny that the mighty God has presided at the formation of the universe, and pretend that he has only brought a crowning contribution to a common work; that he has only contributed some small portion to the genesis of beings; they are incapable, from the debasement of their reasonings, of raising their glances to the height of truth. Here, below, arts are subsequent to matter—introduced into life by the indispensable need of them. Wool existed before weaving made it supply one of nature's imperfections. Wood existed before carpentering took possession of it, and transformed it each day to supply new wants and made us see all the advantages derived from it, giving the oar to the sailor, the winnowing-fan to the laborer, the lance to the soldier.

But God, before all those things which now attract our notice existed, after casting about in His mind and determining to bring into being that which had no being, imagined the world such as it ought to be, and created matter in harmony with the form which He wished to give it. He assigned to the heavens the nature adapted for the heavens, and gave to the earth an essence in accordance with its form. He formed, as he wished, fire, air and water, and gave to each the essence which the object of its existence required.

Finally, he welded all the diverse parts of the universe by links of indissoluble attachment and established between them so perfect a fellowship and harmony that the most distant, in spite of their distance, appeared united in one universal symphony. Let those men, therefore, renounce their fabulous imaginations, who in spite of the weakness of their argument, pretend to measure a power as incomprehensible to man's reason as it is unutterable by man's voice.

God created the heavens and the earth, but not only one-half of each; He created all the heavens and all the earth, creating the essence with the form. For He is not an inventor of figures, but the Creator even of the essence of beings. Further, let them tell us how the efficient power of God could deal with the passive nature of matter, the latter furnishing the matter without form, the former possessing the science of the form without matter, both being in need of each other; the Creator in order to display his art, matter in order to cease to be without form and to receive a form. But let us stop here and return to our subject.

"The earth was invisible and unfinished." In saying "In the beginning God created the heavens and the earth" the sacred writer passed over many things in silence—water, air, fire, and the results from them, which, all forming in reality the true complement of the world, were, without doubt made at the same time as the universe. By this silence history wished to train the activity of our intelligence, giving it a weak point for starting, to impel it to the discovery of the truth.

Thus, we are told of the creation of water; but, as we are told that the earth was invisible, ask yourself what could have covered it and prevented it from being seen? Fire could not conceal it. Fire brightens all about it, and spreads light rather than darkness around. No more was it air that enveloped the earth. Air by nature is of little density and transparent. It receives all kinds of visible objects and transmits them to the spectators. Only one supposition remains: that which floated on the surface of the earth was water, the fluid essence which had not yet been confined to its own place.

Thus the earth was not only invisible; it was still incomplete. Even to-day excessive damp is a hindrance to the productiveness of the earth. The same cause at the same time prevents it from being seen and from being complete, for the proper and natural adornment of the earth is its completion: corn waving in the valleys, meadows green with grass and rich with many-colored flowers, fertile glades and hilltops shaded by forests. Of all this nothing was yet produced; the earth was in travail with it in virtue of the power that she had received from the Creator. But she was waiting for the appointed time and the divine order to bring forth.

"Darkness was upon the face of the deep." A new source of fables and most impious imaginations may be found by distorting the sense of these words at the will of one's fancies. By "darkness" these wicked men do not understand what is meant in reality—air not illumined, the shadow produced by the interposition of a body, or finally a place for some reason deprived of light. For them "darkness" is an evil power, or rather the personification of evil, having his origin in himself in opposition to, and in perpetual struggle with, the goodness of God. If God is light, they say, without any doubt the power which struggles against Him must be darkness, "darkness" not owing its existence to a foreign origin, but an evil existing by itself. "Darkness" is the enemy of souls, the primary cause of death, the adversary of virtue. The words of the prophet, they say in their error, show that it exists and that it does not proceed from God. From this what perverse and impious dogmas have been imagined! What grievous wolves, tearing the flock of the Lord, have sprung from these words to cast themselves upon souls! Is it not from hence that have come forth Marcions and Valentinuses and the detestable heresy of the Manicheans which you may, without going far wrong, call the putrid humor of the churches!

O man, why wander thus from the truth and imagine for thyself that which will cause thy perdition? The word is simple and within the comprehension of all. "The earth was invisible." Why? Because the "deep" was spread over its surface. What is "the deep?" A mass of water of extreme depth. But we know that we can see many bodies through clear and transparent water. How, then, was it that no part of the earth appeared through the water? Because the air which surrounded it was still without light and in darkness. The rays of the sun, penetrating the water, often allow us to see the pebbles which form the bed of the river, but in a dark night it is impossible for our glance to penetrate under the water. Thus, these words, "the earth was invisible," are explained by those that follow: "the deep" covered it and itself was in darkness. Thus the deep is not a multitude of hostile powers, as has been imagined; nor "darkness" an evil sovereign force in enmity with good. In reality two rival principles of equal power, if engaged without ceasing in a war of mutual attacks, will end in self-destruction.

But if one should gain the mastery it would completely annihilate the conquered. Thus, to maintain the balance in the struggle between good and evil is to represent them as engaged in a war without end and in perpetual destruction, where the opponents are at the same time conquerors and conquered. If good is the stronger, what is there to prevent evil from being completely annihilated? But if that be the case, the very utterance of which is impious, I ask myself how it is that they themselves are not filled with horror to think that they have imagined such abominable blasphemies.

It is equally impious to say that evil has its origin from God; because the contrary can not proceed from its contrary. Life does not engender death; darkness is not the origin of light; sickness is not the maker of health. In the changes of conditions there are transitions from one condition to the contrary; but in Genesis each being proceeds from its like and from its contrary. If, then, evil is neither uncreated nor created by God, from whence comes its nature? Certainly, that evil exists no one living in the world will deny. What shall we say, then? Evil is not a living animated essence: it is the condition of the soul opposed to virtue, developed in the careless on account of their falling away from good.

Do not, then, go beyond yourself to seek for evil, and imagine that there is an original nature of wickedness. Each of us—let us acknowledge it—is the first author of his own vice.

Among the ordinary events of life, some come naturally, like old age and sickness; others by chance, like unforeseen occurrences, of which the origin is beyond ourselves, often sad, sometimes fortunate—as, for instance, the discovery of a treasure when digging a well, or the meeting of a mad dog when going to the market-place.

Others depend upon ourselves; such as ruling one's passions, or not putting a bridle on one's pleasures; the mastery of anger, or resistance against him who irritates us; truth-telling or lying, the maintenance of a sweet and well-regulated disposition, or of a mood fierce and swollen and exalted with pride. Here you are the master of your actions. Do not look for the guiding cause beyond yourself, but recognize that evil, rightly so called, has no other origin than our voluntary falls. If it were involuntary, and did not depend upon ourselves, the laws would not have so much terror for the guilty and the tribunals would not be so pitiless when they condemn wretches according to the measure of their crimes.

But enough concerning evil rightly so called. Sickness, poverty, obscurity, death, finally all human afflictions, ought not to be ranked as evils, since we do not count among the greatest boons things which are their opposites. Among these afflictions some are the effect of nature, others have obviously been for many a source of advantage. Let us be silent for the moment about these metaphors and allegories, and, simply following without vain curiosity the words of Holy Scripture, let us take from darkness the idea which it gives us.

But reason asks, Was darkness created with the world? Is it older than light? Why, in spite of its inferiority, has it preceded it? Darkness, we reply, did not exist in essence; it is a condition produced in the air by the withdrawal of light. What, then, is that light which disappeared suddenly from the world so that darkness should cover the face of the deep? If anything had existed before the formation of this sensible and perishable world, no doubt we conclude it would have been in the light. The orders of angels, the heavenly hosts, all intellectual natures named or unnamed, all the ministering spirits, did not live in darkness, but enjoyed a condition fitted for them in light and spiritual joy.

No one will contradict this, least of all he who looks for celestial light as one of the rewards promised to virtue—the light which, as Solomon says, is always a light for the righteous, the light which made the apostle say, "Giving thanks unto the Father, which hath made us meet to be partakers of the inheritance of the saints in light." Finally, if the condemned are sent into outer darkness, evidently those who are made worthy of God's approval are at rest in heavenly light. When, then, according to the order of God, the heaven appeared, enveloping all that its circumference included, a vast and unbroken body separating outer things from those which it enclosed, it necessarily kept the space inside in darkness for want of communication with the outer light.

Three things are, indeed, needed to form a shadow: a light, a body, a dark place. The shadow of heaven forms the darkness of the world. Understand, I pray you, what I mean, by a simple example—by raising for yourself at midday a tent of some compact and impenetrable material, you shut yourself up in sudden darkness. Suppose that original darkness was like this, not subsisting directly by itself, but resulting from some external causes. If it is said that it rested upon the deep it is because the extremity of air naturally touches the surface of bodies, and as at that time the water covered everything, we are obliged to say that darkness was upon the face of the deep.

"And the Spirit of God moved upon the face of the waters." Does this Spirit mean the diffusion of air? The sacred writer wishes to enumerate to you the elements of the world, to tell you that God created the heavens, the earth, water and air, and that the last was now diffused and in motion; or rather, that which is truer and confirmed by the authority of the ancients, by the Spirit of God he means the Holy Spirit. It is, as has been remarked, the special name, the name above all others that Scripture delights to give to the Holy Spirit, and by the Spirit of God the Holy Spirit is meant, the Spirit, namely, which completes the divine and blessed Trinity. You will always find it better, therefore, to take it in this sense. How, then, did the Spirit of God move upon the waters? The explanation that I am about to give you is not an original one, but that of a Syrian who was as ignorant in the wisdom of this world as he was versed in the knowledge of the truth.

He said, then, that the Syriac word was more expressive, and that, being more analogous to the Hebrew term, it was a nearer approach to the Scriptural sense. This is the meaning of the word: by "moved" the Syrians, he says, understand brooded over. The Spirit cherished the nature of the waters as one sees a bird cover the eggs with her body and impart to them vital force from her own warmth. Such is, as nearly as possible, the meaning of these words—the Spirit moved: that is, prepared the nature of water to produce living beings: a sufficient proof for those who ask if the Holy Spirit took an active part in the creation of the world.

"And God said, Let there be light." The first word uttered by God created the nature of light; it made darkness vanish, dispelled gloom, illuminated the world, and gave to all being at the same time a sweet and gracious aspect. The heavens, until then enveloped in darkness, appeared with that beauty which they still present to our eyes. The air was lighted up, or ether made the light circulate mixed with its substance, and, distributing its splendor rapidly in every direction, so dispersed itself to its extreme limits. Up it sprang to the very ether and heaven. In an instant it lighted up the whole extent of the world, the north and the south, the east and the west. For the ether also is such a subtle substance and so transparent that it needs not the space of a moment for light to pass through it. Just as it carries our sight instantaneously to the object of vision, so without the least interval, with a rapidity that thought can not conceive, it receives these rays of light in its uttermost limits. With light the ether becomes more pleasing and the water more limpid. These last, not content with receiving its splendor, return it by the reflection of light and in all directions send forth quivering flashes. The divine word gives every object a more cheerful and a more attractive appearance, just as when men pour in oil in to the deep sea they make the place about them smooth. So, with a single word and in one instant the Creator of all things gave the boon of light to the world.

"Let there be light." The order was itself an operation, and a state of things was brought into being than which man's mind can not even imagine a pleasanter one for our enjoyment. It must be well understood that when we speak of the voice, of the word, of the command of God, this divine language does not mean to us a sound which escapes from the organs of speech, a collision of air struck by the tongue; it is a simple sign of the will of God, and, if we give it the form of an order, it is only the better to impress the souls whom we instruct.

"And God saw the light, that it was good." How can we worthily praise light after the testimony given by the Creator to its goodness? The word, even among us, refers the judgment to the eyes, incapable of raising itself to the idea that the senses have already received. But if beauty in bodies results from symmetry of parts and the harmonious appearance of colors, how, in a simple and homogeneous essence like light, can this idea of beauty be preserved? Would not the symmetry in light be less shown in its parts than in the pleasure and delight at the sight of it? Such is also the beauty of gold, which it owes, not to the happy mingling of its parts, but only to its beautiful color, which has a charm attractive to the eyes.

Thus, again, the evening star is the most beautiful of the stars: not that the parts of which it is composed form a harmonious whole, but thanks to the unalloyed and beautiful brightness which meets our eyes. And further, when God proclaimed the goodness of light, it was not in regard to the charm of the eye, but as a provision for future advantage, because at that time there were as yet no eyes to judge of its beauty.

"And God divided the light from the darkness." That is to say, God gave them natures incapable of mixing, perpetually in opposition to each other, and put between them the widest space and distance.

"And God called the light day, and the darkness he called night." Since the birth of the sun, the light that it diffuses in the air when shining on our hemisphere is day, and the shadow produced by its disappearance is night. But at that time it was not after the movement of the sun, but following this primitive light spread abroad in the air or withdrawn in a measure determined by God, that day came and was followed by night.

"And the evening and the morning were the first day." Evening is then the boundary common to day and night; and in the same way morning constitutes the approach of night to day. It was to give day the privilege of seniority that Scripture put the end of the first day before that of the first night, because night follows day: for, before the creation of light, the world was not in night, but in darkness. It is the opposite of day which was called night, and it did not receive its name until after day. Thus were created the evening and the morning. Scripture means the space of a day and a night, and afterward no more says day and night, but calls them both under the name of the more important; a custom which you will find throughout Scripture. Everywhere the measure of time is counted by days without mention of nights. "The days of our years," says the Psalmist; "few and evil have the days of the years of my life been," said Jacob, and elsewhere "all the days of my life."

"And the evening and the morning were the first day," or, rather, one day. Why does Scripture say "one day," not "the first day?" Before speaking to us of the second, the third, and the fourth days, would it not have been more natural to call that one the first which began the series? If it, therefore, says "one day," it is from a wish to determine the measure of day and night and to combine the time that they contain. Now, twenty-four hours fill up the space of one day— we mean of a day and of a night; and if, at the time of the solstices, they have not both an equal length, the time marked by Scripture does not the less circumscribe their duration. It is as tho it said: Twenty-four hours measure the space of a day, or a day is in reality the time that the heavens, starting from one point, take to return thither. Thus, every time that, in the revolution of the sun, evening and morning occupy the world, their periodical succession never exceeds the space of one day.

But we must believe that there is a mysterious reason for this? God, who made the nature of time, measured it out and determined it by intervals of days; and, wishing to give it a week as a measure, he ordered the week to resolve from period to period upon itself, to count the movement of time, forming the week of one day revolving seven times upon itself: a proper circle begins and ends with itself. Such is also the character of eternity, to revolve upon itself and to end nowhere. If, then, the beginning of time is called "one day" rather than "the first day," it is because Scripture wishes to establish its relationship with eternity. It was, in reality, fit and natural to call "one" the day whose character is to be one wholly separated and isolated from all others. If Scripture speaks to us of many ages, saying everywhere "age of age, and ages of ages," we do not see it enumerate them as first, second, and third. It follows that we are hereby shown, not so much limits, ends, and succession of ages as distinctions between various states and modes of action. "The day of the Lord," Scripture says, "is great and very terrible," and elsewhere, "Woe unto you that desire the day of the Lord: to what end is it for you? The day of the Lord is darkness and not light." A day of darkness for those who are worthy of darkness. No; this day without evening, without succession, and without end is not unknown to Scripture, and it is the day that the Psalmist calls the eighth day, because it is outside this time of weeks. Thus, whether you call it day or whether you call it eternity, you express the same idea. Give this state the name of day; there are not several, but only one. If you call it eternity still it is unique and not manifold. Thus it is in order that you may carry your thoughts forward toward a future life that

Scripture marks by the word "one" the day which is the type of eternity, first-fruits of days, the contemporary of light, the holy Lord's day.

But while I am conversing with you about the first evening of the world, evening takes me by surprise and puts an end to my discourse. May the Father of the true light, who has adorned day with celestial light, who has made to shine the fires which illuminate us during the night, who reserves for us in the peace of a future age a spiritual and everlasting light, enlighten your hearts in the knowledge of truth, keep you from stumbling, and grant that "you may walk honestly as in the day." Thus shall you shine as the sun in the midst of the glory of the saints, and I shall glory in you in the day of Christ, to whom belong all glory and power forever and ever. Amen.[58]

PREACHING IN THE WEST

The Western half of the Catholic Church has made its own unique contributions to the development of Christian doctrine and practice. The West fostered no school like the famed centers of scholarship in the East, namely Alexandria and Antioch. The focus of the Western Church was the city of Rome, the center of ecclesiastical life, and residence of the pope. The West suffered from the various Gothic invasions as the Roman Empire gradually fell apart.

Fortunately, men like Ambrose, Augustine, Leo the Great, and Gregory the Great were there to assist the Church in these chaotic centuries. Their writings and their leadership enabled the Church to weather the storms of controversy, and grow in understanding of the mysteries of salvation. Unlike Eastern churches, the Western Church is often at odds with secular society. Like the Eastern Church, the West holds seven sacraments directly instituted by Christ. It focuses on the atoning nature of the death and Resurrection of Christ. Its liturgical life is marked by a noble simplicity, and an emphasis on the understanding of the biblical text. Celibacy is mandatory for priests (with some exceptions), unleavened bread is used in the Mass, and there is less chant in the liturgy. Its preachers have their own philosophical and theological emphases.

Saint Ambrose of Milan: Man of Ten Talents

Saint Ambrose (ca. 339–397) is one of the guiding lights of the early Church. He has been called a "Man of Ten Talents," referring to the parable in Saint Luke's Gospel (19:11–27).[59] He was multi-talented and put his talents to good use. He resisted Arianism, lay interference in clerical life, abuse of authority, and invasion by Ostrogothic pagans. He had a remarkable ecclesiastical career. He was born in Trier on the Moselle River in Germany, of noble parents. Classically educated, his speaking and other abilities were recognized early in his life. He became the governor in Milan, where he was known for his fair and courageous leadership. His ecclesiastical life developed rapidly. Incredibly, he was ordained a priest, and then a bishop by popular acclaim on December 7, 374, one week after his baptism! He was 35 years old at the time. He gave up all his worldly goods and titles, and proceeded to educate himself in Scripture, and the writings of the Church Fathers, especially Saint Basil the Great. His allegorical Scriptural exegesis and rhetorical skill made him an outstanding preacher. He was a defender of orthodoxy against Arianism, and he brought the emperor Theodosius to public penance, after his revenge massacre of seven thousand persons at Thessalonica. Ambrose composed several liturgical hymns (so-called "Ambrosian Hymns"). He also authored the Ambrosian liturgical rite, still used in that diocese. His homilies led to the conversion of Augustine, who became bishop of Hippo Regius in North Africa. He died in 397 on Holy Saturday, at the age of 57. Along with Jerome, Augustine, and Gregory I, Ambrose is one of the four great Doctors of the Latin Church. His feast day is December 7.

The Preaching of Saint Ambrose of Milan

Ambrose dedicated his life to God with fervor and devotion. He studied the works of Tertullian, Cyprian, Lactantius, Origen, Athanasius, Didymus the Blind, and Basil the Great. His most famous works are *De sacramentiis* and *De mysteriis*.

He wrote a series of homilies on the Gospel of Saint Luke, which gives us some insights into his preaching philosophy. Ambrose was strongly influenced by Origen and other Eastern writers. He introduces chapter four of Luke's Gospel by discussing the temptations of Ulysses and contrasting them with those of Christ. Later he contrasts Adam and Christ "in a series of antithetical phrases which so delighted the devotees of Roman literature."[60]

> From the virgin earth came Adam;
> from the Virgin Mary came Christ.
> Adam was made in the image of God;
> Christ was the image of God Himself.
> Adam had authority over all animals;
> Christ had authority over all creation.
> Adam was made foolish through a woman;
> Christ was made wise through the virgin.
> Adam tasted death through a tree;
> Christ bought death through a cross. (Ambrose, *On Luke* 4.7)

From the standpoint of literary form, this sermon follows the tradition of the classic expository sermon, first developed in the Jewish synagogue and later in the Christian pulpit.[61] Our preacher chose a passage of twelve verses, which followed directly the passage on which he had preached in the previous service, and continued the passage to its logical conclusion.[62] His faithful adherence to the literary form of the Hebrew expository sermons underscores his respect for the Church's homiletical traditions.[63]

In the homilies on Luke's Gospel, we see examples of Ambrose's use of allegory. The healing of Peter's mother-in-law (Luke 4:38–39) shows that the woman's affliction is regarded as a figure of the fever which our flesh suffers from different desires (1 Cor. 7:9). Giving into the desires of the flesh can ruin one's spiritual health. God, who is patient and kind, works tirelessly for our salvation, and His plan brings spiritual, and sometimes physical, healing (Ambrose, *On Luke* 4.65).

Ambrose held a strong doctrine of the power of faith and grace, which leads Hughes Old to suggest that Augustine learned his doctrine of grace from Ambrose.[64] He had a talent for combining various elements into a natural thematic unity in the course of a sermon.[65]

An interesting example of Ambrose's preaching is found in his *Sermon Against Auxentius*. It is a rare example of a sermon modeled on the orations of Cicero. Auxentius was an Arian bishop who demanded Ambrose turn over his basilicas over to the Arians. He was supported by the empress Justina. In response, Ambrose mounted the pulpit of Milan and denounced the state interference in ecclesial affairs. He used 1 Kings chapter 21 and Luke chapter 19 as the biblical basis for his defense of ecclesiastical rights. As the stones cried out if the Lord was silent, so too Ambrose felt the need to denounce the unreasonable Arian demands. As with the Naboth vineyard story, he declared that the Church had no right to surrender her patrimony. *De sacramentis* is a collection of six catechetical sermons explaining the Christian mysteries. These sermons were given to the newly baptized members of the Church. He explains the *ephpheta* prayer, pre-baptismal anointing, renunciation of sin and Satan, blessing of the font, the baptism, the post-baptismal anointing and blessing, and First Communion. These homilies were liturgical or mystagogical, gradually unfolding the mysteries for his listeners.

De mysteriis is a series of talks given on the sacred mysteries of Baptism, Confirmation and Eucharist. These talks explain the nature and symbolism of the mysteries to the catechumens, but unlike *De sacramentis*, it adds a commentary on the seven petitions of the Lord's Prayer and discussion of the virtue of prayer.

Catechetical preaching in general recounted the history of salvation, beginning with the Old Testament. Saint Paul employed this kind of preaching in the synagogue, as we see in Acts 13:16–43. It included instruction in morality as well. New Testament precedents for this type of preaching appear in 1 Peter chapters 3–5, 1 Timothy, and Ephesians chapter 5. Doctrinal instruction occurred as well, focusing on the Creed. In Milan, at the end of the fourth century, the bishop delivered a special sermon called the *traditio symboli*, explaining the Creed; and the candidates would return the next day and recite it (the *redditio symboli*).[66]

Hughes Old believes that Ambrose read, interpreted, and preached three classics of Greek homiletical literature: Basil's *Hexaemeron*, Origen's *Sermons on Luke,* and Cyril's *Mystagogical Catecheses*. Ambrose, following a well-established Christian tradition, explained the sacraments in terms of typology. *Typology* is the use of "types" or "figures" to explain Christian truths. For example, the crossing of the Red Sea and the Great Flood were types of baptism. The stories of Elijah's servant, who loses the head of his ax in water are a type of the cross (2 Kings 6:1–7). The cross frees us from "our infirmities."[67] The sweetening of the bitter waters of Marah, which Moses healed by throwing wood into the water (a symbol of the power of the cross), thus sanctifying the waters of baptism (Exod. 15:22–25; Num. 33:8). He makes the point that the saving power comes from the consecration by Christians and not the magic associated with the initiation rites of the Hellenistic mystery religions. Strictly speaking, these stories from the Eljiah cycle are allegories rather than types. Ambrose, as a faithful disciple of Origen, turned the types into allegories, and *De Sacramentiis* is an early example of "allegorical interpretation of worship."[68]

The following homily centers on Christ the Good Shepherd, the principal theme for the fourth Sunday of Easter. Like a good shepherd, Christ seeks us, finds us, and brings us back to our true Home.

Homily: The Good Shepherd

In the teaching of our Lord which preceded this Gospel reading you learned that we are to put away all carelessness, to avoid conceit, to begin to be earnest in religion, not to be held fast to the things of this world, not to place fleeting things before those that endure forever. But though human frailty finds it hard to maintain a firm foothold in this so uncertain world, the Merciful Judge does not withhold the hope of His forgiveness, and as a Good Physician made known to you the remedies even against going astray.

And so it was not without design that the holy Luke places in order before us three parables: that of the sheep that strayed and was found, that of the silver piece that was lost and also was found, that of the son who was dead (through sin) and who returned to life; so that sustained by this threefold cure we may seek to cure our own wounds: for a triple rope does not break.

Who are these three persons: the shepherd, the woman, the father? Is not Christ the Shepherd, the Church the woman, and God the Father? Christ, who took upon Himself your sins, bears you upon His own Body; the Church searches for you; the Father receives you back. As a shepherd He brings us back, as a mother He looks for us, as a Father He clothes us. First, mercy, second, intercession, third, reconciliation; each to each; the Redeemer comes to our aid, the Church intercedes for us, the Creator restores us to Himself. It is the same divine mercy in each operation; but grace varies according to our merits.

The sheep that strayed is brought back by the Shepherd. The silver piece that was lost is found. The son turns back fully repentant from his sinful wanderings, and retraces his footsteps to his father. Because of this was it fittingly said: *Men and beasts thou wilt preserve, O Lord* (Ps. xxxv. 7). Who are those beasts? The prophet tells us: *I will sow the house of Israel and the house of Judah with the seed of men, and with the seed of beasts* (Jer. xxxi. 27). And so Israel is saved as a man; Judah is gathered in as though it were a sheep. I would prefer to be a son than a sheep; for a sheep is brought back by a shepherd, the son is honoured by the Father.

Let us therefore rejoice because that sheep which had fallen by the way in Adam is uplifted in Christ. The shoulders of Christ are the arms of His Cross. There have I laid down my sins; upon the neck of that sublime yoke of torment have I found rest. This sheep is one in kind, but not one in outward appearance. For we are all one body, but many members; and so it was written: *Now you are the body of Christ and members of member* (1 Cor. xii. 27). So therefore *the Son of Man is come to seek and to save that which was lost* (Lk. xix. 10); that is, all men: for *as in Adam all die, so also in Christ all shall be made alive* (1 Cor. xv. 22).

Rich then is that Shepherd of whose portion all we are but a hundredth part. For He has besides the innumerable flocks of the Archangels, of the Dominations, of the Powers, of the Thrones and all the rest whom He left upon the mountains. And since they are rational flocks, they [fittingly] rejoice because of the redemption of men. Let this also incite us to a just and upright life, that each one shall believe that his own conversion to God is pleasing to the angelic choirs, whose protection he should seek, and whose good will he should fear to lose. Be ye therefore a joy to the angels; let them have cause for rejoicing in your own return.

Neither is it without significance that the woman rejoices because of the silver piece that was found. For this is no ordinary piece of silver, upon which is the figure of the Prince. And because of this, the Image of the King is the wealth of the Church. We are His sheep; let us pray that He will place us amid *the waters of his refreshment* (Ps. xxii. 2). We are, I say, His sheep; let us seek of Him *a place of pasture*. We are pieces of silver; let us jealously cherish our value. We are children; let us hasten to our Father, who with the Son and the Holy Ghost liveth and reigneth world without end. Amen. (*Sunday Sermons*, 3:195–96)

Saint Augustine of Hippo: Preacher of Grace

Saint Augustine (354–430) is one of the most famous and interesting figures in early Church history. He is featured prominently in many standard historical works, both Catholic and Protestant. His writings and life story have inspired countless Christians through the centuries as they wrestle with the issues with which he dealt.

Augustine was born in Tagaste, a small town in North Africa. He lived a wild and reckless life as a youth, embracing Manichaeism, a heresy which downplayed the importance of the body. His conversion came about in part because of his mother Monica, who prayed thirty years for his soul.

While in the city of Milan, Augustine heard the eloquent homilies of Bishop Ambrose, which changed his life. He repented of his sinful ways and was baptized on Easter 387, by Ambrose. On the way home, Monica died at Ostia, the port of Rome.

On his return to Africa in 388, Augustine and his friends formed a semi-monastic community at Tagaste. In 391, Augustine visited the city of Hippo Regius on the North African coast, and popular demand secured his ordination as priest to assist the Bishop Valerius, a Greek who struggled to preach in Latin. Lest their brilliant preacher should be called elsewhere, the people in 395 secured Augustine's consecration as coadjutor to Valerius, whom he succeeded in 396. For the rest of his life he was known as a pastor, preacher, and administrator. He was also a prominent figure in the councils of the African Church, partly because of his close friendship with Bishop Aurelius of Carthage. He fought the Donatist and Manichaeist heresies, and authored hundreds of homilies and other works. Among his famous works are *City of God*, *Confessions*, and *De Catechizandis Rudibus,* as well as hundreds of letters. Augustine died in 430. His feast day is August 28.

The Preaching of Saint Augustine of Hippo

"As the Father has loved me, so I have loved you. Live on in my love" (John 15:9). This Scripture verse perhaps best sums up Saint Augustine's theology and spirituality. He is called "The Doctor of Grace" because of the importance he attached to this gift of God's life and love. Grace was a gift he deeply appreciated because through grace he found a deep relationship with Christ, and the means to help others grow in their relationship with Him. For the purpose of this book, he is called a "Preacher of Grace." His own conversion experience illustrates the primacy of grace in our lives.

Augustine was a great orator and faithful servant of the Gospel. Hughes Old notes, "Great oratory was not his aim. His preaching was worship, a service to God that the People of God might be nourished by the Word of God."[69] Augustine was most concerned with proclaiming the Word of God. He saw the Christian life as a bond between God and His People, and the primary purpose of preaching was to strengthen that bond. Augustine's intellectual and spiritual qualities were recognized early in his ministry. Blessed John Paul II remarked:

> It is well known how much Augustine loved Sacred Scripture, proclaiming its divine origin, its inerrancy, its depth and inexhaustible riches. But the aim of his own study, and of his promotion of study by others, is the entirety of Scripture, so that the true thought, or as he says, the 'heart' of Scripture may be indicated, harmonizing it where necessary with itself.[70]

Paul Scott Wilson highlights these aspects of Augustine's preaching:
- Augustine accepts the standard early Church understandings of biblical interpretation: The Old Testament is revealed in the New; the New Testament is concealed in the Old.
- The preacher pours the healing ointment of God's Word by the use of "similar things" (e.g., preaching humility is an antidote to the sin of pride).
- Some teachings of Scripture should be taken literally. Translations preferring ambiguity, when clarity is possible, are misleading at best and harmful

at worst. Consulting the original text in the original language is the best way to clarify its meaning.

- The primary principle for the interpretation of a figurative passage is the "rule of love." One should study the text until an interpretation consistent with the virtue of charity is produced. Augustine defines love as "the motion of the soul toward the enjoyment of God for His sake, and the enjoyment of one's self and one's neighbor for the sake of God." One cannot understand the Scriptures if he fails to grasp the meaning of love.

- Five qualities are needed to correctly interpret Scripture, namely, fear of God, piety, knowledge, fortitude, and mercy.

- "The purpose of preaching is to teach, to delight, and to persuade." Teaching is primary; delight and persuasion are secondary. The preacher "should not consider the eloquence of his teaching but the clarity of it. . . . Sermons should not be prepared word for word and memorized, for that can hinder effective communication," Augustine said.

- Three rhetorical styles were recognized by classical orators: "subdued, temperate and grand." Any one style may dominate any sermon, but the others may be used to provide variety and stimulate interest. The *subdued* or plain style was for proof (i.e., to teach), the *temperate* style was for pleasure (to delight), and the *grand* style was for emotion (to persuade) (Wilson, 61–63).

Augustine was a classic expository preacher. We are fortunate to have some five hundred sermons available to us, including a lengthy series on St. John's Gospel, the Psalms, and the Church's liturgical feasts.

The Sermons on the Gospel of John show Augustine to be "an artist at work on a big canvas."[71] They follow the grammatical-historical approach of the city of Antioch. Old compares Augustine on John to a gardener of a large plantation, a fine artist showing the beauty of creation and revelation, bringing it to fruit and flower. The biblical text is the same but the preacher brings different fields to fruit and different fields to flower at various times of the year.

More than a hundred sermons on John's Gospel exist, but only fifty or so are complete homilies; the rest are abbreviated because of the cost of publishing them. In them he explores the doctrine of Christ's divinity, bringing out moral and philosophical implications of Christian teaching. Augustine calls them *discourses*—in other words, a complete, systematic treatment of a subject. This was an ancient literary technique. Cicero gave them on such topics as old age, friendship, and the nature of the gods; and Seneca gave them on mercy, anger, and providence.[72] A sermon, however, is an exposition or discourse on Sacred Scripture. Old calls this series "Christian expository discourses." They are a comprehensive treatment on Christ's divinity. In Matthew, Jesus is portrayed as the Promised Messiah; in Mark, as the Servant of the Lord; in Luke, as the Divine Physician; and in John, as the Son of God. Augustine uses the Son of God image in his series.

Old points out that Augustine's use of rhetoric dates back to his training as a lawyer and philosopher. He never entered the pulpit with a prepared text, but instead spoke at length from prepared thoughts and engaged in a dialogue with his listeners, a practice many found engaging.

In one sermon during the Easter Octave, Augustine addresses the catechumens:

> I speak to you who have just been reborn in baptism, my little children in Christ, you who are the new offspring of the Church, gift of the Father, proof of Mother Church's fruitfulness. All of you who stand fast in the Lord are a holy seed, a new colony of bees, the very flower of our ministry and fruit of our toil, my joy and my crown. It is the words of the Apostle that I address to you: *Put on the Lord Jesus Christ, and make no provision for the flesh and its desires,* so that you may be clothed with the life of him whom you have put on in this sacrament." (*Sermo 8 in octava Paschale* 1,4; PL 46, 838, 841)

Hughes Old identifies several reasons for the effectiveness of Augustine's homilies.[73] The first is his focus on great religious ideas, such as Christian hope, sin, and redemption. This focus enabled him to explore the depths of Scripture, and present his findings for his congregation.

The second is Augustine's sense of the divine authority of his message. His power and effectiveness came from grace, that free gift of God given out of love and designed to produce good fruit.

The third was that Augustine involved himself in a dialogue with his congregation through rhetorical questions, rather than a personal display or individual performance. For example, commenting on 1 John 2:6, "He who abides in him ought to walk in the same way in which he walked," he asks, "How is it, brethren? How is it that we are admonished? He who says he abides in him? Is John telling us to walk on the sea? Certainly not! Surely what we are being told to do is walk in righteousness."

The fourth reason for Augustine's effectiveness is simplicity. He uses a clear, simple Latin style in sacred oratory. For example, he compares the love of God entering a human heart to a needle entering a cloth, and, passing through, pulling the thread with it. Such language appealed to his congregation and communicated his message well.

The fifth reason was the variety of his presentations and styles. Augustine covered doctrinal, polemical, pastoral, and moral subjects. He used history and allegory in speaking. He was no mundane predictable speaker. This variety appealed to the imagination and challenged both his listeners' intellects and hearts.

Vitality was a sixth reason. He who was on fire with the love of God spread that fire to the hearts of his listeners. The zeal of Augustine was contagious and many caught that spark.

The following homily is one of the most magnificent examples of Augustine's didactic skills. It is clear, precise, and inspiring. The sermon's theme was the Blessed Trinity in the Baptism of Jesus.

Homily: The Trinity in the Baptism of Christ

I—1. *God the Trinity placed before us in Christ's Baptism.* This Gospel places before us that on which we shall speak to Your Charity as though the Lord had commanded us, and He has truly commanded us. For my heart has waited as it were for His command to speak, that by this I might understand that He wills me to speak on that which He has also willed should be read to you. Therefore let you listen with earnestness and with devotion; and may God our Lord Himself help me in my task.

For here by the river Jordan we behold, and we contemplate as in a divine scene set before us, Our God made known to us as a Trinity. For when Jesus came, and had been baptized by John, the Lord by the servant—and this He did as an example of humility: for He showed us that it was in humility charity was made perfect; and when John said to Him: *I ought to be baptized by thee, and thou comest to me,* He answered: *Suffer it to be so now. For so it becometh us to fulfill all justice*—when then He had been baptized the heavens opened, and the Holy Spirit descended upon Him in the form of a Dove. Then a Voice followed from heaven, saying: *This is my beloved Son, in whom I am well pleased.*

Here then we have the Trinity, brought before us as it were separately: the Father in the Voice, the Son in the Man, the Holy Ghost in the form of a Dove. There was need to bring it to our mind in this way: for to see is the easiest thing to do. For clearly, and beyond any shadow of doubt, the Trinity is here placed before us. For the Lord Christ Himself, coming in the form of a servant to John, is truly the Son: for it cannot be said He is the Father, nor can it be said He is the Holy Ghost. *Jesus,* it says, *came;* that is, the Son of God. And who can doubt about the Dove; or who can say, What does the Dove mean, since the Gospel itself tells us most clearly: *The Spirit of God descended upon Him in the form of a dove?* And likewise, who can doubt that it is the Father's, since it reads: *This is my beloved Son?* Here then we have the Trinity distinguished One from the Other.

II—2. *A difficulty concerning the Inseparable Trinity.* And if we consider one place with another, I shall venture to say (and though I say it with diffidence, I shall venture to say it) that the Trinity is as it were separable, the one from the other. When Jesus came to the river, He came from one place to another. The Dove descended from heaven to earth; from one place to another. Even the Voice of the Father sounded neither from the earth, nor from the waters, but from heaven. The three were as it were separate in place, in purpose, and in work.

Some one will say to me: 'Show the Trinity to be inseparable. Remember, you who speak to us, that you are a Catholic, that you are speaking to Catholics. For this is our faith, that is, the true faith, the right faith, the Catholic faith, which comes not from private judgement (*opinione presumptionis*), but from the testimony of the Scriptures, not based on faltering heretical rashness, but on Apostolic Truth. This we know; this we believe. And although we do not see it with our eyes, nor yet with the heart, while being purified by faith, yet by this very faith we most truly and most strongly hold that the Father and the Son, and the Holy Spirit are an inseparable Trinity: One God, not three Gods. They are One God, yet so that the Son is not the Father, that the Father is not the Son, that the Holy Spirit is neither the Father nor the Son, but the Spirit of the Father and of the Son. We know that this ineffable Divinity, abiding within itself, renewing all things, creating, re-creating, sending, recalling, judging, delivering, this Trinity is, we know ineffable and inseparable.'

3. What then are *we* to do? Here is the Son comes separately in His humanity, the Holy Spirit descends separately in the form of a Dove, the Voice of the Father sounds separately from heaven, saying: *This is my beloved Son.* Where then is your inseparable Trinity? God has made you attentive, through my words. Pray for me, and open your own hearts, that He may give to me to fill what you have opened. Let us work together. For you see what we have undertaken; and you see not alone what I am but who I am, and of what it is I desire to speak, and how I am situated, how I dwell within *a corruptible body that is a load upon the soul,* and in an earthly habitation that presses upon the mind as it muses on many things (Wisd. ix. 15). When therefore I withdraw this mind from the many things, and apply it to the One God, the Inseparable Trinity, that I may understand something so as to speak of it, do you think that in this body which weighs upon the soul I shall be able to speak, so as to say something worthy of this sublime theme? *To thee, O Lord, I have lifted up my soul* (Ps. lxxxv. 5). May He help me, may He lift it up with me. For I am weak before Him, and a burthen to myself.

III—4. *The Works of the Father and the Son Inseparable.* This is a question that is wont to be propounded by learned brethren, and spoken of in the conversation of the lovers of God's word; for this there is much knocking at God's door, with men saying: Does the Father do anything which the Son does not do; or does the Son do something the Father does not do? For the present let us speak of the Father and the Son. And when He to Whom we say, *Be thou my helper, forsake me not* (Ps. xxvi. 9), shall have helped our effort, then shall we understand that the Holy Ghost also is in no way excluded from the work of the Father and the Son. Hearken then, Brethren, to what we have to say of the Father and the Son. Does the Father do anything without the Son? We answer, No. Do you doubt this? For what does He do without Him, *by whom all things are made*? *All things,* says the Scriptures, *were made by him.* And impressing this to repletion upon the slow of mind, upon the unlearned, upon the disputatious, it added. *And without him was made nothing that was made.*

5. *The Father makes and rules all things by the Son.* What then do we mean, Brethren, by *All things were made by Him*? We understand that the whole Creation made by the Son, the Father made by His Word, God wrought through His power and Wisdom. Are we then to say that all things, when they were made, were made by Him, but that the Father does not now make all things by Him? By no means. Far from the hearts of the faithful be such a thought, let it be banished from devoted souls, from pious minds! It cannot happen that He created though Him, and will not govern through Him. Let it be far from our minds that the Father should rule creation without Him, when, that it might be, He made it.

But let us show you, and this by the testimony of Scripture, that not alone were all things made by Him, as we recalled from Scripture—*All things were made by him, and without him was made nothing that was made,* is ordered and governed by Him. You confess that Christ is the Power and the Wisdom of God. You know what is said of Wisdom: *She reacheth from end to end mightily, and ordereth all things sweetly* (viii. 1). Let us not doubt that by Him all things are ruled, by Whom all things were made. Accordingly, the Father does nothing without the Son, the Son nothing without the Father.

6. *Is the Son's Birth and Passion also the Father's? Heresy of the Patripassiani.* A question then arises which we shall take upon ourselves to answer in the Lord's Name, and by His permission. If the Father does nothing without the Son, and the Son nothing without the Father, does it not follow that we must say that the Father also was born of the Virgin Mary, that the Father suffered under Pontius Pilate, that the Father rose from the dead, and ascended into heaven? Far from it. We do not say this, because we do not believe it. *I have believed, therefore have I spoken; we believe also, for which cause we speak also* (Ps. cxv. 10; II Cor. iv. 13). What does the Creed say? That the Son, not the Father, was born of the Virgin. Again what does the Creed say? That the Son, not the Father, suffered under Pontius Pilate, and that He died. Have we forgotten that there are certain persons, misunderstanding this, called Patripassiani, who say that the Father was born of woman, that the Father suffered, that the Father and the Son are the same: they are two names, not two things? And these persons the Church has cut off from the Communion of Saints, that they may deceive no one, but, apart from her, may dispute among themselves.

7. *The Difficulty.* Let us bring before your minds the difficulty of this question. Someone may say to me: You have said that the Father does nothing without the Son, nor the Son without the Father, and you have proved from Holy Scripture the Father does nothing without the Son, because all things were made by Him, and that what was made is not ruled without the Son, since He is the Wisdom of the Father, reaching from end to end mightily, and ordering all things sweetly. Now you tell me, contrary as it were to what you are saying, that the Son, not the Father, was born of the Virgin; that the Son, not the Father, died; that the Son, not the Father, rose from the dead? Here then I behold the Son doing something which the Father does not do. Then you must confess, either that the Son does something without the Father, or that the Father was born, suffered, died, rose again. Say either one thing or the other: choose which of the two.

I choose neither. I shall say neither the one nor the other. I shall neither say the Son does something without the Father: for should I say that I would lie; nor say that the Father was born, suffered, rose again; for were I to say this I should again lie. How then, he will say, will you free yourself from this contradiction?

IV—8. *Christ alone born of the Virgin: but This was wrought by both Father and Son.* The question placed before you pleases you. May God assist me so that its answer may also please you. See what I am saying: that He may free both you and me! For we stand together in the one faith in the Name of Christ, and we dwell in One House under One Lord, and we are members of One Body, under One Head, and we live by One Spirit. And this I say: so that the Lord may deliver from the entanglement of this most tedious question, both me who am speaking to you, and you who listen to me: The Son it was, and not the Father, that was born of the Virgin Mary; but this very birth of the Son, not of the Father, from the Virgin Mary, was wrought by the Father and the Son. It was not the Father Who suffered; the Son did. Yet both the Father and the Son wrought the Passion of the Son. The Father did not rise; the Son did. But the Resurrection of the Son was the work of both Father and Son. We seem then to be delivered from the difficulty; but perhaps only from my words. Let us see if this be so from the divine words also.

Now it rests on me to prove to you, from the testimonies of the Holy Books that the Birth of the Son was the work of both the Father and the Son; and the same with regard to the Passion; likewise the Resurrection: that while it is the Son's Birth, Passion, and Resurrection, yet these three works, which relate to the Son alone, nor the Son alone, but in every way of both Father and Son.

Let us prove each point singly; you listen as judges; the case has been stated; let the witnesses come forward. Let your court say to me what is wont to be declared by those who handle causes: Make good what you allege. This with God's help I shall clearly show you; and I shall quote for you from the written books of the law of heaven. You have listened carefully as I set out the matter; Listen more carefully while I prove it.

9. *The Nativity of the Son made by the Father. Paul and authority on Divine Law.* We must first show you with regard to the Birth of Christ, how the Father wrought it, and the Son wrought it, though what both Father and Son wrought related only to the Son. I shall quote Paul, a fitting authority on Divine Law. For advocates have today a Paul who is an authority on the laws of litigants as well as of Christians. I shall quote for you, I say, Paul, who is an authority on the laws of peace, not of strife. Let the holy Apostle show us how the Father has wrought the Nativity of the Son. *But when,* he says, *the fullness of time was come, God sent His Son, made of a woman, made under the law: That he might redeem them who were under the law: that we might receive the adoption of sons* (Gal. iv. 4, 5). You have heard, and because what was said is clear and direct, you have understood. Behold how the Father made the Son to be born of a Virgin. For when the fulness of time had come, God sent his son; the Father truly sends Christ. How did He send him? *Made of woman, made under the law.* The Father therefore made Him from a woman, under the Law.

10. This puzzles you perhaps: That I said, of a Virgin, and Paul said, *of a woman?* Let it not trouble you. We shall not stop at this point; and neither am I speaking to the uninstructed. The Holy Spirit says both; both *from a Virgin,* and *from a woman.* When from a Virgin? *Behold a Virgin shall conceive, and bear a Son* (Isa. vii. 14). And, *of a woman,* you have already heard: there is no contradiction. For the Hebrew tongue gives the name woman, not merely to non-virgins, but to all females. You have proof of this in Genesis, when Eve herself was first made: *The rib he took from Adam he formed into a woman* (Gen. ii, 23). In another place Holy Scripture says also that God bade the woman he set apart who had not known the bed of a man (Num. xxxi. 18; Jgs. xxi. 11). This should be known to you already, and need not detain us, so that we may with God's help explain other things which deserve to be explained.

11. *The Son's Nativity also made by the Son.* We have therefore proved that the Birth of the Son was wrought by the Father; let us prove that it was also

wrought by the Son. Now what is the Birth of the Son from the Virgin Mary? Is it not simply the taking of the form of a servant in the womb of the Virgin? Is the Birth of the Son anything other than the taking of the form of a servant in the womb of the Virgin? Hear then how this is also the work of the Son: *Who being in the form of God, thought it not robbery to be equal to God; but emptied himself taking the form of a servant* (Phil. ii. 5, 6). *But when the fullness of the time was come, God sent his son, made of a woman; who was made to him of the seed of David, according to the flesh* (Gal. iv, 4; Rom. i. 3). We see therefore that the Birth of the Son was wrought by the Father, but since the Son emptied Himself, *receiving the form of a servant*, we see that the Birth of the Son was also the work of the Son. This then is proved. Let us go on from here. Give your attention now to another question which comes next in order.

12. Let us prove that the Passion of the Son was made by the Father, and made by the Son. That the Father wrought the Passion is evident: *He that spared not even his own Son, but delivered him up for us all* (Rom. viii. 32). That the Son also wrought the Passion: *Who loved me, and delivered himself for me* (Gal. ii. 20). The Father delivered up the Son; the Son delivered Himself up. The Passion was wrought for One, but it was the work of both. As the Birth was not wrought by the Father without the Son, so likewise the Passion. What did Judas work in it but his own sin? Let us pass on from here also and come to the Resurrection.

13. *The Same is shown of the Resurrection of Christ.* We shall see the Son, not the Father, rising from the dead, but both Father and Son accomplishing the Resurrection of the Son. The Father works the Resurrection of the Son: For which cause God also hath exalted him, and hath given him a name which is above all names (Phil. ii. 9). The Father therefore has raised up the Son, exalting Him, and *quickening Him* from among the dead. But has the Son not raised Himself? He has truly raised Himself. For He said of the Temple, as of the figure of His own Body: *Destroy this temple, and in three days I will raise it up* (Jn. ii. 19).

Next, as the laying down of His life refers to the Passion, so the taking it up again relates to the Resurrection, let us see if the Son truly laid down His life, and if the Father truly restored it to Him, not He to Himself? That the Father restored it to Him is evident. For of this the psalmist says: *But, Thou, O Lord, have mercy on me, and raise me up again* (Ps. xl. 11). But what need to look to me for a proof that the Son likewise restored to Himself His own life? Let Him tell us: *I have power to lay down my life.* I have not yet, I know, made good what I promised. I said *laying down life*; already you are shouting it out, because you are ahead of me. Well taught in the school of the Heavenly Master, listening attentively to the lessons and, devoutly reciting them, you are not unacquainted with what follows: *I have power*, He says, *to lay down my life: and I have power to take it up again. No man taketh it away from me; but I lay it down of myself* (Jn. x. 18).

V—14. We have made good what we promised. We have proved our assertions with, I think, the solidest documentary proof. Hold firmly to what you have heard. I shall briefly sum it up, and commit it to you, to be retained carefully in your mind as something, in my opinion, supremely profitable.

The Father was not born of the Virgin; nevertheless this Birth of the Son from the Virgin was the work of both the Father and the Son. The Father did not suffer on the Cross; yet the Passion of the Son was the work of both Father and Son. The Father did not rise from the dead; yet the Resurrection of the Son was wrought by both Father and Son.

You have then both a distinguishing of Persons, and Their inseparableness in work. Therefore let us not say that the Father does something without the Son, or the Son something without the Father. But perhaps the miracles Jesus wrought give you anxiety, lest perhaps He wrought some the Father did not? And then what of His words: *The Father who abideth in me, he doth the works?* (Jn. xiv. 10). All we have said was plain to you, only needing to be repeated. We had not to labour to make you understand; but we had to take care it should be brought to your remembrance.

15. We must not think of God as occupying space like a body. I would like to speak of another point, and here I earnestly ask for your very close attention, and for recollection of the Presence of God. Only material bodies fill or occupy material space. The Godhead is beyond all space; let no one seek It as though it were in space. Everywhere It is Invisible and indivisibly present. Not greater in one direction, lesser in another; but whole and entire in all places, and no where divided.

Who can see this? Who can comprehend it? Let us humble ourselves; keep in mind who we are, of Whom we speak. Let this truth or that truth, or wherever it is that God is, be devoutly believed, piously meditated on, and, as far as it is given us, as well as we can, understood in silence. Let words cease, let the tongue be at rest, but let the heart be enkindled, let the heart be uplifted. For It is not such as enters into the heart of man, but whither the heart of man may ascend. Let us turn our minds towards creation. *For the invisible things of him, from the creation of the world, are clearly seen, being understood by the things that are made* (Rom. i. 20), to see if perhaps we may find there, in the things God has made, and with which we have a certain measure of intimacy, some similitude, by means of which we may show that there are three things which reveal themselves to us as separate, and which are yet inseparable in operation.

VI—16. *God is Incomprehensible.* Come then, Brethren, attend with all your mind. Consider first what I am putting before you: to see if I may find this in creation; for the Creator is remote above us. And it may be that one among us, whose mind the lightning of truth has as it were blinded with its brilliance, may cry out the words: *I said in the excess of my mind—what said you in the excess of your mind? I am cast away from before thy eyes* (Ps. xxx. 23). For it seems to me that he who said this had uplifted his soul to God, *had poured out his soul* within him, while they said to him day by day: *Where is thy God* (Ps. xli, 4. 11)?—that he had by some touching of the Spirit attained to that Unchangeable Light, and in his infirmity could not bear to look upon It, and had fallen back again as it were into his own languor and weakness, and had compared himself with It, and saw that the eye of his soul could not yet be adjusted to the light of the Wisdom of God.

And because he had done this in ecstasy, while caught up from the body's senses, brought unawareness before God, when recalled in a manner from God to man, he cried: *I said in the excess of my soul.* For in my ecstasy I saw I know not what, which I could not long endure, and returning to my moral members, and to the many thoughts of mortal men (Ps. xix. 21), from this body that weighs upon the soul, I cried. What did you cry? *I am cast away from before thy eyes.* Thou art far above; I am far below.

What then, Brethren, are we to say of God? For if you have grasped what you wish to say, it is not God. If you had been able to comprehend it, you would have comprehended something else in the place of God. If you had been *almost* able to comprehend it, your mind has deceived you. That then is not He, if you have understood It. But if it is He, you have not understood It. What therefore would you say of that which you could not understand?

17. *The Similitude of God to be looked for in Us.* Let us see then if we may find in created things something by means of which we may prove that there are three things which may be both shown to us as separate and which are inseparable in operation. Whither shall we turn? To the heavens, that we may consider the sun, the moon, and the stars? To earth, to speak perhaps of its fruits, of the trees and the living things that fill the earth? Or shall we speak of both heaven and earth which contain all things that are in heaven and earth? How long, man, will you wander through creation? Turn back to yourself; look at yourself; consider yourself; speak of yourself! You are searching throughout creation for three things which must be shown to be separate, and are yet inseparable in operation. If you search among creatures, first search within yourself. For are you not a creature? You are searching for a similitude. Will you search among cattle? For it was of God you were speaking, when you were searching for a similitude. You were speaking of the Ineffable Majesty of the Trinity; and since you availed nothing in divine things, and with fitting humility have confessed your own infirmity, you have come to man. Try there. Look among cattle, seek in the sun, search among the stars! Which of these is made in the *image and likeness* of God? Look then within yourself to see whether the image of the Trinity may not possess some imprint of the Trinity.

And what kind of *image* is it? A created image, though one far removed. A *likeness* nevertheless, and an image, however far removed. Not such an Image as the Son is, Who is What the Father is. One is the image in a son, another that we find in a mirror. They are far apart. In a son your image is yourself; for by nature your son is what you are. In substance the same as you, in person different. Man therefore is not an image like the Only-begotten Son, but is made in a certain image and in a certain likeness. Let him seek whether he can find some things within himself, which may be made known as separate and which are yet inseparable in operation. I shall search; let you seek with me. I shall not seek it in you, but I seek it in myself, and you in yourselves. Let us seek for it together, and let us together examine our common nature and our common substance.

VII—18. *Our Soul was made in God's image.* Reflect, O Man, and consider if what I say be true. Have you a body, have you flesh? I have, you say. For how else am I here, how am I in one place, how do I move from place to place? How do I hear the words of someone who is speaking to me, except through the ears of my body? How do I see the mouth of the speaker, unless with the eyes of my body? You have a body, it is plain; nor need we trouble further about something so evident.

Reflect on something else; consider what it is that is acting through the body. For you hear by the ear, but it is not the ear hears. Within is someone who hears by the ear. You see by the eye: look at it. Do you see the house, and pay no heed to the occupant? Does an eye see by itself? Is there not someone within who sees by the eye? I do not say that the eye of a dead man, from whose body it is apparent the occupant has departed, does not see, but that the eye of a man thinking of something else does not see the face of someone in front of him.

Look then at your interior man. It is there rather the similitude is to be looked for, of three things that are to be shown to be separate, and which are inseparable in their operation. What are the properties of your mind? Should I search I may find many things there. But there is something of great import, readily known. What is it your soul possesses? Recall it to mind; remember. I am not asking you to believe me in what I am going to say. Do not accept what I say, if you do not find these things within you. Look inward then; but first let us see something we overlooked; namely, whether man is not the image of the Son only or of the Father only, but of both Father and Son, and then of the Holy Ghost likewise? Genesis tells us. *Let us*, it says, *make man to our image and likeness* (i. 26). The Father therefore did not make him without the Son, nor the Son without the Father. *Let us make man to our image and likeness.* It says, *Let us make*, not I shall make; or, make; or let him make, but *Let us make man to our image*, not to your image or to mine; but, *to our image*.

19. *The Similitude of the Trinity in Man.* I am enquiring into, I am speaking now of something dissimilar to ourselves. Let no one say: Look, he is comparing us with God. I have said this already, I began by saying it; I cautioned you, and I have myself been cautious. They are *far* removed, the one from the other: as the lowest is from the highest, the changeable from the Unchangeable, the created from Those Who are creating, the human from the Divine. I am drawing your attention to this from the start, so that no one may speak against me, because that of which I am about to speak is so remotely different. Since therefore, while I am asking for your ears, someone else may be getting ready his teeth (i.e., *to attack him*), take note that I promise but this: to show you, that there are three things in us, which are known to be separate, which work inseparably. I am not considering now how like or how unlike they may be to Omnipotent Trinity; but in this lowest of creatures, in this changeable creature, we find three certain things, which can be shown, to be separate and yet work inseparably.

O unspiritual of mind! O obstinate and unbelieving mentality! Why do you doubt in this Ineffable Majesty of what you could discover within your own self? Here now I say to you, I now ask you. Man, have you a memory? If you have not, how do you keep in your mind what I said to you? But perhaps you have already forgotten what I said to you a moment ago. Even these two words, *I said*, you could not keep in your mind except by the aid of memory. How would you know they were two, if while the second is sounding in your ears you had forgotten the first? Why do I linger so long on this? Why do I insist so much? Why am I striving to make this clear? It is manifest why. Because you have a memory.

I wish to know something else. Have you an understanding? I have, you will say. If you had not a memory, you could not retain what I said. If you had not an understanding, you would not know what it was you retained. So you have this also. You apply your understanding to that you hold in your mind, and you reflect upon it, and perceiving it you are instructed, so that you are said to know. I wish to know a third thing. You have a memory, by which you retain what is said to you. You have an understanding, by which you grasp what you retain. But as to these two, I ask you: was it not through willing that you both retained and understood? Of course it was by willing, you will say. You have a will then. These therefore are the three things which I undertook to make known to you and to your minds. These are the three things which you can number, but cannot separate. These three: memory, understanding, and will. Observe, I say, that these three are made known to us separately, and yet inseparable in operation.

VIII—20. *Memory, intellect, and Will are proved separate, yet are inseparable in operation.* The Lord will aid me, and I know He is near at hand. From your understanding I perceive that He is present. For from your very voices (i.e., *acclamations*!) I can see in what measure you have understood me; and it is my hope He will continue to assist you, that you may understand all that I say. I have undertaken to place before you three things that are known to us separately, which operate inseparably.

Now I knew not what was in your mind, but you revealed it to me by saying, 'Memory.' This word, this sound, this utterance, came forth from your mind to my ears. For this 'memory' you were wont to think of to yourself only; you did not speak of it. It was within you, but it had not yet come forth to me. But that what was in you might be communicated to me, you told me its name, namely, Memory (*Memoria*). I heard it. In the name, Memory, I heard these three syllables. It is a word, a noun of three (four) syllables; it sounded, it proceeded to my ear, it made known something to my mind. The sound by which it was made known has passed away; what was made known remains.

But let me ask you this: when you spoke this name of memory, you are no doubt aware that this name refers only to memory. For the other two faculties have their own names. For one is called, understanding (intellectus), the other, will (voluntas), not memory: this other faculty is alone called memory. But that you should say this, that you should give utterance to these three (four) syllables, from what source has it come that you should do this? This word, which relates but to memory alone, was wrought within you, by the memory, that you might retain what you said, by the understanding, that you might know what you retained, by the will, that you might communicate what you know.

Thanks be to the Lord our God! He has helped us; He has been near at hand both in you and in me. I declare truly to Your Charity that it was with the greatest trepidation that I undertook to discuss and make this known to you. I feared it might please only those of larger understanding, and greatly weary those whose minds were slower. Now I see, as well by the attention with which you listened to me as by the quickness of your understanding, that you have not alone grasped what I said, but that you have been ahead of me, in what I was about to say. Thanks be to God!

IX—21. *By these three things the Mystery of the Trinity is explained.* You see then that it is with an untroubled mind I now put before you that which you have already understood. I have not taught something that was unknown to you, but am recalling to your minds what you already knew. Now one thing is referred to by these three; the name used refers but to one thing. Memory is the name of one of these three things; yet it was these three made it the name of this one of the three. It could not be named by memory alone, unless through the work of will, memory and understanding. Understanding by itself could not be named unless through memory, will and understanding working together. Will of itself could not be named will, unless by the common action of will, memory and understanding.

I think I have explained what I undertook to explain: that what I made known to you as separate, I have employed inseparably in my mind. The three together have made one thing of all of them. Yet this one thing the three made does not relate to the three, but to one of them. The three made the name, memory. But this name relates solely to memory. The three made the name, understanding; but it relates only to the understanding. The three made the name, will; but this belongs solely to the will. So the Trinity made the Flesh of Christ; but this belongs to Christ alone. The Trinity made the Dove from heaven; but this refers to the Spirit alone. The Trinity made the Voice from heaven; but the Voice itself belongs only to the Father.

22. *Which of these relates to the Father, which is the Son, and Holy Ghost is left to recollection.* Now let no one say to me, let no bothersome person try to pin down my poor self, saying: Which then of the three things you show are in our mind or soul, which of these relates to the Father, that is, as it were the *likeness* of the Father, and which has the likeness of the Son, and which of them is made in the likeness of the Holy Ghost? I cannot tell you, I cannot find out. Let us leave something to those who meditate; and let us yield something to silence. Enter into yourself, and withdraw yourself from all strife. Look within you; see if you possess there some sweet inner sanctuary of the soul's awareness, where there is no disquiet, no strife, no contest, where you give no thought to harshness or discord. There, *be meek to hear the word, that thou mayst understand* (Ecclus. v. 13). It may be that then you will say: *To my hearing thou wilt give joy and gladness*: and the bones that have been humbled shall rejoice (Psl i. 10); the bones that have been humbled, not exalted.

X—23. *By this can be sufficiently understood, that the Persons of the Trinity can be shown to be separate but that they work together inseparably.* It is enough then that we have shown that there are three things known to us separately, that are inseparable in work. If you have found this within you, if you have found it in man, if you have found it in any person walking this earth, bearing about *a frail body that is a load upon the soul* (Wisd. ix. 15), believe then that the Father and the Son and the Holy Ghost may, through certain single imperceivable things, by means of certain images borrowed from a creature, be shown as separate, and as inseparable in operation.

Let this suffice. I do not say, the Father is Memory, the Son is Understanding, the Spirit is will. This I do not say. Let each one understand it as he pleases; I do not presume to say. Let us leave the greatest questions to those who are capable of them; but we who are weak, to the weak we make known what we can. I do not say that these things are to be compared with the Trinity, in a sort of proportion (*ad analogiam*); that is, that they are to be considered as a ground of comparison. This I do not say. But what do I say? I say this: that I have found within you three things shown to be separate, yet inseparable in operation. And that of these three, each single name was made by the three together; but would yet belong, not to the three, but to some one of the three.

Believe there (i.e. in the Trinity) what you are unable to see, if here you have learned of it, have seen it, and have understood it. For what is in yourself, you may know; but what is in Him Who made you what you are, whatever you are, how can you know? And if you ever shall be able, you are not yet able. And even when you will be able, will you, do you think, be able so to know God as He knows Himself? Let this suffice. Your Charity. All we could say we have said. I have made good my promises to those who required them of me. As to what remains to be added, so that you may *grow* in knowledge, seek it from the Lord.

May then the power of His mercy strengthen our heart in His truth. May it confirm and calm our souls. May This grace abound in us, may He have pity on us, and remove obstacles from before us, and from before the Church, and from before all those who are dear to us, and may He by His power and in the abundance of His mercy, enable us to please Him forever, through Jesus Christ His Son our Lord, who with Him and the Holy Ghost lives and reigns world without end. Amen. (*Sunday Sermons*, 3:69–81)

Saint Leo the Great: A Most Brilliant Ray in the Sunset of Classic Civilization[74]

Nation will rise against nation, and kingdom against kingdom; there will be famines and earthquakes from place to place. All these are the beginning of the labor pains.
. . . the sun will be darkened,
and the moon will not give its light,
and the stars will fall from the sky,
and the powers of the heavens will be
shaken. (Matt. 24:7–9, 29)

These are the words of Jesus, describing the final test and period of the coming of the Son of Man. But they could just as easily be used to describe the end of the Roman Empire in the fifth and sixth centuries after Christ.

Saint Leo the Great (ca. 400–461) lived in a time of transition. The society and empire he once knew was falling as he was rising in position and influence in the Church and world. Leo was one of the great popes and Doctors of the early Church. He was born in Rome. Even as a deacon, other Church leaders looked to him for guidance and explanations of the faith. He was also known as a great peacemaker. He was often sent to settle arguments between leaders. He was in Gaul on just such a mission when Pope Sixtus III died. Leo was then called by the people and clergy to be the new pope. He helped the Church stay united at a time when it was being assaulted by heretics on the inside and warring tribes on the outside. In 452, the Huns, led by Attila, marched toward Rome to destroy it. Pope Leo went to meet Attila and convinced him to spare the eternal city in exchange for an annual tribute. Three years later, the Vandals marched on Rome. Leo again met their leader but was only able to prevent the burning of the city. For two weeks, the Vandals pillaged and looted Rome while the people sought shelter in their churches. Leo helped rebuild the city after the invaders departed. He sent missionaries to Africa to minister to those who were captured by the Vandals. He was an eminent pastor and great defender of the Roman primacy. He combated the Pelagian and Manichaean heresies. His *Tome* on Christ's nature was adopted by the Council of Chalcedon (461). At that council, a famous saying was born: "Peter has spoken through Leo." He died in 461, and his feast day is celebrated on November 10.

The Preaching of Saint Leo the Great

Saint Leo the Great has been called "a consummate statesman who more than once saved the Eternal City."[75] Leo was an able politician, an articulate Church spokesman and a gifted orator. He lived in a dying civilization and led people to an eternal Kingdom.

Leo strongly supported the Chalcedonian creed (461), which teaches that Christ is both divine and human, and that He transforms and glorifies human nature and us in Him. Human society as a result is highly important as a reflection of the wonder and beauty of God.

The pope's preaching style was "authoritative and majestic, his words few but weighty."[76] We possess ninety-six of his sermons, some heavily edited. Leo's sermons are more like the panegyrics of classical oratory than the expository sermons of the early Church. They include reflections on the mysteries of Christmas, the Epiphany, the beginning of Lent, the Transfiguration, Passion Sunday, Wednesday of Holy Week, Easter, Ascension, Pentecost, the solemnity of Saints Peter and Paul, the feast of Saint Lawrence, and the Ember days.[77] These solemnities were appropriate times for the faithful to hear their bishop speak, and Leo never disappointed his listeners.

Leo's sermons were liturgical, in other words, an expounding of the Christian mysteries. Unlike those of Origen, Basil or Ambrose, these sermons defined the mysteries we celebrate annually. With the preaching of Leo, the "festal sermon has become the chief sermon genre."[78] His sermons contain "marvelous paradoxes, parallelisms, and antitheses, all in the best tradition of classical oratory."[79]

At the beginning of Lent, the pope "encouraged the faithful to keep the spiritual disciplines of the season" (e.g., works of charity, fasting, frequent prayer, Scripture study).[80] Leo said much in few words. His sermons are not as long as Augustine's or Origen's, but they still contain material of profound depth and insight. One splendid example is the preaching of Leo on the Beatitudes, excerpts of which are in *The Liturgy of the Hours*, volume IV. First, he speaks of the setting for the Beatitudes:

> In order, therefore, to transform outward healings into inward remedies, and to cure men's souls now that he had healed their bodies, our Lord separated himself from the surrounding crowds, climbed to the solitude of a neighboring mountain, and called the apostles to himself. From the height of this mystical site he then instructed them in the most lofty doctrines, suggesting both by the

very nature of the place and by what he was doing that it was he who long ago had honored Moses by speaking to him."[81]

Then he discusses each Beatitude:

Blessed . . . are the poor in spirit, for theirs is the kingdom of heaven. . . . The kingdom of heaven is to be given to those who are distinguished by their humility of soul rather than by their lack of worldly goods. . . .

Blessed are they who mourn, for they shall be comforted. But the mourning for which he promises eternal consolation, dearly beloved, has nothing to do with ordinary worldly distress; for the tears which have their origin in the sorrow common to all mankind do not make anyone blessed. There is another cause for the sighs of the saints, another reason for their blessed tears. Religious grief mourns for sin, one's own or another's; it does not lament because of what happens as a result of God's justice, but because of what is done by human malice. . . .

Blessed are the meek, for they shall inherit the earth. To the meek and gentle, the lowly and the humble, and to all who are ready to endure any injury, he promises that they will possess the earth. . . . The earth that is promised to the meek and which will be given to the gentle for their own possession is none other than the bodies of the saints. Through the merit of their humility their bodies will be transformed by a joyous resurrection and clothed in the glory of immortality. . . .

Blessed are those who hunger and thirst for righteousness, for they shall be filled. This hunger is not for any bodily food, this thirst is not for any earthly drink; it is a longing to be blessed with righteousness, and, by penetrating the secret of all mysteries, to be filled with the Lord himself. . . .

Blessed are the merciful, for God will be merciful to them. . . . Mercy itself wishes you to be merciful, righteousness itself wishes you to be righteous, so that the Creator may shine forth in his creature, and the image of God be reflected in the mirror of the human heart as it imitates his qualities. . . .

Blessed are the pure of heart, for they shall see God. . . . Who are the clean of heart if not those who strive for those virtues we have mentioned above? What mind can conceive, what words can express the great happiness of seeing God? Yet human nature will achieve this when it has been transformed so that it sees the Godhead *no longer in a mirror or obscurely but face to face*". . . . The blessedness of seeing God is justly promised to the pure of heart. For the eye that is unclean would not be able to see the brightness of the true light, and what would be happiness to clear minds would be a torment to those that are defiled. . . .

Blessed are the peacemakers, for they shall be called sons of God. . . . These then are the peacemakers; they are bound together in holy harmony and are rightly given the heavenly title of *sons of God, coheirs with Christ.* And this is the reward they will receive for their love of God and neighbor: when their struggle with all temptations is finally over, there will be no further adversities to suffer or scandal to fear; but they will rest in the peace of God, undisturbed.[82]

As the years went on and Roman society deteriorated, Leo's preaching adapted to meet new challenges. Adult baptisms were fewer, and the threat of barbarian invasion became greater. The need for repentance applied to adults preparing for the sacraments of initiation. In the midst of opposition and conflict, the need to repent and do penance was great. Peoples' lives were being turned upside down, and their society was crumbling. With the end near, many thought of the afterlife and the need to reform their lives. The annual sermons of their pastor assisted them in this preparation.

Leo's preaching reflected his own asceticism. Almsgiving, sobriety, and chastity were stressed in order to obtain God's mercy, lest one's life become like the society in which he lived (see Matt. 7:24–29).

Leo was a transitional figure. His sermons are best understood in light of the dying culture in which he lived. He remained faithful to his calling throughout his life, ever mindful of the need to reassure frightened people that Christ was in their midst as the storms of persecution and chaos raged all around them (see Mark 4:38–41).

The following homily is found in *The Liturgy of the Hours* for the Feast of the Epiphany of the Lord. Of particular interest is the unfolding and gradual revelation of God's hidden plan. At the end Leo talks about the humble service of the star, which leads us to the Savior, and which is a model for the Christian disciple.

Homily: The Lord has made his salvation known

The loving providence of God determined that in the last days he would aid the world, set on its course to destruction. He decreed that all nations should be saved in Christ.

A promise had been made to the holy patriarch Abraham in regard to these nations. He was to have a countless progeny, born not from his body but from the seed of faith. His descendants are therefore compared with the array of the stars. The father of all nations was to hope not in an earthly progeny but in a progeny from above.

Let the full number of the nations now take their place in the family of the patriarchs. Let the children of the promise now receive the blessing in the seed of Abraham, the blessing renounced by the children of his flesh. In the persons of the Magi let all people adore the Creator of the universe; let God be known, not in Judea only, but in the whole world, so that *his name may be great in all Israel.*

Dear friends, now that we have received instruction in this revelation of God's grace, let us celebrate with spiritual joy the day of our first harvesting, of the first calling of the Gentiles. Let us give thanks to the merciful God, *who has made us worthy,* in the words of the Apostle, *to share the position of the saints in light; who has rescued us from the power of darkness, and brought us into the kingdom of his beloved Son.* As Isaiah prophesied: *The people of the Gentiles, who sat in darkness, have seen a great light, and for those who dwelt in the region of the shadow of death a light has dawned.* He spoke of them to the

Lord: *The Gentiles, who do not know you, will invoke you, and the peoples, who knew you not, will take refuge in you.*

This is *the day that Abraham saw, and rejoiced to see,* when he knew that the sons born of his faith would be blessed in his seed, that is, in Christ. Believing that he would be the father of the nations, he looked into the future, *giving glory to God, in full awareness that God is able to do what he has promised.*

This is the day that David prophesied in the psalms, when he said: *All the nations that you have brought into being will come and fall down in adoration in your presence, Lord, and glorify your name.* Again, *the Lord has made known his salvation; in the sight of the nations he has revealed his justice.*

This came to be fulfilled, as we know, from the time when the star beckoned the three wise men out of their distant country and led them to recognize and adore the King of heaven and earth. The obedience of the star calls us to imitate its humble service: to be servants, as best we can, of the grace that invites all men to find Christ.

Dear friends, you must have the same zeal to be of help to one another; then, in the Kingdom of God, to which faith and good works are the way, you will shine as children of the light: through our Lord Jesus Christ, who lives and reigns with God the Father and the Holy Spirit for ever and ever. Amen. (*Sermo 3 in Epiphania Domini,* 1–3, 5; PL 54, 240–244)

SUMMARY

The first eight centuries were a formative period in Church history. These centuries were a time when the Apostles moved beyond the confines of Jerusalem to spread the Gospel message to the ends of the earth. In doing so, they founded churches around the world, refuted heresies, combated challenges to the Faith, and built a body of doctrine from which we still benefit.

This period was characterized by the break with Judaism, great doctrinal controversies and the challenge of heresy, the legalization and spread of Christianity throughout the Mediterranean basin, and the collapse of the Roman Empire. Preaching was rooted in Scripture and offered listeners solid spiritual and doctrinal content.

Early Church preachers carried on the mission of Christ in the expectation of His Coming. The Second Coming did not occur, but what did occur was preaching based on and rooted in the ministry of Jesus. Scripture passages were used to show the fulfillment of the Old Testament in the New and the foreshadowing of the New Testament in the Old. As we move into the Middle Ages, we will see how this technique developed, and how biblical knowledge and understanding of the mysteries of the Eucharist, the Blessed Virgin Mary, and other topics developed; and how they were disseminated by means of the sermon.

NOTES

1. Boniface Ramsey, *Beginning to Read the Fathers* (New York: Paulist Press, 1985), 4–7.
2. Ibid., 7–8.
3. Ibid., 39.
4. Old, *Reading and Preaching of the Scriptures*, 2:171–2.
5. Ibid., 2:173.
6. Ibid.
7. Ibid.
8. Ibid.
9. Wilson, 41.
10. Old, *Reading and Preaching of the Scriptures*, 2:167.
11. Ibid.
12. Ibid., 2:168.
13. Ibid.
14. Ibid., 2:169.
15. Ibid., 2:170.
16. Wilson, 43.
17. Ibid., 44.
18. Old, 2:189.
19. Ibid., 2:190.
20. Ibid., 2:191.
21. Chrysostom, *On the Statues, nn.* 2.1, 2.2, 2.5, 2.8, 2.13, cited in Old, 2:191–93.
22. Ibid., 2:198.
23. Ibid.
24. Ibid., 2:201.
25. Ibid., 2:249.
26. Kathleen McVey, trans., introduction to *Ephrem the Syrian: Hymns*, Classics of Western Spirituality (New York: Paulist Press, 1989), 5.
27. Ibid., 5–6.
28. Ibid., 13.
29. Ibid., 4–5.
30. Ibid., 42.
31. Benedict XV, *Principi Apostolorum Petro*, no. 8.
32. Ibid., no. 4.
33. Ibid., no. 11.
34. Ibid., no. 10.
35. Ibid., no. 14.
36. Ibid., no. 21.
37. Old, *Reading and Preaching of the Scriptures*, 2:252.
38. Ibid., 2:253.
39. Ibid., 2:253–54.
40. Ibid., 2:257.
41. Ibid.
42. Ibid., 2:259–60.
43. Ibid., 2:262.
44. Ibid., 2:264.

45. Ibid., 2:265.

46. Ibid., 2:266.

47. Ibid., 2:268.

48. Ibid., 2:34.

49. Ibid.

50. Ibid., 2:38.

51. Ibid.

52. Ibid., 2:38–39.

53. Ibid.

54. Ibid., 2:44.

55. Ibid., 2:45.

56. Ibid., 2:55.

57. Ibid., 2:49.

58. Grenville Kleiser, *Basil to Calvin*, vol. 1 of *The World's Greatest Sermons*, (London: General Books, 2010), 4–11.

59. Ibid., 2:300.

60. Ibid.,.2:303.

61. Ibid., 2:304.

62. Ibid., 2:304–5.

63. Ibid., 2:305.

64. Ibid., 2:311.

65. Ibid., 2:313.

66. Ibid., 2:319.

67. Ibid., 2:322.

68. Ibid., 2:323.

69. Ibid., 2:344.

70. John Paul II, Apostolic Letter on St. Augustine of Hippo *Augustinum Hipponensem* (August 28, 1986), 4 (Boston: Daughters of St. Paul, 1986), 33–34.

71. Old, 2:346.

72. Ibid., 2:349.

73. Ibid., 2:362–68.

74. Ibid., 2:401.

75. Ibid.

76. Ibid., 2:402.

77. Ibid., 2:403.

78. Ibid.

79. Ibid., 2:404.

80. Ibid., 2:405–6.

81. Leo the Great, *Sermo 95* in *Liturgy of the Hours*, Ordinary Time Weeks 18–34, 4:206.

82. Ibid., 4:207–26.

Chapter 6
Preaching in the Middle Ages

This is the writing that was inscribed:
MENE, TEKEL, and PERES. These words mean: MENE, God has numbered your kingdom
and put an end to it; TEKEL, you have been weighed in the scales and found wanting;
PERES, your kingdom has been divided and given to the Medes and Persians.

Daniel 5:25-28

THE MEDIEVAL PERIOD was a time of contrasts. In these centuries, new heights were reached in scholarship, music, poetry, law, and art. At the same time, age-old problems of truth and authority were highlighted.

The Church saw great progress and great loss. The flourishing churches around the eastern and southern Mediterranean were overrun by Muslims, Mongols, and Turks. At the same time, Spain was reconquered for the faith, and a wide arc of territory from Gaul to the British Isles, to Scandinavia, through central and southern Europe, was evangelized.

The Middle Ages began with the collapse of the Roman Empire in AD 476, and ended with the fall of Constantinople in 1453. This period of history witnessed the spread of Islam in the West, the development and growth of new religious orders, the rise and fall of the Carolingian Empire, the Crusades, the growth of towns and universities, the rise and decline of the feudal system, and the split between the Christian East and West.

Preaching in the Middle Ages generally followed ecclesiastical, cultural, and spiritual developments. Two developments in particular so influenced Medieval preaching, that they could be called the twin pillars of Medieval scholastic development. The first is the growth of monasteries and religious life. The High Middle Ages marked an unsettled period of history, writes Dominican Simon Tugwell:

There were a lot of people milling about in the towns, and a lot of people on the move, such as merchants, pilgrims, and students, whether they were serious students in pursuit of learning or just the rowdy clerics whom ecclesiastical authority was constantly trying to curb, and marauding soldiers, often no better than bandits. But amid all this seething mass of humanity, there was one class of people that was expected to remain tranquil and aloof: the religious.[1]

In these turbulent times, the Cistercians emphasized quiet prayer, detachment from material things, and community life as an antidote to the poison of worldliness all around them.

The Mendicants later also emphasized a return to the early Church model of deep prayer, communal living, and evangelical preaching. The Cistercians in the twelfth century, and the Mendicants in the thirteenth to the fourteenth centuries, were two of many orders that flourished at the time. Medieval monasteries were heavily influenced by the Church Fathers. Jean Leclerq talks about the connection between the Patristic and Medieval cultures: "Its foundation was Christian, it was based on Holy Scripture, and this was apparent in the domain of thought and imagination as well as in verbal expression."[2] He goes on to say:

Monastic language is, first of all, a biblical language, fashioned entirely by the Vulgate. Monastic culture was also based on patristics, as is revealed in the topics for reflection, in the allegorical method of exegesis, in the vocabulary and even more so in the general 'style' of literary works.[3]

Monasteries did the exacting, patient work of compiling and arranging patristic texts. They preserved and developed ecclesial culture through their efforts. This collection and arrangement of material gave an impulse to thought and methods of inquiry, which bore fruit in the schools and universities of the twelfth and thirteenth centuries.

This is the second development that shaped Medieval homiletics. The scholastic method emerged from the *florilegium*. In its simplest form, the *florilegium* was an attempt to solve, by patient criticism and careful distinction, the problems posed by the juxtaposition of related but often divergent passages in the works of the Church's great writers. It was the attempt of the intellect to discover and articulate the whole range of truth, discoverable or hinted at, in the seminal works of Christianity. This process was slowly fashioned in the twelfth century and advanced rapidly thereafter. With the growing intellectual movement of the Middle Ages, preaching was heavily influenced by the rise of colleges and universities in England, Italy, Spain, and elsewhere. The practice of the Christian religion—the ordered life of Church service, the maintenance of discipline, the formulation of doctrine, and the work of Church governance—required a large and varied body of learning, penetrating every field of inquiry.

There are two great intellectual influences on the thought of the period. One was the influence of the traditional syllabus of Christian studies, which had come down from classical times. The second was the impulse to thought provided by the practical difficulties of organized life, whether in religious communities, or in the Church as a whole, or in secular society. The assimilation of Aristotle's logic was the greatest intellectual task of the period, from the end of the tenth to the end of the twelfth century. The universities developed systems of thought, and gathered the greatest minds in Europe to study and learn. A systematic presentation of Scripture was now possible.

MONASTIC PREACHING

It is a fact that the monks of the Church saved Christian civilization. How? By preserving Christian heritage found in books and manuscripts. The libraries were ecclesial repositories for learning. The devastation wrought by marauding Gothic tribes would have been far worse, if these monks had not preserved ancient texts and Christian writings in their libraries. The monks spent their lives copying manuscripts, studying Scripture, and reflecting on the Christian mysteries. They further developed knowledge and insight into the Christian faith. Preaching was part of their ministry. Medieval preaching articulated the Faith as understood by these monastic scholars. We can scarcely imagine what Western civilization would look like without the monks. The impact of medieval monks reaches far beyond the monastic enclosure to touch the lives of Christians who appreciate and reflect upon their words.

Venerable Bede: Candle of the Church lit by the Holy Spirit[4]

Saint Bede (ca. 673–735) was a famous English theologian and historian. He was born in 673 in England. He became a monk at age seven at the monastery of Wearmouth, in Northumbria, under the rule of Saint Benedict Biscop. He was transferred to the monastery of Jarrow around 681, where he spent most of his life. He was ordained a deacon around 692 and a priest around 703. He was a devoted Biblical scholar, teacher, and writer. His early works included *De Orthographia*, and *De Arte Metrica,* and appear to have been written for his students in the monastery. He also wrote *Life of Cuthbert* and *Lives of the Abbots of Wearmouth and Jarrow*. Some of his greatest works were his biblical expositions, which were founded on the writings of Saints Ambrose, Augustine, Jerome, and Gregory the Great.

His magnum opus was *The Ecclesiastical History of the English People.* In this work, Bede describes the development of the Church in Anglo-Saxon England. In simple yet attractive terms, he discusses the geography of England, the arrival of Saint Augustine from Rome, the Northumbrian Council, the acceptance of Christianity, the achievements of Abbess Hilda, and the poet Caedmon. The book provides a clear and accurate picture of the history of the Church of early England and Ireland. Bede's insight, empathy, and conciseness are evident throughout the book. Bede used papal letters, episcopal lists, and conciliar decrees as well as oral accounts to support his thesis that England's history progressed from diversity to unity. From a variety of tribes and tongues, England became unified in the Catholic Church. He saw the Church as an instrument of England's unification, especially in the sacred liturgy and the Church's liturgical calendar. This explains his account of the Synod of Whitby in Book 3, chapter 25. That synod codified the Roman Rite as the official liturgical rite in England. It also explains his concern over the controversy regarding the date of Easter. Bede puts his weight behind the attempt to abolish Celtic usages in favor of Roman ones, but he gives credit to the Celtic missionaries for their fervor and devotion. Bede combines various sources in this compelling narrative of English ecclesiastical history.

Author Frank Stenton comments:

> The quality which makes his work great is not his scholarship nor the faculty of narrative which Bede shared with many contemporaries, but his astonishing power of co-ordinating the fragments of information which came to him through tradition, the relation of friends, or documentary evidence.[5]

In other words, Bede was a collector and organizer more than an originator of ecclesiastical history. Bede relied on Eusebius's *Ecclesiastical History of the Church* as a model for his account of England's Church history. Bede's biblical scholarship shaped his presentation of this history. For example, Bede's history contains miracle stories, which reveal God's power and care. Bede provides scholars and historians a guide to the development of English ecclesiastical history.

Bede also wrote Scriptural expositions, commentaries, and homilies. He received the title "Venerable" less than a century after his death and is known as "The Father of English History." The Age of Bede was a more diverse and important reality than Bede himself. He was, in the words of Saint Boniface, "the candle of the Church lit by the Holy Spirit, and he is our first guide in the study of his age."[6] In 1899, Pope Leo XIII declared Venerable Bede a "Doctor of the Church." His feast day is May 25.

The Preaching of Saint Bede

The Abbey of Jarrow was the center of learning in Anglo-Saxon England. This was true in part because of Benedict Biscop's acquisition of books from Italy and France. In 716, the abbeys of Wearmouth and Jarrow housed around six hundred monks. These men devoted their time to prayer and study. Bede benefited from the strong organization provided by the Benedictine Rule, a solid Christian foundation in England laid by Saint Augustine of Canterbury, and strengthened by Cuthbert and Aidan, as well as from having a vast library. This remarkable library contained the writings of such Latin Fathers as Saints Augustine, Jerome, and Gregory. Bede's preaching reflects his deep study of

Sacred Scripture. He used the tremendous resources of the monastery library in his studies, and produced Latin grammar books, histories, hagiographies, and patristic commentaries on the Bible.

Bede regarded himself primarily as a biblical commentator. The number and size of these works exceed all others. His sermons reveal him as "a contemplative scholar whose life was spent reflecting on the mysteries of the Christian faith."[7] His commentaries on nearly every book of the Bible "have seemed unoriginal and derivative to many, but they at least provide useful digests of patristic commentary to preachers in England and overseas in an age when books were scarce and expensive."[8] He carefully studied the Church Fathers (especially Saints Augustine and Jerome), and creatively adapted their insights into his commentaries and homilies on Scripture. Bede studied not only the Scriptures themselves, but also the tradition of their interpretation. Unlike Origen in Caesarea, Chrysostom in Antioch, or Jerome in Bethlehem, Bede lived far from the setting of the Scriptures. He made up for this deficit by a thorough study of the materials. Hughes Old describes Bede as

> not a creative thinker, but rather a master of the tradition; he did not come up with new ideas but passed on the ideas of others. It was because of this that he was able to shape the tradition in such a way as to make it accessible to his contemporaries. Be that as it may, Bede has to be recognized as an extraordinary biblical scholar.[9]

His primary audience was composed of the monks of Wearmouth-Jarrow. Some fifty of his homilies are extant. Hughes Old notes, "The individual sermons are true to the forms of expository preaching, although the cycle is defined by the liturgical calendar."[10] He then analyzes Bede's homiletic style:

> He takes the appointed passage for the day and goes through it verse by verse, making learned comments. His explanation of Scripture by Scripture is outstanding, showing his profound mastery of every facet of the sacred writings. He often speaks of the literal sense of the passage and then the spiritual sense, but in such a way that the two are balanced. Bede's insights into the meaning of the passages he interprets are often solid. These sermons were surely helpful to the monks to whom he preached, and all down the Middle Ages they were read and reread, copied and recopied, for centuries heard all across Europe. They became models for other preachers and, even more importantly, were simply preached by thousands of other preachers.[11]

Bede's sermons were cyclical, treating diverse themes in diverse seasons (e.g., penitential themes in Lent, joyful themes in Easter). They include homilies for Advent, Christmas, Epiphany, the Octave of Pentecost, and Saints Peter and Paul. They were incorporated into the Church's *Liturgy of the Hours* because of their spiritual insights.

The following table shows some of Bede's homily topics in Book One:

Table 6.1 Some of Bede's homily topics.

TOPIC	BIBLICAL TEXT	SUNDAY
John the Baptist	Mark 1:4–8	Advent
The Annunciation	Luke 1:26–38	Advent
Birth of Christ	Matthew 1:18–25	Christmas Vigil
Appearance of the shepherds	Luke 2:1–14	Christmas

Source: *The Reading and Preaching of the Scriptures,* vol 3. Hughes Oliphant Old, Wm. B. Eerdmans, 1999.

These homily excerpts focus on the call of the Apostle Matthew, described in chapter 9 of his Gospel. It is found in the Lectionary in three places: on Saint Matthew's Feast, September 21; on Friday of the thirteenth Week in Ordinary Time; and on the tenth Sunday in Ordinary Time, Year A.

Homily: The Call of Matthew

Jesus saw a man called Matthew sitting at the tax office, and he said to him: Follow me. Jesus saw Matthew, not merely in the usual sense, but more significantly with his merciful understanding of men.

He saw the tax collector and, because he saw him through the eyes of mercy and chose him, he said to him: *Follow me.* This following meant imitating the pattern of his life—not just walking after him. Saint John tells us: *Whoever says he abides in Christ ought to walk in the same way in which he walked.*

And he rose and followed him. There is no reason for surprise that the tax collector abandoned earthly wealth as soon as the Lord commanded him. Nor should one be amazed that neglecting his wealth, he joined a band of men whose leader had, on Matthew's assessment, no riches at all. Our Lord summoned Matthew by speaking to him in words. By an invisible, interior impulse flooding his mind with the light of grace, he instructed him to walk in his footsteps. In this way Matthew could understand that Christ, who was summoning him away from earthly possessions, had incorruptible treasures of heaven in his gift.

As he sat at table in the house, behold many tax collectors and sinners came and sat down with Jesus and his disciples. This conversion of one tax collector gave many men, those from his own profession and other sinners, an example of repentance and pardon. Notice also the happy and true anticipation of his future status as apostle and teacher of the nations. No sooner was he converted than Matthew drew after him a whole crowd of sinners along the same road to salvation. He took up his appointed duties while still taking his first steps in the faith, and from that hour he fulfilled his obligation and thus grew in merit.

To see a deeper understanding of the great celebration Matthew held at his house, we must realize that he not only gave a great banquet for the Lord at his earthly residence, but far more pleasing was the banquet set in his own heart which he provided through faith and love. Our Savior attests to this: *Behold I stand at the door and knock; if anyone hears my voice and opens the door, I will come in to him and eat with him, and he with me.*

On hearing Christ's voice, we open the door to receive him, as it were, when we freely assent to his promptings and when we give ourselves over to doing what must be done. Christ, since he dwells in the hearts of his chosen ones through the grace of his love, enters so that he might eat with us and we with him. He ever refreshes us by the light of his presence insofar as we progress in our devotion to and longing for the things of heaven. He himself is delighted by such a pleasing banquet. (Homily 21; CCL 122; 149–151)

Saint Bernard of Clairvaux: The Mellifluous Preacher

Saint Bernard of Clairvaux (1090–1153), Abbot and Doctor of the Church, is known as the "Mellifluous Doctor." *Mellifluous* means "flowing with honey or sweetness." The word "mellifluous" can be misleading in this context. The title "Mellifluous Doctor" was not bestowed on Saint Bernard because his sermons delighted the ear (or were as sweet as honey). Instead, it reflected an idea originating with Origen and developed by Bernard, that one draws hidden meanings from the literal biblical text, just as honey flows from a honeycomb, or as Moses drew water from the rock (Exod. 17:6).[12] Saint Bernard's life and writings reflect the flow of grace from God to His Church and beyond.

Before discussing Saint Bernard's life, it might be helpful to situate it within the context of Cistercian reform as a whole. Cistercian reform was an important renewal movement within the Western Church. Its preaching was marked by "devotional insight, its theological integrity, and its evangelical fervor, and from the standpoint of its literary quality."[13] The Cistercians cultivated the literary arts in order to spread the Gospel and nourish Christian piety and devotion. Cistercians desired to recover monastic piety as expressed in the Benedictine Rule. The earliest Cistercians wanted to restore balance among "prayer, manual work, study, and contemplation."[14] They sought to recover monastic poverty, humility and charity. They were critical of the material comforts, ceremonialism, and lax discipline that had crept into Western Monasticism and stifled the spirit of monastic life.

The Cistercian reform sought a return to the sources of traditional monastic spirituality, especially the Benedictine Rule. Cistercian monks gave renewed attention to the study of Sacred Scripture and Patristic writings. Liturgical simplicity was another thrust of the Cistercian reform movement. A whole host of activities had been added to the praying of the Divine Office. For example, the saying of the seven Penitential Psalms was added to the saying of Prime, and the

Office of the Dead was recited each day. New feasts were added and the celebration of the liturgical year became increasingly elaborate.[15] The Cistercians trimmed these services: "processions were reduced to a minumum, musical settings were simplified, and the altar was kept bare."[16]

While not a founder of Citeaux, Bernard became its chief spokesman. Like Saint Thomas Aquinas with the Dominicans, he brought clarity of expression to the Order. Saint Bernard was one of the leaders of the late Gregorian reform. He was born in the year 1090. His family belonged to the minor nobility of Burgundy, France. He grew up with five brothers and one sister. His father was a knight. Bernard attended a small school run by the Canons Regular of Saint Vorles near Dijon. He emerged from their school a remarkable thinker and well-trained Latinist after devoting himself to literary and theological studies. After finishing his studies, Bernard returned to the family estate at Fontaine-les-Dijon.

Saint Bernard lived in one of the most interesting times in Church history. Monasteries and convents were rapidly expanding. Former soldiers and landowners were giving up their wealth and property to enter monasteries and devote themselves to the service of God. Many followed the rule of Saint Benedict, the founder of Western Monasticism.

In 1111, at the age of twenty-one, Bernard decided to become a monk of Citeaux, the Cistercian proto-monastery, located a few miles from his own birthplace. He did not enter alone. His enthusiasm for monastic life spurred him to bring his uncle, his brothers, and a group of young noblemen into Citeaux.[17] He even persuaded his sister Humbeline to leave her husband and become a nun.[18] Three years later he was sent to the monastery of Clairvaux in Champagne and became abbot.

Bernard was one of the early signers of Citeaux's first organizational charter, the *Carta Caritatis*. He became the principal promoter of the Cistercian Order. He influenced the abbot of Cluny in reforming his own congregation. Bernard created sixty-eight foundations which, by the time of his death, comprised some 350 houses, of which 164 were accountable to him directly. These extended from Scandinavia to southern Portugal, from northern England to central Europe. There were between eight hundred and nine hundred monks at Clairvaux by the time Bernard died.

Saint Bernard played an active role in healing the schism of 1130–1138 in France and Italy. Through his constantly growing correspondence with the leading personalities of Western Christendom, through his ever more frequently requested and obtained intervention in ecclesiastical crises, Bernard gradually became an influential advisor to both Church and state. He became involved in disputes regarding political rivalries, doctrinal disputes, monastic life, and clerical reform. His friends and relatives soon occupied the most influential positions in the Church. Bernard was well connected with the Roman Curia because of his friendship with the chancellor Aimeric. He was a powerful influence on the Cluniac, Premonstratensian, and Carthusian orders. He collaborated in the writing of the constitution of the Knights Templars. Pope Eugene III gave him the

commission to preach a crusade in France, which he first did at Vezelay on
March 31, 1146.

Bernard's spiritual prestige was enormous. He had long been interested in
the Crusades, and had already taken a large part in drawing up the "Rule of the
Knights Templars."[19] He preached the Wend Crusade, and preached against the
Albigensian heresy in southern France. The Albigensians denied the goodness of
the created world and downplayed the beauty of God's work in creation. Bernard fought this spiritual and doctrinal poison with the antidote of Scripture and
the Church's Tradition.

He preached the Second Crusade primarily for spiritual reasons. The purpose of the Crusade, according to Bernard, was for atonement of sin and the
glory of God, rather than money, power, or fame. He convinced Louis VII of
France to lead it. In a dramatic gesture, Bernard tore off his own habit to provide
material so that more crosses might be fashioned. It was in no idle boast that he
could write to the pope a few days later: "You ordered; I obeyed . . . I opened
my mouth; I spoke; and at once the Crusaders have multiplied to infinity."[20]
Bernard delivered his message from Vezelay to Lorraine, Flanders, and
throughout Germany, even convincing the emperor Conrad III to take up the
banner of the Crusaders and set off to liberate the Holy Land.[21]

Bernard mediated disputes until the end of his life. After mediating a dispute at Metz, Bernard returned to his monastery, where he died on August 20,
1153. He is the patron of Gibraltar and his feast day is August 20.

The Preaching of Saint Bernard

"The nature of true, pure contemplation is such that, while kindling the
heart with divine love, it sometimes fills it with great zeal to win other souls for
God. The heart gladly gives up the quiet of contemplation for the work of
preaching," Bernard wrote in one of his sermons on the Song of Songs (57,9).[22]
Bernard's preaching was an expression of His love for God and zeal for souls.
"The Last of the Fathers," as Bernard has been called, left a bulky corpus of
letters, sermons, and treatises, masterpieces of spiritual and theological literature. Most of the treatises deal with questions of monastic spirituality, such as
the *Steps of Humility and Pride*, *On Consideration*, the *Defense of the Cistercian
ideal of life in comparison with that of Cluny*, several works on *The Love of
God*, and a treatise on *Grace and Free Will*.

In 1135, Bernard began his chief work, *The Sermons on the Canticle of
Canticles*, eighty-six of which he finished by the time of his death. These sermons are actually treatises on the Song of Songs, which are more a reflection on
his own personal experience, than an exegesis of the biblical text. Bernard's
spirituality focused on devotion to Mary and the humanity of Christ. He stressed
the love of God as a reaction to the rationalistic emphasis of Peter Abelard. That
love provided him with ceaseless impulses that determined his activity, as well

as his contemplation. An author observed that the theme of love was not confined to the religious sphere:

> In Christian Europe in the twelfth century, love was cultivated in both secular and religious circles. It flourished in [both] the court and in the cloister. In southern France before the twelfth century, troubadour poets had begun to awaken a romantic strain, singing the glories and the sorrows of the love between man and woman. . . . Storytellers recounted the tragic love between Launcelot and Guinevere, between Tristan and Isolde.[23]

The cloister, however, produced a spirituality of love, linking it to its ultimate source, God Himself. Bernard preached and proclaimed this spirituality, and manifested it throughout his life.

Saint Bernard's homilies make up an important part of his written work. The festal sermons, which have been called "medieval preaching in its distilled essence" and "the prototype of lectionary preaching," are some of the most interesting.[24] These sermons were given on the occasion of great feasts, such as Christmas and Easter. Bernard delivered many sermons to his monks, none of which were written down. Instead, his listeners jotted down notes and preserved them for future reflection.[25] We do not possess an actual written text of Bernard's sermons. In addition to his listeners, Bernard dictated to a secretary, who edited and publicized them. These texts are critical source material for scholars, religious and historians who wish to understand Bernard's spirituality and doctrine.

Saint Bernard's sermons are concerned primarily with the mysteries and biblical texts proclaimed in the sacred liturgy.[26] They focus on virtues and vices, monastic observances, and the truths of the Faith. Gradually Bernard grouped them into categories, "reflecting the development of the liturgical cycle."[27] Toward the end of his life, Bernard put together a vast collection of his sermons, which forms a "commentary on the liturgical year."[28] Beginning with Advent and going through to the mysteries celebrated at the end of the liturgical calendar in November, Bernard discusses the liturgical seasons and the feasts of Our Lord, Our Lady, and the saints. He wrote an actual treatise for each of the major Church feasts. He "began with Old Testament events, then explained their dogmatic content and significance in terms of the New Testament, and concluding with their moral and spiritual application."[29]

Bernard often asks rhetorical questions in his preaching. For example, on the Epiphany: "What are you doing? Magi! What are you doing? Are you worshipping a baby in the lap of his mother? In a stable? Is this supposed to be God? The Scriptures tell us that God dwells in his temple, the Lord has his throne in the heavens (Ps. 11:4), and you, you look for him in a dirty stable?"

Bernard was steeped in the tradition of Catholic preaching. He was well acquainted with Scripture, and the way the Church interpreted it through the centuries. For example, on Epiphany, he interpreted the three gifts brought by the

Magi as follows: the offering of gold was made to Christ the King, incense acknowledged Him as God, and myrrh acknowledged him as a priest. Bernard
thought with the mind of the Church (*sentire cum ecclesia*).

Bernard also exhorted his listeners to live the Christian life. Again on
Epiphany, he exhorted them to be people of faith and trust like the Magi, rather
than be suspicious and skeptical like Herod. Bernard invited his followers to
behold the Child Jesus in the arms of His Mother and to seek the simplicity of a
child and the reserve of a virgin.

An interesting interpretation that Bernard uses, typical of medieval preachers, is the symbolic meaning of the six stone water jars at the Wedding Feast of
Cana (John 2:6). Bernard explains them in terms of six steps of repentance
(since they were used for purification): (1) sorrow for sin; (2) confession of sin;
(3) the generous giving of alms; (4) forgiving those who sin against us; (5) the
mortification of our flesh; and (6) new obedience (Bernard, *In Epiphania*, Sermo
V, 4).

In another sermon, this one for monks, Bernard interprets the water jars as
symbolizing: (1) chastity, (2) fasting, (3) manual labor, (4) keeping of vigils, (5)
silence, and (6) obedience (Bernard, *In Epiphania* Sermo VI, 7). He later says
the water symbolizes the fear of the Lord under the Law of Moses, which was
replaced by the wine of love in the coming of the Christ.

Saint Bernard's preaching often addressed the intimate love between the
Bride and the Bridegroom, between the soul and Christ. With great tact and sub-
tlety, Bernard distinguished attitudes underlying human relationships. For example, fear motivates a slave toward his master, desire for gain motivates a
worker toward his employer, knowledge motivates a pupil toward his teacher,
respect motivates a son toward his father. "But the one who asks for a kiss is a
lover."[30] "This affection of love," Bernard says, "excels among the gifts of nature, especially when it returns to its source, which is God."[31] Bernard used the
full power of his passionate rhetoric to describe the heights of mystical union
between God and the soul.

Patristic and Medieval preachers looked on allegory as a means of more
deeply understanding Scripture. They saw the Hand of God in the deeper spiritual meanings found in the biblical text. In this view, God imprinted certain
spiritual meanings on the physical universe, meanings that could be discovered
through heightened contemplation. Patristic and Medieval homilists brought that
meaning out and applied it to peoples' lives.

Saint Bernard wanted to mine the rich spiritual depths of the Bible and present these treasures to his listeners. A cursory examination of his writings will
convince the reader that he succeeded. There is a tremendous amount of material
for spiritual and theological reflection. In his symbolic interpretation of the Song
of Songs, Bernard "situates himself in an ancient tradition," the roots of which
go back to Origen in the third century.[32] Like his predecessor, Bernard highlights the allegory of the bride and bridegroom as symbolic of God's relationship with the soul. Bernard emphasized the bride as the individual soul, but like

Origen, he brings out a second meaning of the bride as symbolic of the Church. In a beautiful passage, Bernard writes the following of the worship of the Church:

> There are three perfumes by which the bride is anointed, which please the Bridegroom. The first is the broken-hearted sorrow for sin, the second is thanksgiving for the work of redemption, the third is lovingkindness [sic], expressed on one hand by loving acts of mercy and on the other by the preaching of the Gospel.[33]

Saint Bernard once gave a preacher this counsel: "If you are wise, be a reservoir, not a conduit, be full yourself of what you preach and do not think it enough to pour it out for others" (*In Cant. Serm.* 18). He then added: "Today we have in the Church a profusion of conduits, but how few are the reservoirs!"

For Bernard preaching was not just delivering a well-prepared message. It was a presentation of the results of a deep reflection on a sacred text and the spiritual lessons that could be drawn from it. The purpose of this presentation was to encourage the listener to meditate on Scripture and experience the joy of mystical contemplation.

Bernard understood that spiritual and theological reflection went hand in hand. A preacher needed to know Scripture, but he also needed to be grounded in solid spirituality. If the homilist didn't grow spiritually, it would be difficult, if not impossible, to help the listener take the message from head to heart. Growth in spirituality took place by meditating on the sacred mysteries and listening to the quiet voice of the Savior.

In the homily below, Saint Bernard uses the text John 2:1–11, which is proclaimed on the Second Sunday after Epiphany in the 1962 calendar, and on the second Sunday of Year A in the 1970 calendar. He talks about Our Lord's relationship with His Church through the Gospel.

Homily: The Spiritual Nuptials of the Gospel

> 1. A simple consideration of the works of the Lord will nourish simpler minds; but they whose souls are more exercised find within a food more nourishing, more flavoured, and as *the fat and marrow of corn.* For the works of God are lovely in their outward seeming, and yet more lovely in their inward perfection; as He outwardly was beautiful among the sons of men (Ps. xliv. 3), but within Him possessed the splendour of eternal light, surpassing the countenances of the angels (Wisd. vii. 26). For to outward eyes He appeared as a man without stain, flesh without sin, a lamb without blemish. How beautiful are the feet of him that bringeth good tidings, and that preacheth peace (Is. iii. 7): yet more beautiful, more precious, His head; since God is the Head of Christ.
>
> Most beautiful was He in His outward form of man, on whom sin hath not fallen, and blessed are the eyes that saw Him; yet more blessed are the clean of heart, for they shall see God (Mt. v. 8). And lastly, the Apostle, when he had come to the final inwardness of things reckoned this as but a potsherd, though

beautiful indeed, saying: *And if we have known Christ according to the flesh; but now we know him so no longer* (II Cor. v. 16). And this no doubt he said because the Lord Himself had foretold: *The flesh profiteth nothing, it is the spirit that quickeneth* (Jn vi. 64). This however is a wisdom that Paul speaks among the perfect, not among those to whom we read that he said: *For I judged not myself to know anything among you but Jesus Christ, and him crucified* (I Cor. ii. 2).

All sweet is He, all wholesome, and most lovely, as the voice of the Spouse declaims (Cant. v. 16). And as He is there shown to us, so will you find Him in His works. For as in His outward look, as seen by others, He is indeed lovely, yet should one break the nut within he will find what is yet more lovely, and still more desirable. This you find not among the Fathers of the Old Testament. For in their works what is beautiful is their mystical meaning; considered in themselves they are sometimes found less worthy; as in the deeds of Jacob, the adultery of David, and many similar things. Precious indeed the trays, but not so precious the vases. And perhaps for this it was said: *Dark waters in the clouds of the air*; since these were indeed dark clouds: while of the Lord there is added: *At the brightness that was before him the clouds passed* (Ps. xvii. 12).

2. I believe that you have now seen why I desire to say these things. For today you have heard of the miracle that was performed at the wedding feast, which was the beginning of the Lord's miracles; of which indeed the account is wonderful, yet more wondrous is its significance. It was a truly great sign of divine power, that at the word of the Lord water is changed into wine; but there is a more perfect change wrought by the hand of the Almighty which He prefigured in this wonder. For we are all of us invited to spiritual nuptials, in which the Bridegroom is none other than Christ the Lord: for in the psalm we sing: *And He as bridegroom coming out of his bridal chamber* (Ps. xviii. 6). And we are the Spouse, and, if this does not appear incredible to you, all together we are one Spouse, and the soul of each single one of us is itself a Spouse. But when can our misery know this of its God, that He loves us as the Bridegroom loves the Spouse? This Spouse is far below Her Bridegroom, in degree, in appearance, and in dignity. Yet for this Ethiopian the Son of the Eternal King has come from afar, to espouse Her, and feared not to die for Her.

Moses also espoused an Ethiopian, but he could not change her colour; but Christ loved His Spouse, lowly and stained though She be, that He might present Her to Himself, a glorious Church, without spot or wrinkle (Eph. v. 27). Let Aaron murmur, and Mary, not the new, but the old; not the Mother of the Lord, but the sister of Moses (Num. xii); not, I repeat, our Mary, for She was anxious only that nothing be wanting at the wedding feast. But though the priests murmur, and the Synagogue murmurs, let you remember to give thanks with all your heart.

3. Whence is this to thee, O Human Soul, whence to thee? Whence to thee this immeasurable glory, that you should merit to become the spouse of Him on Whom the angels desire to look? Whence is it to thee that He is thy Bridegroom Whose beauty the sun and moon reflect with wonder, at whose nod all things are moved? What wilt thou render to the Lord for all that He has rendered to thee (Ps. cxv. 12), who art the companion of His table, the sharer of

His Kingdom, the consort of His bridal chamber, and at the end the King will bring you into His House?

Behold how much already you perceive of the Lord, how much you have already tasted of Him; see with what eagerness of love bestowed must He be embraced and loved in return, Who has deemed thee worthy of so much, nay, Who for thee has done so much? From His side He refashioned thee, when for thee He slept upon the Cross, and for thee accepted the sleep of death. For thee He went forth from His Father, departed from the Synagogue His mother, that cleaving to thee, you might become one with Him in spirit.

And hearken thou, O Daughter, and see, and reflect (Ps. xliv. 11), and consider how great is the condescension of thy God to thee, and forget thy people and thy father's house. Depart from the loves of the flesh, unlearn the ways of the world, withhold thee from thy former sins, and forget thy evil habits. And why you may wonder? Does not an angel of God stand by thee, who shall cut thee in two (Dan. xiii. 59), should you, which God forbid, accept another lover?

4. For thou art already espoused to Him, and now is the nuptial breakfast: the supper is prepared in heaven, in the eternal banquet hall. And shall wine be wanting there? Far from it. For there we shall be inebriated with the abundance of Thy House, and drink of the torrent of Thy pleasures (Ps. xxxv. 9). For thou has prepared for Thy nuptials a torrent of wine; of wine, I say, that will gladden the heart, for the stream of the river maketh the city joyful (Ps. xiv. 5).

But now we partake of the breakfast here, for great is the way that still remains to us, but we partake not with great abundance, for fullness and satiety pertains to the eternal supper. Here the wine sometimes fails, that is, the grace of devotion, the fervour of love. How often, have I Brethren, after your miserable complainings, had to implore the Mother of mercy that she remind Her most gentle Son that you had no wine? And She, I declare to you, Beloved Brethren, if devoutly implored by us will not be wanting in our necessities: for She is merciful and the Mother of mercy. For if She had compassion on the embarrassment of those who invited her to the wedding, much more will she have compassion on us if he devoutly beseech Her. For She is pleased with our nuptials, and they concern her more closely than theirs: since it was from her womb, as from His chamber, that the heavenly Bridegroom came forth (Ps. xviii. 6).

5. But whom does it not move that at these nuptials the Lord made answer to His kind and most holy Mother, saying: *Woman, what is it to me, and to thee? My hour is not yet come.* What is it to Her and to Thee, O Lord? Does not what concerns the mother concern also the son? Why do you ask what is it to Her, since Thou art the Blessed fruit of her immaculate womb? Is it not She that with modesty undefiled conceived Thee, and without corruption brought Thee forth? Is it not She in whose womb for nine months Thou didst abide, at whose virginal breast thou hast drunk milk with whom at twelve years old Thou hast gone down from Jerusalem, and was subject to Her? Why now, O Lord, dost Thou complain to Her, saying: *What is it to Me, and to Thee?* Much indeed, and for every reason. But yet do I see that it is not as though annoyed, or as seeking to trouble the tender reserve of the Virgin Mary that Thou hast said, *What is it to me, and to thee*, since it was at the word of Mary the waiters came to Thee, and without delay Thou didst that which She had laid before Thee.

Why then, Brethren, why then did He thus reply at first? It was especially because of us, so that being given over to the service of God anxiety regarding our earthly parents might not be allowed to trouble us, and that their needs must not stand in the way of our spiritual service. As long as we are of the world it is true that we are debtors to our parents. But having abandoned our own selves, how much more are we freed from anxiety concerning them? Regarding which we read of a certain one of the brethren, who lived as a hermit, who when approached for aid by his brother in the flesh replied, that he ought rather seek aid from their other brother since he himself had died. And he who had come was so impressed that the other should answer that he had died, that he made answer that he too now died.

Perfectly therefore did the Lord teach us that we also should not be solicitous for our kindred more than religion requires, when He said to His Mother, and to such a Mother: *Woman, what is it to me, and to thee?* So also in another place, when it was said to Him that His Mother and His brethren stood without seeking to speak with Him, He answered: *Who is my mother and who are my brethren?* (Mt. xii. 48). Where then do they stand who so unspiritually and so unwisely are wont to be concerned with their kindred in the flesh, as though they were still living among them?

6. But let us see what follows. There were, the Evangelist tells us, *six water pots of stone, according to the manner of the purifying of the Jews.* From this you can see that the nuptial feast was not at the stage of completion but of preparation, where there was yet need for the purifications. They were therefore the nuptials of betrothal and not of union. Far be it from us to believe that there will be water pots of purification at those nuptials where Christ will present to Himself a glorious Church, having neither spot nor wrinkle, or any such thing (Eph. v. 27). For what stain will purification be necessary? Now indeed is the time to wash one's self, now it is evident that purification is necessary for us, since no one is free from stain, not even an infant whose life upon the earth is but one day. Now the Spouse is being washed clean, now is she to be purified, so that in these celestial nuptials she may be presented without stain to Her heavenly Bridegroom.

Let us therefore seek for the six water pots of stone, in which the ablution of the Jews, that is, of those who believe, becomes a purification. For if we say that we have no sin we deceive ourselves, and there is not in us that Truth Which alone makes us free, alone redeems us, alone washes away our sins. But if we confess our sins there will not be wanting to the true Israelite vessels of purification, since God is faithful, to forgive us our sins, and to cleanse us from all iniquity (I Jn. i. 8, 9).

7. For my part I believe the six jars are the six observances which the holy Fathers laid down for the purification of the hearts of the faithful, and all of them unless I am mistaken we shall find here. The first jar is the self-restraint of chastity, by which whatsoever before was stained by sensuality is washed away. The second is abstinence: so that what gluttony has stained abstinence may now clean. Through sloth and laziness which are enemies of the soul, we have defiled ourselves with much filth; against the command of God, we are bread that came from the sweat of another's brow, and not of our own (Gen. iii.

19); and for this cause also is the third jar *set there*, that these stains may be washed away by the labour of our own hands.

So likewise through excessive sleep and other works of the night and of the darkness we have offended much; therefore the fourth jar, the nightly watch, is placed there, so that by rising by night to praise the Lord we may buy back the nights of other times that were not well spent. Now indeed as to the tongue who is it that does not know how much we soil ourselves through idle talk and lies, through detraction and flattery, through malicious talk and idle boasting? For all these the fifth jar is necessary, namely silence, the safeguard of religion, and wherein is our strength. The sixth jar is discipline, whereby we live not by our own but by another's will, so that we may wipe away that of which we have been guilty through disordered living.

The jars are of stone, they are hard, but we must be cleansed in them, unless we wish to receive from the Lord a bill of divorce *because of our uncleanness* (Deut. xxiv. 1). Yet in this that they are said to be of stone, not alone hardness, but even more, durability may be understood; since these will not wash us unless they remain firm and steadfast.

8. Then the Lord said to the waiters: *Fill the water pots with water.* What does this mean, O Lord? The waiters are concerned with the shortage of wine, and You say to fill up the vessels with water. They are thinking of the drinking cups: and You bid them fill up the water pots of purification. So Jacob desiring the embrace of the promised Rachel was given Leah by her father. To us, Brethren, who are your waiters and servants Christ has given orders to fill up the watering pots with water, as often as wine is wanting. It is as if He says: these seek devotion, they desire wine, they crave to serve with love, but My hour is not yet come: fill the stone water pots with water. For what is the water of saving wisdom, though not so pleasant, if not *the fountain of life*, and the beginning of wisdom that is the fear of the Lord? To the servants is it therefore said: Awaken fear, and fill up not alone the watering pots but mens' hearts with the spirit of fear: for to come to love they must begin by fear, so that they too may say: from the fear of thee have we conceived, O Lord, and brought forth the spirit of salvation (Is. xxvi. 18).

But how are the jars filled up? For the Evangelist says: *containing two or three measures apiece.* What are the two measures, and what is the third? There is indeed a common twofold fear, and known to all; and a third that is less frequent, and less known. The first is fear lest we be tormented in hell. The second is the fear of being shut out from the inestimable glory of the vision of God. The third fills every anxious soul with deepest dread: lest it be forsaken by grace.

9. As water puts out fire, so every fear of the Lord puts out the concupiscence of sin, but especially this fear, since it rises up at every temptation, lest having once lost grace a sinner may then be abandoned to himself, and day by day fall from one evil to a greater, from lesser guilt to more grievous, such as many we see, who being filthy are left in filth (Apoc. xxii. 11). For against this fear the soul cannot deceive itself, either on the grounds of the smallness of the offence, or with the hope of future amendment; for with such blandishments we may quiet the two other kinds of fear.

The Lord therefore commands us to fill the stone jars with water; for sometimes they stand empty, and filled with wind. If anyone is so foolish as to remain in this state through vanity, the holy exercises of which we have spoken to you are deprived of their enduring reward, and such are as foolish virgins in whose vessels there was no oil (Mt. xxv. 3).

Sometimes, and this is a greater evil, they are full: but filled with the poison which is envy, murmuring, bitterness of soul, detraction. Lest therefore it should happen that these evils enter when the wine is wanting, we are ordered, so that the commandments of the Lord be obeyed in fear, to fill up the jars with water, which is then changed into wine, since fear is cast out by charity (I Jn. iv. 18), and all things are filled with fervour of spirit and joyful in their obedience, by the grace and mercy of Our Lord Jesus Christ, Who with the Father and the Holy Spirit liveth and reigneth world without end. Amen. (The Sunday Sermons of the Church Fathers, 1:281–86)

MENDICANT PREACHING

Mendicants were religious on the move, always taking the Gospel to new frontiers, and bringing new life to old communities throughout Italy and France. Mendicant friars were members of religious communities which did not own property in common. In the Middle Ages, they worked or begged for a living, and carried out their evangelical mission primarily in towns. The Dominicans and Franciscans are two examples of Mendicant orders. These religious orders came about in part because of the spiritual decline of monastic orders like the Cistercians and the canons regular. There was an urgent need to proclaim the Gospel in urban areas of Europe. Mendicant religious fulfilled that need through preaching, teaching, and service.

Saint Dominic: Mendicant Preacher

Dominic de Guzman (1170–1221) was a priest who lived in the thirteenth century. He was born in Caleruega, Spain, the son of Felix Guzman and Blessed Joan of Aza. He studied at the University of Palencia, and was ordained there while pursuing his studies. In 1203, he accompanied Bishop Diego de Avezedo of Osma to Languedoc, where Dominic preached against the Albigensians, and helped reform the Cistercians. While in Toulouse, France, he founded the Order of Preachers in 1214, which today numbers some 6,500 religious. Known as the Dominican Order, it is an elective, religious, fraternal form of community life, dedicated to contemplation, study, and preaching. He preached in Italy, Spain, and France, attracting new members to the Order, and establishing houses. Pope Benedict XV called him "an invincible champion of the faith."[34]

One of Dominic's important tasks was to bring the Albigensians back to the Church through preaching and evangelical poverty. The Albigensian heresy spread like a plague through southern France, in part because of the lack of sound doctrinal formation on the part of the laity, and ineffective leadership on the part of the clergy. The Albigensian doctrine was based on a dualism of two eternally opposing principles: good and evil. All matter was regarded as evil, and the creator of the material world was a devil. All spiritual things were regarded as good, and created by God. Hence, they denied the doctrine of the Incarnation, and the seven sacraments. In order to become "pure," a person had to abstain from sexual relations (which were seen as base), and restrict his eating and drinking. Starvation by suicide was seen as a noble act. The Albigensians convinced many to join them, and a military as well as spiritual crusade was waged against them. Dominic responded to the Albigensians, in part by asceticism. He rarely ate anything except bread and soup. He drank some water, however. He slept on the floor or even on a road. He lived on alms. He believed that the preacher had to live the Gospel before he preached the Gospel, or be exposed as a fraud.

His example reinforced his message. There is a story that illustrates the power of his words. Dominic was on his way to Denmark on an mission for the king in 1203. While in the city of Toulouse, he met an Albigensian heretic at an inn where he was staying. The two struck up a conversation, which lasted through the night. The next morning the man converted and returned to the Catholic fold. The reason: Dominic's charity won him over. From that day, it seems that Dominic knew that God required him to actively preach the charity of God in the world. The Dominican Order adopted the rule of Saint Augustine. The order's ideal is *contemplata tradere* ("to hand on to others what is contemplated").

"In addition to cultivating poverty, innocence of life, and religious discipline, [Saint Dominic] commanded his Order in a strict and solemn manner to be zealous in the study of Christian doctrine and the preaching of the truth," said Pope Benedict XV.[35] One of Dominic's most successful strategies was to take over from the enemy his own instruments, grasp his enemy's spiritual concerns, and make them his own. Like Jesus, Dominic proclaimed *verbo et exemplo*, glad tidings by word and example to those with whom he came in contact. For example, Dominic, joined by a few companions, took charge of a house established at Prouille by Bishop Diego. They lived a common life of pious poverty in the midst of the heretical *Cathari* (who, like the Albigensians, held that whatever is material was evil and only the spiritual was good). This pious life was a powerful witness to the message Dominic and his companions proclaimed. In his bull of canonization, Pope Gregory IX said Dominic lived according to the "rule of the apostles," and was a "man of the Gospel in the footsteps of his Redeemer."

Saint Dominic combined a keen intellect, strict asceticism, and fidelity to the chosen rule. He was a born preacher who spent hours on the road, talking to anyone who would listen. He was model for his brothers and a faithful apostle, a theologically equipped apologist. He died at Bologna on August 6, 1221, and was canonized in 1234.[36] His Order of Preachers spread to Paris and Spain, and beyond. Today there are forty-one provinces world-wide, and a considerable number of vicariates, especially in the Third World. St. Dominic's feast day is August 8.

The Preaching of Saint Dominic

From his first encounter with the Cathari of the Midi, it was clear to Dominic that a solid theological formation was essential for preaching. A clear grasp of dogmatic and moral theology was necessary for the renewal of the preaching of Christian doctrine. Early on this approach gained for Saint Dominic many companions from the university circles, for example, Blessed Jordan of Saxony (1222–37), who studied in Paris. Under Blessed Jordan, the Order spread to Syria and Scotland. For Dominic, the Gospel and the Church went together.

In his encyclical *Fausto Appetente Die* (1921), Pope Benedict XV identified three qualities of Dominican preaching: great solidity of doctrine, the fullness of fidelity towards the Apostolic See, and piety towards the Blessed Mother. Saint Dominic studied Sacred Scripture carefully, and, in particular, the writings of the Apostle Paul. Dominic used his deep knowledge of Scripture and doctrine to refute heretics. He established his Order's houses near universities, so the brethren could make use of every branch of learning. "It's special mission was always to care for the various wounds of error, and to diffuse the light of Christian Faith, seeing that nothing is such a hindrance to eternal salvation as the ignorance of the truth and perversity of doctrine," Benedict said.[37]

Thomas Agni of Lentini, in a homily on Saint Dominic, identified five characteristics of Dominic's teaching: it was *savoury* and therefore *useful* (like the "salt of the earth"); it was *radiant* (like the "light of the world"); it was *solid* (like the "mountain that cannot be hidden"); it should be *on fire* ("like the lamp shining for all to see"); and it was *effective and complete*, as the Lord said ("Do not think I have come to abolish the Law").[38]

The second great quality of Dominican preaching was a supreme reverence for the Apostolic See. It is said that, prostrate at the feet of Innocent III, Dominic vowed himself to the defense of the Roman Pontificate, and that, the following night, Pope Innocent in a vision saw him sustain on his courageous shoulders the tottering pile of the Lateran Basilica. The Dominican virgin Catherine of Siena later convinced the Roman Pontiff to return to Rome, and thus end the "Babylonian Exile of the Church."

Finally, Dominican preaching is characterized by devotion and piety towards the Mother of God. The rosary was decisive in the naval victory at Lepanto (1570). But it was also helpful in repelling other kinds of attacks on the Christian world. The Albigensians attacked, among other dogmas, the Divine maternity and the virginity of Mary. Dominic vigorously defended the Blessed Mother with the words: "Make me worthy to praise thee, Sacred Virgin; give me strength against thine enemies."[39]

There are few documents that tell us anything about early Dominican preaching. One such document is the Commission given to Dominic by Bishop Fulk of Toulouse. This document tells us that preaching is to provide basic Christian teaching, especially on the Creed, Lord's Prayer, Hail Mary, and the

Ten Commandments. We know that Dominic's preaching was backed up by the solid witness of a pure and simple lifestyle.

Unlike the papal legates, Dominic and his followers wore simple clothes and begged for their food. Dominican preaching was in part a devout and intellectual response to the challenge of the Albigensians. Dominican teaching was more reasonable and faithful to the Gospel. It was committed to the exposition of Christian doctrine, dedicated to systematic theology, and devoted to the development of Christian philosophy. Their words and witness were effective, and they successfully liberated several towns in southern France from the Albigensian scourge.

Dominic established followers as early as 1217, at universities in Paris and Bologna. His work bore fruit in the writings of such greats as Albert the Great and Thomas Aquinas, and continues to inspire Dominicans today to preach and defend the Faith.

Unfortunately, we do not possess any of Dominic's homilies or any of his writings other than a brief letter to Dominican nuns in Madrid, and two succinct letters regarding the situations of converted heretics. He is included in this history because he founded the Order of Preachers, and because the principles he espoused are useful for homilists.

Saint Anthony of Padua: Repository of Holy Scripture [40]

Saint Anthony of Padua (1195–1231) is one of the most beloved Franciscans in the Church, in part because he is the patron of those who lose objects. He was born in Lisbon, Portugal, and was baptized Ferdinand. His parents were Martin, an army officer, and Mary, a virtuous woman. Educated by priests, Anthony decided to enter the Order of the Augustinians at age fifteen. He lived in an Augustinian monastery outside of Lisbon, where he read the Bible and the Church Fathers, and cultivated a life of asceticism and devotion to God.

In the year 1220, Ferdinand witnessed an event that caused him to change religious orders and the direction of his life. The bodies of five Franciscans who had been tortured and martyred in Morocco were brought home for burial. As he listened to the adventures of these heroic men, a flame of zeal grew in Anthony's heart. He decided to join the Franciscans and sailed to Morocco. The African climate was difficult for Anthony. He became ill and decided to return to Portugal. A storm, however, knocked his boat off course and he landed in Sicily. After a few months he made his way to Assisi, where Franciscan priests and brothers were holding an important meeting. He attended that meeting and probably met Saint Francis himself, who by then was a frail, old man.

Anthony joined the Italian Franciscans, and took the name Anthony after the fourth-century desert monk Saint Anthony of Egypt. He lived a quiet life of prayer, and worked in the kitchen, until he attended an ordination Mass in 1224, at which the priest who was to give the homily failed to appear. At the last minute Anthony was asked to preach. That homily was a turning point in his life.

When the people heard him speak, they were impressed with his message and faith. Anthony became a teacher of Franciscans and then a preacher in Italy, France, and Belgium. His fame spread throughout the world. His sermons are noted for their learning and gentleness.

He converted so many heretics through his preaching and works of charity that he was called "The Hammer of the Heretics" and the "Wonder Worker." He is also called "Finder of Lost Articles," "Holy Matchmaker," and the "Guardian of Mail." Pope Gregory IX called him the "Ark of the Testament" and the "Repository (or armory) of Holy Scripture."[41] Long before John Wesley drew huge crowds, this gifted speaker drew crowds numbering up to thirty-thousand. His homilies were so powerful that they inspired enemies to reconcile, thieves to confess, and heretics to convert. Anthony also pleaded for the poor, and tried to secure the release of people imprisoned because of debt.

The fast and frantic pace of Anthony's work ruined his health. At the end of Lent in 1231, Anthony's health began to decline. Following the example of his patron, he retreated to a remote location with two companions to pray for a peaceful death. Forced to return to the Franciscan monastery at Padua because of his worsening condition, Anthony was surrounded by devoted crowds. After receiving the Last Rites, Anthony prayed the seven penitential psalms, sang a hymn to the Blessed Mother, and died at the age of thirty-six. Anthony's holiness, miraculous deeds, and theological depth led Pope Gregory IX to canonize him one year after his death. Pope Pius XII proclaimed Anthony a "Doctor of the Universal Church" in 1946.[42] Anthony ranks with the likes of Patrick, Christopher, and Francis as one of the best known and invoked saints to this day, and his influence continues in our time. His feast day is June 13.

The Preaching of Saint Anthony

Saint Anthony of Padua was one of the great homilists of the thirteenth century. His sermons show a mastery of the art of preaching as it had been developed in the schools of that time. Anthony was a pure and holy man, filled with the fire and zeal of youth, who, through disciplined academic study, preached the Scriptures with a holy and profound understanding.

Saint Anthony was sent into northern Italy in 1222 to preach to the *Humiliati* and other quasi-heretical groups. The *Humiliati* were proponents of an austere form of Christianity, that tended toward extreme forms of penance. They condemned the pride and wealth of the Church, and the laxity of the clergy, to the point that they seriously undermined the attachment of the people to the institutional Church. Anthony responded by emphasizing basic Christian teachings in his homilies. He succeeded, through careful biblical exposition and practical application, in restoring peoples' confidence in their shepherds.

Having succeeded in this mission, Anthony was sent to southern France to combat the Albigensians and Waldensians. The Albigensians were extremely ascetical people who, as we saw earlier, deprecated the material world. The Waldensians preached a simple gospel and provided a strong moral witness, but failed to secure the Church's permission to preach (unlike the Dominicans), and today are part of the Italian Protestant community. Politicians had fought the Albigensians with political and military force. But Anthony fought them with the "sword of the Spirit" and the text of the Bible, and largely succeeded.

One development that greatly influenced Anthony's preaching was the growth of cities. Anthony preached in cities, where commerce, industry, and schools and universities produced a rich culture. Both Dominicans and Franciscans made the cities the focal point of their ministries. They preached in the marketplaces, built communities in the cities, and constructed large churches. They challenged city inhabitants to repent of fornication, theft, usury, dishonesty, violence, and insurrection.

Anthony succeeded as a preacher because of his sincerity. He called people to repentance and faith, both of which he lived himself. He offered a message of hope for forgiveness and assurance of God's grace. Anthony spoke with authority, God's authority. He was a witness to the truth of God's word, which was the key to his effectiveness.

Father Larry Landini, O.F.M., has written an excellent article on Saint Anthony titled, "Saint Anthony of Padua: Portrait of the Ideal Preacher," in which he talked about the preaching of this saint. He called Anthony "one of the most celebrated preachers in Northern Italy, famed for moving souls to conversion and for working miracles."[43]

Among the miracles attributed to Saint Anthony is this story from the thirteenth century: A woman living in Lisbon, Portugal, was afflicted with convulsions of a type attributed to demoniacal possession. Her husband blamed her affliction on guilt for immoral behavior. She resolved to commit suicide, and, on her way to commit the act, she stopped in a church and prayed to Saint Anthony, as it was his feast day. She fell into a trance and had a vision of the saint giving her a piece of paper, which he said would free her from Satan's power. She awoke, finding a parchment in her hand, with these words from Revelation: "Behold the Cross of the Lord! Fly all hostile powers! The Lion of the tribe of Juda, the Root of David, hath conquered, Alleluia. Alleluia!" [Rev. 5:5]. Immediately, she was calmed, and the temptation to suicide vanished. She confessed her sins, returned home to her husband, and remained at peace as long as she kept the paper in her possession.

There are available two cycles of sermons in Latin which Anthony wrote "at the requests and love of the brothers, who have pressed me to this work." The two cycles are known as the *Sermones Dominicales* and *Sermones Festivi.* These *Sermones* reveal the depth of his theological knowledge of the Scriptures as well as giving a portrait of the ideal preacher.[44] Landini discusses two factors in Anthony's preaching. One was his membership in the Order of Friars Minor, "which was rooted in the new understanding of the apostolic life as an indigent and itinerant life dedicated to preaching." The second was the Conciliar reform inaugurated by Pope Innocent III at the Fourth Lateran Council (1215), which called for "the reform of the laity through an informed clergy who were capable of preaching doctrinal sermons to offset heresies."[45] Medieval preaching was carried out by wandering friars dedicated to ecclesial renewal and spiritual formation.

> At the affective level, the Mendicant preachers attempted to deepen the peoples' love for Christ in the mystery of His humanity and suffering. Practically, they strove to move the hearts of their hearers away from evil to the love of God and to works of charity.[46]

Landini quotes D. L. d'Avray regarding the impact of Anthony and other friars, who dedicated their lives to conversion and the salvation of souls:

> They were able to attract urban congregations, promote lay spirituality, and channel volcanic eruptions of religious enthusiasm because they were highly effective as preachers and confessors. In both roles they brought to the religious scene a fresh and re-invigorating change of energy.[47]

How would one describe the *Sermones*? They are a manual designed to prepare the Friars for preaching. In the Prologue, Anthony says that he has undertaken this work for the friars who have asked him to write so that they may effectively preach and correctly minister the sacraments.[48] Anthony's sermons thus provide not only "a learned plan of outlines for the development of a Sunday or Feast Day theme, but also popular, concrete examples taken from nature, the meaning of words, and literature."[49] He used poetry, song, and the arts and sciences in his sermons.

Anthony's sermons were better when they were heard, than when we read them today. For each sermon, Anthony presents material drawn from biblical or liturgical texts. He picks out key words from the Introit, Epistle, Gospel, and even from the Sunday lessons of the Divine Office. Anthony himself describes his Sunday sermons as a four-wheel chariot. "The whole Bible was his sphere; the Breviary and the Missal were his guides."[50] He begins with a biblical text and picks out certain key words from it; then he explains the meaning of these words by referring to other texts from Sacred Scripture. Thus, *catenae*—links or connections with other Scripture texts—were established. Anthony thus illustrates the monastic principle that "the best commentary on Sacred Scripture is Sacred Scripture itself, as well as commentaries taken from Patristic sources."[51]

He also presents material drawn from mythology and folklore, a popular tradition in Mendicant preaching. Anthony breaks open the meaning of Scripture according to four classical senses, which for him come down to answering these questions: "What does the text literally mean? What are the Scriptures saying about Christ? What challenge is the Word of God offering to us in terms of conversion? And to what hope-filled goal are the Scriptures pointing us?"[52]

Anthony used allegory frequently in his preaching. Anthony's mystical teaching flows from his extensive knowledge of Saints Ambrose, Augustine, Gregory the Great, Jerome, John Damascene, Isidore, Bede, and Bernard of Clairvaux.[53] In addition, he knew Cicero, Seneca, Ovid, and other ancient non-Christian writers.

Landini identifies several characteristics of the ideal preacher found in Saint Anthony's *Sermones*:

1. The ideal preacher is above all animated by love. The empowering love is God's love. "The Good News of Christ's love," says Anthony, "is like sweet music on the tongue of the preacher." Only through God's love can the preacher seek the glory of God, the defense of one's neighbor, and the overthrow of the devil.

2. The ideal preacher witnesses to a holy way of life. Only the gift of personal holiness gives authority to the preacher's words. "The word is alive when it is accompanied by works," Anthony says, and then he laments that many preachers "are full of words but empty of good works." . . . Faith, love, patience and zeal must be modeled by preachers. Only then can sinners be lifted from the mud and made into a living stone of God's Temple, the Church. . . .

3. The ideal preacher must possess wisdom and knowledge. Preachers are like the columns supporting the temple of God. To be sturdy, the bronze of eloquence must be mixed with the gold of wisdom and knowledge. Only with wisdom and knowledge can the preacher uphold truth and scatter ignorance. Wisdom also instructs the preacher to adapt his knowledge to the time and place and, above all, to the people.

4. The ideal preacher must also be a person of courage who speaks frankly. The preacher should fear no one. Because the Church is crucified and put to death daily by the devil, the preacher must not compromise with sin. . . .

Anthony stands in the great prophetic tradition of preaching. In the spirit of Francis, he courageously announces vices and virtues, punishment and salvation. He knows the role of speaking *for* God *to* the people and of speaking *to* God *for* the people. He does not shrink from the task of forming the consciences of the people. Conscience is for Anthony the table on which a person plays the cards of his moral choices, and it is on the basis of the choices made by conscience that the person is either just or sinful. . . .

5. The ideal preacher suffers for the Gospel. The preacher prepares for such opposition by voluntary mortification of himself. He must, like Paul and Francis, be vested in the purple of the Crucified. He must bear the wounds of Jesus by a life of penance on behalf of sinners. (*Josephinum Journal* 56–57)

Saint Anthony lived each of these principles. He was a man animated by love and filled with the Holy Spirit. His strong but loving message brought about conversions in droves. He combined solid doctrine with the virtue of loving outreach to his listeners, and they responded. He was formed and transformed by the Word he preached and proclaimed. Sacred Scripture was the starting point for his private prayer and public preaching. Anthony knew that prayer, study, and conversion were essential elements of the preaching apostolate.

Prayerful reflection also deepened one's commitment to Christ and the sacred ministry He gave preachers. Only through contemplation does the preacher come to feel in his own heart the "triple darts of fear, sorrow, and love."[54] The depth of a man's preaching can be measured by the amount of time and effort he spends with the Scriptures. "Like a bee, he must drink from the many flowers of Revelation."[55]

For Anthony, conversion resulted from pardon, which is there for all those "who are truly penitent, a pardon born of spiritual poverty, fraternal love, tears of regret, bodily mortification, the sweetness of contemplation, contempt for worldly prosperity, love of adversity, and the intention of persevering to the end."[56] Anthony, like Christ, enfleshed the Living Word of God in his preaching and pastoral ministry. The thirst to see and hear Christ took flesh in Anthony for all those who came to see him with the anguished cry: "Sir, we would like to see Jesus" (Jn. 12:21).

In this homily, delivered on "Low" (today called "Divine Mercy") Sunday, the Second Sunday of Easter, Saint Anthony discusses the account of the Lord's appearance to the Apostles in the Upper Room. He talks about the three-fold gift of peace. He connects the Lord's appearance with the sacrament of reconciliation in a masterful way.

Homily: The Gift of Peace

> At that time: "When it was late that same day, the first day of the week, and the doors were closed, where the disciples were gathered together, for fear of the Jews, Jesus came and stood in their midst, and said to them: 'Peace be with you.'" (Jn. 20:19).
>
> In the Acts of the Apostles Peter says: "I was in the city of Joppa praying, and I saw in an ecstasy of mind a vision, a certain vessel descending, as it were a great sheet let down from heaven by its four corners, and it came to me. I watched it attentively and saw fourfooted creatures of the earth, and wild beasts, and reptiles, and birds of the air. And I heard a voice saying to me: 'Arise, Peter, kill and eat' (11:5–7). Peter signifies the preacher who ought to be at prayer "in the city of Joppa"—the name means beauty—that is, in Church unity, in which resides the beauty of virtue, and outside of which is the leprosy of unbelief. This is the first thing the preacher must do, give himself to prayer; afterwards follows the transport of mind and heart, the rising above worldly things, and in that transport he sees "a certain vessel like a great sheet," etc. In the vessel and the great sheet the grace of preaching is denoted; and aptly is it called "vessel" for it contains the wine of compunction that fills the hearts of the faithful; "great sheet," too, because it wipes away the sweat of labor and re-freshes to aid in tolerating sufferings. "By its four corners," the teachings of the four evangelists, it is "let down from heaven," for "every worthwhile gift, every genuine benefit comes from above" (Jm. 1:17). "And it came to me." This em-phasizes the very special privilege of the preacher, for the vessel of preaching is sent to him specially from heaven. In this vessel are the "fourfooted creatures of earth," the intemperate and the self-indulgent; "wild beasts," so–called be-

cause they devastate, such as traitors and murderers; and "reptiles," the avaricious and the usurers; and "birds of the air," the haughty, those aloft on the wings of vainglory. This vessel is the net dropped into the sea, gathering every kind of fish (cf. Mt. 13:47), about which the preacher is told: "Arise, kill and eat." Arise to proclaim the good news, kill them to the world; mortify them and offer them up that you might make of them a sacrifice to God, so that snatched from their old way of life they might pass over into something new; and eat, that is, receive them into the unity and togetherness of the body of the Church. Today's gospel speaks of this unity and togetherness: "When it was late that same day, the first day of the week," etc.

Note that five points are highlighted in this gospel: (1) the coming together of the disciples, introduced by "when it was late, etc."; (2) the recommendation of a threefold peace, as the text continues: "Jesus came and stood in their midst and said to them: 'Peace be with you'"; (3) the power of binding and loosing that is given to the apostles: "And when he had said this, he breathed on them, etc."; (4) the doubt of Thomas: "But Thomas, one of the twelve, etc."; (5) Thomas' own acknowledgement and the confirming of our faith: "And after eight days, etc."

Note, too, that on this Sunday we read the Epistle of John: "Everything that is born of God overcomes the world" (1 Jn. 5:4); and during Matins, following the ritual of the Roman Church, the book of the Acts of the Apostles is read. We want briefly to touch upon five factual incidents mentioned there and establish a correlation between these and the five points of the gospel mentioned above. The five episodes are: (1) the apostles' coming together in Jerusalem, "then they returned to Jerusalem from the mount that is called Olivet" (1:12); (2) "in those days Peter stood up in the midst of the brethren, etc." (1:15); (3) the story of the man lame from his mother's womb, to whom Peter said: "Gold and silver I have none," etc. (3:1–11); (4) the conversion of Saul (9:1–19); (5) the stories of the eunuch and Cornelius the centurion (8:26–38; 10:1–48).

1. The Coming Together of the Disciples

We begin with: "When it was late that same day, etc." (Jn. 20:19). In this opening line there are five notable points: it was late; that same day; the first day of the week; closed doors; disciples gathered together for fear of the Jews. Day, so named from "dia," which means brightness, signifies the bright glory of worldly vanity. Of such, in John's gospel the Lord says: "I do not receive glory from men" (5:41). And Jeremiah says: "I have not desired the day of man, you know that" (17:16), while Luke has, "And now in this your day," and not my day, "There are things which lead to your peace" (19:42), but not to mine. And in the Acts of the Apostles: "On the next day, when Agrippa and Bernice had come with great pomp" (25:23), that is, with a great crowd attending them; the Gloss comments here that the Greek text has "With great *phantasia*." The name Agrippa means "a sudden gathering," Bernice means "a daughter moving about with elegance." Agrippa signifies the worldly rich man who amasses wealth quickly through usury and dishonesty but, as Job says, "The riches which he has swallowed, he shall cough up, and God shall make him vomit it from his belly" (20:15). Bernice signifies fleshly luxury; she is a daughter of the devil excited by exterior elegance that causes others to be aroused. Agrippa and Bernice, then, the wealthy and the lovers of luxury, appear in the daylight of worldly vanity "with much pomp" deluding themselves in this fantasy; for whereas it seems "to be something, it is nothing" (Ga. 6:3), and so while they believe they have something, in truth they are being deceived.

"When it was late, therefore, that same day," The late time of this day, the evening, is repentance, in which the sun of worldly glory turns into darkness, and the moon of carnal concupiscence into blood. For this reason, Peter says in the Acts of the Apostles, using the Lord's words in the prophet Joel: "I will show wonders in the heaven above and signs on the earth beneath, blood and fire, and vapor of smoke. The sun shall be turned into darkness, and the moon into blood" (Acts 2:19–20; Jl. 3:3–4).

Interpreted allegorically: the Lord gave signs in heaven and on earth when he descended into earth through the blood of the cross; and in the fire when he sent the Holy Spirit into the apostles; and consequently the smoke of compunction arose. Hence it says in Acts: "They had compunction in their hearts, and said to Peter, and to the other apostles: 'What shall we do, men and brothers?' Peter said to them: 'Do penance and be baptized everyone of you in the name of Jesus Christ'" (2:37–38).

Interpreted morally: in blood is the subduing of flesh, in fire is the ardor of charity, and in vapor of smoke is compunction of heart. The Lord gives the signs "in heaven," i.e. in the just, and "on earth," i.e. in the sinner.

You have a concordance with these three signs in today's epistle: "There are three who give testimony on earth: the spirit, and the water, and the blood" (1 Jn. 5:8). Interpreted allegorically: the spirit is the human soul, which Jesus Christ gave up in his passion; the water and blood is that which flowed from his side, which occurrence was possible only because he was endowed with authentic human flesh.

Interpreted morally: the spirit is charity, the water is compunction, the blood is the subduing of the flesh. You also have a concordance with these three in Exodus, where it says: "All Mount Sinai was smoking because the Lord had come upon it in fire, and the smoke arose from it as out of a furnace, and the whole mountain shook terribly. And the sound of the trumpet grew louder and louder, and was drawn out at a great length" (19:18–19). Mount Sinai is the penitent's heart. When the Lord comes down upon it in the fire of charity, of which he himself said, "I have come to cast fire upon the earth" (Lk. 12:49), the whole mountain smokes and the fume of compunction arises from it as from a furnace, that is from the ardor of the soul's heart. And thus the whole mountain shakes terribly with the penancing of the flesh; or it is terrible to unclean spirits. For this reason the Book of Job says: "No one spoke a word to him; for they saw that his sorrow was very great" (2:13). And the "sound of the trumpet," that is, confession, gradually "grew greater, and was drawn out at great length," because when the penitent confesses he begins first with illicit thoughts, then words, and adds afterwards his deeds.

And staying with the text from Acts: "The sun will be turned into darkness, and the moon into blood" (2:20). The sun will be turned into darkness when worldly glory is darkened by the sackcloth of penance; and the moon will be turned into blood when concupiscence is castigated by penancing, vigils and abstinence. Appropriately, therefore, it says: "When it was late that day, the first day of the week." In Exodus, the Lord says about this: "Remember, keep holy the sabbath day" (20:8).

A person sanctifies the sabbath day when that person remains in peace of spirit and keeps himself from illicit works. "And the doors were closed." The doors are the five senses of the body, which we must close with the slide-bolt of divine love and fear of the Lord, lest befall to us what Paul threatens in the Acts of the Apostles: "I know that after my departure, ravening wolves will enter in among you, not sparing the flock" (20:29). The name Paul means humble. Once humility leaves the heart, "ravening wolves," or carnal desires, enter through the doors of the five senses devouring the flock of simple thoughts. "Where the disciples were gathered together for fear of the Jews." The disciples stand for the mind's best thoughts, which must be gathered into one "On account of fear of the Jews," i.e. demons, so that they do no harm to them. For this reason the Canticle says: "You are beautiful and lovely, daughter of Jerusalem, fearful as an army drawn up for combat" (Sg. 6:4). The daughter of Jerusalem is the soul, beautiful in her faith and lovely in her charity; that will be a cause of fear to the unclean spirits if she so sets in order the thoughts of her mind and the intentions of her heart so as to be like a battle line of soldiers ready to meet the enemy.

Concerning this gathering together you have a concordance in the Acts of the Apostles: "Then they returned to Jerusalem from the mount that is called Olivet, which is near Jerusalem, within a sabbath day's journey. And when they had come in they went up into the upper room where were staying Peter and John, James and Andrew, Philip and Thomas, Bartholomew and Matthew, James of Alpheus, and Simon the Zealot, and Jude the brother of James. All these were persevering with one mind in prayer with the women, and Mary the mother of Jesus, and with his brethren" (1:12–15). Mount Olivet is about a mile from Jerusalem, a sabbath day's journey, or a thousand paces, beyond which it was illicit for Jews to walk on the sabbath. The upper room is called the third roof, according to the Gloss on this text, and stands as a figure of charity, of built-up faith and of hope. We must go up to this upper room and remain there with the disciples and "persevere with one mind in prayer" and contemplation, and in shedding tears so that we might merit to receive the grace of the Holy Spirit. For which the Lord says in Luke: "Stay in the city until from on high you are vested with power" (24:49), or with the Holy Spirit.

If, therefore, the day of worldly glory will have come to a close and have gotten dark in the evening of repentance, in which a person must rest from evil doing, as if it were the sabbath; and if the "doors" of the five senses will have been "closed," and all Christ's disciples, or Christians, or the thoughts of any holy person, will have been gathered into one, then we will be brought from darkness to light, from labor to rest, from being scattered to being gathered together in the heavenly Jerusalem, by Jesus Christ who is blessed forever and ever. Amen.

2. On the Threefold Gift of Peace

The gospel text continues: "Jesus came, and stood in the midst of the disciples and said to them: 'Peace be with you.' And when he had said this, he showed them his hands and side. The disciples therefore were glad when they saw the Lord. He said therefore to them again: 'Peace be with you. As the Father has sent me, I also send you'" (Jn. 20:19–21).

Note first of all that in this gospel "Peace be with you" is said three times on account of the triple peace which Christ formed again between God and man, by reconciling him to God the Father in his blood; between angel and man, by taking to himself human nature and raising it above the choirs of angels; and between man and man, by bringing the Jewish and Gentile peoples together in himself the cornerstone (Ep. 2:20).

Note, too, that in this word "*pax,*" peace, there are three letters and one syllable, which denotes trinity and unity. In P is seen the Father; in A, the prime vocalic, we hear the Son who is the voice of the Father; in X, the double consonant, is understood the Holy Spirit proceeding from the first two. Therefore, when Jesus said, "Peace be with you," he commended to us faith in the Trinity and Unity.

"Jesus came and stood in their midst" Jesus' proper place is always in the middle: in heaven, in the Virgin's womb, in the crib between the animals, on the gibbet of the cross. In heaven, as the Apocalypse says, "The lamb who is in the midst of the throne," i.e. in the bosom of the Father, "shall rule them, and lead them to the fountains of the waters of life" (7:17), i.e. or the fullness of heavenly joy.

In the Virgin's womb, since as *Isaiah* says, "Rejoice and exalt, O habitation of Zion, for great in your midst is the Holy One of Israel" (12:6). O blessed Mary, you who are the habitation of Zion, i.e. of the Church, which established for herself a dwelling place of faith in the Incarnation of your Son, rejoice in your heart, exult in your eloquent words, "My soul proclaims the greatness of the Lord, etc." (Lk. 1:46). "For the great one," yet the small and humble one, "the Holy One of Israel," the sanctifier, is "in your midst," that is, in your womb.

In the crib of the animals, for as we read in [Habakkuk], "In the midst of two animals you will be known" (3:2). And furthermore Isaiah says, "The ox knows its master, and the ass his master's crib" (1:3).

On the gibbet of the cross, for as John describes: "they crucified him with two others, one on each side, and Jesus in the middle" (Jn. 19:18).

"Jesus came and stood in their midst," "I am," he says, "in your midst as the one who serves you" (Lk. 22:27). He stands in the middle of every heart; he stands in the middle so that from him, as from a center, all lines of grace might stretch outward to us who are at the circumference, revolving and moving about him.

You have a concordance for this in the Acts of the Apostles: "In those days Peter rose up in the middle of the brethren—now the number of persons together was about a hundred and twenty—and he said, 'Brethren, etc'" (1:15), which lines are read in the section about the election of Matthias. Christ rising from the dead stood in the middle of the disciples; and Peter, who previously had fallen by denying Jesus, rose up in the middle of the brethren, signifying by this that we too, rising from sin, might stand in the middle of the brethren, because charity is medial, extending itself both to friend and to enemy. "Jesus came, therefore, and stood in the middle of the disciples, and said to them: 'Peace be with you.'"

Note that peace is three-fold. There is a temporal peace, and about this we are told in the First Book of Kings, that "Solomon had peace on all his borders round about" (5:4). There is a peace of heart, and a Psalm speaks of it thus, "In peace I lie down, and fall asleep at once" (4:9). Also, in the Acts of the Apostles: "Now the Church enjoyed peace throughout all Judea, and Galilee, and Samaria; it was being built up, walking in the fear of the Lord, and was filled with the consolation of the Holy Spirit" (9:31). "Judea" is interpreted to mean confession, "Galilee" is a passing over, and "Samaria" is a keeper or guardian. The Church, that is, the faithful soul, has peace on all these three points: in confessing, in passing over from vices to virtues, and in keeping the divine precepts and the gift of grace. And in this way it is built up, walking from virtue to virtue in a filial, not a servile, fear of the Lord and it is filled with the consolation of the Holy Spirit in every tribulation. The third peace is the eternal one: "He has made peace your end" (Ps. 147:14).

You should have the first peace with your neighbor; the second peace with yourself; and so you will have, on the octave of the resurrection, the third peace with God in Heaven. Stay "in the middle," therefore, and you will have peace with your neighbor. If you do not stay in the middle, you will not be able to have peace, for those on the circumference there is neither peace nor tranquility, but motion, rather, and continual change. It is said of elephants that if at any time they fight in battle, they take good care of their wounded. For they gather the tired and the injured into the center of the herd. In the same way, you should receive into the center of your love the wearied and the wounded, as did that prison guard of whom the Acts of the Apostles speaks. "Taking Paul and Silas at that same hour of the night he washed their wounds . . . and he brought them into his own house, and set a table for them, and rejoiced with his whole house, believing in the Lord" (16:33–34).

"Jesus, therefore, stood in the midst of the disciples and said to them: 'Peace be with you.' And when he had said this he showed them his hands and side." Luke says it this way: "See my hands and my feet, see that it is I myself" (24:39). It seems to me that the Lord had four reasons for showing the Apostles his hands, feet and side: (1) to show that he had truly risen, and take away from us all doubt; (2) in order that the dove, namely the Church or the faithful soul, might make a nest in his wounds as if in the clefts of the rock (cf. Sg. 2:14), and hide herself from the face of the hawk searching to seize her; (3) to impress our hearts with the most notable signs of his passion; (4) he showed them to us, asking that we become compassionate and not crucify him again with the nails of sin. As he shows us his hands and side, he is effectively saying: 'Here are the hands that formed you, see them pierced with nails. Behold the side, out of which you faithful, my Church, have been born, as Eve was brought forth from the side of Adam; it has been opened by a lance so that it might open for you the gate of paradise which had been shut by a Cherub with fiery sword.' The power of the blood flowing from Christ's side removed the angel, and dulled the sword, and the water put out the fire. 'Do not, therefore, crucify me again and esteem unclean the blood of the testament in which you have been sanctified, and offer and insult to the Spirit of grace (cf. Heb. 6:6; 10:29). If you should heed well and listen to these things, O man, you will be at peace with yourself.' "And then, after the Lord showed them his hands and side, he again said: 'Peace be with you.' As the Father has sent me" to sufferings, even though he loves me, "I send you," with that same love as it were, to the evils to which the Father has sent me. May he who is blessed forever grant us patience here in these evils, and eternal peace in the world to come. Amen.

3. On the Power of Absolution Given to the Apostles

"When he had said these things, he breathed on them, and said to them: 'Receive the Holy Spirit; whose sins you shall forgive, they are forgiven them, etc." (Jn. 20:22–23). His breathing on them signified that the Holy Spirit proceeds from him, as well as from the Father. Gregory says about this text: "The Spirit is given 'on earth' so that the neighbor might be loved; he is given 'from heaven' so that God might be loved." Jesus says, "Receive the Holy Spirit; whose sins . . .," that is, whomever you will find worthy of forgiveness by the two keys, namely of power and judgment, that is, by exercising authority and discernment. Understand that the measure and order must be observed in the power of binding and loosing. Let us see in what way, in fact, a priest forgives sins and absolves a sinner.

Anyone who sins mortally has already established a place for himself in hell; he is already bound by a chain of eternal death. But after the fact contrition may occur; and the truly contrite person proposes then to confess. Immediately, the Lord absolves him from the fault and from eternal death, which because of the contrition is changed into a purgatorial debt of punishment. Contrition could also be so intense, as in the case of Magdalene and the thief on the cross, that were the sinner to die he would go immediately to heaven. The contrite then goes to the priest and confesses; the priest imposes on him a temporal penance; this temporal penance replaces the purgatorial punishment. If the temporal expiation is authentically completed, the person is ready to enter into glory. Thus God and the priest together forgive and absolve.

Concerning this you have a concordance in the Acts of the Apostles, where Peter says: "'Silver and gold I have none; but what I have, I give you. In the name of Jesus Christ of Nazareth arise and walk.' And taking him by the right hand, he lifted him up, and right away his feet and soles received strength. He jumped up, stood for a moment, and began walking about, and went with the disciples into the Temple in Jerusalem" (3:6–8).

Blessed Bernard, writing to Pope Eugene, says: "Consider the legacy your fathers left; the testator's will allotted you none of the things like silver and gold. Hear the voice of your predecessor as he says, 'Gold and silver I have none.'" The Gloss on this text comments further, that the first covenant contained ritual justifications and with that an earthly sanctuary richly adorned with gold and silver. But the blood of the new covenant is more precious and has more brilliance than all the details of the law. For a people, who had laid weak before the golden doors, enters now into the celestial temple in the name of Jesus Christ crucified. Jerome adds: If you want to bring gold and silver back into the Church, bring back the bloody sacrifices which the ancients offered for which they were promised those glittering things. But as matters stand, the poor Christ has consecrated poverty in his own body, and has promised his followers not temporary but heavenly rewards.

"In the name of Jesus Christ, etc." "There is a sense of ascending perfection here: first, the one who had laid a cripple arises; then he eagerly takes the path of virtue; and thus he enters the gate of the kingdom with the apostles." Note the words "arise," through contrition, and "walk," through confession, and thus, "having grasped his right hand, Peter lifted him," i.e. absolved him, and sent him away in peace.

In the same Acts of the Apostles you have another concordance concerning this, where it says that "Peter found at Lydda a man named Aeneas, a paralytic who had been bedridden for eight years. And Peter said to him: 'Aeneas, may Jesus Christ heal you; arise, and set your bed in order.' Aeneas got up immediately" (9:32–34). Aeneas means poor and miserable, and signifies the sinner in mortal sin; he is poor in virtue and miserable because he is a slave of the devil. This sinner is a paralytic; he lies in a bed of carnal concupiscence with all his members dissolute. Peter's vicar must say to him: Aeneas, poor and miserable, let Jesus Christ heal you; "Arise" through contrition, and "set your things in order," through confession. You yourself, not another, must get yourself in order. And immediately he arose, "absolved from every bond of sin."

You will have still another concordance where "Peter says; 'Tabitha, arise.' And she opened her eyes; and giving her his hand, he lifted her up" (Ac 9:40–41). Tabitha means gazelle and even the word-sound suggests 'gaze eluder.' This is a timid and faint-hearted animal of the goat family. It signifies the timorous and faint-hearted soul of the sinner who is fleeing from the hand of the heavenly Father. It is said to her: "Arise," through contrition; and then "she opens her eyes," through confession; and she sits up and humbles herself through satisfaction; and thus "she is lifted up," through the absolution of her sins. May the true priest and supreme pontiff Jesus Christ, who is blessed forever, do the same for us. Amen.

4. On the Doubt of Thomas

"Thomas, however, one of the twelve, who is called Didymus, was not with them when Jesus came. Therefore, the disciples said to him: 'We have seen the Lord.' But he said: 'Unless I see in his hands the print of the nails, and put my fingers in the place of the nails, and put my hand into his side, I will not believe'" (Jn. 20:24–25).

'Thomas means abyss, for by doubting he gets to know more deeply, and to stand more securely. Didymus is Greek for double, because he was doubtful. It is not by chance, but by divine dispensation that Thomas was missing and did not believe the things he heard." O divine dispensation, O loving doubt of the disciple. Thomas said, 'Unless I will see in his hands,' etc. He desired to see David's reconstructed tent, which had fallen, and of which the Lord speaks in Amos the prophet: "In that day I will raise up again David's tent, that is fallen, and I will repair the openings in its walls" (9:11).

By "David," which means sturdy of hand, divinity is understood; by "tent" is understood the body of Christ himself, in which divinity dwelt as if in a tent. And this body had fallen through his passion and death. "The openings in the walls mean the wounds of the hands and feet and side. The Lord has repaired these in the resurrection. Thomas says of them: "Unless I will see in his hands," etc. The good Lord did not want to leave the doubting disciple in that doubt, for he was going to be a vessel of election. He mercifully removed all darkness of doubt from Thomas as he removed the blindness of Saul's unbelief.

Hence, you have a concordance in the Acts of the Apostles when Ananias says: "'Brother Saul, I have been sent by the Lord Jesus who appeared to you in the way here that you might see and be filled with the Holy Spirit.' And suddenly, there fell from his eyes scales, as it were, and he received his sight; and rising up he was baptized. And when he had taken food, he was strengthened" (9:17–19). Herein, Isaiah's prophesy is fulfilled: "The wolf and the lamb [shall feed together]" (65:25), in other words, Saul with Ananias, which means sheep. The body of a serpent is covered with scales. The Jews are "serpents and a brood of vipers" (Lk. 3:7). Saul followed in their unbelief; he had as it were covered the eyes of his heart with the serpent's skin; but when the scales fell, under the hand of Ananias, it was obvious in his face that he had received light in his mind. So too, under the hand of "Ananias," i.e. Jesus Christ, who was led "as a lamb to the slaughter" (Is. 53:7), the scales of doubt fell from Thomas' eyes and he received the sight of faith. May he who is blessed forever grant that we, enlightened by the sight of faith, may merit to see the light of glory. Amen.

5. On Thomas' Confession of Faith and the Confirming of Ours

"And after eight days the disciples were inside again, and Thomas was with them. Jesus came, though the doors were shut, and stood in their midst, and said: 'Peace be with you.'" (Do not go over what has already been explained.) "Then he said to Thomas: 'Put your finger in here, and see my hands; and bring your hand here, and put it into my side. And do not be faithless any longer, but believing.' Thomas answered and said to him: 'My Lord and my God.' Jesus said to him: 'Because you have seen me, you have believed. Blessed are they who have not seen and have believed'" (Jn. 20:26–29).

In Isaiah the Lord says: "I have written you in my hands" (49:16). Note that for writing three things are necessary: paper, ink, and pen. The hands of Christ were the paper as it were; his blood the ink; the nails the pen. Christ has inscribed us in his hands, therefore, for three distinct reasons: (1) to show the scars of the wounds he bore for us to the Father, thus inviting the Father to show us mercy. (2) In order not to forget us. For this reason he says in Isaiah: "Can a woman forget her infant, and not have pity on the son of her womb? And if she should forget, yet I will not forget you. Behold, I have written you in my hands" (49:15–16). (3) He has written in his hands what kind of people we should be and in whom we should believe. "Do not be faithless," therefore, O Thomas, O Christian, "but be instead a believer."

"Thomas answered: 'My Lord, and my God'" etc. The Lord does not say, because you touched, but "because you have seen . . ." Because sight in a certain way is a general sense and we usually speak of 'seeing' concerning the other four senses. The Gloss says that perhaps Thomas did not dare to touch, but by looking only, or also by touching, he saw. He saw and touched a man, and beyond this he believed him to be God, and his doubt being removed now, he confessed what he did not see. "Thomas, you have seen me" a man, and "you have believed me" to be God.

"Blessed are they who have not seen and have believed." In this he commends the faith of the Gentiles, but he uses the past tense as one who in his foreknowledge knew already what was going to be. About the Gentile faith you have a concordance in the Acts of the Apostles in the episode of the eunuch of Queen Candace of Ethiopia, whom Philip questioned: "'Do you believe with your whole heart?' He answered: 'I believe that Jesus Christ is the son of God'" and Philip baptized him (8:37–38). There is another concordance in Cornelius the centurion whom, along with his whole family, Peter baptized in the name of Jesus Christ (cf. Acts 10:47–48). These two men believing in Christ prefigured the Church of the Gentiles that had to be reborn in sacred baptism, and was going to believe in the name of Jesus Christ. It is to such as these that Peter speaks in the Introit of today's Mass, saying: "Like new born infants, reasonable, without guile, desire nothing but milk" (1 Pt. 2:2).

"Infant is so-called because it does not yet know how to speak, or is non-speaking, '*non fans.*' The faithful of the Church who are born of water and the Holy Spirit should be '*infantes,*' that is, not speaking in the tongue of Egypt. Isaiah speaks of this: "This Lord," he says, "shall lay waste the tongue of the sea of Egypt" (11:15). 'Tongue' represents eloquence, 'sea' philosophical wisdom, and 'Egypt' represents the world. The Lord, then, lays waste the tongue of the sea of Egypt when, through the simple and unlettered, he shows the eloquence and wisdom of the world to be hollow and foolish.

"Reasonable, and without guile." Something is reasonable that is done with reason. "Reason is an aspect of the mind by which it beholds truth, not by means of the body, but by itself; or it is the direct contemplation of truth, not through the body; or again, it is the very truth itself which it is contemplating." We should, therefore, be "reasonable" as to God and as to ourselves, and "without guile" as to our neighbors.

We should also "desire milk," namely that about which Augustine speaks: "The bread of angels has become the milk of little ones." "Milk is so named [*lac*] from its color, because it is a white liquid; '*leuchos*' is the Greek word for white. The substance of this liquid is produced from blood. For after birth whatever blood has not yet been consumed as nourishment in the uterus flows by a natural transfer into the breasts where it becomes white and takes on the characteristics of milk." And here it will be food for the newborn. For the matter out of which generation occurs is the same matter from which one is fed. Milk is blood transformed and digested; there is nothing corrupt about it. In the blood, which is dreadful to look at, the wrath of God is designated; in milk, which is sweet-tasting and of pleasant odor, the mercy of God is designated. The blood of wrath was converted into milk of mercy in the breast, that is, in the humanity of Jesus Christ. This is the reason why the prophet says: "He has made the lightning into rain" (Ps. 135:7). When the Word was made flesh (cf. Jn. 1:14), the lightning of divine wrath was turned into a soft rain-shower of mercy.

Interpreted morally: the Ethiopian eunuch and Cornelius the centurion signify converted sinners. Cornelius is interpreted as understanding circumcision. The two figures of Cornelius the centurion and the eunuch go well together. For penitents make themselves eunuchs for the sake of the kingdom of heaven (cf. Mt. 19:12), i.e. they circumcise away carnal desires from themselves and, believing in the name of Jesus Christ, they wash themselves in the living fountain of penance, and renew themselves by a baptism of repentance. They do as those elephants about whom Solinus writes: "The females do not know sexual relations before ten years of age, the males not before five years. They mate for a period of two years, and they do not have coition more than five times a year; and they do not return to the herd before they have cleansed themselves in running waters." In a similar way, penitents and upright men, if they have offended in any way, are ashamed to return to the number of the faithful unless they are washed first by the living waters of tears and repentance.

Let us ask, therefore, dearest brothers, and humbly entreat the mercy of Jesus Christ, so that he might come and stand in our midst. May he grant us peace, absolve us of our sins, and take away all doubt from our hearts. And may he imprint in our minds faith in his passion and resurrection, so that with the apostles and faithful of the Church we might merit to receive eternal life. May he grant this, he who is blessed, laudable, and glorious through all ages. Let every faithful soul say: Amen. Alleluia. (Marcil, *Anthony of Padua*, 89–104)

SCHOLASTIC PREACHING

Preaching in the so-called "High Middle Ages" must be seen within the context of scholastic thought. Scholastic thought refers to the organized and systematic historical theology characteristic of the eleventh, twelfth and thirteenth centuries. Scholasticism developed as individual questions and particular answers surfaced in this historical period. While theological questions date to the earliest centuries of the Church, Scholasticism systematized these historically disparate questions and answers. Philosophers and theologians such as Saint Anselm (1033–1109), Hugh (d. 1142) and Richard (d.1173) of Saint Victor, Alexander of Hales (1186–1245), and Saint Bonaventure (1217–1274) contributed to theological development in this period. Scholastic preaching reflected the organized textbook theology and thesis method of learning characteristic of the period.

Saint Thomas Aquinas: Scholastic Preacher

Saint Thomas Aquinas (ca.1225–1274) is one of the most well known Christian writers. He was a master of theology, who lived at the height of the Middle Ages, the thirteenth century. He was born in 1225 in southern Italy. He was a brilliant student, but he was also quiet and soft-spoken. As a result, his fellow students called him "the dumb ox." Thomas' wealthy family sent him at age five to be taught by the Benedictines, hoping that he would one day join their community, and perhaps become an abbot. He decided at age nineteen to become a Dominican friar instead. The Dominicans' life of prayer and study attracted Thomas more than the Benedictines', so he joined the Dominicans instead. This news greatly upset his family. As a result, they imprisoned him in a family castle for two years. They also sought to lure him away from his vocation by locking him up in a room with a harlot, an act that failed to achieve its intended purpose. Realizing that they weren't going to change his mind, they released him, and he followed his holy desire. He eventually was ordained a Dominican priest. He studied the natural sciences under Albert the Great, but preferred theology. He was ordained, and appointed as the doctrinal student for one of two professorships assigned to the Dominicans at the University of Paris. As a professor (1256–59), he would have taught in the three areas of study: homiletics, commentary on Peter Lombard's *Sentences,* and theological debate.

During the next decade of teaching in Italy, Thomas wrote his famous *Summa Theologiae*, a systematic and dialectical summary of theology. In it, he addresses a question, arguments against his position, and then arguments for it. It was the classic mode of medieval disputation. He returned to Paris for a second term, and died before he was fifty. The great irony is that he who earned the nickname "Dumb Ox" for his early silence as a student, became the most articulate theologian of his age. As Albert the Great had predicted to Thomas' detractors, "he will yet bellow so loud in doctrine that his voice will resound through the whole world."

The early Church tried to synthesize Greek ideas and Christian Revelation. Aquinas now sought to reconcile the rediscovered Aristotelian philosophy with Christianity. He argued that nature and reason should be kept distinct from revelation. Rational science, based on empirical evidence gathered by the senses, confirmed revealed knowledge about God. However, there are some truths or mysteries, such as the Blessed Trinity and the Incarnation, that could never be demonstrated. Reason supports rather than undermines the faith. The four virtues that remained after the Fall (prudence, justice, fortitude, temperance) are adequate for reading Sacred Scripture, and for living a good life. Salvation, on the other hand, requires more than virtue: the forgiveness of sins, and the restoration of friendship with God are essential to salvation (CCC, no. 1129). Through the gift of God's free and unmerited grace, received exclusively through the sacraments, the three Christian virtues (faith, hope and love) are bestowed, enabling men to do acts deserving of merit. Grace and merit were the primary concepts of medieval piety.

Thomas spent most of his time in study, prayer, and writing. He could dictate to four secretaries at the same time on different subjects. He was known as the "Angelic Doctor" because of the beauty of his writings. In addition to the *Summa Theologiae*, he wrote the Eucharistic hymns *Adoro te devote*, *O Salutaris*, and *Pange lingua*. Saint Thomas died on March 7, 1274, while on his way to the Council of Lyons. He is the patron of Catholic colleges and universities, philosophers, theologians, and booksellers. His feast day is January 28.

The Preaching of Saint Thomas Aquinas

Saint Thomas was an articulate preacher as well as a brilliant theologian. He lived at a time referred to as "The Age of Synthesis" because philosophers and theologians synthesized Christian and non-Christian thought in their writings. If the thirteenth century was "The Age of Synthesis," St. Thomas was "The Master Synthesizer." We are not talking about *syncretism* here, which attempts to fuse or accommodate diverse and often opposing and contradictory views and beliefs. Rather, we are speaking of the search for truth in all places. Saint Thomas drew on Christian and non-Christian sources alike in his *Summa*, a monumental piece of thought and study. By this time the Church had gone beyond simply using the Fathers to support their teaching. Anselm of Canterbury had devised a method of applying reason to support matters that were already decided by faith. Peter Abelard (1079–1142) demonstrated in *Sic et Non* (Yes and No) the contradictions among the Fathers, and Peter Lombard (d. 1160) "adopted Abelard's *dialectical method* as he compiled and discussed ancient and contemporary ideas."[57] Christopher Dawson goes a step further. In *The Formation of Christendom,* he argues that Aquinas was a launching pad toward a revitalization of thought in future centuries. Saint Thomas, in fact, anticipated the Renaissance.

Although he is primarily remembered as a systematic theologian who placed a high value on the power of intellect, Aquinas understood that reason alone could not lead to the whole truth of man's existence. Thomas saw man as a natural being with a supernatural end. While reason can discover some truths about God, it does not provide the knowledge necessary for man to understand his final end, and to attain his salvation. Hence, faith and divine revelation are necessary for man to achieve his supernatural end, viz., union with God.

Aquinas showed great respect for the literal, historical sense of Scripture. He says it is the only sense of Scripture from which one can argue, because it derives from images having to do with the body's physical senses, from which our knowledge springs. The other spiritual senses are interpretations of the literal and presuppose it. As with Saint John Chrysostom, the literal sense was what the author intended, and though it includes a metaphorical meaning, it cannot contain what is false. One consequence of this view of knowledge was Aquinas' insistence that the Garden of Eden was an historical fact.

The preaching of Catholicism's greatest theologian is a treasure that has yet to be discovered by students of homiletics. His homilies come to us in the form of sermon outlines, and homiletic aids for students to transcribe and develop, in part or in whole, complete with valuable and numerous additional texts to consult. They represent a skeletal version of his clearly ordered thought.

We know his preaching was powerful and effective. When preaching in Naples and Rome, he repeatedly moved people to tears, and he had to pause to allow the congregation to weep. He appealed to both intellectuals and nonintellectuals alike.

We may observe three things from his sermons: First, every detail in a statement he makes is supported by a Scripture quotation—this is partly because he links the allegorical or symbolic readings back to other texts read literally; second, every quotation, including the initial text, stands on its own as a literal complete truth without support from its context; third, his use of allegory is sometimes more subjective than that of earlier preachers, although at times it functions more as a simile than as an absolute one-on-one correspondence.

Aquinas' sermons are early examples of what came to be known as "university sermons" because of their numerous and elaborate divisions (points and sub-points). His homiletic method is as follows: Start with a Scripture verse; either make several main points (headings) from it and support these with verses from other texts; or start by finding verses from other texts that are similar to the first one, and then use them instead to make as many main points as necessary.

His next step is to make sub-points in the same manner, if they are necessary, using the new or additional textual verses. He develops each point in turn, develops the idea early before going on to proof text, and shapes the whole by his doctrinal understanding. His sermons moved from discussion of a particular doctrine (e.g., the Transfiguration) to a final application to our lives.

His homiletic style was characterized by his use of proof texts and allegory; his rooting of homilies in the Bible; his clear organization; his singular appeal to reason and experience; his easy assumption of the objective truth of his argument or theme. In his sermons, Aquinas reached out to common as well as highly educated people, by promoting different senses that have emotional as well as logical appeal.

Wilson provides a modern example of Aquinas' preaching:

> Start with a need in the congregation (e.g., to establish a mission for the poor); identify the underlying issue or barrier (e.g., we do not want to enter the suffering of others); clarify a doctrine that speaks to the issue (e.g., Christ has entered our suffering); point to the consequences of that truth in each of our lives (e.g., because we have experienced God meeting our needs, we are here); and move back to the original need, this time with a fresh perspective (e.g., we are stronger for entering the suffering of others for there we encounter Christ).[58]

Saint Thomas mastered the art of catechetical instruction. Fortunately, the Church possesses a series of his catechetical sermons. These include thirty-one sermons on the Ten Commandments, two on the Hail Mary, eleven on the Lord's Prayer, and fifteen on the Creed. One is tempted to think that catechetical sermons originated in the Middle Ages, but in fact they date back to Christian antiquity. As stated earlier, Saint Thomas preached in the university setting. Universities were located in large cities. Saint Thomas and others sought to revitalize the Christian faith in part through preaching. They instructed merchants, housewives, shopkeepers, burghers, and artisans in Naples and other cities. The Dominicans rose to the challenge of teaching a Western Christendom ignorant of basic Christian teaching.

Saint Thomas would preach his catechetical sermons in the late afternoon or early evening, a time when an Italian town comes alive, and the populace is outdoors after siesta. There were two advantages to preaching at this time: One was that he was not obliged to follow the Lectionary readings. He could select his own biblical passages and cover topics not found in the Lectionary cycle. The other was that people had more time to hear him preach. They didn't have to rush off to work, and could listen to his preaching in a more relaxed fashion.

Aquinas preached on basic Christian doctrines: the Blessed Trinity, the humanity and divinity of Jesus, and the Incarnation. These mysteries were present from the beginning, but the Church Fathers clarified and explained them in response to heretical attacks. Saint Thomas drew new insights into them for his listeners.

Of preachers in history, we possess different types of recorded sermons. In some cases we have exact stenographical reports of what was said. In other cases we have embellishments composed by the homilist himself. Sometimes we have abbreviated sermons or sermon notes. In the case of Saint Thomas, we have abbreviations. Saint Thomas brought profound theological reflection to his preaching ministry, and the Church is blessed to have his works.

Saint Thomas' approach to catechetical analysis can be seen in his Sermons on the Creed. Thus, considering Christ's suffering and death on the cross, Thomas discusses five ways in which Our Lord's death is a remedy for sin: (1) It is a remedy for the stain of sin. Sin disfigures the soul, but the Passion of Christ removes this disfigurement. "For Christ with his passion makes a bath of his blood by which sinners are cleansed," Thomas says.[59] (2) The Lord's Passion excuses the offense against God. Sin offends God. But the Lord's Passion satisfies Him. His justice is now fulfilled and the offense is no more. (3) The Lord's Passion strengthens us for the new life of grace we receive. Original Sin caused weakness and infirmity to plague man, but the Passion strengthens us so we may not be completely dominated by our sins. (4) The Passion takes away the punishment due to sin by Christ's bearing it Himself. We incur punishment when we sin. But Jesus' suffering was so powerful that it expiated the sins of the whole world, a power that is continued in the forgiving ministry of priests. (5) By His Passion Christ opens the gates of Paradise once again. When Adam and Eve sinned, they were expelled from the Garden of Paradise. Christ came to reopen the Garden and reconcile us to the Kingdom.[60]

In his sermon on the Resurrection, Aquinas discusses the differences between the resurrection of Lazarus and Our Lord's Resurrection. (1) Christ's Resurrection came about by His own strength and power. Others require the strength of Christ or the prayers of the saints in order to rise. But the Son of God, who laid down His life freely, took it up again freely. (2) Christ rose to a glorious and incorruptible life, whereas Lazarus and others rose to the same life they had before they died. The life of the risen Christ is a new life rather than a resumption of the old life. (3) Because of the power of the Resurrection of Christ, all people rise. Saint Paul calls it the "first fruits" of those who have risen again. Christ's Resurrection opens the door to more resurrections. (4) Christ rose on the third day, whereas the resurrection of others is deferred until the end of time. The resurrection is a sign of man's passage from this world to the Father.

Saint Thomas clearly emphasizes the doctrine of redemption in his sermons. They are enlightening and interesting. Saint Thomas drew on the wisdom of those who had preceded him, and the Church is better as a result.

The following homily summary is taken from the First Sunday after Pentecost (Holy Family Sunday C in the revised calendar). It is based on the text: "And Jesus advanced [in] wisdom and age and favor before God and man" (Luke 2:52).

Homily: The Four Growths of Christ

1. *Jesus the model of youth*: All the works of the Lord were a salutary example to us, as he testified himself (John 13.15). Christ, as a youth, gives that example to young people to show them how they should grow and learn.

2. *The four growths of Christ*: We can observe four growths in Christ: in age, so far as his body was concerned; in knowledge, in the intellect; in grace of soul; and finally, in the sight of men. It is to be admired that the Eternal One should grow in age, the infinitely wise, in wisdom, the author of grace increase in it, and all this in the sight of men, instead of men growing in his sight.

The growth in age is easy to understand, but the others are more difficult, for if his glory was like that of the only-begotten Son of God, full of grace and truth, then he would be full all the time, since he was always the only-begotten Son of God.

But a person is said to grow in knowledge not merely when he is acquiring it, but also when he manifests it. In such a way did Christ conform to the condition of our human nature that he manifested his wisdom in accordance with natural growth. There is a natural parallel between the growth of the body and that of the soul, because if it were not so, then the growth would be abnormal, as happens when one member grows more quickly than another. "When I was a child I spoke as a child . . . but now I am a man I have put away the things of a child" (1 Cor. 13. 11). We are only bidden to keep two of our childhood qualities, its simplicity and humility.

It would also be a pernicious growth. The merchant who lets the time of the annual fair go by, or the student who does not assist at the best lectures, both feel that they have suffered a great loss. For more important things than these God has given us the gift of time. Eye has not seen, nor ear heard, neither has it entered into the heart of man to conceive what things God has prepared for them who love him. For which reason we are warned not to deprive ourselves of the good things of the day (Ecclus. 14: 13–14).

God has given you your strength so that you may fight against the devil and thus gain your reward. If you use that strength to serve Satan then you have handed to him that which might have been your reward and the good things which you may have done will be of profit to others, perhaps, but not to you. Then indeed, your growth will cost you a great effort, because it will be much harder for you to correct your ways afterwards. The farm laborer ploughs easily because he has been accustomed to it from his youth; for which reason we are told to instruct the child in his ways, and he will not depart from them in his old age (Prov. 22. 6).. If then you live an evil life in your youth, either you will despair of salvation later or at least you will have prepared a difficult task for yourselves.

A dangerous growth because God will demand an account of you for everything at every step of your life. While thou art yet young, take thy fill of manhood's pride, let thy heart beat high with youth, follow where thought leads and inclination beckons, but remember that for all this God will call thee to account (Eccles. 11. 9). How then did Christ grow in age and spirit? By growing in wisdom and grace. Even though the texts speaks first of growth in wisdom we shall deal first of all with growth in grace, which is its cause.

3. *Growth in grace—peace*. Hidden causes, such as grace, are known by their effects which are visible, and there is none so visible as that of peace. There is no peace for the wicked, says the Lord (Isaiah 48.22). Go then, youths, as Jesus did on coming to the use of reason, to Jerusalem, city of peace. Man is at peace when he has won the victory in the struggle between the flesh and the spirit.

The conditions necessary for peace are: first of all, that it should be at a high level, because if the soul is subjected to the flesh, then it will be nothing but a low and false peace. Peace at a high level consists in the subjection of the body to the soul by means of mortification, without consenting to the lower nature, since servants as vile as this one are never satisfied; given one scrap of liberty, they clamour for more. So far as external manifestations are concerned, those which can be seen by others, be content with those which are common among people of good conscience. God does not like singularity. Peace must endure, be both constant and watchful against the allies of the body, such as relatives and dangerous companions . . . .

4. *Growth in wisdom through contemplation. Its conditions*: Wisdom is acquired through contemplation, and the place for such contemplation is the temple. There Jesus was found. Let us see what he did to teach us contemplation.

(a) *Listen carefully*: This knowledge is so profound that no one can hope to acquire it without being taught. Do not think that you are already wise, because there is no man so wise that he cannot learn by listening to another. Jesus gave us an example by listening to the doctors of the law.

(b) *With constancy*: No one attains wisdom in one lesson. His parents found the Child after three days.

(c) *Hear many people*: Because God has divided his graces among many. St. Gregory gives lessons in morality; Augustine solves difficulties; Ambrose is a master of allegory; One who is just beginning should listen to one master until he has attained the fundamentals of knowledge; but once he is proficient in those, then he should pluck his flowers from various gardens. Thus the Child was found in the midst of the doctors, as one who would judge them and choose the best.

(d) *Seek and inquire*: Merchants are always active; but wisdom is worth more than all their products. Where should you seek wisdom? In three places, mainly. First, in your master, who is also your father, because he has given you birth. Then by asking questions of those who are absent, such as the ancient writers. Observe nature, in which God has written the lesson of his wisdom as creator. The third way of increasing your wisdom is by teaching others. Experience tells us that there is no one who does not learn by teaching. The very fact of having to reply to questions makes one define concepts more carefully.

But to reply to questions there is need of a three-fold prudence. First, that of accommodating the doctrine to one's own capacity; the second to reply to the question without wandering. The Child Jesus caused admiration at the wisdom of his answers. Thirdly, and this is the mother of all prudence, we must meditate carefully. Our Lady was a model of prudence, because she kept all the words in her heart. (*The Preacher's Encyclopedia IV: Advent to Quadragesima* 284–86)

SUMMARY

We now come to the end of the Medieval Period. Since the days of Gregory the Great, "Christendom" experienced periods of darkness and of light. The Christian faith grew in many places, and contracted in many others. Various invasions disrupted the life of the Church; nonetheless, the Church continued to grow intellectually and spiritually. While schisms had taken place in the early centuries of Church history, the great schism of the eleventh century divided East and West in profound ways. Then a few centuries later, the Western Church itself would be divided.

The Muslim invasions of the West constricted, and, in some cases obliterated, the Eastern churches which had given Christian thought and life its glory and luster. The reduction of Christian lands by the sword, and the attempt to reconquer them are prominent features of Medieval history.

The Scholastics and Monastics each had a great influence on the development of preaching. In addition to preserving the intellectual heritage of Western civilization during the Dark Ages, they synthesized the Scriptures, and patristic and ancient sources; at the same time, they continued to provide new insights into ancient texts. The new religious orders also contributed to the liturgical prayer and pastoral service of the Church.

The Church in the Middle Ages was in a period of self-reflection, as it tried to see the world and religion as a unified whole. In this process, new heights of intellectual development were reached, as a result of the emergence of monastic and university study. At the same time, doctrinal controversies continued to erupt in the Church.

Homilies developed in remarkable ways as the Middle Ages came to an end. Classical vocabulary, syntax, and diction were gradually eclipsed by medieval expressions of thought. In addition, and more importantly, the content of homilies changed in the Middle Ages. The thematic sermon became less important, and the proclamation of God's saving works became more important in Medieval homiletics. The homily itself began to reflect the praise of God in liturgical worship, rather than dialectical arguments over points of doctrine or morality. This development would continue as the Church in the West faced a great crisis in the coming centuries.

As we will see in the next chapter, the Protestant Reformation greatly impacted the life and preaching of the Church. Sermons preached during and after the Council of Trent dealt with matters of morality and ethics. They emphasized the importance of Christian virtue, and dealt with issues affecting day-to-day living. We now examine preaching at the time of the Reformation, and in its aftermath.

NOTES

1. Simon Tugwell, ed., Introduction to *Early Dominicans, Selected Writings*, Classics of Western Spirituality (New York: Paulist Press, 1982), 6.

2. Leclerq, Jean. *The Love of Learning and The Desire for God: A Study of Monastic Culture.* (New York: Fordham University Press, 1982), 141.

3. Ibid.

4. D. H. Farmer, Introduction to Bede, *Ecclesiastical History of the English People* (London: Penguin Books, 1990), 35.

5. Ibid., 22.

6. Ibid., 35.

7. Ibid., 21.

8. Ibid.

9. Old, *Reading and Preaching of the Scriptures*, 3:122.

10. Ibid.

11. Ibid.

12. John Farina, ed., *Saint Bernard of Clairvaux,* Classics of Western Spirituality (New York: Paulist Press, 1987), 33.

13. Old, *Reading and Preaching of the Scriptures*, 3:253.

14. Ibid., 3:254.

15. Ibid., 3:255.

16. Ibid.

17. John Farina, ed., *St. Bernard of Clairvaux*, 17.

18. Ibid.

19. Martin Scott, *Medieval Europe* (New York: Dorsett Press, 1964), 142–43.

20. Ibid., 143.

21. Ibid.

22. John Farina, ed., *St. Bernard of Clairvaux*, 51.

23. Ibid., 7.

24. Old, 3:258.

25. John Farina, ed., *St. Bernard of Clairvaux*, 28.

26. Ibid., 29.

27. Ibid.

28. Ibid.

29. Ibid.

30. Ibid., 9.

31. Ibid.

32. Ibid.

33. Old, 3:274.

34. Benedict XV, Encyclical on St. Dominic *Fausto Appetente Die* (June 29, 1921), no. 2. http://www.vatican.va

35. Ibid., no. 3

36. *Oxford Dictionary of the Christian Church*, s.v. "Saint Dominic."

37. *Fausto Appetente Die*, no. 6.

38. Simon Tugwell, ed., *Early Dominicans*, 63.

39. *Fausto Appetente Die*, no. 11

40. Lawrence C. Landini, "Saint Anthony of Padua, Portrait of the Ideal Preacher," *Josephinum Journal of Theology* 4, no. 2 (1997): 51.

41. Ibid.

42. Ibid.
43. Ibid.
44. Ibid.
45. Ibid., 52.
46. Ibid.
47. Ibid., 53.
48. Ibid., 53–54.
49. Ibid., 54.
50. Ibid.
51. Ibid.
52. Ibid., 55.
53. Ibid., 58–59.
54. Ibid.
55. Ibid., 58.
56. Ibid.
57. Wilson, 78.
58. Ibid., 84–85.
59. Thomas Aquinas, *The Sermon-Conferences of St. Thomas Aquinas on the Apostles' Creed*, trans. Nicholas Ayo (Notre Dame: University of Notre Dame Press, 1988), cited in Old, 3:419n.
60. Old, 3:419–23.

Chapter 7
Preaching in the Reformation Period and Beyond

As we have said before, and now I say again,
if anyone preaches to you a gospel other than the one that you received,
let that one be accursed!

Galatians 1:9

R EFORM WAS THE BANNER carried by both Protestants in Germany and Switzerland, and Catholics in Italy in the sixteenth century. The rebellion of Luther, Calvin, Zwingli, and others, produced a deep split in the Western Church. The Church responded to the Lutheran challenge by convening the Council of Trent (1545–63). The years after Trent were a period of retrenchment, following the Protestant revolt. In addition, the Council addressed the need for reform in the Church. This period also saw a new missionary zeal and a renewed emphasis on the fundamentals of Catholicism. In the West, the Church was expanding. The sixteenth and seventeenth centuries witnessed one of the great missionary movements, with the Church branching out beyond the Mediterranean basin, to the Caribbean, Indian, and Pacific Oceans. The Spanish took the Gospel to the New World; Saint Francis Xavier spread the Faith in the Indies and China. In the East, the Church was struggling against the Turks, and prevailed at the Battle of Lepanto, a victory attributed largely to the power of the rosary. The successes of the experimental sciences in the seventeenth and eighteenth centuries undermined the Aristotelian world view, and ushered in the Enlightenment, providing new challenges to the Faith..

In this chapter, we examine several Catholic homilists who were distinguished for their eloquence and spiritual depth. They were part of a great movement within the Church to respond to the Protestant Reformation and its aftermath. The preachers of the Counter-Reformation moved away from the Scholastic (thematic) approach to homilies, and toward a more evangelical and ethical approach. In places like Italy, the principles of classic rhetoric were being studied and applied to sacred oratory in a new and unique way. We will see examples of this new approach in the homilies that follow.

PASTORAL PREACHING

The Protestant Reformation, the Catholic Counter-Reformation, and the spreading of the Gospel to the New World were the three key developments of the sixteenth century. Questions of doctrine, such as the Real Presence, the Sacrifice of the Mass, and the ministerial priesthood were raised, along with questions about the missionary methodology that took place when Spanish, Portuguese, French, and other European nations landed on the shores of the New World. Pastoral preaching was tied into the spread and defense of Catholic doctrine and practice. The Catholic Reform movement of the sixteenth century had both an inward and outward flow. The inward flow was in the direction of internal Church reform. The dynamic forces of the Catholic Counter-Reformation were medieval piety, Christian humanism, Scholasticism, and deep veneration for the Church as the bride of Christ. The "internal mission" of the Church was its attempt to reform itself in light of Protestant critiques. Then there was an outward movement of the Church. This was the spread of the Gospel to the Americas, Africa, and Asia. Christian missionaries, Franciscans and Jesuits in particular, accompanied public officials, merchants, and soldiers across the globe to plant the flag of Christian nations in the far corners of the earth. This movement required missionaries to adapt to the native customs and languages they found. Educating the young, bringing Protestants back to the Church, defending the Faith, translating the Gospel into new languages, and serving the poor were characteristic tasks of sixteenth-century evangelists.

Saint Anthony Zaccaria: Reforming Preacher

Saint Anthony (1502–1539) was born in Cremona in Lombardy in 1502. His life was dedicated to the service of others. He studied medicine at Padua, and received a medical doctorate at age twenty-two. Later he decided to devote his life to saving souls rather than bodies. He entered the seminary and was ordained at the age of twenty-six. In Milan, he worked for the reform of a decadent society. He took Saint Paul for his model and patron. His days were filled with activity, preaching in churches and on street corners among the people. After his ordination to the priesthood, he founded the Society of Clerics Regular of Saint Paul, also known as the Barnabites. At the very time that Martin Luther was dividing the Church in Germany, Anthony and his followers were drawing half-hearted

Catholics back to their faith. He encouraged the collaboration of lay people in the work of the apostolate, frequent Communion, Forty Hours devotions, the ringing of church bells at 3:00 pm on Fridays, the hour of Our Lord's death. In addition, he had his priests conduct parish missions. He stirred up the flame of faith in the Catholic people. His Society did much to reform the morals of the faithful. He died at Cremona in 1539 at the age of thirty-six, exhausted from his work of preaching, teaching, and traveling. His feast day is July 5.

The Preaching of Saint Anthony

Saint Anthony's preaching was typical of many in the sixteenth century. It was clear, colorful, rooted in Sacred Scripture, and faithful to the Church's Magisterium. But there is also a spiritual quality that reflects the depth of his spirituality. There was renewed enthusiasm for literary and oral eloquence during the Italian Renaissance. Ancient writers were carefully studied, and oral techniques were refined. This enthusiasm reached its peak in the sixteenth and seventeenth centuries in Italy, France, Spain, and elsewhere. Saint Anthony shared this enthusiasm, and his homilies reflect his understanding of rhetoric and its employment in ecclesiastical settings.

In the following homily (excerpts of which are presented here), Saint Anthony talks about being "fools" for the sake of Christ. It is based on readings found on Saturday of the twenty-second week in Ordinary Time, Year II.

Homily: The follower of the apostle Paul

We are fools for Christ's sake: our holy guide and most revered patron was speaking about himself and the rest of the apostles, and about the other people who profess the Christian and apostolic way of life. But there is no reason, dear brothers, that we should be surprised or afraid; *for the disciple is not superior to his teacher, nor the slave to his master.* We should love and feel compassion for those who oppose us, rather than abhor and despise them, since they harm themselves and do us good, and adorn us with crowns of everlasting glory while they incite God's anger against themselves. And even more than this, we should pray for them and not be overcome by evil, but overcome evil by goodness. We should heap good works *like red-hot coals* of burning love *upon their heads*, as our Apostle urges us to do, so that when they become aware of our tolerance and gentleness they may undergo a change of heart and be prompted to turn in love to God.

In his mercy God has chosen us, unworthy as we are, out of the world, to serve him and thus to advance in goodness and to bear the greatest possible fruit of love in patience. We should take encouragement not only from the hope of sharing in the glory of God's children, but also from the hardships we undergo.

Consider your calling, dearest brothers; if we wish to think carefully about it we shall see readily enough that its basis demands that we who have set out to follow, admittedly from afar, the footsteps of the holy apostles and the other soldiers of Christ, should not be unwilling to share in their sufferings as well. *We should keep running steadily in the race we have started, not losing sight of Jesus, who leads us in our faith and brings it to perfection.* And so since we have chosen such a great Apostle as our guide and father and claim to follow him, we should try to put his teaching and example into practice in our lives. Such a leader should not be served by faint-hearted troops, nor should such a parent find his sons unworthy of him. (J.A. Gabutio, *Historia Congregationis Clericorum Regularium S. Pauli*, 1,8)

Saint Robert Bellarmine: Champion of the Counter-Reformation

Saint Robert Bellarmine (1542–1621) was a bishop and Doctor of the Church in the sixteenth century. He was a brilliant theologian, and a vigorous advocate of the Counter-Reformation. At a time when the Church was reacting strongly to the Protestant revolt, Bellarmine developed an effective antithesis to Protestant teachings, and recovered some of the Church's own treasures in the process. Robert Bellarmine was born in the foothills of central Italy, Montepulciano, south of Florence. He was the third of ten children in a noble family where prayer and service were stressed. He came under the influence of the Jesuits early in his life, and joined the order in 1560. After finishing his studies in Rome, Robert was sent to teach in a Jesuit school in the Piedmont. There he studied and taught Greek, focusing on Greek orators and rhetoricians, such as Demosthenes and Isocrates, Old writes.[1] He continues, "The Jesuits were enthusiastic supporters of the humanistic studies of the Renaissance, and the study of Greek orators would be almost as important as the Latin orators Cicero and Quintilian."[2]

Bellarmine earned a reputation as an eloquent homilist early in his priestly ministry. He went to study at the University of Louvain in Flanders, Belgium, in 1569, spending seven years there, and was the first Jesuit to be appointed chair of theology.[3] He is most noted for his three-volume *Disputationes de controversiis Christianae Fidei adversus hujus temporis haereticos*, published between 1586 and 1593. His sermons were so powerful that people came from across Europe to hear them, and many hearts were converted. He was a professor of theology at the Roman College for twelve years. There he wrote a work of several volumes defending the faith. He also composed two catechisms that were used for several generations. In 1598, Robert was named a cardinal against his wishes, and was appointed to the see of Capua in 1602, where he served as an outstanding pastor.

Cardinal Bellarmine was an advisor to five popes and was involved in the Galileo controversy. Galileo sought to prove the Copernican theory that the earth revolved around the sun, known as the *heliocentric* theory. Galileo and Bellarmine were friends; but the Cardinal was given the unpleasant task of informing Galileo of the findings of a council of theological advisors to Pope Paul V. That council ruled in February 1616 that it was bad science, and probably heresy, to teach as fact that the sun is the center of the universe, that the earth is not at the center of the world, and that it moves.

This ruling was in accord with the accepted science, and with the opinions of both Catholic and Protestant biblical interpreters, of the time. Bellarmine met with Galileo, advised him of the panel's ruling, and ordered him to cease teaching his theories as fact. He also urged Galileo to refrain from discussion of biblical interpretations of such matters. In the end, Galileo recanted, but his theory that the earth revolved around the sun proved largely correct. Bellarmine struggled with his duty, but performed it out of love for Holy Mother Church.

He died in 1621, and was declared a Doctor of the Church in 1931. Bellarmine is the patron saint of catechists and catechumens. His feast day is September 17.

The Preaching of Saint Robert Bellarmine

There is much we can learn from the sermons of St. Robert Bellarmine. He emphasized the preaching of the Word as one of the most important functions of his priestly office. Bellarmine saw biblical examples of great preaching in Saint John the Baptist (Matt. 3:3), the Apostle Peter (Acts 3:14–41), and the Apostle Paul (1 Cor. 1:17). Recalling the ancient practice of the preacher delivering his sermon while seated in his *cathedra* as the congregation stood, Bellarmine said the people are responsible for receiving the message delivered by the preacher.[4] In speaking of the utility of God's Word, Bellarmine draws our attention to three images Scripture uses for preaching the Word. He calls God's Word *the seed* from which we are born again, *the bread* by which we are nourished, and *the sword* by which we are defended.[5] Bellarmine refers to several New Testament texts (e.g., Luke 8:11, James 1:21, and 1 Pet. 1:23), and concludes that faith grows, and conversion from sin is brought about, by the preaching of the Word.[6]

Bellarmine clearly identified preaching as a source of conversion and renewal in the Church. He deeply appreciated the power of the Word to touch hearts and win souls. As the tiny *mustard seed* produces a large tree, Bellarmine's preaching produced results well beyond his immediate sphere of influence (Matt. 13:31–32). For Bellarmine, the truth preached and proclaimed in the Word enlightens minds and nourishes hearts. As *bread* feeds the body, so the "bread" of Bellarmine's preaching satisfied hungry souls. As a sword cuts, so the "sword" of Bellarmine's teaching "cut to the heart" of his subjects. Old, taking up Ephesians 6:17, calls the Word of God "the sword of the Spirit."[7] He adds the word of Hebrews 4:12, "Indeed, the word of God is living and effective, sharper than any two-edged sword." For Bellarmine, the two "edges" of the sword are the threats of God on one side and the promises of God on the other.[8] The threats temper and restrain the listener, and the promises sustain and encourage the listener.

Bellarmine gave a series of sermons on the Beatitudes in Capua. He displays his profound understanding of biblical exegesis as well as his love for patristic sources. He continues the practice of using "examples, illustrations, and anecdotes that had become widely used in the sermons of the preaching orders of the Middle Ages."[9] Christ (in particular, His death on the cross) is the "ultimate exemplum" for the Christian.[10]

Cardinal Bellarmine wrote a short essay on preaching titled *De ratione formandae concionis.* This brief essay provides insights into the ministry of the Word as the Counter-Reformation proclaimed it. He begins by explaining two reasons for preaching: first, preaching presents the virtues that ought to be cultivated and vices that ought to be avoided. "Second, preaching should motivate people to live the virtues they have been taught."[11] Here he echoes the decrees of the Council of Trent, which stressed preaching as the primary office of bishops (Council of Trent, 5th Session, nn. 1203–05 [1546]). Bellarmine saw himself as a moral catechist above all, and he saw the purpose of his sermons as being to persuade his listeners to live according to Christian teaching. Bellarmine defined preaching as "the art of persuasion."[12] Therefore, he and other Christian preachers turned to the ancient writer and lawyer Cicero to learn rhetorical skills.

Speakers in the Counter-Reformation Church thus found their literary model in the orations of the law court. "The oration of antiquity took shape in the court of law, where the object was to convince jurors."[13] Sermons, then, became orations or moral appeals, and Counter-Reformation homilists used this model to persuade their listeners to live according to Christian doctrine and morality.

Hughes Old describes the process Bellarmine used to prepare sermons:

> Regarding the actual preparation of a sermon, Bellarmine tells us, the first thing a preacher needs to do is figure out the scope his sermon should have as a whole and then how its different parts fit in. Having decided that, he needs to gather together the reasons, applications and examples which are helpful in achieving his purpose. When it comes to teaching . . . one must search out the genuine and literal sense of the passage. From there one needs to speak of the dogmas of the faith and the rules for living that have been developed by the Church.[14]

Old tells us that Bellarmine noted three qualities of an effective homilist: "zeal, wisdom, and eloquence." Bellarmine provided a biblical figure for this, saying these qualities are "symbolized by the tongues of fire, which appeared above the Apostles on the Day of Pentecost. . . . The heat of this Pentecostal fire points to zeal, the splendor to wisdom, and the form of tongues to eloquence."[15]

The Pentecostal image and setting are highly appropriate images for preaching. This Medieval symbolism shows preaching to be "a divine anointing, a charism conferred by the outpouring of the Holy Spirit, and a divinely given gift," according to Old.[16]

Bellarmine talks about the importance of prayer and study for the preaching ministry. Prayerful contemplation must be accompanied by formal study in order to produce the effects the homilist desires. Both of these aspects enhance the quality of the homilist himself, which itself produces better preaching.

He distinguishes three kinds of sermons. The *expository sermon*, "the purpose of which is to explain Scripture," is the first kind. Augustine's sermons on John's Gospel, Basil's sermons on the *Hexaemeron*, and Chrysostom's sermons on Genesis are examples of expository preaching. The second kind of sermon is the *thematic sermon*, which "treats a particular subject or theme." Examples include Chrysostom's sermons to the people of Antioch, and the sermons of Augustine, Leo, and the other Church Fathers. Finally, there is the *explanation/exhortation sermon*, which "partly explains Scripture and partly exhorts people to virtue and living a good Christian life."[17] Chrysostom's sermons on the Pauline epistles are a good illustration of this kind of preaching.[18]

Robert Bellarmine brought rhetorical eloquence, intellectual discipline, and prayerful asceticism to his pulpit ministry. He spoke from and to both the head and the heart, as he addressed his congregations. His methods are best understood in the context of the Counter-Reformation/Baroque era. He is an excellent example of Jesuit preaching, and a fine model for homilists in our era.

The following is a brief summary of a sermon the saint gave on the Third Sunday after Easter (1962 calendar). It discusses the text 1 Peter 2:11–19. He talks about the fruits of conversion and the need for good example.

Homily: On Good Example

1. Argument: St. Peter teaches us: (a) that we should abstain from carnal desires; (b) the reason—because we are pilgrims on this earth and this is not our home; (c) the effect produced—conversion of evil-doers and their greater respect for us.

2. Abstain: From carnal desires—not merely sexual, but any desire which is not in accordance with the principles of redemption, such as excessive desires for honours, riches, etc. (Cf. Gal. 5:19). We must not consent to these desires—that is what is meant by abstaining from them. This we must do, not from human respect or fear, but to dry up the fountain of temptation.

3. The cause: Pilgrims do not bother very much about the land through which they are passing, neither do they purchase stable goods such as houses or lands there, but only enough to support life. They spend as little as possible, they do not desire to be well-known, on the contrary, they try to pass unobserved; they remember and long for their homeland, making their way thither as soon as possible, especially if they know that their time is short and that the way into that country may be closed to them. Thus lived our Lord and the saints, careless of worldly things.

In order to know if we are on the right road as pilgrims we have only to ask ourselves if we are living an honest life, if we are constantly looking towards our fatherland and if we are increasing in the knowledge of God.

Our knowledge of God can increase either extensively, that is, by an increase in the things we know about God, or intensively, by an ever deeper penetration into those things we already know. He who has but a confused notion of what is meant by God, the Judgement, eternity, etc., needs to perfect himself in the knowledge of these things in order to reach love and fear. Many, even after a long life, have hardly advanced at all in their knowledge of the future life, and we must repeat to them constantly those words: "Finish your journey while you still have the light, for fear darkness should overtake you" (Jn. 12:35).

The impediments on the road are carnal desires, which blind the intellect, so that we do not reach the knowledge we should have. They can change a man into a chained beast who is as blind as was Samson, one who is always going round in circles without reaching anything definite. We must mortify ourselves always—a difficult thing, because we are made up of soul and body.

4. The fruit: Kindness towards sinners—a difficult thing at times. Yet Lot could live respected in Sodom.

The conversion of sinners, who even when they murmur against the good cannot but admire them, and this is often the first preparation to receive the grace of God. How many times did St. Paul praise the patience of St. Stephen, and St. Augustine that of his mother!

The acquisition of true liberty, even though one may be a subject, a slave even. It is the liberty of the sons of God, those who are in a state of grace and so free from sin and capable of earning merits for heaven. Lastly we shall obtain the final and true liberty of the eternal joys of heaven. This is the liberty which comes from the mortification of carnal desires and which purifies our minds to know that truth which alone can make us free (Jn. 8:32). (*The Preacher's Encyclopedia*, vol. 1, 572–3.)

Saint Charles Borromeo: Pastoral Preacher

Saint Charles Borromeo (1538–1584) was a greatly respected bishop and Counter-Reformation figure. Born in Italy on October 2, 1538, he was a talented and serious young man. He had no formal theological training, but a good background in literature and law. He read many classical and patristic authors, and by the time he was twenty-one, he held doctorates in civil and canon law. Within a period of one year, he was called to Rome by his uncle, Pope Pius IV, and made cardinal and administrator of Milan, and Secretary of State. He worked closely with the pope at the Council of Trent, when many topics led to heated arguments. Several times it seemed as if the Council would break up and everyone would return home. Charles, working behind the scenes, kept people together and on task.

Borromeo zealously implemented the reforms of the Council of Trent in the Diocese of Milan, where he lived in 1565. He founded three seminaries in his diocese, and he promoted the work of the Confraternity of Christian Doctrine (CCD) in his parishes. He held five provincial councils and eleven diocesan synods. The first, second, and fourth Provincial Synods of Milan touched on preaching in their various decrees.[19] He set up orphanages, homes for neglected women, hospitals, and colleges. He tried to reform the lives of priests and religious. He founded a group of priests called the Oblates of Saint Ambrose (now the Oblates of Saint Charles) to assist him. Once Charles tried to reform a religious order whose members became so angry they tried to kill him. The attempt, made while he prayed, failed.

In 1567, a plague broke out in Milan and famine accompanied it. So many people were ill and dying that even city officials fled the area—but not Charles. He stayed with the sick and cared for them. He ate little and slept only a few hours a night on boards. During the plague, he sold all his possessions and borrowed large sums of money so he could feed the sixty- to seventy-thousand people who came to him for help.

Charles died on November 3, 1584, at age forty-six, worn out from caring for others, and bearing the burdens of his position. He was considered a model pastor by many, including Saint Francis de Sales. He is a patron of catechists and catechumens. His feast day is November 4.

The Preaching of Saint Charles Borromeo

Saint Charles has long been recognized as an important contributor to the history of preaching. He was a forceful and articulate preacher. He spoke from deep love and concern for his congregation, whether they were priests or lay people. In his day, the material content of sermons was shifting. "Besides the themes of vices and virtues, punishment and reward," Frederick J. McGinnis tells us, "the matter necessary for salvation" was to be emphasized. Preachers were encouraged to "proclaim the truth and avoid debate with Protestants on controversial topics." McGinnis continues:

> In asserting Catholic truth, the [preacher] is to demonstrate this with texts from Scripture and passages from the Fathers. The result will not be the (traditional) "scholastic" sermon, in which a question is raised (utrum) at the outset and then argfued to its conclusion, but teaching the faith by proclamation and authority, confirming tyhis with Scripture, substantiating it from tradition, and (as will be the case in later decades) asserting the right to do so on the vasis of the apostolic succession, the decrees of the councils, and the writings of the Fathers.[20]

Saint Charles reflected this trend in his episcopal ministry. He wrote a work titled *Instructiones*, in which he proposes the content for sermons. They include mortal and venial sins, occasions of sin, virtues, the sacraments, and sacramentals of the Church.[21] As he sees it, the Christian congregation is beset by the forces of Satan, and so needs a message of conversion and renewal. The moralistic, vaguely Stoical, framework of Borromeo's preaching stands in stark contrast to the doctrinal and affective emphasis in preaching in certain parts of Catholicism, especially early in the sixteenth century.

Despite a natural aversion to public speaking, and despite a weak voice and a slurred speech pattern that often made him difficult to understand, Saint Charles eventually overcame his reservations, and preached on a regular basis.[22]

Borromeo led by example. He expected his priests and fellow bishops to prepare their homilies well. In addition, he expected them to be authentic witnesses of the Gospel they proclaimed. Therefore, he put these things into practice first in his own life.

Hughes Old describes his preaching in this way:

> [Borromeo] was a competent preacher and he preached frequently, sometimes as many as three or four times a day. His sermons were usually homilies in the patristic sense. He moved away from the thematic sermons of Scholasticism. His sermons do, on the other hand, have elements of high oratory in the sense of classical rhetoric. The important thing was that he set the example. He actually became a preaching archbishop, as Ambrose of Milan, his ancient predecessor had been. In fact, the parallels between the two men are remarkable.[23]

Old makes several other important points about Charles Borromeo's preaching, with respect to his fulfillment of the decrees of the Council of Trent. First, Trent called preaching "the principal office of bishops." This statement was in response to the decline of preaching by bishops, who became feudal rulers who led armies, and managed large estates, while leaving the ministry of the Word primarily to others.

Second, Trent declared that bishops were responsible for leading and controlling the preaching ministry. They set the guidelines, and issued norms and directives for this vital ministry.

Third, Trent defined preaching as exhorting congregations to live Christian virtues and avoid anti-Christian vices. "The Counter-Reformation pulpit constantly threatened the punishments that would fall on sinners and heretics, and pointed to the glories which would be the reward of the faithful and the virtuous," Old says.[24] Borromeo applied these points, and the other aspects of the Council, to his diocese of Milan.

Fourth, Trent established the seminary system in order to standardize and regulate the training of future priests, whose training had been sporadic, and often poorly executed, in the centuries preceding it. Borromeo "wanted his seminarians to get beyond the old Scholastic method of preaching, and adapt a more humanistic and patristic approach."[25] Borromeo provided them with the writings of such famous Christian writers as Ambrose, Augustine, Leo the Great, Chrysostom, and Gregory the Great. He expected preachers to be knowledgeable in theological matters, and also to possess pastoral skills.

Borromeo defined an able preacher as one well-versed in theological topics; the apostolic and ecclesiastical traditions; and the writings and homilies of the Fathers, their ordinances, spiritual interpretations, and ecclesiastical rites and rituals. He also considered it necessary to know Church history; the ancient canons, laws of popes, and conciliar decrees; the precepts of mystical theology; methods and practices of mental prayer; matters of conscience; and the pertinent passages on Christian mores and virtues that could "enkindle the faithful with pious desires."[26] Knowledge of Hebrew and Greek would also be highly useful and were strongly recommended.

Finally, Borromeo encouraged the writing of preaching manuals using the literary methods of Christian humanism, rather than the literary methods of Scholasticism. Therefore, ancient writers such as Aristotle, Cicero, and Quintilian, as well as Augustine's *De doctrina Christiana,* were carefully studied.[27]

Old summarizes Charles Borromeo's influence as follows:

> If Scholasticism showed the preacher how to teach the people Christian moral-
> ity and if the Protestant Reformers showed preachers how to expound the Word
> of God, the Counter-Reformation showed preachers how to move the wills of
> their congregations. This was the direction in which the new spirituality of the
> Jesuits was pointing the Catholic Church. The problem was the will, as the
> Jesuits saw it, and it was the will which had to be moved.[28]

The post-Reformation preachers saw their mission as moving the will, to bring about contrition, and

> to effect moral reform and a return to the Church's channels of grace. The
> Catholic preacher, moreover, could measure repentance by the numbers of
> Christians returning to the confessional, taking whipcords, shedding tears, and
> receiving the Eucharist. Sinners could give visible evidence of an active coop-
> eration with God's grace in the warfare against vices.[29]

Charles Borromeo epitomized an entire shift in thinking and emphasis. As the nephew of a Medici pope, and as a lawyer trained in Renaissance humanism, he understood the power politics of his day and how preaching could play a role in it. He knew that, as a successor of Ambrose of Milan, he was in a position to shape Christian society, and with single-hearted devotion he gave his life to doing just that.

The following sermon was given during the last synod he attended. In this homily, Charles talks about the importance of preparation for spiritual activities. It is partly based on Wisdom 7:7, which is read on the 28th Sunday of Year B.

Homily: Practice what you preach

> I admit that we are all weak, but if we want help, the Lord God has given us the
> means to find it easily. One priest may wish to lead a good, holy life, as he
> knows he should. He may wish to be chaste and to reflect heavenly virtues in
> the way he lives. Yet he does not resolve to use suitable means, such as pen-
> ance, prayer, the avoidance of evil discussions and harmful and dangerous
> friendships. Another priest complains that as soon as he comes into church to
> pray the Office or celebrate Mass, a thousand thoughts fill his mind and distract
> him from God. But what was he doing in the sacristy before he came out for the
> office or for Mass? How did he prepare? What means did he use to collect his
> thoughts and to remain recollected?

Would you like me to teach you how to grow from virtue to virtue and how, if you are already recollected at prayer, you can be even more attentive next time, and so give God more pleasing worship? Listen, and I will tell you. If a tiny spark of God's love already burns within you, do not expose it to the wind, for it may get blown out. Keep the stove tightly shut so that it will not lose its heat and grow cold. In other words, avoid distractions as well as you can. Stay quiet with God. Do not spend your time in useless chatter.

If teaching and preaching is your job, then study diligently and apply yourself to whatever is necessary for doing the job well. Be sure that you first preach by the way you live. If you do not, people will notice that you say one thing, but live otherwise, and your words will bring only cynical laughter and a derisive shake of the head.

Are you in charge of a parish? If so, do not neglect the parish of your own soul, do not give yourself to others so completely that you have nothing left for yourself. You have to be mindful of your people without being forgetful of yourself.

My brothers, you must realize that for us churchmen nothing is more necessary than meditation. We must meditate before, during and after everything we do. The prophet says: *I will pray, and then I will understand.* When you administer the sacraments, meditate on what you are doing. When you celebrate Mass, reflect on the sacrifice you are offering. When you pray the Office, think about the words you are saying and the Lord to whom you are speaking. When you take care of your people, meditate on the Lord's blood that has washed them clean. In this way, *all that you do becomes a work of love.*

This is the way we can easily overcome the countless difficulties we have to face day after day, which, after all, are part of our work: in meditation we find the strength to bring Christ to birth in ourselves and in other men. (*Acta Ecclesiae Mediolanensis, Mediolani* 1599, 1177–1178)

Jacques Benigne Bossuet: French Pulpit Master

Jacques Bossuet (1627–1704) was a famous French preacher, theologian, and the bishop of Meaux in northern France. The fifth son of a judge in the Parliament of Dijon, he was educated at the Jesuit school at Dijon, and later attended school at Metz. In 1642, he went to Paris, where he entered the college of Navarre to study for the priesthood. He studied under Vincent de Paul, and was ordained in 1652. His first assignment was in Metz, where he studied and engaged in controversy with Protestants.

Bossuet moved back to Paris in 1659. His fame grew, and he became a preacher at the royal court. Bossuet was largely responsible for the conversion of Marshal Turenne from Protestantism in 1668. The next year he was appointed Bishop of Condom [sic] in Gascony, southern France, and delivered his first great "Funeral Oration." He was consecrated in 1670, but resigned when elected to the French Academy in 1671. For the next eleven years he tutored the nine-year-old Dauphin (1670–81). He published three classical works: *Discourse on*

Universal History, Treatise on the Knowledge of God and Oneself, Art of Governing Drawn from the Words of Holy Scripture.

In 1681, Bossuet transferred to the see of Meaux. At a clerical assembly in 1682, he was instrumental in securing French clerical support for the Four Gallican Articles, which he himself wrote. In his zeal for the Catholic faith, he approved the Revocation of the Edict of Nantes (1685), and directed many publications against Protestants. At the same time, he worked for the reunion of Christians. He conducted a long correspondence with the philosopher, G. W. Leibniz (1646–1716). He also wrote French devotional literature. Bossuet died in 1704.

The Preaching of Jacques Benigne Bossuet

Jacques Bossuet was one of the most brilliant homilists in French history. His preaching must be seen in the context of the Counter-Reformation, and the flowering of French culture associated with the reign of Louis XIV, the Sun King. Louis encouraged and supported eloquent preaching. He appreciated the importance of sacred oratory, and invested time and money in it. Bossuet and other French homilists "preached the Word of God in such polished eloquence that even the most cultured despisers of the Christian faith listened with admiration," writes Hughes Old.[30]

The preaching of Bossuet and others was a response to the learned sermons of the Reformers, and in response to the needs of French intellectuals. Jacques Bossuet was an eloquent orator, a deep thinker, a leading theologian, and an adviser to the King. He was also a great spokesman for the Church. He addressed Protestants and Catholics alike in an attempt to articulate the Catholic faith. He possessed both outward and inward gifts for preaching. He had an impressive presence, a pleasing voice, an easy manner, and a clear presentation. He was a precise thinker and a passionate defender of the Faith. He studied ancient Greek and Latin literature, including the writings of St. Augustine. The fire of his passion was fueled by hours spent with the Lord in prayerful contemplation of the sacred mysteries of salvation. He also inspired a humble parish priest, who would become the model for parish priests two centuries later.

We can learn much by studying the sermons of Bossuet. He quotes ancient and contemporary sources in introducing his homily (e.g., the Christian emperor Theodosius). In a sermon for the Feast of the Presentation, for example, he distinguishes three kinds of law: directive, constraining, and enticing. Jesus and Mary submitted to a *directive law*, which required them to perform certain rituals regarding their first-born son; Simeon submitted to a *constraining law* of death, which limits our earthly existence; and Anna through her bodily penance, overcame the *enticing law* of sin, which tempts us to rebel against God.[31] In addressing the intellectuals of his day, he analyzes law in terms of freedom from pleasures, passions, and sensual delights. By regulating life, God acknowledges man's intelligence and free will. He goes on to discuss the figures of Simeon and Anna in relation to these laws.

Bossuet often uses three-point homilies. For instance, in a sermon on the virtue of honor, he urges his listeners: (1) to be mature in their thinking, (2) to avoid outward honor for the purpose of concealing inward evil, and (3) to recognize that true honor needs no praise.

Hughes Old concludes that Bossuet was an "evangelistic preacher" and an "apologist for the faith," rather than a "great expositor." He had a good grasp of the Old Testament prophets; his sermons were topical or thematic. Old remarks: "If Bossuet saw Louis XIV as the Theodosius of his day, he never followed the example of Ambrose and confronted the Sun King with his all too public sins. In the end he was more the courtier than the prophet. And yet he was a great orator."[32] His greatness lay in the eloquence and clarity he brought to preaching, as well as his determination to convince his congregation of the correctness of his position. All good homilists need to persuade their listeners to live out the Word preached and proclaimed. Bossuet tells us this can be done tactfully and effectively.

The following is a detailed outline of a sermon Bossuet preached in Paris, at the chapel of the Daughters of Providence, in 1659. It was based on readings used for Septuagesima Sunday in the 1962 calendar, and on the twenty-fifth Sunday in Ordinary Time, Year A, in the 1970 calendar. He talks about the relationship between the rich and the poor, and their place in the Kingdom.

Homily: The last will be first

1. *The last and the first*: The world clings to the fortunate ones of this earth while it abandons the poor to their misery, which is why the prophet says: "The poor are in thy hands" (Ps. 9. 14). God sees and takes care of the poor, that is why, as priest, as preacher and advocate of the poor, I am going to speak to you of them. The phrase of the Lord about the "last [being] the first" will be completely fulfilled when those just who were despised by the world occupy the first places in heaven. But it also begins to be fulfilled in this life with the foundation of the Church, a wonderful city, whose foundations were laid by God. Christ, on coming into this world, in order to organize a revolt against the order established by pride, inaugurated a policy completely opposed to that of the world. This opposition can be reduced to three things:

(a) In the world, the advantages and the first places are reserved for the rich; in the kingdom of Christ, to the poor.

(b) In the world the poor serve the rich, and would even appear to have been born for that purpose; in the Church the rich are only admitted on condition that they serve the poor.

(c) In the world the favors and privileges are reserved for the powerful; in the Church the blessings are for the poor.

2. *The citizens in the Church*: In the time of the synagogue, to encourage them, besides heaven they were promised worldly goods; but in the Church there is no word about the latter, riches are despised and the affliction of the

cross is substituted for them. The rich, who had the first places in the synagogue, do not exist as a class apart in the Church, whose citizens are the poor.
Do you wish to see this in our Lord's preaching? Then listen to those words in
which he orders his servants to go out and bring in from the highways the poor
and the needy.

Christ was sent to preach the Gospel to the poor (Lk. 4:18). To fulfill his
mission it is to them mainly that he directs his preaching, and in his greatest
sermon, that on the Mount, he does not address the rich except it be to reprove
their pride. "Blessed are you who are poor," he says to them, "the kingdom of
heaven is yours" (Lk. 6:20). If heaven belongs to the poor, then so does the
Church; and if she belongs to them, it is because they are the first to enter. So it
was, in fact, as St. Paul proves (1 Cor. 1. 26). The early Church was practically
a Church of the poor, and the rich who entered it had to strip themselves of
their goods and lay them at the feet of the apostles. So far did the Holy Spirit go
in his efforts to make clear the essence of the Christian religion and the privileges of the poor as members of Christ . . . .

3. *The rich, servants of the poor*: If Christ promised nothing but afflictions
and crosses, then there is no reason to point out that he does not need the rich.
Why should he want them within his kingdom? So that they can build him temples of gold and precious stones? Do not imagine that he esteems such things
very highly. He accepts them merely as signs of piety and religion. When he
founds his religion directly, as distinct from that of the Old Law, he chooses the
most simple elements, such as water, bread, oil . . . . Instead of surrounding
himself with pomp, Christ has the poor around him.

Here is a secret I will make known to you (1 Cor. 15:51). Christ does not
need anything, and yet he has need of all things. He does not need anything because he is omnipotent; he needs all things, because he is merciful. Just as the
mercy of our innocent Jesus led him to load upon himself the miseries and
crimes of us all, so now, that same Jesus carries the same miseries in the persons of his poor . . . .

But if there were only poor within the Church, then who would help them?
That is why the rich are admitted. He could have used the angels for this task,
but he chose that men should be aided by their fellows. The love for his sons,
the poor, made him permit the entry of strangers, the rich. Do you see the miracle of poverty? The rich were strangers, and the service of the poor has given
them nationality. The rich had a contagious disease, and God permitted their
riches to act as a cure for it. Rich and poor should help one another. The poor
carry a heavy burden, and the task of the rich is to help them bear it. But the
rich also carry a burden. As Augustine says: Who would believe that the burden
of the poor is their necessity and that of the rich their abundance?

I know that there are worldly people who long for such a burden as this;
but a day will come when such worldly errors end and they come to a judgement in which they will know the true weight of those riches they coveted. Do
not wait until that dreadful hour. Help one another to carry your burdens. You
rich, carry something of the weight of the poor, and remember that, as you
lighten his burden, so do you remove some of the weight of your own . . . .

Without this share in the privileges of the poor there is no salvation for the
rich. And privileges do belong to the poor, for theirs is the kingdom and the
first places in it. It is easy to understand. In every kingdom, privileges are re-

served for those who are nearest to the Ruler, either by birth or office. It is the ruler who distributes them. You know perfectly well that those nearest and dearest to Christ are the poor. The crown of his monarch is one of thorns, his throne a manger and a cross; his whole life one of suffering. Therefore it is not the rich who are nearest to him or who enjoy his privileges. Do not despise poverty; for it the world thinks of it as something foul, the King of glory has taken it for his spouse and has granted it his favours.

4. *The right use of riches*: And what does the Gospel reserve for the rich? Read it through and you will find nothing but reproof. Woe to you, rich! (Lk. 6:24). Do you not tremble at this curse hurled at you by the very instrument of our salvation? However, hold fast to your hope because if the privileges are the right of the poor, still you can enjoy them also, provided you draw near to the poor to receive them at their hands. You who are rich know now the source from which you can obtain heaven's graces: the poor. Do you wish to wipe away the memory of your sins? Then redeem them with almsdeeds (Dan. 4:24). Do you long for God's mercy? Seek it at the hands of the poor by being merciful to them! Do you wish to enter into the kingdom? The door is open wide to you, says Christ, provided you have the poor to lead you in.

Therefore grace, mercy, pardon of sin and the very kingdom itself are all in the hands of the poor, and the rich cannot enter unless they are received by the poor. How rich you are, you who are poor! And in what real misery you live who are rich! If you live attached to your worldly goods then you will find yourselves deprived for ever of the graces of the New Testament and the only thing left to you will be that terrible curse: Woe to you who are rich.[33]

MISSION PREACHING

Christ the Lord spent His life proclaiming the Gospel and spreading the Kingdom. He gave the Church a missionary mandate to continue His work. Mission work was first carried out by the twelve Apostles. Through them, the Gospel was carried to the distant corners of the world (e.g., Spain, Russia, Ethiopia, India). This missionary character was a key component of Europe's dynamic influence on world history.

Christopher Dawson describes the spread of Christianity in Europe:

Christianity first entered Western Europe as a missionary movement which originated in the Hellenistic cities of the Levant, and for centuries the men from the East—Paul, Irenaeus, Athanasius, Cassian, Theodore of Tarsus, and the Greek and Syrian Popes of the eighth century—played a leading part in laying the foundations of Western Christianity. In the age which followed the fall of the Empire, this process of transmission was continued, by the Christians of the Western provinces toward the barbarian peoples, as we see in St. Patrick's mission to Ireland, St. Amand's evangelization of Belgium and above all in the epoch-making work of Gregory the Great for the conversion of England.[34]

Preaching in the seventeenth to the eighteenth centuries was tied into several important historical developments. These developments caused tremendous upheavals in the Church and in the world, the effects of which are felt in our day. This period was marked by the Baroque, the Enlightenment, the fragmentation of science, and the ascendancy of rationalism.

The Baroque refers to an ornate style of art and architecture, which flourished in Italy, France, and Spain at this time, and which reflected the faith of the artists. The Enlightenment refers to a scientific spirit championed by men such as Locke, Hume, and Newton. This movement was generally hostile to Christianity as it over-emphasized the importance of reason, and cast doubt on the value of faith. Science and reason detached from faith and morality led to questions about human existence, questions with which we struggle in the twenty-first century.

The French Revolution, which caused the collapse of both the Church and the monarchy in France, deepened the skepticism held by many thinkers of this period. The revolution produced schism, war, moral depravity, and intellectual rejection of long-held truths. Preaching in this era aimed at strengthening the faith of believers and promoting a virtuous life. It laid the foundation for the modern era, in which the Church and world struggled to understand and relate to one another.

Saint Alphonsus Ligouri: Mission Preacher

Saint Alphonsus Maria Ligouri (1696–1787) was one of the great bishops of the eighteenth century. He was born on October 5, 1696, in Naples, Italy. He had a sharp mind, which he put to good use. From his earliest years, he cultivated Christian virtues and acquired a vast knowledge of sacred literature. Alphonsus acquired degrees in civil and canon law at age sixteen. He practiced law until he lost an important case through oversight, confusing one kind of law for another.

Disillusioned with the justice system, Alphonsus banded together with a group of mission preachers, and studied theology privately. Over his father's objections, he was ordained to the priesthood in 1726. He sought to spread the Gospel by word and deed. He devoted himself to Mary, the Mother of God. He visited the sick in hospitals, and spent many hours hearing confessions, and celebrating the other sacraments. He lived an active and vigorous life. He wore a hair shirt and exercised great discipline, including attaching small iron chains to his body. Pope Clement XIII promoted him to the Episcopal see of *Agata de Goti* (Saint Agatha of the Goths), which he presided over for thirteen years.

In 1732, Alphonsus reorganized a group of priests. When he suggested that he would draw up a rule whereby they would live in poverty and utmost simplicity, most of the priests deserted him. He stood his ground, however, and the numbers grew. With papal approval in 1749, they became known as the Congregation of the Most Holy Redeemer (the Redemptorists). They were a preaching order, dedicated to imitating Christ, particularly through evangelizing the poor.

In 1750, Pope Benedict XIV approved the rule and institute for women as well. The Redemptorists today number some 5,600 members.

In 1762, he was ordained a bishop, and continued his work in the Church. Controversies that dogged his Order throughout his lifetime were not settled before his death. He wrote approximately 100 books on subjects ranging from preaching to science. Among his writings are *The Glories of Mary* (1750), *The Great Means of Prayer* (1759), and *The Way of Salvation* (1767). He was recognized as a teacher in systematic and moral theology, which was intended to help both preachers and priests who were hearing confessions.

He died in 1787, and was declared a Doctor of the Church in 1871. He is the patron saint of confessors and moral theologians. His feast day is August 1.

The Preaching of Saint Alphonsus Ligouri

The Protestant Reformation of the sixteenth century sent shock waves all across Europe. The spirit of reform that helped foster it continued within the Catholic Church. An example of that spirit was the formation of the Oratory of Divine Love, under the leadership of Catherine of Genoa and others in the 1500s. The fruits of the Counter-Reformation included the renewal of religious orders, and the appearance of new societies, such as the Jesuits under St. Ignatius Loyola; a rebirth of mission work; a renewed emphasis on preaching; clarification of doctrine and discipline at the Council of Trent (1545–63); and an overhaul of the administrative machinery of the Church. Trent produced a seminary system, a catechism, a revised Latin liturgy, and a new Breviary, as well as an army of bishops and priests ready and willing to defend the Church against the Protestant reformers.

Saint Alphonsus Liguori was a key figure in the progress of the reforms in Italy. His gift for preaching was quickly recognized.

Saint Alphonsus published *Instructions to Preachers*, a work which laid out his methodology of preaching. Among the various suggestions he offers are:

- The homilist should purpose solely to seek the salvation of souls and pray to God for good fruits from his preaching.
- The homilist must be inflamed with God's love so he can set others on fire.
- Sermons should often cover the Last Things (Death, Judgment, Heaven, Hell), and move the sinner toward the love and mercy of God.
- Preachers should inculcate love and devotion to the Blessed Mother.
- Preachers should address the topic of bad confessions and the terrible consequences of making one.
- He lays out the parts of a discourse: the exordium, the proposition, the division, the introduction, the proof, the confutation, the amplification, the peroration or conclusion, the epilogue, and the appeal to the passions.
- There ought to be two or three central points in the homily.
- Scripture references should be clear and brief.

- Transitions should be clear.
- Homilists should suggest practical means of living the faith. Daily Mass, visits to the Blessed Sacrament and the Virgin Mary, the Act of Contrition, and invoking the names of Jesus and Mary are some examples.
- He recommends that young preachers write out their sermons and develop them in their own manner.
- Modulation of voice and succinctness of manner are important.
- The homilist should avoid gestures that are affected or too vehement.
- The length of sermons: Lenten sermons should not exceed an hour and the Sunday sermon no more than forty-five minutes.[35]

Paul Scott Wilson talks about Alphonsus' fascinating and detailed homiletic, which is collected in one volume of Alphonsus' *Works*. He describes various aspects of mission preaching, some of which are listed below:

First, missions would last for two or three weeks, led by two to twenty priests, and would be repeated every three or four years. They would follow the same pattern. There would be preaching for more than an hour in the morning and in the evening (Alphonsus himself would do the latter if he were present). His first sermon was on mortal sin and the need for confession. For several days thereafter he would preach *di terrore*, that is, on the fear of the Last Things (death, judgment, hell). For several additional days he preached on the discipline of the devout life. The remaining days would be occupied with the community, in turn, of children, unmarried women, married men and women. Meanwhile during the mission days, priests heard confessions and taught catechetical classes to small groups. Priests could neither take money nor ask for food, but were allowed to request shelter.

Second, in addition to the hour-long "great sermons," priests were to be skilled at four other kinds of exhortation. Daytime and evening exhortations were a form of 15- to 30-minute street preaching to encourage people to come to the church to hear the sermon. These were usually based on the words of a preceding hymn and followed a set structure: introduction and proposition, amplification, moral application, announcement of the mission's purpose and concluding with a "terrible Sentence" warning of the judgment that approached. In these last days of the mission there were exhortations to acts of peace and reconciliation.

Third, the structure of the "great sermon" followed a classic rhetoric rewritten by Alphonsus and inspired mainly by Quintilian and the Apostle Paul.

Fourth, near the end of the sermon the preacher might encourage the congregation to kneel and repeat words in an Act of Contrition. The preacher would also strike himself with a rope as an act of penance on behalf of the congregation. A blessing would then be given with a crucifix.

Fifth, visual aids were used (e.g., the rope as a scourge in acts of contrition; a human skull in the sermon on death; a large picture of someone damned for a sermon on hell).

Sixth, the "bread of the divine word" was broken open for the people in a manner that ensured they understood, as directed by the Council of Trent. Latin quotations were to be kept to a minimum. Ornateness of style, abstract ideas and any seeking of applause were forbidden. Alphonus was not tolerant of priests whose preaching failed to meet his expectations. He once stopped one of his priests in mid-sermon and required him to do penance for speaking too abstractly.

Seventh, Scripture was read for its moral lesson. His approach was often allegorical. Two Liguouri sermons are based on the Book of Jonah. In the first, Jonah stands for our sin that must be thrown overboard to stop the tempest of God's scourge. In the second, Jonah's story is an allegory of God punishing us in this life to spare us in the next.

Eighth, the purpose of the sermon was to delight the congregation. The purpose of delight was to encourage the practice of what was learned. Homilists were to aim their sermons at the uneducated and to provide them with specific practical instructions they might follow.

Finally, while the terrors and judgments of hell were to be proclaimed, the preacher was also to speak of the love of God in order that obedience might be done out of faith in God rather than fear of punishment. (Wilson, 116–19)

Alphonsus' missions were thoroughly organized in a sophisticated manner, with instructions for all matters and occasions of public speaking. He insisted on simplicity in preaching, and advocated such topics as Eucharistic Adoration, frequent Confession, daily prayer, and attendance at Mass. He understood that good preaching leads to delight, delight leads to obedience, and obedience brings about fulfillment in the Christian life.

Morality is an important topic for homilies today. With issues like human cloning, embryonic stem-cell research, abortifacients masquerading as new forms of contraception, and the creation of babies in petri dishes, all Christians need clear teaching and guidance on ethics and morality. St. Alphonsus Ligouri is an inspiring example for us.

Below is a homily he preached on the Fifth Sunday after Pentecost (sixth Sunday of the Year A in the revised calendar). It deals with the sin of anger, which Saint Alphonsus compares to a fire and a door.

Homily: On the Sin of Anger

"But I say to you, whosoever is angry with his brother, shall be in danger of the judgment"— *Matt.*, v. 22.

Anger resembles fire; hence, as fire is vehement in its action, and, by the smoke which it produces, obstructs the view, so anger makes men rush into a thousand excesses, and prevents them from seeing the sinfulness of their conduct; and thus exposes them to the danger of the judgment of eternal death. "Whosoever is angry with his brother, shall be in danger of the judgment." Anger is so pernicious to man, that it even disfigures his countenance. No matter how comely and gentle he may be, he shall, as often as he yields to the passion of anger, appear to be a monster and a wild beast full of terror. "Iracundus",

says St. Basil, "humanam quasi figuram amittit, ferae speciem indutus"—*hom.*
xxi. But, if anger disfigures us before men, how much more deformed will it
render us in the eyes of God! In this discourse I will show, in the first point, the
destruction which anger unrestrained brings on the soul; and, in the second,
how we ought to restrain anger in all occasions of provocation which may occur to us.

First point. The ruin which anger unrestrained brings on the soul.

1. St. Jerome says that anger is the door by which all vices enter the soul.
"Omnium vitiorum janua est iracundia"—*Inc., xxix, Prov.* Anger precipitates
men into resentments, blasphemies, acts of injustice, detractions, scandals, and
other iniquities; for the passion of anger darkens the understanding, and makes
a man act like a beast and a madman. "Caligava ab indignatione oculus
meus"—*Job,* xvii. 7. "My eye has lost its sight, through indignation." David
said: "My eye is troubled with wrath."—*Ps.,* xxx. 10. Hence, according to St.
Bonaventure, an angry man is incapable of distinguishing between what is just
and unjust. "Iratus non potest videre quod justum est, vel injustum." In a word,
St. Jerome says, that anger deprives a man of prudence, reason, and understanding. "Ab omni consilio deturpat, ut donce irascitur, insanire crediatur." Hence
St. James says: "The anger of man worketh not the justice of God"—*St. James,*
i: 20. The acts of a man under the influence of anger cannot be conformable to
the divine justice, and consequently cannot be faultless.

2. A man who does not restrain the impulse of anger, easily falls into hatred towards the person who has been the occasion of his passion. According to
St. Augustine, hatred is nothing else than persevering anger. "Odium est ira di-
uturno tempore perseverans." Hence St. Thomas says that "anger is sudden, but
hatred is lasting"—*Opusc.,* v. It appears, then, that in him in whom anger per-
severes, hatred also reigns. But some will say: I am the head of the house; I
must correct my children and servants, and, when necessary, I must raise my
voice against the disorders which I witness. I say in answer: It is one thing to be
angry against a brother, and another to be displeased at the sin of a brother. To
be angry against sin is not anger, but zeal; and therefore it is not only lawful but
it is sometimes a duty. But our anger must be accompanied with prudence, and
must appear to be directed against sin, but not against the sinner; for, if the person whom we correct perceive that we speak through passion and hatred towards him, the correction will be unprofitable and even mischievous. To be angry, then, against a brother's sin is certainly lawful. "He," says St. Augustine,
"is not angry with a brother, who is angry against a brother's sin." It is thus, as
David said, we may be angry without sin. "Be ye angry and sin not,"—*Ps.,* iv.
5. But, to be angry against a brother on account of the sin which he has committed, is not lawful; because according to St. Augustine, we are not allowed to
hate others for their vices. "*Nec propter vitia* (licet) *homines odisee*'—In *Ps.,*
cxviii.

3. Hatred brings with it desire of revenge; for, according to St. Thomas,
anger, when fully voluntary, is accompanied with a desire of revenge. *Ira est
appetitus vindictae.* But you will perhaps say: If I resent such an injury, God
will have pity on me, because I have just grounds for resentment. Who, I ask,
has told you, that you have just grounds for seeking revenge? It is you, whose
understanding is clouded by passions, that say so. I have already said, that anger obscures the mind, and takes away our reason and understanding. As long

as the passion of anger lasts, you will consider your neighbour's conduct very unjust and intolerable; but, when your anger shall have passed away, you shall see that his act was not so bad as it appeared to you. But, though the injury be grievous, or even more grievous, God will not have compassion on you if you seek revenge. No; he says: vengeance for sins belongs not to you, but to me; and when the time shall come, I will chastise them as they deserve. "Revenge is mine, and I will repay *them* in due time"—*Deut.*, xxxii. 35. If you resent an injury done to you by a neighbour, God will justly inflict vengeance on you for all the injuries you have offered to him, and particularly for taking revenge on a brother whom he commands you to pardon. "He that seeketh to revenge himself, shall find vengeance from the Lord. . . . Man to man reserveth anger, and doth he seek remedy of God? . . . He that is but flesh nourisheth anger; and doth he ask forgiveness of God? Who shall obtain pardon for his sins?" —*Eccl.*, xxviii. 1, 3, 5. Man, a worm of flesh, reserves anger, and takes revenge on a brother: does he afterwards dare to ask mercy of God? And who, adds the sacred writer, can obtain pardon for the iniquities of so daring a sinner? "Qua fronte," says St. Augustine, "indulgentiam peccatorem obtinere poterit, qui praecipienti dare veniam nec acquiescit." How can he who will not obey the command of God to pardon his neighbor, expect to obtain from God the forgiveness of his own sins?

4. Let us implore the Lord to preserve us from yielding to any strong passion, and particularly to anger. "Give me not over to a shameful and foolish mind"—*Eccl.*, xxiii. 6. For he that submits to such a passion is exposed to great danger of falling into a grievous sin against God or his neighbour. How many, in consequence of not restraining anger, break out into horrible blasphemies against God or his saints! But, at the very time that we are in a flame of indignation, God is armed with scourges. The Lord said one day to the Prophet Jeremias: "What seest thou, Jeremias? And I said: I see a rod watching'"—*Jer.*, i. 11. Lord, I behold a rod watching to inflict punishment. The Lord asked him again: "What seest thou? And I said: I see a boiling cauldron"—*ibid.*, v. 13. The boiling cauldron is the figure of a man inflamed with wrath, and threatened with the rod, that is, with the vengeance of God. Behold, then, the ruin which anger unrestrained brings on man. It deprives him, first, of the grace of God, and afterwards of corporal life. "Envy and anger shorten a man's days"—*Eccl.*, xxx. 26. Job says: "Anger indeed killeth the foolish"—Job v. 2. All the days of their life, persons addicted to anger are unhappy, because they are always in a tempest. But let us pass to the second point, in which I have to say many things which will assist you to overcome this vice.

Second point. How we ought to restrain anger in the occasions of provocation which occur to us.

5. In the first place, it is necessary to know that it is not possible for human weakness, in the midst of so many occasions, to be altogether free from every motion of anger. No one, as Seneca says, can be entirely exempt from this passion. "Iracundia nullum genus hominum excipit"—*l.* III. c. xii. All our efforts must be directed to the moderation of the feelings of anger which spring up in the soul. How are they to be moderated? By meekness. This is called the virtue of the lamb—that is, the beloved virtue of Jesus Christ. Because, like a lamb, without anger or even complaint, he bore the sorrows of his passion and

crucifixion. "He shall be led as a sheep to the slaughter, and dumb as a lamb before his shearer, and he shall not open his mouth"—*Isa.*, liii: 7. Hence he has taught us to learn of him meekness and humility of heart. "Learn of me because I am meek and humble of heart"—*Mat.*, *xi.* 29.

6. Oh! how pleasing in the sight of God are the meek, who submit in peace to all crosses, misfortunes, persecutions, and injuries! To the meek is promised the Kingdom of Heaven. "Blessed are the meek; for they shall possess the land"—Mat., *v.* 4. They are called the children of God. "Blessed are the peace-makers; for they shall be called the children of God"—*ibid.*, *v.* 9. Some boast of their meekness, but without any grounds; for they are meek only towards those who praise and confer favours upon them; but, to those who injure or censure them, they are all fury and vengeance. The virtue of meekness consists in being meek and peaceful toward those who hate and maltreat us. "With them that hated peace, I was peaceful"—*Ps.*, cxix. 7.

7. We must, as St. Paul says, put on the bowels of mercy towards all men, and bear one with another. "Put on ye the bowels of mercy, humility, modesty, patience, bearing with one another, and forgiving one another, if any have a complaint against another"—*Col.*, *iii.* 12, 13. You wish others to bear with your defects, and to pardon your faults; you should act in the same manner towards them. Whenever, then, you receive an insult from a person enraged against you, remember that "a mild answer breaketh wrath"—*Prov.*, xv. 1. A certain monk once passed through a corn field: the owner of the field ran out, and spoke to him in very offensive and injurious language. The monk humbly replied: "Brother you are right; I have done wrong; pardon me." By this answer the husbandman was so much appeased, that he instantly became calm, and even wished to follow the monk, and to enter into religion. The proud make use of the humiliations they receive to increase their pride; but the humble and meek turn the contempt and insults offered them into an occasion of advancing in humility. "He," says St. Bernard, "is humble, who converts humiliation into humility"—*ser.* xxiv., *in Can.*

8. "A man of meekness," says St. Chrysostom, "is useful to himself and to others." The meek are useful to themselves: because, according to F. Alvarez, the time of humiliation and contempt is for them a time of merit. Hence, Jesus Christ calls his disciples happy when they shall be reviled and persecuted. "Blessed are ye when they shall revile you and persecute you"—*Mat.*, v. 11. Hence, the saints have always desired to be despised, as Jesus Christ has been despised. The meek are useful to others; because, as the same St. Chrysostom says, there is nothing better calculated to draw others to God than to see a Christian meek and cheerful when he receives an injury or an insult. "Nihil ita conciliat Domino familiares ut quod illum vident mansuetudine jucundum." The reason is, because virtue is known by being tried; and, as gold is tried by fire, so the meekness of men is proved by humiliation. "Gold and silver are tried in the fire, but acceptable men in the furnace of humiliation"—*Eccl.*, ii. 5. "My spikenard," says the spouse in the Canticles, "sent forth the odour thereof"—i. 11. The spikenard is an odoriferous plant, but diffuses its odours only when it is torn and bruised. In this passage the inspired writer gives us to understand, that a man cannot be said to be meek, unless he is known to send forth the odour of his meekness by bearing injuries and insults in peace and without anger. God wishes us to be meek even towards ourselves. When a per-

son commits a fault, God certainly wishes him to humble himself, to be sorry for his sin, and to purpose never to fall into it again; but he does not wish him to be indignant with himself, and give way to trouble and agitation of mind; for, while the soul is agitated, a man is incapable of doing good. "My heart is troubled; my strength hath left me"—*Ps.*, xxxvii. 11.

9. Thus, when we receive an insult, we must do violence to ourselves in order to restrain anger. Let us either answer with meekness, as recommended above, or let us remain silent; and thus, as St. Isidore says, we shall conquer. "Quamvis quis irritet, tu dissimula, quia tacendo vinces". But, if you answer through passion, you shall do harm to yourself and others. It would be still worse to give an angry answer to a person who corrects you. "Medicanti irascitur", says St. Bernard, "qui non irascitur sagittanti"—*ser.*, vi., *de Nativ.* Some are not angry, though they ought to be indignant with those who would harm their souls by flattery; and are filled with indignation against the person who censures them in order to heal their irregularities. Against the man who abhors correction, the sentence of perdition has, according to the Wise Man, been pronounced. "Because they have despised all my reproofs, . . . the prosperity of fools shall destroy them"—*Prov.*, i. 30, *etc.* Fools regard as prosperity to be free from correction or to despise the admonitions which they receive; but such prosperity is the cause of their ruin. When you meet with an occasion of anger, you must, in the first place, be on your guard not to allow anger to enter your heart. "Be not quickly angry,"—*Eccles.*, vii. 10. Some persons change colour, and get into a passion, at every contradiction: and when anger has got admission, God knows to what it shall lead them. Hence, it is necessary to foresee these occasions in our meditations and prayers; for, unless we are prepared for them, it will be as difficult to restrain anger as to put a bridle on a horse while he is running away.

10. Whenever we have the misfortune to permit anger to enter the soul, let us be careful not to allow it to remain. Jesus Christ tells all who remember that a brother is offended with them, not to offer the gift which they bring to the altar, without being first reconciled to their neighbour. "Go first to be reconciled to thy brother; and then coming thou shalt offer thy gift"—*Mat.*, v. 24. And he who has received any offense, should endeavour to root out of his heart not only all anger, but also every feeling of bitterness towards the persons who have offended him. "Let all bitterness," says St. Paul, "and anger, and indignation . . . be put away from you"—*Eph.*, iv. 31. As long as anger continues, follow the advice of Seneca—"When you shall be angry, do nothing, say nothing which may be dictated by anger." Like David, be silent, and do not speak, when you feel that you are disturbed. "I was troubled, and I spoke not"—*Ps.*, lxxvi. 5. How many, when inflamed with anger, say and do what they afterwards, in their cooler moments, regret, and excuse themselves by saying that they were in a passion? As long, then, as anger lasts, we must be silent, and abstain from doing or resolving to do anything; for, what is done in the heat of passion will, according to the maxim of St. James, be unjust. "The anger of man worketh not the justice of God"—i. 20. It is also necessary to abstain altogether from consulting those who might foment our indignation. "Blessed," says David, "is the man who hath not walked in the counsel of the ungodly"—*Ps.*, i. 1. To him who is asked for advice, Ecclesiasticus says: "If thou blow the spark, it shall

burn as a fire; and if thou spit upon it, it shall be quenched"—*Eccl.*, xxviii. 14. When a person is indignant at some injury which he has received, you may, by exhorting him to patience, extinguish the fire; but, if you encourage revenge, you may kindle a great flame. Let him, then, who feels himself in any way inflamed with anger, be on his guard against false friends, who, by an imprudent word, may be the cause of his perdition.

11. Let us follow the advice of the apostle: "Be not overcome by evil, but overcome evil by good"—*Rom.*, xii. 21. *Be not overcome by evil*: do not allow yourself to be conquered by sin. If, through anger, you seek revenge or utter blasphemies, you are overcome by sin. But you will say: *I am naturally of a warm temper.* By the grace of God, and by doing violence to yourself, you will be able to conquer your natural disposition. Do not consent to anger, and you shall subdue the warmth of your temper. But you say: *I cannot bear with unjust treatment.* In answer I tell you, first, to remember that anger obscures reason, and prevents us from seeing things as they are. "Fire hath fallen on them, and they shall not see the sun"—*Ps.*, lvii. 9. Secondly, if you return evil for evil, your enemy shall gain a victory over you. "If," said David, "I have rendered to them that repaid me evils, let me deservedly fall empty before my enemies"— *Ps.*, vii. 5. If I render evil for evil, I shall be defeated by my enemies. "*Overcome evil by good.*" Render every foe good for evil. "Do good," says Jesus Christ, "to them that hate you."—*Matt.*, v. 44. This is the revenge of the saints, and is called by St. Paulinus, *heavenly revenge.* It is by such revenge that you shall gain the victory. And should any of those, of whom the Prophet says, "The venom of asps is under their lips"—*Ps.*, cxxxix. 4, ask how you can submit to such an injury, let your answer be: "The chalice which my Father hath given me, shall I not drink it?"—*John*, xviii. 11. And then turning to God, you shall say: "I opened not my mouth, because thou hast done it."—*Ps.*, xxxviii. 10; for it is certain that every cross which befalls you, comes from the Lord. "Good things and evil are from God"—*Eccl.*, xi. 14. Should any one take away your property, recover if you can; but if you cannot, say with Job: "The Lord gave, and the Lord hath taken away"—i. 21. A certain philosopher, who lost some of his goods in a storm, said: "If I have lost my goods, I will not lose my peace." And do you say: "If I have lost my property, I will not lose my soul."

12. In fine, when we meet with crosses, persecutions, and injuries, let us turn to God, who commands us to bear them with patience; and thus we shall always avoid anger. "Remember the fear of God, and be not angry with thy neighbour"—*Eccl.*, xxviii. 8. Let us give a look at the will of God, which disposes things in this manner for our merit, and anger, shall cease. Let us give a look at Jesus crucified, and we shall not have courage to complain. St. Eleazar being asked by his spouse, how he bore so many injuries without yielding to anger, answered: "I turn to Jesus Christ, and thus I preserve my peace." Finally, let us give a glance at our sins, for which we have deserved far greater contempt and chastisement, and we shall calmly submit to all evils. St. Augustine says, that though we are sometimes innocent of the crime for which we are persecuted, we are, nevertheless, guilty of other sins which merit greater punishment than that which we endure. "Esto non habemus peccatum, quod habitur: habemus tamen, quod digne in nobis flagelletur"—*in Ps.*, lxviii.[36]

SUMMARY

As we conclude the Reformation Era, and move into the Modern and Contemporary Era, we note the subtle shift in homiletic method from a Scholastic approach to an evangelical approach. This shift in approaches was tied into the great missionary movements of the sixteenth and seventeenth centuries. These movements vastly expanded the scope of the Church's outreach. Technological developments enabled people to move from Europe to the far reaches of South America, Asia and Africa with relative ease. While journeys to these places were long, improved ship design enabled explorer and evangelist alike to reach new shores.

In these centuries, the Church was concerned with implementing the decrees of the Council of Trent, while it took seriously the Lord's missionary mandate and spread the Gospel to the far reaches of the globe. Homilies had a new pastoral and spiritual emphasis in these centuries. They went from being argument/proof texts to being inspiring, moral and spiritual exhortations. Preaching in this era addressed the skepticism and atheism held by Enlightenment thinkers and French revolutionaries. Like their predecessors, each featured homilist drew on images and ideas from the contemporary culture to preach and proclaim the Gospel. They emphasized themes touching peoples' daily lives. We will see this method develop through the next two hundred years.

NOTES

1. Old, 4:194.
2. Ibid.
3. Ibid.
4. Ibid., 4:201.
5. Ibid., 4:201–4.
6. Ibid., 4:201.
7. Ibid., 4:203.
8. Ibid., 4:203–4.
9. Ibid., 4:214.
10. Ibid., 4:215.
11. Ibid., 4:218.
12. Ibid., 4:219.
13. Ibid.
14. Ibid.
15. Ibid., 4:220.
16. Ibid., 4:220–1.
17. Ibid., 4:221-22.
18. Ibid., 4:222.
19. John W. O'Malley, *Religious Culture in the Sixteenth Century*, art. 6, 142.

20. Frederick J. McGinness, *Right Thinking and Sacred Oratory in Counter-Reformation Rome* (Princeton, NJ: Princeton University Press, 1995), 37.

21. O'Malley, *Religious Culture*, art. 6,142.

22. Ibid., 143.

23. Old, 4:224.

24. Ibid., 4:225.

25. Ibid., 4:226.

26. McGinness, *Right Thinking,* 43.

27. Old. 4:226.

28. Ibid., 4:226–27.

29. McGinness, *Right Thinking,* 33.

30. Old, 4:475.

31. Ibid., 4:481.

32. Ibid., 4:497.

33. *Preacher's Encyclopedia*, Volume IV 608–610.

34. Christopher Dawson, Religion and the Rise of Western Culture (Garden City, NJ: Doubleday, 1958), 18–19,

35. Alphonsus Liguori, *Instructions to Preachers*, in *Sermons of St. Alphonsus Liguori*, 4th ed. (Rockford, IL: Tan Books, 1982), xxiii–xxxii.

36. *Sermons of St. Alphonsus Liguouri*, 254–62.

Chapter 8
Preaching in the Modern
and Contemporary Era

Take no part in the fruitless works of darkness;
rather expose them.
Ephesians 5:11

TECHNOLOGICAL INNOVATION and advances in science and knowledge marked the modern and contemporary era. This period is shaped by the Church's relationship with the modern world. A flood of socialist ideologies brought in its wake revolutions and anti-Church states. Darwin and Marx became famous world-wide. The nineteenth century saw the Industrial Revolution outside the Church, and the development of the Liturgical Movement within the Church. The twentieth century was characterized by the rise and fall of both Communism and Fascism, two world wars and a host of smaller wars, the technological revolution and the Second Vatican Council.

Vatican II returned to the sources of Christian Tradition, and recovered many lost customs, ideas, and rituals. The purpose of Vatican II was to promote Christian unity, implement internal Church reform, and create a new relationship of dialogue and respect with the modern world. The implementation of Vatican II, specifically, the liturgical reforms, created an enormous spiritual and ecclesiastical upheaval, which reverberates still into the twenty-first century.

At points in her history, the Church has been anti-worldly. Recently, she has engaged in dialogue with the world, seeing it as more of a partner to be engaged than an enemy to be opposed. Modern and contemporary preachers have addressed how Catholics should deal with the world in which we live. Some are hostile; others are more accommodating. The notion of witness in the world is an important theme in contemporary preaching. We now examine the lives and homiletic styles of several modern and contemporary preachers, in order to better understand the concept of preaching, and the context in which it occurs.

PREACHING IN THE MODERN ERA

By the modern era, I refer to the nineteenth century. This century was marked by the Industrial Revolution, political upheavals in Europe in the 1840s, the rise of Marx and Darwin in secular thought, the Civil War in the United States, and the decline of the Papal States in Italy and France. Preaching in this era had a strong pastoral character. Saint John Vianney in France, and Saint John Newman in England, represent attempts by the Church to reach Catholic communities with a relevant Gospel message.

Saint John Mary Baptiste Vianney: Parochial Preacher

Saint Jean Marie Baptiste Vianney (1786–1859) is one of the most beloved priests in Church history, and the model for parish priests. Vianney lived in a time of social turmoil and political upheaval, but within those turbulent times he transformed a town and touched a nation, by sharing the light of Christ which burned brightly in him. He was born on May 8, 1786, of poor parents in southern France. When he was young, he hid from French authorities who were looking for religious practitioners during the French Revolution. He began his studies for the priesthood at the age of nineteen, and was ordained after many failures and difficulties, even being tutored by Matthias Loras, the future bishop of Dubuque, Iowa. He struggled with Latin and the study of theology.

Vianney was ordained in 1815. He spent two years as an assistant in Ecully, under Monsignor Bellay. He was appointed pastor of the small agricultural village of Ars, north of Lyons, where the faith had practically vanished while depravity remained. On February 9, 1818, he entered the village and began what became a forty-one-year parish ministry. He labored in that village for the rest of his life, gaining a worldwide reputation as a preacher, spiritual director, confessor and teacher. He became known as the "Curé of Ars."

The Curé of Ars lived in abject poverty: all his resources went to improving his church, to helping the poor, and to educating children. He opened a girls' school called La Providence, for this very purpose, in 1824. He was a compassionate counselor who spent eleven to eighteen hours a day in the confessional; he was a physical as well as spiritual builder of the Church. After many trials, including harassment by the devil himself, Father Vianney, exhausted by his labors and penance, went to the Lord on August 4, 1859, and was canonized in 1929.

His life and work met three important needs: the need of Ars for inspiration and transformation, the need of France for renewal and conversion, and the need of the Universal Church for a model of holiness and pastoral care in its parish priests. John Vianney fulfilled these spiritual needs in exceptional ways. That is one reason he is the patron of priests and parish clergy. His feast is August 4.

The Preaching of Saint John Vianney

Saint John Vianney was a model parish priest. Like the Master, he was humble, ascetical, and deeply committed to the salvation of souls. He brought a tremendous passion and dedication to his preaching ministry. Vianney studied the Church Fathers, and used the homilies of Bishop Jacques Bossuet, sometimes verbatim. A few sermon manuals, nearly all of which he acquired before 1830, were among the more than four hundred books in his personal library. St. John Vianney struggled to deliver effective sermons. But his most persuasive speech was not the precise language of his sermons, but rather the mute eloquence of his holy life. This holy man converted hundreds of thousands to the faith. People heard him preach, informally at the morning catechism lesson, and at greater length on Sundays, and were fascinated by his words.

In February 1818, as he approached Ars, John Vianney met a young shepherd boy named Antoine Givre. He asked Antoine where Ars was located. When the boy pointed out the village, Vianney said, "My little friend, you have shown me the way to Ars. I will show you the way to Heaven." He spent the rest of his life doing just that: pointing out the heavenly Kingdom, and leading souls to Christ.

But many struggles and obstacles awaited him. In his early days at Ars, this young priest had to rekindle in his people the flame of faith, which had died down considerably through the years. The people of Ars possessed the faith, but were exceedingly lax in its practice. It was easy for them to skip Sunday Mass, or engage in excessive drinking and obscene behavior, because their consciences had become lax. It pained him deeply to hear the carts go by his tiny parish church as he preached on Sunday. He knew they were headed out to work in the fields to earn money, so they could come into town and drink. And some who came to Sunday Mass showed their lack of interest in the way they conducted themselves, for example, yawning out loud. This pastoral situation was a challenge, to say the least. Saints embrace rather than flee pastoral challenges. John Vianney resolved to change this situation by converting hearts and minds. His early sermons dealt with morality, the sinfulness of drinking and dancing, the need for repentance, the terrors of Hell and the joys of Heaven, the value of prayer, and the power of the sacraments. He spoke on the proper way to behave in church, keeping the Sabbath, the purpose of work, and other topics.

Vianney's sermons are rather severe in tone, and some claim they are tinged with Jansenism. Father George Rutler, in his fine biography *The Curé D'Ars Today* (1988), strongly refutes this charge. He defines Jansenism as a "form of rigorism, a truncated view of human nature and creation, or what is known as deontological spirituality, endemic in many modern spiritual movements."[1] It was named after Cornelius Jansen, the seventeenth century Bishop of Ypres. It was primarily associated with the convent of Port-Royal, "whose nuns were 'pure as angels and proud as devils,' and had a pronounced influence lasting long after its condemnation by the bull *Unigenitus* in 1713."[2] Jansenism "is not so much a wrong body of doctrines as it is a wrong doctrine of the body."[3] Rutler rejects the suggestion that John Vianney was tinged with this pernicious heresy. He argues that Vianney did not preach or condone heresy, but rather followed his religion scrupulously, and called others to do the same. Vianney's strictness must be seen in the context of his times. His seminary training emphasized the serious nature of mortal sin and the importance of strict adherence to God's Law. Vianney's preaching and teaching were no stricter than those found in other parishes of his day.

How did the patron of parish priests prepare his Sunday sermons? We know that he spent a considerable amount of time on them. With the aid of certain reference books, he wrote out his sermons, often on the vestment cabinet of the sacristy. He occasionally took breaks to kneel before the Blessed Sacrament. He spent hours in church meditating, praying, and refining his homily. Vianney spent so much time in the pulpit (and later in the confessional), because he recognized the power of the Word preached and proclaimed well. Having written out his homily (which was anywhere from thirty to forty pages long and took an hour to deliver), he then memorized it. After doing so, he would recite his homily in the church or the churchyard out loud late on Saturday night, and more than once, to his embarrassment, was "caught in the act."[4]

The congregation at the beginning of his pastorate at Ars was sparse. A few old peasant women, the lady of the manor, a couple of men, and some children made up his flock. He spoke loudly and clearly, so they could not sleep. After the Gospel at the sung Mass on Sunday mornings, when he removed his chasuble and ascended the rickety wooden steps to the pulpit, they knew he would be there for a good hour. Vianney celebrated Mass slowly, often beginning around eight o'clock and ending at eleven on Sunday morning.

There are at least eighty-five complete written sermons of the Curé of Ars. In later years, he stopped writing them down beforehand, and preached without the set form he first adopted. A cursory review of an index of Vianney's sermons is revealing.[5] It lists the extant homilies of John Vianney by title. His most frequently preached topics include: the good God, God the Father, Jesus Christ, Christ the Savior, the Holy Spirit, the Devil, the Blessed Virgin Mary, Saint Paul, the Hebrew People, the Desert Fathers, Baptism, the Commandments, the Cross, the Church, Eucharist, the Passion of Christ, Confession, Priesthood, and the Sacraments. The breadth of his preaching is amazing. He covers a variety of other topics as well, including: Divine Love; the prophet Amos; Saint Gregory the Great; Jesus, Son of Justice; the Old Testament figure Noah; the Angel Raphael; the Gentiles; the Scapular; and others.

John Vianney based his homilies on the biblical texts proclaimed throughout the liturgical year. A perusal of his topics on different days reveals that for him no topic was out of bounds. The homilist had to proclaim the message of salvation in its fullness. Vianney was duty-bound and inspired by the love of God to proclaim the entire message of Christ. He is a paragon of homiletic integrity.

Table 8.1 Some of Saint John Vianney's Homily Topics

TOPIC	BIBLICAL TEXT	SUNDAY READING
Behold, thy King	Matthew 21:5	Palm Sunday
Called to the Faith	Matthew 2:2	Epiphany
Detraction	Mark 7:35	Eleventh Sunday after Pentecost
Easter Confession	John 6:4	Low Sunday
Extreme Unction	John 4:47	Twentieth Sunday after Pentecost
Fear of Man	Matthew 11:6	Third Sunday of Advent
Hope	Matthew 22:37	Fourth Sunday after Pentecost
Humility	Luke 18:14	Sixteenth Sunday after Pentecost
Indulgences	Luke 11:24	Third Sunday of Lent
Last Judgment	Luke 21:27	First Sunday of Advent
Penance	Luke 3:8	Fourth Sunday of Advent
Prayer	John 16:23	Fifth Sunday after Easter
Second Commandment	Exodus 20:7	Fifth Sunday after Pentecost
The Soul	Luke 19:41	Ninth Sunday after Pentecost
Three-fold Love	John 21:20	Sunday in the Octave of Christmas

Source: *Sermons of the Ven. Curé of Ars.* Neumann Press, 1901.

John Vianney was a simple man who spoke to simple folk. Like our Lord, he was a master of the use of imagery in his homilies. A sampling follows:

We should imitate the shepherds in the fields of winter—life is truly a long winter!—they make a fire, but from time to time to keep it lighted, they run about gathering wood from all sides. If like the shepherds, we knew how to keep the fire of God's love alight by prayers and good works, it would never go out.[6]

Crosses transformed into the flames of love are like a bundle of briers which are thrown into the fire and consumed to ashes. The briers are hard but the ashes are soft.[7]

The Holy Spirit has told us that the Lord brings his people out of Egypt and, leading it to the Promised Land, compares Himself to 'an eagle who flies around his little ones to encourage them to fly, and takes them and carries them on his wings.' Here precisely, my brethren, is what Jesus Christ does for us. He stretches forth His wings, inciting us by His lessons and by His examples to detach ourselves from this world, that we may be raised up to Heaven by Him.[8]

The damned fall into Hell fast as the snow flakes on a winter day.[9]

A poor creature, directly it is on a slanderer's tongue, is like a grain of wheat under a millstone. It is torn, crushed and entirely destroyed.[10]

Margaret Trouncer commented on Vianney's preaching in her biography of the Curé of Ars:

He stormed and wept in the pulpit. He strained his poor voice until it cracked. He employed all the arts of oratory and mime to bring these poor souls back to God. And if, as was sometimes their unpleasant practice, the parishioners began leaving before the sermon, he would have recourse to a trick, for he was a wily peasant. For example, preaching about restitution of stolen goods: 'My brethren, I am going to preach against thieves. Any among you who feel guilty would do well to go out, because I have some hard truths to tell.' Of course, no one dared to leave.[11]

Vianney promoted devotion and love for the Blessed Sacrament in his sermons. He would often repeat the words "He is there! He is there!" pointing to the Blessed Sacrament. John Vianney, like his patron, always pointed to Jesus Christ, the Lamb of God who takes away the sins of the world (John 1:29). He directed his words and even his gestures to the Savior locked in the tabernacle, and called his flock to follow their Master.

Two twentieth-century popes devoted letters to the topic of Saint John Mary Vianney. The first was Blessed John XXIII. On August 1, 1959, he released the encyclical *Sacerdoti Nostri Primordia* (The First Days of our Priesthood). He comments on two important aspects of Saint John Vianney's preaching: perseverance and hard work:

Because, as is recorded, 'he was always ready to care for the needs of souls,' St. John Vianney, good shepherd that he was, was also outstanding in offering his sheep an abundant supply of the food of Christian truth. Throughout his life he preached and taught Catechism . . . his first sermons to the people kept him up for whole nights on end. How much the ministers of the Word of God can find here to imitate! . . . They would be much better off if they would imitate the great perseverance of soul with which the Curé of Ars prepared himself to carry out this great ministry to the best of his abilities; which, as a matter of fact, were not quite as limited as is sometimes believed, for he had a clear mind and sound judgment . . . Would that all pastors of souls would exert as much effort as the Curé of Ars did to overcome difficulties and obstacles in learning, to strengthen memory through practice, and especially to draw knowledge from the Cross of Our Lord, which is the greatest of all books.[12]

Blessed John XXIII quotes his predecessor, Pope Pius XII:

The holy Curé of Ars had none of the natural gifts of a speaker that stand out in men like P. Segneri or B. Bossuet. But the clear, lofty, living thoughts of his mind were reflected in the sound of his voice and shone forth from his glance, and they came out in the form of ideas and images that were so apt and so well fitted to the thoughts and feelings of his listeners and so full of wit and charm that even St. Francis de Sales would have been struck with admiration.[13]

Finally, the pope comments on Vianney's ability to move people:

When, towards the end of his life on earth, his voice was too weak to carry to his listeners, the sparkle and gleam of his eyes, his tears, his sighs of divine love, the bitter sorrow he evidenced when the mere concept of sin came to his mind, were enough to convert to a better way of life the faithful who surrounded his pulpit.[14]

Blessed John Paul II devoted his 1986 Holy Thursday letter to the topic of Saint John Vianney. He comments on significant aspects of Vianney's forty-one-year ministry. "The Curé of Ars was also careful never to neglect in any way the ministry of the Word, which is absolutely necessary in predisposing people to faith and conversion," he wrote. "He even said: 'Our Lord, who is truth itself, considers his Word no less important than his Body!'"[15] The pope continued:

We know how long he spent, especially in the beginning, in laboriously composing his Sunday sermons. Later on he came to express himself more spontaneously, always with lively and clear conviction, with images and comparisons taken from daily life, and easily grasped by his flock.

John Paul accentuated Vianney's courageous denunciation of evil:

He had the courage to denounce evil in all its forms; he did not keep silent, for it was a question of the eternal salvation of his faithful people. 'If a pastor remains silent when he sees God insulted and souls going astray, woe to him! If he does not want to be damned, and if there is some disorder in his parish, he must trample upon human respect and the fear of being despised or hated.'

The pontiff pointed out, however, that Vianney preferred to show "the attractive side of virtue rather than the ugliness of vice."[16]

Vianney's humble attitude is illustrated in the following story. There was once a meeting of the parish priest of Ars and the great Dominican Père Lacordaire. On the morning of May 4, 1845, Lacordaire was staying at a chateau in Ars. He met John Vianney in the sacristy and Father Vianney expressed his joy at seeing him. He embraced Lacordaire warmly, clasped his hands for a long time, and thanked him for his visit. Then, in an expression of his usual warm hospitality, Vianney brought out his finest vestments, chalice, and missal for his guest. Lacordaire was deeply impressed by Vianney's sermon on the Holy Spirit. Afterwards, Lacordaire went up to Vianney and said, "You have taught me how to know the Holy Ghost." Then it was the Curé's turn to listen to Lacordaire. He listened most attentively, and afterwards exclaimed: "Ah, today two extremes have met: the extreme of knowledge [Lacordaire] and the extreme of ignorance [Vianney]."[17]

This homily was delivered on the Third Sunday after Pentecost (pre-1962 calendar). It deals with the mercy of God and takes its material from the parable of the Good Shepherd in Luke, chapter 15. Vianney talks about the greatness of God's mercy and our efforts to receive it.

Homily: The Mercy of God

By His demeanor during His earthly life Jesus Christ indicated the abundance of His mercy toward sinners. We see how everyone sought His society, and He not only not repulsed them, or at least kept them at a distance, but on the contrary, He took every possible opportunity of being among them, so as to win them for the Father. He seeks them by giving them remorse of conscience, leads them by means of His grace, and conquers them by His kindness. His kindness toward them is so great that He even becomes their advocate before the doctors and Pharisees, who condemned them, and who would not suffer them to approach Jesus Christ. Furthermore, He justifies His behavior toward sinners by a parable which gives evidence of His great and beautiful love for sinners, when He says:

"A good shepherd, who has a hundred sheep and loses one of them, leaves all the others behind and seeks the stray one, and when he has found it he takes it upon his shoulders to spare it the difficulties of the way, and when he has brought it back to his sheepfold he invites all his friends, that they may rejoice with him over the finding of the sheep which was thought to be lost."

Again, the parable of the woman who had ten pennies, and having lost one, lighted a lamp so as to look for it in all the corners of the house, and after she had found it invited all her friends, that they might take part in her joy. "Even so," He adds, "does the whole court of heaven rejoice at the return of the sinner who is converted and does penance. I [did] not come to save the just, but sinners, those who are well need not a physician, but those who are sick." As you see, Jesus Christ applies both of these parables to Himself as illustrations of His compassion for the sinner. O what a happiness it is for us to know that God's mercy is infinite! Our heart should compel us to throw ourselves at the feet of God, who will be so glad to receive us. If we go to perdition, dear brethren, we shall have no excuse, for Jesus Christ Himself told us that His mercy was ever ready to forgive us, no matter how deeply we had fallen. To impress these facts upon our hearts and minds I will show you to-day:

I. The greatness of God's mercy toward sinners.

II. What we must do on our part to merit it.

I. Yes, dear brethren, the way in which God concerns Himself with us is consoling, but it imposes obligations upon us. Although we are guilty His patience waits for us, His love invites us to rise from our sins and to return to Him. His mercy protects us. "With patience," says the prophet Isaiah, "the Lord waits for us, to show us His mercy. As soon as we commit sin, we deserve to be punished at once. Nothing is more deserving of punishment than sin." As soon as a man revolts against God all creation demands vengeance, saying: "Lord, wilt Thou that we destroy this sinner who has offended Thee? Wilt Thou, cries the sea to Him, that I should bury him in my depths?" The earth says: "Lord, wilt Thou that I open and bury him alive in hell?" The air says: "Lord, shall I suffocate him?" The fire asks: "O Lord, I pray Thee, let me consume him, and all creation cries for vengeance." "But no," replies this good Jesus, "leave him upon earth until the moment which my Father has ordained for him; perhaps I shall have the happiness of seeing his conversion."

Contemplate, for instance, the mercy of God toward the world before the deluge, when the vices of men covered the earth and it was steeped in the filthy waters of the most abominable vices. The Lord felt Himself obliged to punish it, but what warnings, what admonitions, what delays did He not give them before the chastisement! Long before He threatened them, so as to arouse them and bring them to their senses. When he saw that their crimes increased from day to day He sent Noe to them, whom He commanded to build an ark, which should take him a hundred years to build, and to all those who should ask him the reason of this construction he was to say that the Lord was about to destroy the whole world by a flood, but that, if they would be converted and do penance, He would alter His determination. Only when He saw that His admonitions were of no avail, that men mocked at His menaces, He found Himself obliged to step in with His chastisement. And even then we see how the Lord declared that He regretted having created them, thereby expressing the greatness of His mercy. He wished to say: "I would rather not have created you, now that I find myself obliged to punish you." Tell me, dear brethren, could God Almighty, as He is, have shown greater mercy?

From the beginning of the world, dear brethren, until the advent of the Messiah, we behold but mercy, grace, and kindness. And yet we may say that under the law of grace of the New Testament the benefits which He is lavishing upon the world are still more abundant and more precious. What commiseration on the part of the eternal Father, who had an only Son, and who consented that

the only Son should give His life to redeem us all! Ah, dear brethren, if we remembered the Passion of Jesus Christ with proper feelings of gratitude, how
many tears would we shed? As you see, the mercy of God could go no farther,
for He had *one* only Son, and He sacrificed Him to save us—this Son who was
the dearest that He had. But what shall we say when we consider the love of the
Son? He goes willingly, to suffer torments and even death to procure for us the
blessedness of Heaven. What did He not do for us during His life upon earth?
He is not satisfied to call us by His grace, and to place all means of salvation at
our disposal. Behold how He seeks after the strayed sheep! See how He trav-
erses cities and villages in quest of them, to lead them to the abode of His
mercy! Behold how He leaves His Apostles and waits for the Samaritan woman
at Jacob's well, where He knew that He would meet her! He appeared before
her and begins to speak to her, so that the gentleness of His speech, combined
with His grace, should touch and console her. He asks her for a drink of water,
that she herself may venture to implore Him for something far more precious,
namely, for His grace. So pleased was He at the conversion of this soul that He
declined, when His Apostles asked Him to partake of some food, as if to say: "I
am not thinking of material food; I am so rejoiced at having gained a soul for
my Father!"

Look in at the house of Simon the leper. He does not go there to eat, but
because He knows that He will find there Mary Magdalene, a sinner. For this
reason, dear brethren, He appears at this feast. Observe the joy revealed by His
countenance as Mary Magdalene throws herself at His feet and washes them
with her tears and dries them with her hair. But the Redeemer repays her abun-
dantly by pouring out the fulness of His grace into her heart. Behold how He
takes her in opposition to those who are scandalized by her! His compassion is
so great that He not only forgives her her sins, and drives out the devils who
had taken possession of her heart, but He chooses her to be one of His companions. He desires that she should accompany Him during His entire life's journey, and that in the whole world, wherever the Gospel should be preached, it
should be related what she did for love of Him. He will speak no more of her
sins, which He has already washed away by the merits of His most adorable
blood, which He is to shed.

Why do we find Him on the road to Capharnaum? Is it not to meet Matthew the tax collector and make him a zealous Apostle? Why on His way to
Jerico? It is to convert the publican Zachaeus. Ask Him why He walks in the
public square and He will tell you it is to defend the adulteress and to convert
her. Reflect how He weeps when approaching the city of Jerusalem, which is
an image of the sinner, for of it He said: "Ungrateful Jerusalem who hast mur-
dered the prophets and put to death the servants of God. O that thou mayest accept to-day the graces which I bring thee!" See, my brethren, how God weeps
over the loss of our souls when He sees that we will not be converted. How can
we, after seeing all that Christ has done to save us, doubt of His mercy, when
we are sure of His forgiveness if we give up sins and repent of them, no matter
how numerous they may be? Yea, and even deeply though you may have
fallen, so that in the eyes of God you are in a worse condition than was the
prodigal son, who from a noble, rich youth was reduced to a servant to feed the
swine and had not anything wherewith to satiate himself, not even the husks the

swine left over. Yet how did the father anticipate his coming—even prepared a feast for again finding the lost son. Thus will your heavenly Father act toward you from the very moment that you form the resolution of being converted; at the first step which you take toward that happy end the divine heart is moved to compassion, to mercy. He receives you with endearment.

Jesus Christ, in speaking of these sinners through the mouth of His servant, says: "Let this Christian, who is converted, be clothed with the robe of baptismal grace which he had lost; let him be clothed with Jesus Christ, with His justice, His virtues, and His merits." See, dear brethren, how Jesus Christ treats us when we are so happy as to forsake our sins and to abandon ourselves to Him. O how great is God's mercy! (Sermons of the Curé of Ars, 185–89)

John Henry Newman: Convert Preacher

John Henry Newman (1801–1890) was one of the most influential figures in modern Catholicism. He was an Anglican priest who later became a Cardinal of the Catholic Church. He was brought up in the Church of England under Evangelical influence. He entered Trinity College at Oxford in 1816, became a Fellow of Oriel in 1822, and was ordained to the deaconate in 1824. Newman was ordained a priest of the Church of England the next year. He was appointed vice-principal of Alban Hall in 1826, and two years later was appointed vice-principal of St. Mary's, Oxford. He toured southern Europe in the early 1830s, and became associated with the Tractarian or Oxford Movement upon his return home. That movement, which sought to return Anglicanism to the Fathers of the Church, profoundly influenced his thinking, philosophy, and spirituality. Newman was not the founder of the Oxford Movement, but he was one of its most famous and influential members.

Newman began to have doubts about the principal claims in the Thirty-Nine Articles of the Anglican Church, and from 1841 onwards, he gradually distanced himself from Oxford. In 1842, he set up a quasi-monastic establishment at St. Mary's, where he lived in retirement with a few friends. In late September 1843, he preached a celebrated sermon titled "The Parting of Friends," and two years later he was received into the Catholic Church. Soon afterward, he issued his *Essay on the Development of Christian Doctrine*, in defense of his change of allegiance. He was ordained a Catholic priest on Trinity Sunday, May 30, 1846.

In 1848, Newman established the Oratorians at Birmingham. In 1851, he became rector of Catholic University at Dublin, where he remained for three years before returning home. He published his *Apologia pro vita sua* in 1864, which won him many Catholic friends. Six years later, he published his *Grammar of Assent*, a work containing much of his best thought. His strengths lay in his psychological analysis and moral perception, rather than profound spirituality. He had deep insight into the nature and motives of religious faith as well.

Newman struggled within the Anglican Communion, and later in the Catholic Church, in his quest for truth and understanding. Men like Gerard Manly

Hopkins, Edward Pusey, John Keble, Isaac Williams, and Robert Wilberforce left the Church of England, and followed Newman back to Rome.

John Henry Newman was made a cardinal in 1879. His motto was *Cor ad cor loquitur* ("heart speaks to heart"). He died on August 11, 1890, in Birmingham. His epitaph reads *Ex umbris et imaginibus in veritatem* ("Out of shadows and pictures into truth").

Because of his writings on the laity in the life of the Church, and other topics, Father Karl Rahner called Vatican II "Newman's Council." John Newman was a man ahead of his time in many respects. For example, he anticipated the Church's renewed emphasis on the role of the laity in ecclesial life. Pope Benedict XVI canonized Newman on a papal journey to the United Kingdom on September 19, 2010. The impact of Cardinal Newman continues to this day, and can be seen in the growing number of Anglican converts to Catholicism. His feast day is October 9, the date he entered the Church.

The Preaching of John Henry Newman

John Henry Newman once said: "In the primitive Church, the chalices were of wood, and the prelates of gold; but now the chalices are of gold, and the prelates are wooden." John Newman was anything but wooden. He was both a prolific writer and speaker. Among his writings, we possess eight volumes of *Parochial and Plain Sermons*, preached while Newman was at St. Mary's, Oxford (1828–43), and were delivered before his entrance into the Church. A contemporary listener has given the following description of the church on a Sunday evening, as the congregation waited eagerly for Newman to begin his sermon:

> The great church, the congregation which barely filled it, all breathless with expectant attention. The gas light, just at the left hand of the pulpit, lowered that the preacher might not be dazzled; themselves perhaps standing in the half-darkness under the gallery, and then the pause before those words in the 'Ventures of Faith' thrilled through them—"They say unto Him we are able."[18]

Vincent Ferrer Blehl tells us that the method and style accounted for the powerful impact of Newman's sermons.[19] He describes Newman's preaching vision as "at once patristic and personal."[20] The *patristic* quality came from reflecting on biblical realities, and the *personal* quality came from reflecting on his own relationship with God. For Newman and the early Church Fathers, the Bible presents "the living drama of God's salvific relations with men."[21] Newman's sermons were a call to holiness, which means conversion of heart, and a commitment to incorporate the values of the Kingdom into one's life. "This is the very definition of a Christian—one who looks for Christ; not who looks for gain or distinction or power, or pleasure or comfort," Newman said.[22]

Newman began his sermons with a general notion, and reflected more deeply until it became concrete and personal. "With keen psychological acumen, he led them through a definite pattern of thought of mind," Blehl writes.[23] The Gospel was intended to produce concrete changes in one's life. "The perfect Christian state is that in which our duty and our pleasure are the same, when what is right and true is natural to us, and in which God's service is perfect freedom," Newman said in one sermon.[24]

"We must become what we are not; we must learn to love what we do not love, and practice ourselves in what is difficult," he wrote in *Parochial and Plain Sermons*.[25] Newman was under no illusion about the difficulty in achieving this lofty goal, but one purpose of his sermons was to aid his listeners to accomplish this transformation.

Vincent Blehl summarizes Newman's style well:

Newman's purpose in the sermons, then, was to lead men to realize vividly for themselves the mysteries of faith, to comprehend authentic Christianity as a concrete way of life, not merely as an abstract programme for living. Christian doctrine and morality were presented in a way that demanded an authentic response, a definite commitment of the entire being to accomplish such a change in the consciousness of his hearers was no easy task. Mere logical reasoning would be ineffectual. Newman employed the more subtle method of implicit reasoning which was, in fact, a personal logic, a logic of conviction rather than a strict proof. By an accumulation of biblical examples, suggestions, analyses of mind, Newman gradually brought his hearers to assimilate the meaning of Christian truths in relation to their personal lives. No longer could they ignore or reject Christian doctrine without a pang of conscience.[26]

The following homily was preached July 13, 1852, in St. Mary's, Oscott, in the first Provincial Synod of Westminster. It is called "The Second Spring" homily, and it is one of Newman's finest sermons.

Homily: The Second Spring

Arise, make haste, my love, my dove, my beautiful one, and come. For the winter is now past, the rain is over and gone. The flowers have appeared in our land. Cant., ii. 10–12.

We have familiar experience of the order, the constancy, the perpetual renovation of the material world which surrounds us. Frail and transitory as is every part of it, restless and migratory as are its elements, never-ceasing as are its changes, still it abides. It is bound together by a law of permanence, it is set up in unity; and, though it is ever dying, it is ever coming to life again. Dissolution does but give birth to fresh modes of organization, and one death is the parent of a thousand lives. Each hour, as it comes, is but a testimony, how fleeting, yet how secure, how certain, is the great whole. It is like an image on the waters, which is ever the same, though the waters ever flow. Change upon change—yet one change cries out to another, like the alternate Seraphim, in praise and in glory of their Maker. The sun sinks to rise again; the day is swallowed up in the gloom of the night, to be born out of it, as fresh as if it had never been quenched. Spring passes into summer, and through summer and autumn into winter, only the more surely, by its own ultimate return, to triumph over that grave, towards which it resolutely hastened from its first hour. We mourn over the blossoms of May, because they are to wither; but we know, withal, that May is one day to have its revenge upon November, by the revolution of that solemn circle which never stops—which teaches us in our height of hope, ever to be sober, and in our depth of desolation, never to despair. And forcibly as this comes home to every one of us, not less forcible is the contrast which exists between this material world, so vigorous, so reproductive, amid all its changes, and the moral world, so feeble, so downward, so resourceless, amid all its aspirations. That which ought to come to nought, endures; that which promises a future, disappoints and is no more. The same sun shines in heaven from first to last, and the blue firmament, the everlasting mountains, reflect his rays; but where is there upon earth the champion, the hero, the lawgiver, the body politic, the sovereign race, which was great three hundred years ago, and is great now? Moralists and poets, often do they descant upon this innate vitality of matter, this innate perishableness of mind. Man rises to fall: he tends to dissolution from the moment he begins to be; he lives on, indeed, in his children, he lives on in his name, he lives not on in his own person. He is, as regards the manifestations of his nature here below, as a bubble that breaks, and as water poured out upon the earth. He was young, he is old, he is never young again. This is the lament over him, poured forth in verse and in prose, by Christians and by heathen. The greatest work of God's hands under the sun, he, in all the manifestations of his complex being, is born only to die.

His bodily frame first begins to feel the power of this constraining law, though it is the last to succumb to it. We look at the bloom of youth with interest, yet with pity; and the more graceful and sweet it is, with pity so much the more; for, whatever be its excellence and its glory, soon it begins to be deformed and dishonoured by the very force of its living on. It grows into exhaustion and collapse, till at length it crumbles into that dust out of which it was originally taken.

So is it, too, with our moral being, a far higher and diviner portion of our natural constitution; it begins with life, it ends with what is worse than the mere loss of life, with a living death. How beautiful is the human heart, when it puts forth its first leaves, and opens and rejoices in its spring-tide. Fair as may be the bodily form, fairer far, in its green foliage and bright blossoms, is natural virtue. It blooms in the young, like some rich flower, so delicate, so fragrant, and so dazzling. Generosity and lightness of heart and amiableness, the confiding spirit, the gentle temper, the elastic cheerfulness, the open hand, the pure affection, the noble aspiration, the heroic resolve, the romantic pursuit, the love in which self has no part,—are not these beautiful? and are they not dressed up and set forth for admiration in their best shapes, in tales and in poems? and ah! what a prospect of good is there! who could believe that it is to fade! and yet, as night follows upon day, as decrepitude follows upon health, so surely are failure, and overthrow, and annihilation, the issue of this natural virtue, if time only be allowed to it to run its course. There are those who are cut off in the first opening of this excellence, and then, if we may trust their epitaphs, they have lived like angels; but wait a while, let them live on, let the course of life

proceed, let the bright soul go through the fire and water of the world's temptations and seductions and corruptions and transformations; and, alas for the in-
sufficiency of nature! alas for its powerlessness to persevere, its waywardness
in disappointing its own promise! Wait till youth has become age; and not more
different is the miniature which we have of him when a boy, when every feature spoke of hope, put side by side of the large portrait painted to his honour,
when he is old, when his limbs are shrunk, his eye dim, his brow furrowed, and
his hair grey, than differs the moral grace of that boyhood from the forbidding
and repulsive aspect of his soul, now that he has lived to the age of man. For
moroseness, and misanthropy, and selfishness, is the ordinary winter of that
spring.

Such is man in his own nature, and such, too, is he in his works. The no-
blest efforts of his genius, the conquests he has made, the doctrines he has
originated, the nations he has civilized, the states he has created, they outlive
himself, they outlive him by many centuries, but they tend to an end, and that
end is dissolution. Powers of the world, sovereignties, dynasties, sooner or later
come to nought; they have their fatal hour. The Roman conqueror shed tears
over Carthage, for in the destruction of the rival city he discerned too truly an
augury of the fall of Rome; and at length, with the weight and the responsibilities, the crimes and the glories, of centuries upon centuries, the Imperial City
fell.

Thus man and all his works are mortal; they die, and they have no power
of renovation.

But what is it, my Fathers, my Brothers, what is it that has happened in
England just at this time? Something strange is passing over this land, by the
very surprise, by the very commotion, which it excites. Were we not near
enough the scene of action to be able to say what is going on,—were we the inhabitants of some sister planet possessed of a more perfect mechanism than this
earth has discovered for surveying the transactions of another globe,—and did
we turn our eyes thence towards England just at this season, we should be arrested by a political phenomenon as wonderful as any which the astronomer
notes down from his physical field of view. It would be the occurrence of a national commotion, almost without parallel, more violent than has happened here
for centuries,—at least in the judgments and intentions of men, if not in act and
deed. We should note it down, that soon after St. Michael's day, 1850, a storm
arose in the moral world, so furious as to demand some great explanation, and
to rouse in us an intense desire to gain it. We should observe it increasing from
day to day, and spreading from place to place, without remission, almost without lull, up to this very hour, when perhaps it threatens worse still, or at least
gives no sure prospect of alleviation. Every party in the body politic undergoes
its influence,—from the Queen upon her throne, down to the little ones in the
infant or day school. The ten thousands of the constituency, the sum-total of
Protestant sects, the aggregate of religious societies and associations, the great
body of established clergy in town and country, the bar, even the medical profession, nay, even literary and scientific circles, every class, every interest,
every fireside, gives tokens of this ubiquitous storm. This would be our report
of it, seeing it from the distance, and we should speculate on the cause. What is
it all about? against what is it directed? what wonder has happened upon earth?

what prodigious, what preternatural event is adequate to the burden of so vast an effect?

We should judge rightly in our curiosity about a phenomenon like this; it must be a portentous event, and it is. It is an innovation, a miracle, I may say, in the course of human events. The physical world revolves year by year, and begins again; but the political order of things does not renew itself, does not return; it continues, but it proceeds; there is no retrogression. This is so well understood by men of the day, that with them progress is idolized as another name for good. The past never returns—it is never good;—if we are to escape existing ills, it must be by going forward. The past is out of date; the past is dead. As well may the dead live to us, well may the dead profit us, as the past return. *This*, then, is the cause of this national transport, this national cry, which encompasses us. The past *has* returned, the dead lives. Thrones are overturned, and are never restored; States live and die, and then are matter only for history. Babylon was great, and Tyre, and Egypt, and Nineve, and shall never be great again. The English Church was, and the English Church was not, and the English Church is once again. This is the portent, worthy of a cry. It is the coming in of a Second Spring; it is a restoration in the moral world, such as that which yearly takes place in the physical.

Three centuries ago, and the Catholic Church, that great creation of God's power, stood in this land in pride of place. It had the honours of near a thousand years upon it; it was enthroned on some twenty sees up and down the broad country; it was based in the will of a faithful people; it energized through ten thousand instruments of power and influence; and it was ennobled by a host of Saints and Martyrs. The churches, one by one, recounted and rejoiced in the line of glorified intercessors, who were the respective objects of their grateful homage. Canterbury alone numbered perhaps some sixteen, from St. Augustine to St. Dunstan and St. Elphege, from St. Anselm and St. Thomas down to St. Edmund. York had its St. Paulinus, St. John, St. Wilfrid, and St. William; London, its St. Erconwald; Durham, its St. Cuthbert; Winton, its St. Swithun. Then there were St. Aidan of Lindisfarne, and St. Hugh of Lincoln, and St. Chad of Lichfield, and St. Thomas of Hereford, and St. Oswald and St. Wulstan of Worcester, and St. Osmund of Salisbury, and St. Birinus of Dorchester, and St. Richard of Chichester. And then, too, its religious orders, its monastic establishments, its universities, its wide relations all over Europe, its high prerogatives in the temporal state, its wealth, its dependencies, its popular honours,—where was there in the whole of Christendom a more glorious hierarchy? Mixed up with the civil institutions, with kings and nobles, with the people, found in every village and in every town,—it seemed destined to stand, so long as England stood, and to outlast, it might be, England's greatness.

But it was the high decree of heaven, that the majesty of that presence should be blotted out. It is a long story, my Fathers and Brothers—you know it well. I need not go through it. The vivifying principle of truth, the shadow of St. Peter, the grace of the Redeemer, left it. That old Church in its day became a corpse (a marvellous, an awful change!); and then it did but corrupt the air which once it refreshed, and cumber the ground which once it beautified. So all seemed to be lost; and there was a struggle for a time, and then its priests were cast out or martyred. There were sacrileges innumerable. Its temples were profaned or destroyed; its revenues seized by covetous nobles, or squandered upon the ministers of a new faith. The presence of Catholicism was at length simply removed,—its grace disowned,—its power despised,—its name, except as a matter of history, at length almost unknown. It took a long time to do this thoroughly; much time, much thought, much labour, much expense; but at last it was done. Oh, that miserable day, centuries before we were born! What a martyrdom to live in it and see the fair form of Truth, moral and material, hacked piecemeal, and every limb and organ carried off, and burned in the fire, or cast into the deep! But at last the work was done. Truth was disposed of, and shovelled away, and there was a calm, a silence, a sort of peace;—and such was about the state of things when we were born into this weary world.

My Fathers and Brothers, *you* have seen it on one side, and some of us on another; but one and all of us can bear witness to the fact of the utter contempt into which Catholicism had fallen by the time that we were born. You, alas, know it far better than I can know it; but it may not be out of place, if by one or two tokens, as by the strokes of a pencil, I bear witness to you from without, of what you can witness so much more truly from within. No longer the Catholic Church in the country; nay, no longer, I may say, a Catholic community;—but a few adherents of the Old Religion, moving silently and sorrowfully about, as memorials of what had been. "The Roman Catholics;"—not a sect, not even an interest, as men conceived of it, —not a body, however small, representative of the Great Communion abroad,—but a mere handful of individuals, who might be counted, like the pebbles and *detritus* of the great deluge, and who, forsooth, merely happened to retain a creed which, in its day indeed, was the profession of a Church. Here a set of poor Irishmen, coming and going at harvest time, or a colony of them lodged in a miserable quarter of the vast metropolis. There, perhaps an elderly person, seen walking in the streets, grave and solitary, and strange, though noble in bearing, and said to be of good family, and a "Roman Catholic." An old-fashioned house of gloomy appearance, closed in with high walls, with an iron gate, and yews, and the report attaching to it that "Roman Catholics" lived there; but who they were, or what they did, or what was meant by calling them Roman Catholics, no one could tell;—though it had an unpleasant sound, and told of form and superstition. And then, perhaps, as we went to and fro, looking with a boy's curious eyes through the great city, we might come today upon some Moravian chapel, or Quaker's meeting-house, and tomorrow on a chapel of the "Roman Catholics": but nothing was to be gathered from it, except that there were lights burning there, and some boys in white, swinging censers; and what it all meant could only be learned from books, from Protestant Histories and Sermons; and they did not report well of "the Roman Catholics," but, on the contrary, deposed that they had once had power and had abused it. And then, again, we might on one occasion hear it pointedly put out by some literary man, as the result of his careful investigation, and as a recondite point of information, which few knew, that there was this difference between the Roman Catholics of England and the Roman Catholics of Ireland, that the latter had bishops, and the former were governed by four officials, called Vicars-Apostolic.

Such was about the sort of knowledge possessed of Christianity by the heathen of old time, who persecuted its adherents from the face of the earth, and then called them a *gens lucifuga*, a people who shunned the light of day.

Such were Catholics in England, found in corners, and alleys, and cellars, and the housetops, or in the recesses of the country; cut off from the populous world around them, and dimly seen, as if through a mist or in twilight, as ghosts flitting to and fro, by the high Protestants, the lords of the earth. At length so feeble did they become, so utterly contemptible, that contempt gave birth to pity; and the more generous of their tyrants actually began to wish to bestow on them some favour, under the notion that their opinions were simply too absurd ever to spread again, and that they themselves, were they but raised in civil importance, would soon unlearn and be ashamed of them. And thus, out of mere kindness to us, they began to vilify our doctrines to the Protestant world, that so our very idiocy or our secret unbelief might be our plea for mercy.

A *great* change, an *awful* contrast, between the time-honoured Church of St. Augustine and St. Thomas, and the poor remnant of their children in the beginning of the nineteenth century! It was a miracle, I might say, to have pulled down that lordly power; but there was a greater and a truer one in store. No one could have prophesied its fall, but still less would any one have ventured to prophesy its rise again. The fall was wonderful; still after all it was in the order of nature;—all things come to nought: its rise again would be a different sort of wonder, for it is in the order of grace,—and who can hope for miracles, and such a miracle as this? Has the whole course of history a like to show? I must speak cautiously and according to my knowledge, but I recollect no parallel to it. Augustine, indeed, came to the same island to which the early missionaries had come already; but they came to Britons, and he to Saxons. The Arian Goths and Lombards, too, cast off their heresy in St. Augustine's age, and joined the Church; but they had never fallen away from her. The inspired word seems to imply the almost impossibility of such a grace as the renovation of those who have crucified to themselves again, and trodden under foot, the Son of God. Who then could have dared to hope that, out of so sacrilegious a nation as this is, a people would have been formed again unto their Saviour? What signs did it show that it was to be singled out from among the nations? Had it been prophesied some fifty years ago, would not the very notion have seemed preposterous and wild?

My Fathers, there was one of your own order, then in the maturity of his powers and his reputation. His name is the property of this diocese; yet is too great, too venerable, too dear to all Catholics, to be confined to any part of England, when it is rather a household word in the mouths of all of us. What would have been the feelings of that venerable man, the champion of God's ark in an evil time, could *he* have lived to see this day? It is almost presumptuous for one who knew him not, to draw pictures about him, and his thoughts, and his friends, some of whom are even here present; yet am I wrong in fancying that a day such as this, in which we stand, would have seemed to him a dream, or, if he prophesied of it, to his hearers nothing but a mockery? Say that one time, rapt in spirit, he had reached forward to the future, and that his mortal eye had wandered from that lowly chapel in the valley which had been for centuries in the possession of Catholics, to the neighbouring height, then waste and solitary. And let him say to those about him: "I see a bleak mount, looking upon an open country, over against that huge town, to whose inhabitants Catholicism is of so little account. I see the ground marked out, and an ample enclosure made; and plantations are rising there, clothing and circling in the space.

"And there on that high spot, far from the haunts of men, yet in the very centre of the island, a large edifice, or rather pile of edifices, appears with many fronts, and courts, and long cloisters and corridors, and story upon story. And there it rises, under the invocation of the same sweet and powerful name which has been our strength and consolation in the Valley. I look more attentively at that building, and I see it is fashioned upon that ancient style of art which brings back the past, which had seemed to be perishing from off the face of the earth, or to be preserved only as a curiosity, or to be imitated only as a fancy. I listen, and I hear the sound of voices, grave and musical, renewing the old chant, with which Augustine greeted Ethelbert in the free air upon the Kentish strand. It comes from a long procession, and it winds along the cloisters. Priests and Religious, theologians from the schools, and canons from the Cathedral, walk in due precedence. And then there comes a vision of well-nigh twelve mitred heads; and last I see a Prince of the Church, in the royal dye of empire and of martyrdom, a pledge to us from Rome of Rome's unwearied love, a token that that goodly company is firm in Apostolic faith and hope. And the shadow of the Saints is there;—St. Benedict is there, speaking to us by the voice of bishop and of priest, and counting over the long ages through which he has prayed, and studied, and laboured; there, too, is St. Dominic's white wool, which no blemish can impair, no stain can dim:—and if St. Bernard be not there, it is only that his absence may make him be remembered more. And the princely patriarch, St. Ignatius, too, the St. George of the modern world, with his chivalrous lance run through his writhing foe, he, too, sheds his blessing upon that train. And others, also, his equals or his juniors in history, whose pictures are above our altars, or soon shall be, the surest proof that the Lord's arm has not waxen short, nor His mercy failed,—they, too, are looking down from their thrones on high upon the throng. And so that high company moves on into the holy place; and there, with august rite and awful sacrifice, inaugurates the great act which brings it thither." What is that act? it is the first synod of a new Hierarchy; it is the resurrection of the Church.

O my Fathers, my Brothers, had that revered Bishop so spoken then, who that had heard him but would have said that he spoke what could not be? What! those few scattered worshippers, *the* Roman Catholics, to form a Church! Shall the past be rolled back? Shall the grave open? Shall the Saxons live again to God? Shall the shepherds, watching their poor flocks by night, be visited by a multitude of the heavenly army, and hear how their Lord has been new-born in their own city? Yes; for grace can, where nature cannot. The world grows old, but the Church is ever young. She can, in any time, at her Lord's will, "inherit the Gentiles, and inhabit the desolate cities." "Arise, Jerusalem, for thy light is come, and the glory of the Lord is risen upon thee. Behold, darkness shall cover the earth, and a mist the people; but the Lord shall arise upon thee, and His glory shall be seen upon thee. Lift up thine eyes round about, and see; all these are gathered together, they come to thee; thy sons shall come from afar, and thy daughters shall rise up at thy side." "Arise, make haste, my love, my dove, my beautiful one, and come. For the winter is now past, and the rain is over and gone. The flowers have appeared in our land . . . the fig-tree hath put forth her green figs; the vines in flower yield their sweet smell. Arise, my love, my beau-

tiful one, and come." It is the time for thy Visitation. Arise, Mary, and go forth
in thy strength into that north country, which once was thine own, and take possession of a land which knows thee not. Arise, Mother of God, and with thy
thrilling voice, speak to those who labour with child, and are in pain, till the
babe of grace leaps within them! Shine on us, dear Lady, with thy bright countenance, like the sun in his strength, *O stella matutina*, O harbinger of peace,
till our year is one perpetual May. From thy sweet eyes, from thy pure smile,
from thy majestic brow, let ten thousand influences rain down, not to confound
or overwhelm, but to persuade, to win over thine enemies. O Mary, my hope, O
Mother undefiled, fulfil to us the promise of this Spring. A second temple rises
on the ruins of the old. Canterbury has gone its way, and York is gone, and
Durham is gone, and Winchester is gone. It was sore to part with them. We
clung to the vision of past greatness, and would not believe it could come to
nought; but the Church in England has died, and the Church lives again. Westminster and Nottingham, Beverley and Hexham, Northampton and Shrewsbury,
if the world lasts, shall be names as musical to the ear, as stirring to the heart,
as the glories we have lost; and Saints shall rise out of them, if God so will, and
Doctors once again shall give the law to Israel, and Preachers call to penance
and to justice, as at the beginning.

Yes, my Fathers and Brothers, and if it be God's blessed will, not Saints
alone, not Doctors only, not Preachers only, shall be ours—but Martyrs, too,
shall reconsecrate the soil to God. We know not what is before us, ere we win
our own; we are engaged in a great, a joyful work, but in proportion to God's
grace is the fury of His enemies. They have welcomed us as the lion greets his
prey. Perhaps they may be familiarized in time with our appearance, but perhaps they may be irritated the more. To set up the Church again in England is
too great an act to be done in a corner. We have had reason to expect that such
a boon would not be given to us without a cross. It is not God's way that great
blessings should descend without the sacrifice first of great sufferings. If the
truth is to be spread to any wide extent among this people, how can we dream,
how can we hope, that trial and trouble shall not accompany its going forth?
And we have already, if it may be said without presumption, to commence our
work withal, a large store of merits. We have no slight outfit for our opening
warfare. Can we religiously suppose that the blood of our martyrs, three centuries ago and since, shall never receive its recompense? Those priests, secular
and regular, did they suffer for no end? or rather, for an end which is not yet
accomplished? The long imprisonment, the fetid dungeon, the weary suspense,
the tyrannous trial, the barbarous sentence, the savage execution, the rack, the
gibbet, the knife, the cauldron, the numberless tortures of those holy victims, O
my God, are they to have no reward? Are Thy martyrs to cry from under Thine
altar for their loving vengeance on this guilty people, and to cry in vain? Shall
they lose life, and not gain a better life for the children of those who persecuted
them? Is this Thy way, O my God, righteous and true? Is it according to Thy
promise, O King of saints, if I may dare talk to Thee of justice? Did not Thou
Thyself pray for Thine enemies upon the cross, and convert them? Did not Thy
first Martyr win Thy great Apostle, then a persecutor, by his loving prayer?
And in that day of trial and desolation for England, when hearts were pierced
through and through with Mary's woe, at the crucifixion of Thy body mystical,

was not every tear that flowed, and every drop of blood that was shed, the seeds of a future harvest, when they who sowed in sorrow were to reap in joy?

And as that suffering of the Martyrs is not yet recompensed, so, perchance, it is not yet exhausted. Something, for what we know, remains to be undergone, to complete the necessary sacrifice. May God forbid it, for this poor nation's sake! But still could we be surprised, my Fathers and my Brothers, if the winter even now should not yet be quite over? Have we any right to take it strange, if, in this English land, the spring-time of the Church should turn out to be an English spring, an uncertain, anxious time of hope and fear, of joy and suffering,—of bright promise and budding hopes, yet withal, of keen blasts, and cold showers, and sudden storms?

One thing alone I know,—that according to our need, so will be our strength. One thing I am sure of, that the more the enemy rages against us, so much the more will the Saints in Heaven plead for us; the more fearful are our trials from the world, the more present to us will be our Mother Mary, and our good Patrons and Angel Guardians; the more malicious are the devices of men against us, the louder cry of supplication will ascend from the bosom of the whole Church to God for us. We shall not be left orphans; we shall have within us the strength of the Paraclete, promised to the Church and to every member of it. My Fathers, my Brothers in the priesthood, I speak from my heart when I declare my conviction, that there is no one among you here present but, if God so willed, would readily become a martyr for His sake. I do not say you would wish it; I do not say that the natural will would not pray that that chalice might pass away; I do not speak of what you can do by any strength of yours;—but in the strength of God, in the grace of the Spirit, in the armour of justice, by the consolations and peace of the Church, by the blessing of the Apostles Peter and Paul, and in the name of Christ, you would do what nature cannot do. By the intercession of the Saints on high, by the penances and good works and the prayers of the people of God on earth, you would be forcibly borne up as upon the waves of the mighty deep, and carried on out of yourselves by the fulness of grace, whether nature wished it or no. I do not mean violently, or with unseemly struggle, but calmly, gracefully, sweetly, joyously, you would mount up and ride forth to the battle, as on the rush of Angels' wings, as your fathers did before you, and gained the prize. You, who day by day offer up the Immaculate Lamb of God, you who hold in your hands the Incarnate Word under the visible tokens which He has ordained, you who again and again drain the chalice of the Great Victim; who is to make you fear? what is to startle you? what to seduce you? who is to stop you, whether you are to suffer or to do, whether to lay the foundations of the Church in tears, or to put the crown upon the work in jubilation?

My Fathers, my Brothers, one word more. It may seem as if I were going out of my way in thus addressing you; but I have some sort of plea to urge in extenuation. When the English College at Rome was set up by the solicitude of a great Pontiff in the beginning of England's sorrows, and missionaries were trained there for confessorship and martyrdom here, who was it that saluted the fair Saxon youths as they passed by him in the streets of the great city, with the salutation, "Salvete flores martyrum"? And when the time came for each in turn to leave that peaceful home, and to go forth to the conflict, to whom did they betake themselves before leaving Rome, to receive a blessing which might nerve them for their work? They went for a Saint's blessing; they went to a calm old man, who had never seen blood, except in penance; who had longed indeed to die for Christ, what time the great St. Francis opened the way to the far East, but who had been fixed as if a sentinel in the holy city, and walked up and down for fifty years on one beat, while his brethren were in the battle. Oh! the fire of that heart, too great for its frail tenement, which tormented him to be kept at home when the whole Church was at war! and therefore came those bright-haired strangers to him, ere they set out for the scene of their passion, that the full zeal and love pent up in that burning breast might find a vent, and flow over, from him who was kept at home, upon those who were to face the foe. Therefore one by one, each in his turn, those youthful soldiers came to the old man; and one by one they persevered and gained the crown and the palm,— all but one, who had not gone, and would not go, for the salutary blessing.

My Fathers, my Brothers, that old man was my own St. Philip. Bear with me for his sake. If I have spoken too seriously, his sweet smile shall temper it. As he was with you three centuries ago in Rome, when our Temple fell, so now surely when it is rising, it is a pleasant token that he should have even set out on his travels to you; and that, as if remembering how he interceded for you at home, and recognizing the relations he then formed with you, he should now be wishing to have a name among you, and to be loved by you, and perchance to do you a service, here in your own land.[27]

PREACHING IN THE CONTEMPORARY ERA

The contemporary era includes the twentieth and twenty-first centuries, bringing us up to the present time. There is no question that the world has witnessed and participated in more technological and social developments in the twentieth century than all the other centuries combined. Consider the development of the airplane, the atomic bomb, microwave ovens, satellite communications, polio vaccine, and the Internet.

In addition to these external changes, the Second Vatican Council brought massive changes within the Church, and in the Church's relations with non-Catholics, non-Christians and non-believers. Technological advances and ecclesial reforms combined to enable the Gospel to be heard by ever-widening audiences, and in a way they could understand. Bishop Fulton Sheen, Blessed John Paul II, and Father Walter Burghardt, each in his own unique way, brought the Gospel to the ends of the earth. In addition, they stimulated thought, discussion, and writing about the most important issues facing humanity.

Bishop Fulton Sheen: Mass Media Preacher

Bishop Fulton Sheen (1895–1979) was one of the most beloved churchmen in the twentieth century. He was probably the most recognized Church leader in the world, thanks to the diffusion of his image on television in the 1950s. Fulton John Sheen was born in El Paso, Illinois, on May 8, 1895. He grew up and served as an altar boy at St. Mary's Cathedral in Peoria. He was blessed with intellectual gifts, which were recognized early in his life. He won a university scholarship while in high school, but turned it down. He knew instead that God wanted him to become a priest. After graduation, Sheen entered St. Viator's College and Seminary in Bourbannais, Illinois (now closed), where he acquired his great communication and debating skills. He attended St. Paul's Seminary in St. Paul, Minnesota, and was ordained to the priesthood for the Diocese of Peoria on September 20, 1919. Sheen earned graduate degrees at the Catholic University of America in Washington, D.C., and at the Catholic University of Louvain, Belgium. There he was strongly influenced by the teachings of Saint Thomas Aquinas. He turned down several teaching offers in obedience to his bishop, and was named assistant pastor of a rural parish.

Fulton Sheen was an extraordinary communicator. His unique ability to be at ease with all audiences was recognized early in his ministry. His bishop allowed Sheen to teach at Catholic University in Washington, D.C., and St. Edmund's College in Ware, England. Sheen met the noted author, playwright, and critic, G. K. Chesterton, while at St. Edmund's. He began the Catholic Hour broadcasts on NBC radio in 1930. Those broadcasts ran for twenty-two years. He spoke at the first religious service ever telecast in 1940. Ten years later, the bishops of the United States invited him to become National Director of the Society for the Propagation of the Faith, where he served for sixteen years. Pope Pius XII appointed him auxiliary bishop of New York in 1951.

From 1951 to 1957, he hosted a highly acclaimed television series, "Life is Worth Living," for which he won an Emmy in 1953. He wrote ninety-six books (including two best sellers, *Peace of Soul* (1949), and *Life Is Worth Living* (1953), as well as hundreds of newspaper columns and articles. People from all faiths watched him on television and enjoyed his wit and wisdom. Sheen carefully designed his broadcasts to reach people of all faiths and people of no faith. His audience looked forward to his goodbye, his blessing, and famous closing line: "Good-bye now, and God love you." In 1966, Pope Paul VI appointed Sheen Bishop of Rochester, New York, where he served until his retirement three years later.

Bishop Sheen was dedicated to promoting the Church's missionary work. To that end, he worked as National Director for the Society for the Propagation of the Faith. He traveled to many countries and founded and edited *Mission* magazine, which revealed the suffering of poor people around the world. He also served on the Commission on the Missions during the Second Vatican Council (1962–65).

Fulton Sheen died at his home in New York City on Dec. 9, 1979, and was buried in the crypt at St. Patrick's Cathedral. Interestingly, Sheen spoke often of his desire to die in the presence of the Blessed Sacrament, on a feast of Our Lady. He went to the Lord in his private chapel on a Saturday, the day after the solemnity of the Immaculate Conception. His broadcasts, books, and articles provide inspiration, and a vast amount of teaching about the Catholic faith. His cause for canonization opened in 2002.

The Preaching of Bishop Fulton J. Sheen

Bishop Sheen outlines his preaching preparation process in his wonderful autobiography *Treasure in Clay*. "All my sermons are prepared in the presence of the Blessed Sacrament," he writes. "As recreation is most pleasant and profitable in the sun, so homiletic creativity is best nourished before the Eucharist."[28] In preparing his homilies, Sheen first formulated his sermon plan. Then he meditated on it by speaking to the Lord aloud.

> Generally there are three different formats to any lecture or sermon [he notes], what is written; what is delivered; and what you wished you had said. That is why 'giving the sermon before Our Blessed Lord' is the best way for me to discover not only its weaknesses, but also its possibilities.[29]

Sheen then gathered material, formulated points, and followed with a mediation or quiet vocalization without referring to notes. Again he tells us, "The material of the sermon is not wholly that which comes from the paper to the brain, but which proceeds from a creative mind to the lips."[30]

Sheen strongly recommends study and reading as part of preaching preparation. He calls the neglect of continuing education "one of the weaknesses of the modern pulpit and lecture platform."[31] "Books are great friends," he continues. "they always have something worthwhile to say to you when you pick them up. They never complain about being too busy and they are always at leisure to feed the mind."[32] He uses the images of food and a building to illustrate good preaching preparation. "When the intellectual larder is empty, it is difficult to prepare a homiletic meal. The higher the building, the more materials have to go into it," he says.[33] Sheen includes literature, science, philosophy of politics, "in a word everything that would be useful for a priest in instructing or discoursing with others, or in supplying material for communication" in his reading repertoire.[34] Specifically, he recommends for the homilist's library William Barclay's seventeen-volume *Daily Study Bible*, Arthur W. Pink's three-volume *Exposition on the Gospel of St. John*, as well as the works of G. K. Chesterton, C. S. Lewis, Hillaire Belloc, Malcolm Muggeridge, and the *Oxford Book of Mystical Verse*.

Sheen makes several interesting comments on the priestly ministry of preaching in his book *The Priest is Not His Own* (1963). First, he talks about the importance of constant spiritual renewal on the part of preachers.

> Contact with the Divine is a privilege that can similarly turn into indifference unless each day one tries to get a step closer to the Lord. Trafficking with the Word of God one Sunday after another without prayer and preparation does not leave a priest the same; it leaves him worse. Failure to climb means to slide

backwards. The only defense against *acedia*, against the tragic loss of divine
reality, is a daily renewal of faith in Christ. The priest who has not kept near the
fires of the tabernacle can strike no sparks from the pulpit.[35]

He warns priests that harsh judgment awaits those who fail to take their
preaching ministry seriously. He suggests that priests meditate each morning on
the subject of next Sunday's sermon, and pray to the Holy Spirit for inspiration
and insight, for five minutes before delivering the homily itself.

Bishop Sheen's preaching was shaped by his profound understanding of the
relationship between faith and reason, his deep appreciation for and insights into
Sacred Scripture, his concern for the growing secularist movement, the decline
of faith in the West, and his strong opposition to Communism.

Sheen identifies repentance as the most important sermon topic. Repentance
was the subject of John the Baptist's preaching (Matt. 3:8), Our Lord's first
sermon (Matt. 4:7), and Saint Peter's first sermon to his fellow Jews (Acts 2:38).
Paul and John the Beloved also spoke on this topic more than once (Acts 20:21;
Rev. 2:5,16). Why preach on repentance? "Because it is the first act of a soul
that turns back to God, the first stroke that severs sin from the heart," he wrote.[36]
He goes on to caution against railing from the pulpit:

> Before the thunder, we see the light. But to thunder against souls without bring-
> ing to them the light of God's truth and the love revealed through the Sacred
> Heart may bring a smile to their lips. It will not, however, bring them to their
> knees in repentance.[37]

Father Timothy Sherwood has written an excellent book on the preaching of
Archbishop Sheen. In it, he discusses Sheen's evangelical outreach using the
media of radio and television. Sheen applied classical methods of rhetoric (e.g.,
organization, memory), and extensive intellectual and spiritual preparation for
both his homilies and his talks to secular audiences. Sherwood examines the
three dimensions of pulpit, audience, and truth in his examination of the substance and style of Sheen's preaching.

The sermons of Bishop Sheen are found in various books, including a number of collections of Sheen's talks published by Our Sunday Visitor. Sermons
delivered in Lent, and on Palm Sunday and Good Friday throughout the 1930s
and 1940s, are most prevalent.

The Sheen Archives in Rochester, New York, has released the homily he
gave on Good Friday in April 1979. It was the last Good Friday homily he delivered. In this homily, delivered at St. Agnes' Church in New York, Bishop
Sheen talks about the three different kinds of spectators at the cross: the spectators of indifference, the spectators of pain, and the spectators of love.

Homily: The Spectators at the Cross

I take your applause as a sign of thanksgiving, for this is the fifty-eighth Good
Friday in which the good Lord has permitted me to talk about His passion and
death. Fifty-eight years. Now in case you're counting them back I started at
four. Each year I have chosen a different topic, and this year our meditation
will be on "Spectators On and About the Cross."

There are three kinds of spectators: the indifferent or "fallen aways," the
spectators of pain, and finally, the spectators of love. *First*, the spectators of indifference. The great French writer Pascal said, "Christ is on the cross until the
end of the world." And the conversion of Saint Paul gives proof of *this*, indeed,
for when the risen Lord spoke from Heaven, as Paul was persecuting His
Church, Our Lord said, "Why are you persecuting me?" So Christ is still on the
cross until the end of time. The Gospel tells us that as He was led to Calvary
there were many spectators. And a very interesting line about them is that
"those who executed him sat and watched, divided his garments and then gam-
bled for the seamless robe." It seems that our Blessed Lord had five garments.
The executioners were four in number, they divided four of the garments, but
the fifth, being seamless, maybe made by His own Mother, and also knowing
perhaps that it had wrought a miracle, decided to shake dice for it. They were
spectators that day.

We are spectators this day. All of us in varying degrees are spectators.
Some are totally indifferent, just like the executioners. They sit and watch.
Someone gave me a canary to be my companion during a long sickness, and
I've often thought as I looked at that bird, "If I told that bird: 'You are in this
tiny little narrow cage, and you have wings, but this is the right place for you,'"
I'm sure the bird would be depressed. If, however, the bird could understand,
and I said to him, "You're in the wrong place. You have the gift of song that
should mount to the heavens, and you have wings that should fly," the bird then
would be happier. And so we're unhappy when we're locked in this little cosmos which could be shattered by a bomb. But if we're told that there's another
world, then life becomes a little bit happier. But the indifferent people sat and
watched.

Now the word "watched" in Scripture does not mean they looked at the
crucifixion because it was interesting to see a man die. It was rather because the
executioners were told that Christ said He would rise again from the dead, and
they were told to be on guard, lest someone steal the Body and say that He was
risen. So it was different kind of watching. Now that's the kind of watching
there is in the indifferent who once had the faith, those among you who had the
faith and who no longer practice it, or who are in bad marriages, or living evil
lives. You're spectators. You say, "Well, I do not believe," but you watch.
Maybe He will rise from the dead, maybe we better sit here, and you spend the
time "dicing," a little pleasure here and there in order to make one forget that
one has given up the faith. But all the while, the grace of God worries you and
disturbs you. We watch. We say we do not believe, but we half-believe, and we
carry with us maybe a few remembrances and relics, like the sign of the cross
on the forehead at night. But as spectators, the Lord will take us, even when we

are unable to walk. If you but stumble into those confessional boxes, He will welcome you back.

So much for the first spectators. They were the indifferent. Remember that famous poem of G. Studdert Kennedy about indifference. He compared Our Lord coming to Calvary and coming to the modern city of Birmingham. He said,

> When Jesus came to Golgotha they nailed Him on a tree,
>
> . . . .
>
> And they crowned Him with a crown of thorns, red were His wounds and deep.
> For those were crude and cruel days, and human flesh was cheap.
> When Jesus came to Birmingham they only passed Him by,
> They would not hurt a hair of Him; they only let Him die;
> For men had grown more tender. They would not give Him pain.
> They only just walked down the street and left Him in the rain.
>
> . . . .
>
> And so it rained. The winter rain that drenched Him through and through;
> And when all the crowds had left the street without a soul to see,
> Then Jesus crouched against a wall and sighed for Calvary.

It was more endurable than the indifference of men.

Now we come to the *second* spectators. They are on the cross. Spectators of pain, and in pain. Pain, anxiety, mental worry, suffering, sadness—all of these disturb the soul, and it was only fitting, therefore, that the good Lord look out on pain and leave us a lesson about it. So on either side of Him were crucified—we call them 'thieves'—they were rather rebels.

Remember that at that particular time, Jerusalem was under the power of Rome, and many a Jew was a loyalist, and opposed to the Roman government; so that as lawless rebels, Pilate made an example of them and had them crucified. They both suffered equally. The crucifixion was such a terrible form of punishment, that Cicero once said he hoped no Roman would ever see one. And no Roman citizen was ever crucified. Saint Paul was a Roman citizen— was stoned to death.

But these two were nailed on either side of Our Lord. They both cursed and blasphemed. So there was no difference between them, at the beginning. The first one, the rebel that was on the left of Our Blessed Lord represents the pain of those who say, "Take me down." The one on the right wanted to be taken up. The one on the left turned his head as much as he could [and] said to Our Lord, "If you are the Son of God, save yourself. Save us." He thought that all our Lord was, was a healer—a healer. You know there are many today who are beginning to believe that that is the essence of Christianity, healing. The Lord does heal, but not always. There will be not a complete healing until the whole cosmos is renewed. Our Lord did not heal Lazarus. He allowed him to die. Our Lord did not release John the Baptist from prison, though He prayed. God will now and then heal, and He does. But healing is not the essence of His coming. That was all, however, that the rebel on the left wanted, just to be healed. As a matter of fact, if he were living today—you see, he never thought of sin. If he had money, he would have spent thousands of dollars on psycho-therapy, and wondered maybe why he was a rebel, why he was a thief. But the thought of sin never entered into his mind—just to be taken down—and he probably would have gone on with the dirty business of stealing, and robbery, and lawlessness.

Few of us think of sin, even when we're sick. As a matter of fact, when-ever I pass a hospital, I always think of how much wasted pain there is; pain that is not offered up because there is no one to love. Love will not kill pain, but it certainly will soften it. When one has no one to love, then one is apt to curse, as he did.

And on the other side, this rebel had a change of heart. It might have been the sight of the Lord's Mother at the foot of the cross, or the word of Our Lord extending forgiveness for sins, but whatever it was, the straw that was there was kindled. And he shouted to his companion. He said, "We are suffering justly for our sins. This man has done no wrong." And then came a burst of faith. "Remember me, when you come into your Kingdom." Imagine! a king-dom—a crown of thorns, a royal diadem, a nail, a scepter, a cross, a throne. But he had that faith, and the Lord answered him back: "This day thou shall be with me in Paradise." One of the first companions of the risen Lord into the King-dom of Heaven. Now this rebel that was on the right—I think it leaves us this great example about pain, that much pain comes to us undeserved, so we say.

But honestly, look into your own heart. I've looked into mine. I've had a great deal of suffering in the eighty-three years of my life, physical suffering, and other suffering, that should never have happened, that lasted over many years; and yet, as I look back, I know very well that I have never received the punishment that I deserved. God has been easy with me. He has not laid on me burdens that were ever equal to my failures. And if we look into our own soul, I think that we will also come to that conclusion. For God speaks to us in various ways. As C. S. Lewis put it: "God whispers to us in our pleasures. He speaks to us in our conscience. And He shouts to us in our pain."

Pain is God's megaphone. Pain is Heaven's loudspeaker. Unlike the rip-ples that are made in a brook or sea when you throw in a stone, the ripples of pain, instead of going out to distant shores, they narrow and narrow and come to a central point where there is less of the outside of the circle, and more of the center, not the ego, but the real person and the real self, and one begins to find oneself alone with God. That is what happens in pain.

The one on the right saw that. And as we look at pain and those in suffer-ing, we only wish that they could understand the mystery of it—why does it happen? You see, I'm sure that that man on the left said, "Well, God is evil." That's why he said, "If you're the Son of God, save us. All your God does anyway is cure." No!

When I was a boy and had a toothache, I would always go to my grand-mother, because she'd give me oil of cloves. And I was afraid to go to my fa-ther because he'd take me to the dentist, and he would hurt me. One day he took me to the dentist, and the dentist said, "You have a very grave infection in your tooth, and it's spreading through your organism. And that tooth has to be pulled, and it's going to give you some pain." The dentist pulled the tooth, my father stood there holding my hand, which really did no good at all—and then, even though I was just a boy, I somehow reasoned that "Why doesn't he stop the dentist? Why does he allow him to make me suffer?" Because he wanted to prevent that infection through my body. And so, the heavenly Father says to His Son on the cross, "You take on the sins and the infections and all the poisons of the world," and the Father was with him, but the Father let Him suffer because of the eventual good that it would do for us in the Resurrection.

But more than that, the man on the central cross was in pain, too. And it was a very unusual kind of pain, which He knew that He would have, which He foretold on many occasions. It was actually the burden of all of our sins. That is why Our Blessed Lord came to this earth. His name "Jesus" means "Savior." He saves us from our sins, so that He took upon [himself] the sin of each and every one of you, whether you know it or not. Now down here before me are two of my doctors who saved my life three or four times, and they've seen me close to death on various occasions. They've been in the Intensive Care wards, and suffered with the patients, as these doctors of mine did. But imagine Our Lord walking through the Intensive Care Ward of the world, and like a great sponge, absorbing into Himself every wounded member, every weak heart, every broken blood vessel, every torn muscle, every battered head; or walking through a battlefield, and drawing to himself all the wounds of those who are wounded. That is what He was doing on that central cross, so that we could never say, "Does God know what it is to suffer? Does He know what it is to be in exile? Does He know anything about poverty, living in a stable? Does He know anything about living under totalitarian governments? If God is good, why does He make me suffer?"

In the end we will discover that sometimes when we're very good, the suffering is to make us better, and we'll have a higher place in Heaven. But in any case, as we see now, as we come to this next word, or rather this next view of spectators, how all of those wounds change.

And the *third* spectators were lovers. It is indifferent that they both were women because we are relating them to love. At the foot of the cross was Mary Magdalene, who is never shown standing. She was too prostrate with grief. Whenever she appears in the Gospel, she's always at the feet of the Lord. And His Blessed Mother. They stand for two kinds of love: one is *need love*; the other is *gift love*. *Need love* is that which we experience because we are imperfect: we need food for the stomach, thought for the mind, music for the ears, friends for the heart. They fill a want. The *gift love* is a love that does not want anything. It just gives, surrenders itself, sacrifices itself.

Now the first kind of love, which the Greeks called *eros*, was the love of friendship, the love of friend for friend, and the love of a good husband and wife, and so forth. *Eros* was a blessed love until Freud changed it into the erotic. Then it became sex. So that today in America whenever the word love is used it is generally used as sex. As a matter of fact, have you noticed that automobiles are now being advertised as sexy? I think the reason is they break down after two years!

Now what is the erotic love, of which Freud spoke, and which Mary Magdalene practiced? The erotic love that Magdalene practiced was a love that was not directed to a person. It was to a pleasure, to a release of energy. It's a love that admits of a substitution. Love that is for a person remains the same. Sex love is transferable. A man walking on Forty-Second Street says he wants a woman. He doesn't want a woman; he just wants a release. The woman makes no difference to him. It is really not love at all, because when you love a person, you love the person in the entirety. It's not the face, the body, or anything else. It is just the totality. And in that love, say of a young man and woman which eventually ends in marriage, there is very little thought, if any at all, in either, about the relations that they may have one another as husband and wife. That comes later. It's the person who's loved. But in this Freudian, erotic, sexy love, the person does not matter. It's just as much as if we suddenly became crazy about feet, and everybody began talking about every one else's feet, and not the least bit concerned about their person.

Well, that's the way Magdalene was. And she changed. How she changed we do not know. She probably heard Our Blessed Lord preach. But in any case, when Our Lord was in Simon's house, just a short time before the crucifixion, she brought a vessel of precious ointment, and it was very expensive, because Judas, who knew the price of everything and the value of nothing, judged it as worth about 300 pieces of silver—about ten times as much as Our Lord was worth. That ointment, that nard that she had, she'd been using in her profession; and she broke it, poured it over His feet, and Our Lord said [that] this was for his burial. And she became completely changed as a result. And the love then became the same kind of love as the other woman that was with her, Our Blessed Mother.

Our Blessed Mother had the *agape* love, sacrificial love. She never lived for herself. Her love was such that from the very moment of her existence she had completely identified herself with Our Lord, completely. And in His providence, He had indicated that to her. Now you who are mothers, imagine yourself at the birth of your son, and your friends bring some myrrh, and funeral spices as a gift. That's what the wise men brought her. Imagine [bringing] embalming fluid to a babe! And His Mother had to look at it, and said, "All right, I'm consecrated to him. He's giving Himself for the life of the world, and I'm going to unite myself with Him as much as I can." And then when He's presented to the Temple at forty days, old Simeon said, "A sword will pierce thy heart, too." In other words, when He was hanging on the cross, and a centurion would pierce His heart, she would be so identified with him that her heart would also be plunged. Then, at the marriage feast of Cana, she asked for a miracle, and He says, "I must be about my Father's business." He began to alienate Himself from her. There was to be no maternal ties of the physical order, and when she's pointed out in the crowd as His Mother, He says, "Who is my mother? Anyone who does the will of my Father in Heaven is my father, my mother, my brother, my sister." There's an entirely new relationship. And then looking down to John, whom He did not call "John," but "the disciple," to indicate that he was not the son of Zebedee, but a follower of Our Lord. We're disciples of our Lord, all of us. So when he was speaking to him, he was speaking to you and to me. And He said, "There's your mother. There she is." So He delivered her over to us. It was a very poor exchange that she was getting, giving up the Son of God merely for us, but she did it. She did it to be our intercessor. Our Lord was really telling us there has to be a feminine principle in religion, and it's going to be my Mother, and when I go to Heaven, I will intercede with the Father. She will intercede with me. You pray to her. She will help you.

And this Lord, whom we saw on the cross, and whom we witnessed as spectators, will come again. We know not when. He said, "You know not the hour or the day." It could be very quickly, when we least expect it. For as the Bible said, "When the sun rose on Sodom and Gomorrah that morning, it was bright. He said He would come like a thief in the night, and when He comes, He will have not wounds but scars, scars on hands and feet and side, and that is the way He will judge us. "Show me your hands. Have you a scar from giving? A scar of sacrificing yourself for another? Show me your feet. Have you gone about doing good? Were you wounded in service? Show me your heart. Have you left a place for divine love?" And that's the way He will know His own. As the poet Shillito put it,

> If I had never sought Thee, I seek Thee now;
> Thine eyes burn through the dark, our only stars;
> we must have sight of thorn pricks on Thy brow,
> We must have Thee, O Jesus of the Scars.

> The heavens frighten us; they are too calm;
> In all the universe we have no place.
> Our wounds are hurting us; where is Thy balm?
> Lord Jesus, by Thy Scars we claim Thy grace.

> If when the doors are shut, Thou drawest near,
> only reveal those hands, that side of Thine;
> We know to-day what wounds are, have no fear,
> Show us Thy Scars, we know the countersign.

> The other gods were strong; but Thou wast weak;
> They rode, but Thou didst stumble to a throne;
> But to our wounds only God's wounds can speak,
> and no God has wounds, but ours alone.

As we say, kneeling, the Act of Contrition: O my God, I am heartily sorry for having offended Thee, and I detest all of my sins because I dread the loss of Heaven and the pains of Hell. But most of all because they offend Thee, my God, who art all good and deserving of all my love. I firmly resolve, with the help of Thy grace, to confess my sins, to do penance, and amend my life. Amen.

God love you. (*His Last Words: Fulton J. Sheen*, 49 min./color)

Blessed John Paul II: Millennial Preacher

Few popes have earned the title "Great." Popes Leo (461) and Gregory (604) are among them. We are fortunate to have had a "great" pope in the twentieth century. John Paul II (1920–2005) was a giant among popes. When he was elected in 1978, he was known to be young, energetic, and orthodox. The cardinals who elected him expected him to do important work for the Church. They had no idea he would live as long as he did, or accomplish as much as he did.

Karol Jozef Wojtyla was born on May 18, 1920, in Wadowice, Poland. His father was an army officer, and his mother was a school teacher. He grew up during a period of relative calm between the two world wars. On September 1, 1939, Nazi Germany invaded Poland and began a nearly six-year reign of terror, exploitation, and annihilation of the Polish people. Wojtyla worked in a quarry and a chemical plant during the war. He studied in an underground seminary, and participated in Polish theater. At one point, as the Germans were retreating from Poland, John Paul had to hide from the Nazis, and narrowly escaped arrest and deportation to the death camps. He studied for the priesthood, and was ordained on All Saints' Day, November 1, 1946. In 1958 he was ordained a bishop, and later participated in the Second Vatican Council. Pope Paul VI made Wojtyla a cardinal of the Archdiocese of Krakow in 1967. He used his authority to promote the Church's interests, and to resist Communism nonviolently.

On October 16, 1978, he was elected the 264th successor of Saint Peter. His papacy coincided with the end of one millennium and the beginning of another. Much of his work in the 1980s and 1990s focused on preparing the Church to enter the third Christian Millennium. More than any previous pope, John Paul tirelessly traveled the globe, drawing on his theatrical skills to present his message to millions. He was fluent in many languages: his native Polish, as well as Italian, French, German, English, Spanish, Portuguese, Russian, Croatian, and, most importantly, Latin. He transformed the papacy into a global pastoral office, addressing youth, artists, civil authorities, Jews, Muslims, and other audiences.

He spent much of his time speaking and teaching. His principle themes, laid out in the encyclical *Redemptor Hominis* (1979), included the dignity of the human person, peace and social justice, the mystery of Redemption, the spiritual importance of the Eucharist and Reconciliation, and the need for solid ethics in public life. He stressed the Church's moral authority in an age that distances God and religious values from the public arena. He was greatly devoted to the Blessed Mother and the Eucharist.

One of the notable features of John Paul's Pontificate was the large number of beatifications and canonizations. John Paul presided at 143 beatification ceremonies and proclaimed 1,339 blesseds. He held 52 canonization ceremonies and made 483 new saints.[38] In his most famous acts, he canonized Pio of Pietrelcina and Jose Maria Escriva, and he beatified Mother Teresa of Calcutta. Another notable feature of this aspect of his papal ministry was that he often performed these ceremonies in the countries where these saints and blesseds lived.

His formidable intellect remained despite the infirmities of old age and Parkinson's Disease. John Paul passed away on Saturday, April 2, 2005, on the eve of Divine Mercy Sunday. His cause for canonization was opened in the summer of 2005, and he was beatified by Pope Benedict XVI on May 1, 2011.

The Preaching of Blessed John Paul II

John Paul's preaching was shaped by many things, including his education in Poland, his experience as a priest, and as bishop in Krakow. His hardships at the hands of Communists and Nazis, his twenty-six-year papacy, his understanding of the Second Vatican Council, and his determination to implement and teach its authentic meaning were other factors that shaped his preaching. His preaching was marked by biblical scholarship, theological reflection, personal prayer, and spiritual insight. He would often greet audiences in their native languages. John Paul viewed the homily as a tremendous catechetical moment; and he understood that the homilist was not just teaching, but proclaiming the Gospel of Jesus Christ. He provided insight for modern hearers into the biblical texts.

As in his encyclicals and other writings, John Paul frequently concluded his homilies with references to our Blessed Mother. They were often simple phrases or exhortations at the end, a reminder that in living the Christian life, one must remember to invoke Mary's intercession, which he saw as invaluable. One example would be a homily he gave on Pentecost 1998. At the end of the homily, he spoke of the prayer of Mary and the Apostles in the Upper Room. "We pray with Mary, sanctuary of the Holy Spirit, a most precious dwelling-place of Christ among us, so that she may help us to be living temples of the Spirit, and tireless witnesses of the Gospel." Pope Benedict has continued this practice in his preaching, a statement of his belief in Mary's continuing importance.

John's Paul's reflections on the topic of preaching have been discussed in the section "Magisterial Documents." He put into practice the principles he taught in the Church's official documents. Perhaps John Paul's most eloquent homily was not one he delivered in a formal address, but rather one he delivered personally as he neared the end of his life. He often spoke of the virtue of hope and the value of suffering. He dedicated an apostolic letter to the topic of Christian suffering (*Salvifici Doloris*). But, in his last years, as he suffered from Parkinson's Disease, and underwent hospitalization for a tracheotomy, he offered his suffering to God, and spoke of the virtue of hope. His attitude and devotion to duty were eloquent testimony to the value of suffering. He totally entrusted himself to Jesus and His Blessed Mother (*Totus Tuus* was his motto).

Blessed John Paul delivered the following homily during his visit to San Antonio, Texas, on September 13, 1987. It encapsulates characteristics of John Paul's preaching, including his fluency with languages, his love for the Eucharist and Reconciliation, and his appreciation of culture and history.

Homily: Address to the People of San Antonio, Texas

My soul, give thanks to the Lord; all my being, bless his holy name. (Ps. 103 (102), 1)

Dear Brothers and Sisters,
Dear Friends,

Citizens of San Antonio and of the State of Texas,

1. It gives me an immense joy to be with you on this Sunday morning and to invoke God's blessings upon this vast State and upon the whole Church in this region.

¡Texas! Este nombre trae inmediatamente a mi memoria la rica historia y desarrollo cultural de esta parte de los Estados Unidos.

En este maravilloso emplazamiento, frente a la Ciudad de San Antonio, no puedo por menos de evocar el recuerdo del Padre Massanet, franciscano, el cual, el 13 de junio de 1691, en la fiesta de San Antonio de Padua, celebró la Santa Misa en las márgenes del río San Antonio para los componentes de una de las primeras expediciones españolas y para un grupo de indios del lugar.

Since then, people of many different origins have come here, so that today yours is *a multicultural society*, striving for the fullness of harmony and collaboration among all. I express my cordial gratitude to the representatives of the State of Texas and the City of San Antonio who have wished to be present at this moment of prayer. I also greet the members of the various Christian Communions who join us in praising the name of our Lord Jesus Christ. A special word of thanks to Archbishop Flores and to the bishops, priests, deacons, religious, and all the Catholic faithful of Texas. The peace of Christ be with you all!

2. *Today is Sunday*: the Lord's Day. Today is like the "seventh day" about which the Book of Genesis says that "God rested from all the work he had undertaken" (*Gen.* 2, 2). Having completed the work of creation, he "rested." God rejoiced in his work; he "looked at everything that he had made, and he found it very good" (*Ibid.* 1, 31). *"So God blessed the seventh day and made it holy"* (*Ibid.* 2, 3).

On this day we are called to reflect more deeply on the mystery of creation, and therefore of our own lives. We are called to "rest" in God, the Creator of the universe. Our duty is to praise him: "My soul give thanks to the Lord . . . give thanks to the Lord *and never forget all his blessings*" (*Ps.* 103(102), 1–2). This is a task for each human being. Only the human person, created in the image and likeness of God, is capable of raising a hymn of praise and thanksgiving to the Creator. The earth, with all its creatures, and the entire universe, call on man to be their voice. Only the human person is capable of releasing from the depths of his or her being that hymn of praise, proclaimed without words by all creation: "My soul, give thanks to the Lord; *all my being*, bless his holy name" (*Ps.* 103(102), 1).

3. What is the message of today's liturgy? To us gathered here in San Antonio, in the State of Texas, and taking part in the Eucharistic Sacrifice of our Lord and Saviour Jesus Christ, Saint Paul addresses these words: *"None of us lives as his own master, and none of us dies as his own master.* While we live we are responsible to the Lord and when we die we die as his servants. Both in life and death *we are the Lord's"* (*Rom.* 14, 7–8).

These words are *concise, but filled with a moving message.* "We live" and "we die." We live in this material world that surrounds us, limited by the horizons of our earthly journey through time. We live in this world, *with the inevitable prospect of death*, right from the moment of conception and of birth. And yet, we must look beyond the material aspect of our earthly existence. Certainly, bodily death is a necessary passage for us all; but it is also true that what from its very beginning has borne in itself the image and likeness of God cannot be completely given back to the corruptible matter of the universe. This is a fundamental truth and attitude of our Christian faith. In Saint Paul's terms: "while we live we are responsible to the Lord, and when we die we die as his servants." We live *for* the Lord, and our dying too is life in the Lord.

Today, on this Lord's Day, I wish to invite all those who are listening to my words, not to forget our immortal destiny: life after death—the eternal happiness of heaven, or the awful possibility of eternal punishment, eternal separation from God, in what the Christian tradition has called hell (Cfr. *Matth.* 25, 41; 22, 13; 25, 30). *There can be no truly Christian living without an openness to this transcendent dimension of our lives.* "Both in life and death we are the Lord's" (*Rom.* 14, 8).

4. The Eucharist that we celebrate constantly confirms our living and dying "in the Lord": *"Dying you destroyed our death, rising you restored our life."* In fact, Saint Paul wrote: "we are the Lord's. That is why Christ died and came to life again, that he might be Lord of both the dead and the living" (*Rom.* 14, 8–9). Yes, *Christ is the Lord!*

The Paschal Mystery has transformed our human existence, so that it is no longer under the dominion of death. In Jesus Christ, our Redeemer, "we live for the Lord" and "we die for the Lord." Through him and with him and in him, *we belong to God* in life and in death. We exist not only "for death" but "for God." For this reason, on this day "made by the Lord" (*Ps.* 119 (118), 24), the Church *all over the world* speaks her blessing from the very depths of the Paschal Mystery of Christ: "My soul, give thanks to the Lord; all my being, bless his holy name. Give thanks... *and never forget all his blessings*" (*Ps.* 103 (102), 1–2).

"Never forget!" Today's reading from the Gospel according to Saint Matthew gives us an example of a man who has forgotten (Cfr. *Matth.* 18, 21–35). He has forgotten the favour given by his lord – and consequently he has shown himself to be cruel and heartless in regard to his fellow human being. In this way the liturgy *introduces us to the experience of sin* as it has developed from the beginnings of the history of man alongside the experience of death.

We die in the physical body when all the energies of life are extinguished. *We die through sin when love dies in us. Outside of Love there is no Life.* If man opposes love and lives without love, death takes root in his soul and grows. For this reason Christ cries out: "I give you a new commandment: love one another. Such as my love has been for you, so must your love be for each other" (*Io.* 13, 34). The cry for love is the cry for life, for the victory of the soul over sin and death. The source of this victory is *the Cross of Jesus Christ: his Death and his Resurrection.*

5. Again, in the Eucharist, our lives are touched by *Christ's own radical victory over sin—sin which is the death of the soul,* and, ultimately, the reason for bodily death. "That is why Christ died and came to life again, that he might be Lord of the dead" (Cfr. *Rom.* 14, 9)—that he might give life again to those who are dead in sin or because of sin.

And so, the Eucharist begins with *the penitential rite.* We confess our sins in order to obtain forgiveness through the Cross of Christ, and so receive a part in his Resurrection from the dead. But if our conscience reproaches us with mortal sin, our taking part in the Mass can be fully fruitful only if beforehand we receive absolution *in the Sacrament of Penance.*

The *ministry of reconciliation* is a fundamental part of the Church's life and mission. Without overlooking any of the many ways in which Christ's victory over sin becomes a reality in the life of the Church and of the world, it is important for me to emphasize that it is above all *in the Sacrament of Forgiveness and Reconciliation that the power of the redeeming blood of Christ is made effective in our personal lives.*

6. In different parts of the world there is *a great neglect of the Sacrament of Penance.* This is sometimes linked to an obscuring of the religious and moral conscience, a loss of the sense of sin, or a lack of adequate instruction on the importance of this sacrament in the life of Christ's Church. At times the neglect occurs because we fail to take seriously our lack of love and justice, and God's corresponding offer of reconciling mercy. Sometimes there is a hesitation or an unwillingness to accept maturely and responsibly the consequences of the objective truths of faith. For these reasons it is necessary to emphasize once again that *"with regard to the substance of the sacrament* there has always remained firm and unchanged in the consciousness of the Church *the certainty* that, by the will of Christ, forgiveness is offered to each individual by means of sacramental absolution given by the ministers of Penance" (Ioannis Pauli PP. II *Reconciliatio et Paenitentia,* 30).

Again I ask all my brother bishops and priests to do everything possible to make the administration of this sacrament *a primary aspect* of their service to God's people. There can be no substitute for the means of grace which Christ himself has placed in our hands. The Second Vatican Council never intended that this Sacrament of Penance be less practiced; what the Council expressly asked for was that the faithful might more easily understand the sacramental signs and more eagerly and *frequently* have recourse to the sacraments (Cfr. *Sacrosanctum Concilium,* 59). And just as sin deeply touches the individual conscience, so we understand why the absolution of sins must be individual and not collective, except in extraordinary circumstances as approved by the Church.

I ask you, dear Catholic brothers and sisters, not to see Confession as a mere attempt at psychological liberation—however legitimate this too might be—but as a sacrament, a liturgical act. *Confession* is an act of honesty and courage; *an act of entrusting ourselves,* beyond sin, *to the mercy of a loving and forgiving God.* It is an act of the prodigal son who returns to his Father and is welcomed by him with the kiss of peace. It is easy, therefore, to understand why "every confessional is a special and blessed place from which there is born new and uncontaminated a reconciled individual—a reconciled world!" (Ioannis Pauli PP. II *Reconciliatio et Paenitentia,* 31, V; cfr. III).

The potential for *an authentic and vibrant renewal of the whole Catholic Church* through the more faithful use of the Sacrament of Penance is immeasurable. It flows directly from the loving heart of God himself! This is a certainty of faith which I offer to each one of you and to the entire Church in the United States.

To those who have been far away from the Sacrament of Reconciliation and forgiving Love I make this appeal: *come back to this source of grace; do not be afraid!* Christ himself is waiting for you. He will heal you, and you will be at peace with God!

To all the young people of the Church, I extend a special invitation to receive Christ's forgiveness and his strength in the Sacrament of Penance. It is *a mark of greatness* to be able to say: I have made a mistake: I have sinned, Father; I am sorry; I ask for pardon; I will try again, because I rely on your strength and I believe in your love. And I know that the power of your Son's Paschal Mystery—the Death and Resurrection of our Lord Jesus Christ—is *greater than my weaknesses and all the sins of the world.* I will come and confess my sins and be healed, and I will live in your love!

7. In Jesus Christ the world has truly known the mystery of forgiveness, mercy and reconciliation, which is proclaimed by God's word this day. At the same time, God's inexhaustible mercy to us obliges us *to be reconciled among ourselves.* This makes practical demands on the Church in Texas and the Southwest of the United States. It means bringing *hope and love wherever there is division and alienation.*

Your history registers *a meeting of cultures,* indigenous and immigrant, sometimes marked by tensions and conflicts, yet *constantly moving towards reconciliation and harmony.* People of different races and languages, colours and customs, have come to this land to make it their home. Together with the indigenous peoples of these territories, there are the descendants of those who came from almost very country in Europe: from Spain and France, from Germany and Belgium, from Italy, Hungary and Czechoslovakia, from Ireland, England and Scotland, and even from my own native Poland—for it was to Texas, and Panna Maria, that the first Polish immigrants came to the United States. There are descendants of those who came in chains from Africa; those from Lebanon, the Philippines and Vietnam, and from every Latin American country, especially from Mexico.

This land is a crossroads, standing at the border of two great nations, and experiencing both the enrichment and the complications which arise from this circumstance. You are thus a symbol and a kind of laboratory testing America's commitment to her founding moral principles and human values. These principles and values are now being reaffirmed by America as she celebrates the Bicentennial of her Constitution and speaks once more about justice and freedom, and about the acceptance of diversity within a fundamental unity—a unity arising from a shared vision of the dignity of every human person, and a shared responsibility for the welfare of all, especially of the needy and the persecuted.

8. Against this background one may speak of a current phenomenon here and elsewhere—*the movement of people northwards,* not only from Mexico but from other southern neighbours of the United States. On this matter also there is work of reconciliation to be done. Among you there are people of great courage and generosity "who have been doing much on behalf of suffering brothers and sisters arriving from the south. They have sought to show compassion in the face of complex human, social and political realities. *Here* human needs, both spiritual and material, continue to call out to the Church with thousands of voices, and the whole Church must respond by the proclamation of God's word and by selfless deeds of service. Here too there is ample space for continuing and growing collaboration among members of the various Christian Communions.

En este contexto, *la comunidad hispana se enfrenta al mayor de los desafíos*. Aquellos de entre vosotros de descendencia hispánica—tan numerosos, presentes en esta tierra desde hace tanto tiempo y bien preparados para poder responder—estáis llamados a oír la palabra de Cristo y a conservarla en vuestro corazón: "Os doy un mandamiento nuevo: que os améis los unos a los otros. Que, como yo os he amado, así os améis también vosotros los unos a los otros" (*Io*. 13, 34). Y Jesús especifica que este amor abraza todo el campo de las necesidades humanas, desde las más pequeñas hasta las más grandes: "Todo aquel que dé de beber tan sólo un vaso de agua fresca a uno de estos pequeños . . . os aseguro que no perderá su recompense" (*Matth*. 10, 42).

La comunidad hispana ha de responder también a sus necesidades propias, y mostrar una solidaridad generosa y eficaz entre sus propios miembros. Os exhorto pues a preservar vuestra fe cristiana y vuestras tradiciones, especialmente en lo que se refiere a la defensa de la familia. Ruego para que el Señor os bendiga con un mayor número de vocaciones al sacerdocio y a la vida religiosa entre vuestros jóvenes.

Ojalá que vosotros, que tanto habéis recibido de Dios, oigáis su llamada a la renovación de la vida cristiana y a la fidelidad a la fe de vuestros padres. Que podáis responder con el espíritu de María, la Virgen Madre que la Iglesia contempla "maternalmente presente y partícipe en los múltiples y complejos problemas que acompañan hoy la vida de los individuos de las familias y de las naciones . . . la ve socorriendo al pueblo cristiano en la lucha incesante entre el bien y el mal, para que 'no caiga' o, si cae, 'se levante'" (Ioannis Pauli PP. II *Redemptoris Mater*, 52).

9. Today's liturgy helps us to reflect deeply *on life and death*, on the victory of life over death. On this earth, in the visible world of creation, *man exists "for death"*; and yet, in Christ, he is called to communion with God, with *the living God who "gives life."* He is called to this communion precisely through the death of Christ—the death which "gives life."

Today, all over the world, countless people—people of many countries and continents, languages and races, are sharing sacramentally in the death of Christ. *We, here in Texas, journey together with them* towards the fulfilment of the Paschal Mystery in life. We journey, conscious of being sinners, conscious of being mortal. But we journey on in hope, in union with the Sacrifice of Christ, through Eucharistic communion with him and *with love* for each other. *We live for the Lord! We die for the Lord! We belong to the Lord! Come, Lord Jesus!* (Cfr. Apoc. 22, 20)

Amen.[39]

Father Walter Burghardt: Preacher of the Just Word

Father Walter Burghardt (1914–2008) was a noted theologian and homilist. He was a Jesuit priest who preached and wrote throughout his life. He inspired countless Catholics by means of his long ministry. His homilies are fortunately available in their entirety.

Father Burghardt was born in Manhattan in 1914. His parents were immigrants from the Austrian-Hungarian Empire. He and his brother attended St.

John the Evangelist's Parish School in New York City. His Jesuit teachers at Xavier High School in New York, inspired Burghardt's initial consideration of the priestly vocation. He was ordained a priest of the Jesuit order in 1941.

Father Burghardt taught at the Jesuit Woodstock Seminary in Woodstock, Maryland (1946–1969), and in New York (1969–1974). He had a professional connection with Union Theological Seminary in New York City, and he taught patristics at Catholic University in Washington, DC (1974–1978). He then accepted an invitation from Father Timothy Healy, President of Georgetown University, to be a "theologian-in-residence." He remained in that position until 1990. Father Burghardt was a Senior Research Fellow at Woodstock Theological Center (now located at Georgetown University, Washington, D.C.). He also served as director of a center for preaching on social justice issues, located in Annapolis, Maryland. Social justice was a lifelong passion for Father Burghardt. He strongly believed that the Church needed to preach and live out her social teachings, and his homilies reflected his deep concern for the topic of justice.

Burghardt was president and co-editor of the homiletic resource, *The Living Pulpit*. From 1946 to 1967, he served as managing editor of the journal *Theological Studies*. When Father John Courtney Murray, S.J., died in 1967, Father Burghardt became editor-in-chief. He contributed to the magazine for forty-four years. He authored many books, including fifteen collections of homilies. His last book is titled *Let Jesus Easter In Us: More Homilies on Biblical Justice* (2006). Father Burghardt died on February 16, 2008, at the Jesuits' infirmary at St. Joseph's University in Philadelphia.

The Preaching of Father Walter Burghardt

Early in his priesthood, Father Burghardt had a special talent for preaching, and was good at it. "A most moving experience was giving the *Tre Ore* at St. Michael's in Buffalo," he related to an author. "That consisted of nine homilies. The first was an introduction, then seven homilies on the seven last words of Jesus, and a concluding sermon. It was a wonderful experience to preach three hours on the passion of Christ," he said.[40] Father Burghardt followed the standard three-point homily, beginning with a brief introduction, making three clear points, and then quickly wrapping up his homily. His homilies were colorful, easy to follow, theologically correct, and well thought-out. His use of inclusive language is troubling for the reader who knows the Church's official Bible translations, but hopefully one can get beyond that to see the depth of his reflections. He once described the process he used in preparing homilies:

> It takes me altogether, including the research I do, about forty to sixty hours to produce what I call an acceptable homily. Those hours of preparation aren't spent just sitting down at a typewriter. I take the experiences of the past week. I try to speak to the needs, the joys, the hopes and the fears of the congregation.[41]

Most priests probably can't spend as much time preparing for homilies as Father Burghardt did, but they can cultivate better research, reflection, and writing skills after his example.

In this homily, Father Burghardt discusses the life and death of Saint Thomas More. It was delivered on June 22, 1998, at the John XXIII Pastoral Center in Charleston, West Virginia.

Homily: The King's Good Servant, but God's First

Four decades ago in America, Thomas More was little more than a name. Yes, he had been canonized in 1935, after Pius XI dispensed with the customary miracles. Yes, Chambers' authoritative biography of More had appeared in 1949. Yes, he has become the patron of Catholic lawyers and university students. And a favored few history buffs may remember that on the scaffold More "moved his tangled gray beard carefully out of the way . . . he said it should not be cut in two, because it had done no treason."

But Thomas More is a household name in America today thanks to theater—because a British playwright, Robert Bolt, staged him as *A Man for All Seasons*. Untold thousands can quote "Man [God] made to serve Him wittily, in the tangle of his mind!" Thousands more repeat or revise More's pained, yet amused response to his betrayer, the perjuring friend Sir Richard Rich: "For Wales? Why, Richard, it profits a man nothing to give his soul for the whole world. . . . But for Wales!"

A play can penetrate to the hidden heart of a human; it's alive, it's vivid, it's imaginative, it puts a face to a name. A homily is more difficult; you hear but you do not see. Still, the man that was More must appear. I mean the More who speaks to us forcefully because his life is peppered with paradox and his death defies dying. Three questions: (1) What was Thomas More? (2) Who was Thomas More? (3) Why and how did Thomas More die?

I. First, what was Thomas More? A humanist. A Renaissance humanist who knew Greek and Latin, believed that the best way to write and speak effectively was to study the ancients. England's outstanding humanist, a leader among humanists then centering in London. Bosom friend of Erasmus, "instrumental . . . in directing Erasmus toward the great works of Biblical and patristic scholarship that were to become his life work." Dear friend of John Colet, who called More "England's only genius."

What was Thomas More? An author. Hundreds of poems and epigrams, a *History of Richard III*, the first *Utopia* in the English language, a treatise on the *Four Last Things*, polemics against English Protestants.

What was Thomas More? A lawyer. Highly competent, a skilful orator, with a reputation for justice and fairness, defender of citizens and guilds, champion of the people in the May Day riots of 1517, royal counselor under Henry VIII, speaker of Parliament, lord chancellor of England. During his two-and-a-half year tenure of the realm's highest office, more than 4000 cases are on file in the public record office.

What was Thomas More? A devoted family man. He wanted the love of his wife and children, and he received it. His home was a strict academy. Erasmus tells us that no one ever quarreled there and that More never let anyone leave in anger. He educated his children and both his wives mercilessly, made his first wife, Alice, "thoroughly miserable by his dogged insistence that she improve her mind." At meals one of the daughters read from Scripture; Thomas conducted a colloquium on the passage; everyone had to speak.

II. Humanist, author, lawyer, family man—but *who* was Thomas More? Here his biographers are not at peace. One searching researcher finds in him "contradictions stark and numerous" that "at times make him a disappointing hero." He claims that

> No one can sit, as I have done at times, in the New England twilight looking at that strong, sad face [Holbein's portrait] and believe that Thomas More will ever be anything but a stranger to those who study him—this divided man who believed in miracles as long as they happened in the remote past, who wore a rough hair shirt next to his skin and made his way steadily in a world of ermine and velvet, a man who flagellated himself with whips and made charming talk at dinner, a man who extolled virginity and married twice, who longed for the monastery and became Lord Chancellor, a man who laughed much in public and nursed a private melancholy, a man who died for an ethereal vision of the sacred that has faded quite away in the electric glow of our modernity.

As early as 12, the world was a stage for Thomas. He had a "natural talent for adopting a role, for entering into a situation and yet remaining curiously detached from it." He was ambitious, but did not want anyone to know. He loved people, but never overcame his early longing for the monk he might have been.

The law intrigued him; he rose steadily in his profession. And yet a career in the Church attracted him; he lived for four years with Carthusian monks. He thought of being ordained, but could not shake off his desire for a wife, decided finally, and surely agonizingly, to become a good husband rather than a bad priest. His spirituality was intense, while his nature was closely connected to the senses. Not for him retirement from the world; he would seek God through and in the world. How? In the law and in marriage; in four children by his first wife, in a second marriage six weeks after the death of his first wife. At one hand, love for literature and the life of the spirit; at the other, legal business and royal missions. Here and elsewhere a ceaseless tension.

Some oppose his "lifelong sensibility and repugnance to physical pain" to his ability to send "heretics to a flaming death with alacrity" and afterwards to mock their torments. Others deny that the charges of intolerant cruelty in heresy cases can be supported; he himself insisted he played no role in the ecclesiastical courts where heretics were tried. From his earliest days he brooded over death. At times he was so fearful of death and hell that his life became a prison from which he yearned to escape, worldly pleasures a trap for the soul. And yet, he loved life with profound passion; in the Tower of London he lamented that he had enjoyed the world so thoroughly. More was a complex spirit, some say a haunted man.

III. Why and how did Thomas More die? One historian concludes that "even his death was irony—he a layman offering his head in witness to the unity of the English church with all Christendom, a unity quickly forsaken by all the English bishops save one, his fellow martyr John Fisher."

But Thomas did not yearn for death, did not ask for martyrdom. He would not have echoed the passionate plea of Ignatius of Antioch to the Christians of Rome on his way to the Coliseum 14 centuries earlier:

> I am writing to all the churches and state emphatically to all that I die willingly for God, provided you do not interfere. I beg you, do not show me unseasonable kindness. Suffer me to be the food of wild beasts, which are the means of my making my way to God. . . . Then only shall I be a genuine disciple of Jesus Christ when the world will not see even my body. Petition Christ in my behalf that through these instruments I may prove God's sacrifice.

No, Sir Thomas did not greet death with a resounding welcome. He found it difficult to face death when his wife did not understand, when he had to leave his dear daughter Meg: "You have long known," he told her, "the secrets of my heart." And given the breadth and depth of his professional life, given the thousands he had known and served, even loved, "He parted with more than most men when he parted with his life."

More loved his church. It was for him a ceaseless miracle, its saints a living presence, its unity over centuries and cultures a stupendous reality—all this "robbed death of its victory, and granted a splendor to life." When Parliament passed the Act of Succession on March 23, 1534, an act that declared Henry's marriage to Catherine null from the beginning and his marriage to Anne lawful matrimony; when all of England had to swear an oath to observe and defend not only this act but also the recognition of Henry as Supreme Head of the church in England, Thomas More was left no legal hiding place. His conscience would not allow him to swear. To the great council of the realm, Parliament, he opposed the sacrosanct council of Christendom, the venerable, unbroken tradition of the Catholic Church.

Somehow during these months in prison, Thomas wrote his last great work, *On the Sadness of Christ*; it has survived in his own hand. It is "art brought to the service of life, a literary discipline to strengthen his mind against the horrors of his imagination . . . a stunning display of More's calm spirit at a time when he was both terribly afraid and indominately resolute." The theme is pain—the sorrow and fear Christ felt before his death, a Christ who does not demand that we be fearless in death's face. "The brave man bears up under the blows that beset him. The senseless man simply does not feel them when they strike."

I close with parts of a prayer Thomas wrote in the Tower; it reveals the "man for all seasons" simply and economically.

> Give me thy grace, good Lord,
> To set the world at nought;
>
> To set my mind fast upon thee,
> And not to hang upon the blast of men's mouths;

To be content to be solitary,
Not to long for worldly company;

Little and little utterly to cast off the world,
And rid my mind of all the business thereof; . . .

Gladly to be thinking of God,
Piteously to call for his help;

To lean unto the comfort of God,
Busily to labor to love him; . . .
To bewail my sins passed,
For the purging of them patiently to suffer adversity;

Gladly to bear my purgatory here,
To be joyful of tribulations;
To walk the narrow way that leadeth to life,
To bear the cross with Christ;

To have the last thing in remembrance,
To have ever afore mine eye my death that is ever at hand;

To pray for pardon before the judge come,
To have continually in mind the passion that Christ suffered for me;

For his benefits incessantly to give him thanks,
To buy the time again that I before have lost;

Recreations not necessary—to cut off,
Of worldly substance, friends, liberty, life and all,
   to set the loss at right nought for the winning of Christ;

To think my most enemies my best friends,
For the brethren of Joseph could never have done him so
   much good with their love and favor as they did him
   with their malice and hatred.[42]

SUMMARY

The preachers of the Modern and Contemporary Era struggled to understand and explain the Gospel message, in light of the challenges posed by ideology, world-wide conflict, the specter of total world destruction, and technological development. They used a variety of styles and methods of preaching. The advances of technology, particularly radio, television, the cell phone, and the Internet, have enabled the Gospel message to reach mass audiences in the far corners of the earth. We can expect these technical advances to continue as the twenty-first century progresses. The possibilities are exciting and frightening at the same time. As is true throughout Church history, the parish is a focal point of concern for the homilists featured in this chapter. The salvation of souls was the top pastoral priority of great homilists. The life and teachings of Jesus Christ inspired these homilists to present God's Word in a clear and comprehensible way. Through prayer, study and reflection, the Church's masterful preachers spread the Gospel to congregations far and wide. As in all centuries, these simple and yet profound skills are necessary if the Gospel is to be effectively transmitted to the ends of the earth.

NOTES

1. George William Rutler, *The Curé d'Ars Today: St. John Vianney* (San Francisco: Ignatius Press, 1988), 102.

2. Ibid.

3. Ibid., 103.

4. Lancelot C. Sheppard, foreword to *The Sermons of the Cure of Ars*, by Una Morrissy (Rockford, IL: Tan Books, 1959), xvii–xviii.

5. Philippe De Peyronnet, Index des Sermons de Saint Jean-Marie Vianney Cure d'Ars (Paris, 1997).

6. Margaret Trouncer, *Saint John-Marie Vianney: Curé of Ars* (New York: Sheed & Ward, 1959), 151.

7. Ibid.

8. Ibid., pp. 151–152

9. Ibid., p. 152.

10. Ibid.

11. Ibid., p. 90.

12. John XXIII, Encyclical on St. John Vianney *Sacerdotii Nostri Primordia* (August 1, 1959), nn.76–78. http://www.vatican.va.

13. Ibid., no. 79.

14. Ibid., no. 80.

15. John Paul II, *Letter to Priests on the Cure of Ars for Holy Thursday 1986* (March 16, 1986), no. 9.

16. Ibid.

17. Trouncer, 164.

18. Vincent Ferrer Blehl, introduction to *Cardinal Newman's Best Plain Sermons* (New York: Herder & Herder, 1964), x–xi.

19. Ibid., 11.

20. Ibid.

21. Ibid, 12.

22. Ibid.

23. Ibid.

24. Ibid., 15.

25. Ibid., 18.

26. Ibid., 13.

27. John Henry Newman, *Sermons Preached on Various Occasions* (New York: Longmans, Green, 1913), 163–83.

28. Fulton J. Sheen, *Treasure in Clay: The Autobiography of Fulton J. Sheen* (Garden City, NY: Doubleday, 1980), 75.

29. Ibid., 76.

30. Ibid.

31. Ibid.

32. Ibid.

33. Ibid.

34. Ibid., 78

35. Fulton J. Sheen, *The Priest is not his own* (San Francisco: Ignatius Press, 1963), 132–33.

36. Ibid., 136.

37. Ibid., 137.

38. *The Wanderer* (St. Paul, MN), April 14, 2005.

39. http://www.vatican.va/holy_father/john_paul_ii/homilies/1987/documents/hf_jp-ii_hom_19870913_messa-san-antonio_en.html

40. Francis P. Friedl and Rex Reynolds, *Extraordinary Lives: thirty-four priests tell their stories* (Notre Dame: Ave Maria Press, 1997), 25.

41. Ibid., 27

42. Walter J. Burghardt, *Christ in Ten Thousand Places: Homilies Toward a New Millennium* (New York: Paulist Press, 1999), 165–70.

Conclusion

PREACHING AND PROCLAIMING the Word of God at Mass are two critically important ministries in the Catholic Church. Each week, thousands of bishops, priests, and deacons around the country step into pulpits in parish churches, shrines, monasteries, cathedrals, convents, and chapels, and reflect on the Scripture readings for that weekend. The quality of these reflections is shaped in large part by the education, experience, and spirituality of the homilist. A homilist who is well educated, in touch with his people, experienced in various ministry fields, and prayerful is both effective and respected. Each of these elements is critical to effective preaching. Homilies are a reflection of the commitment and ability of the homilist.

Catholicism's best homilists are found in every century and culture. They come from all walks of life and were all shaped by the Word they preached. That Word was not a page in a book, but a living reality that changed their hearts, enlightened their minds, purified their souls, and influenced their actions. These preachers cultivated a relationship with the Savior, and shared the rich fruits of their prayer life with the congregations blessed to be in their presence. Their relationship with God was the springboard for a deepening of their congregation's relationship with God.

There are various lenses through which we can look at history (e.g., economic, political, social, spiritual, cultural, theological). The lens of homiletics clarifies various historical periods and possible approaches to contemporary problems. Each of the thirty-one men featured in this book preached in a particular historical context. While generalizations risk oversimplifying complex realities, they do provide some insight for us. We have seen how preaching explained the implications of the covenant between God and Israel in the Old Testament; how New Testament preaching focused on the Person and life of Jesus; and how the post-Apostolic Church dealt with the break from Judaism, various heresies, and the individual Christian's relationship with his pagan neighbors. We saw the Church Fathers use mystagogical preaching to explain the sacred mysteries to the newly baptized, and preachers in the Middle Ages employ the tools of Scholasticism as they dealt with various questions about the Faith. We see that Reformation-era preaching refocused attention on Christian ethics and morality, and that the modern and contemporary era has been shaped by the Church's evolving relationship with the secular world. Preaching has always and will always reflect the time in which it takes place. This is obvious, but nevertheless true.

Spirituality has developed through the course of two millennia of Church history. Spirituality is closely intertwined in the life of the Church and her homilists. Great preachers have a strong desire to learn and grow in union with Jesus Christ. Catholicism's best homilists are men of prayer and spiritual depth. Prayer is their lifeline to God. We know that great preachers nurtured their spiritual lives through Scripture reading, prayerful reflection, and quiet time before the Blessed Sacrament. There is no substitute for prayerful time on one's knees. Archbishop Sheen frequently exhorted priests to make a Eucharistic Holy Hour every day. He led by example, claiming that he never missed a holy hour in his lifetime. His advice is both valuable and timeless. Daily prayer makes the homilist an effective instrument of the Holy Spirit. Good homilists are men of prayer. Great homilists are powerhouses of prayer.

Another quality of great homilists is scholarship. Intellectual preparation is an essential part of effective preaching. While Saint John Vianney was no scholar—he did poorly in seminary and struggled in his study of Latin—he studied after ordination, and his library in Ars was large and diverse. He knew his preaching had to be based on good theology, and he often quoted the Church Fathers in his homilies. Homilies are not biblical commentaries or theological treatises. But in order to "break open the Word" properly, good theological study is indispensable. The homilist needs a well-stocked, regularly updated, well-worn theological library.

Great homilists strive to provide new insight into Scripture. The men featured here provide fascinating insights into the biblical narrative. A worthy goal for every homilist would be to provide our congregation with at least one insight they didn't have before listening to us. That insight is the fruit of prayer, and study of the Scriptures, the Church Fathers, and other ecclesiastical and secular authors. I know from personal experience that having such insight inspires me to live my faith each week. The homilists featured in this book show us how it can be done. We just have to take time to learn from them.

Expression is as important as content in the matter of preaching. History teaches us the value of the study of rhetoric. Ancient rhetoricians are not only good teachers for men like Augustine and Chrysostom; they are good teachers for us as well. Great rhetoric moves the heart as well as the mind of the listener. Communication can facilitate or impede the preaching task.

Various genres of preaching have developed through the ages. Ezekiel exemplifies prophetic preaching, Saint John Chrysostom models expository preaching, Our Lord embodies evangelistic preaching, Saint Augustine exemplifies catechetical preaching, and St. Peter exhibits festive preaching. There is no single style of preaching. All homilists have strengths and weaknesses. They emphasize or highlight the Faith using various means. This is appropriate because the biblical text has come to acquire a variety of meanings and interpretations. This fact is verified by the different preaching styles discussed here. In addition, these styles meet various needs and circumstances in the Church.

A word about homily application is in order. The Church's best preachers sought to break open God's Word and put people in touch with the mysteries of salvation in Christ. However, many homilists did not feel an obligation to provide the faithful with specific weekly applications. For example, they would not recommend writing a journal entry every day, or spending five minutes praying for a particular intention. This is a modern homiletic approach. These homilists wanted the faithful to live out the Gospel message in concrete ways, but those ways were up to the listener to decide. The homilist's main concern was inspiring, enriching, enlightening, and motivating people to action. They encouraged their flocks to study the Word and to live virtuously. You could say they took the faithful from Scripture to doctrine to practice. But the "practice" part was often a generic exhortation (e.g., "Show the abundant virtues in your life," "Let the light of Christ guide you," "Hold out, remain steadfast, endure suffering, bear the burden, carry your cross."), rather than a specific activity (e.g., "Pray for deeper faith every day this coming week," "Make a ten-minute visit to a sick person this week," "Take five minutes at the end of your day to forgive someone who has hurt you."). While the Church's great preachers left specific applications of the biblical message up to the creative initiative of the people, their homilies were not abstract speculation or forms of spiritual entertainment.

This study has taught me, and hopefully teaches the reader, to appreciate the rich history of Catholic homiletics. This history is filled with diverse preachers who collectively touched the lives of millions with their oratorical gifts. This history is not like a museum piece that should be viewed with wonder and awe behind a glass case from a respectable distance. Instead, it should be carefully studied and its insights mined like a precious gem to form and inform contemporary homilists. Effective preaching doesn't "just happen." It requires regular prayer, serious study, and careful thought on the preacher's part. As with so many other things, history is a great tool at our disposal.

Preaching is not a mere liturgical function, but rather an important spiritual and pastoral activity, an opportunity to proclaim God's Word, and apply it to the lives of their listeners. As this book has demonstrated, it doesn't take a saint to be a great homilist. It does, however, take one who loves his vocation, understands the importance of preaching, and applies himself spiritually and intellectually to this task.

Catholicism's finest preachers were in touch with the Holy Spirit. Whether prepared in great cathedrals or in the sacristies of simple country churches, whether by candlelight or fluorescent lamp, whether written with quill pens or on laptop computers, the same Spirit pervaded the homilies preached through the centuries of Church history. The Spirit who inspired masterful preachers touched the hearts of the faithful, and can transform our hearts and lives if we are open and willing to be changed. In the end, the power of effective preaching comes from the Lord, without whom we would not be here to preach, and the cooperation of the minister who must use wisely the intellectual and spiritual gifts he has received from God. To refuse to acknowledge God's power in preaching is prideful arrogance; to refuse to acknowledge human talent is willful naiveté. As in all things, both God and man must cooperate to bring about effective preaching. When we work with the Lord and allow Him to work in and through us, our world can be changed in unbelievable ways. This book has shown how the masters of preaching utilized well the gifts they received. With their prayers and example before us, we can do the same.

Abbreviations

AAS   Acta Apostolicae Sedis. Acts of the Apostolic See

CCC   Catechism of the Catholic Church (1994)

CIC   Codex Iuris Canonici. Code of Canon Law (1983)

EN   Evangelii Nuntiandi. Apostolic Letter of Pope Paul VI on Evangelization in the Modern World (1975)

GIRM   General Instruction on the Roman Missal (2004)

PL   Patrologiae Latinae (The Latin Fathers) (1844-55)

PO   Presbyterorum Ordinis. The Decree on the Life and Ministry of Priests (1965)

SC   Sacrosanctum Concilium. The Constitution on the Sacred Liturgy (1963)

USCCB   United States Conference of Catholic Bishops

VD   Verbum Domini. The Word of God. (2010)

Chronology of Historical Periods and Homilists Covered in this Book

THE OLD TESTAMENT PERIOD (CA. 1571 BC–AD 1)*

ca. 1571–1406 BC	Moses
ca. 650 BC– 570 BC	Jeremiah
ca. seventh century BC	Ezekiel
ca. sixth century BC	Jonah

THE NEW TESTAMENT PERIOD (CA. AD 1–99)

ca. 5 BC–29 AD	John the Baptist
ca. 3 AD–33 AD	Jesus Christ
ca. 1 BC–64 AD	Saint Peter
ca. 6 AD–67 AD	Saint Paul

THE POST–APOSTOLIC PERIOD (100–299)

ca. AD 150	Clement of Rome
185–254	Origen

THE AGE OF THE FATHERS (300–599)

347–407	John Chrysostom
306–373	Ephrem the Deacon
330–379	Basil the Great
339–397	Ambrose of Milan
354–430	Augustine of Hippo
400–461	Leo the Great

THE MIDDLE AGES (600–1499)

673–735	Venerable Bede
1090-1153	Bernard of Clairvaux
1170-1221	Dominic
1195-1231	Anthony of Padua
1225–1274	Thomas Aquinas

THE REFORMATION PERIOD AND BEYOND (1500–1799)

1502-1539	Anthony Zaccaria
1542-1621	Robert Bellarmine
1538-1584	Charles Borromeo
1627-1704	Jacques Benigne Bossuet
1696-1787	Alphonsus Liguouri

THE MODERN AND CONTEMPORARY ERA (1800–PRESENT)

1786-1859	John Mary Vianney
1801-1890	John Henry Newman
1895-1979	Fulton John Sheen
1920-2005	Pope John Paul II
1914-2008	Walter Burghardt

N.B. Dates shown are approximate birth and death dates. Old Testament dates are disputed or internally inconsistent because of disagreements among archeologists, Egyptologists, and others concerning dating methods for events prior to the birth of Christ.

Bibliography

BOOKS

Ackeroyd, Peter R. *Exile and Restoration: A Study of Hebrew Thought in the Sixth Century BC.* Philadelphia: Westminster Press, 1968.

Ahlstrom, Sydney E. *A Religious History of the American People.* New Haven, CT: Yale University Press, 1972.

Allies, Mary Helen Agnes. *Three Catholic Reformers of the Fifteenth Century.* Freeport, NY: Books for Libraries Press, 1972.

Alter, Robert and Frank Kermode, ed. *The Literary Guide to the Bible.* Cambridge, MA: Belknap Press of Harvard University Press, 1987.

Ambrose of Milan. *On the Sacraments : and on the Mysteries.* Translated by T. Thompson. Re-edited by J.H. Srawley. London: SPCK, 1950.

Aquinas Institute of Theology Faculty. *In the Company of Preachers.* Collegeville, MN: Liturgical Press, 1993.

Aquinas, Thomas. *Summa Theologica.* New York: Benziger Brothers, 1947.

Aristotle. *On Rhetoric: A Theory of Civic Discourse.* Translated by George A. Kennedy. New York: Oxford University Press, 1991.

Auerbach, Erich. *Literary Language and Its Public in Late Latin Antiquity and in the Middle Ages.* Translated by Ralph Manheim. Bollingen Series LXXIV. Princeton, NJ: Princeton University Press, 1965.

Augustine. *De catechizandis rudibus.* Edited by Joseph B. Bauer.Vol. 46 of *Corpus Christianorum, Series Latina.* Turnhold, Belgium: Prepols, 1969.

———. *First Catechetical Instruction.* Translated by Joseph Christopher. Vol. 2 of *Ancient Christian Writers.* Westminster, MD: Newman Bookshop, 1966.

———. *On Christian Doctrine.* Translated by Durant Waite Robertson. New York: Macmillan, 1958.

———. *On Christian Doctrine.* Translated by J. F. Shaw. Vol. 2 of *Nicene & Post-Nicene Fathers.* Series 1. Grand Rapids, MI: Wm. B. Eerdmans, 1979.

Bailey, Raymond. *Jesus the Preacher.* Nashville: Broadman Press, 1990.

———. *Paul the Preacher.* Nashville: Broadman Press, 1991.

Bangert, William V. *A History of the Society of Jesus.* St. Louis: Institute of Jesuit Sources, 1972.

Barret, Charles Kingsley. *The First Epistle to the Corinthians.* New York: Harper & Row, 1968.

———. *The Gospel According to St. John.* New York: Macmillan, 1956.

Bayley, Peter. *French Pulpit Oratory, 1598–1650.* Cambridge: Cambridge University Press, 1980.

———. *Selected Sermons of the French Baroque, 1600–1650.* New York: Garland, 1983.

Bede. *Ecclesiastical History of the English People.* Translated by Leo London: Penguin Classics, 1955.

———. *Homilies on the Gospels: Book One, Advent to Lent.* Translated by Lawrence T. Martin and David Hurst. Kalamazoo, MI: Cistercian Publications, 1991.

Bellarmine, Robert. *Robert Bellarmine: Spiritual Writings.* Translated and edited by John Patrick Donnelly and Roland J. Teske. Classics of Western Spirituality. New York: Paulist Press, 1989.

Bellincini, Guido. "Il Predicatore Evangelico Secondo L'Ideale Di Sant' Antonio." *Atti Delle Settimane Antoniane Tenute A Roma E A Padova Nel 1946.* Citta Del Vaticano: Tipografia Poliglotta Vaticana, 1947.

Benedict XVI. *The Fathers.* 2 vols. Huntington, IN: Our Sunday Visitor, 2008, 2010.

Bernard of Clairvaux. *On the Song of Songs.* Translated by Kilian Wasch and Irene Edmonds. 4 vols. Cistercian Fathers Series. Spencer, MA: Cistercian Publications, 1971–80.

———. *Bernard of Clairvaux: Selected Works.* Translated by G. R. Evans. Classics of Western Spirituality. New York: Paulist Press, 1987.

Blehl, Vincent Ferrer, ed. *Cardinal Newman's Best Plain Sermons.* New York: Herder & Herder, 1964.

———. *The Essential Newman.* New York: Mentor-Omega, 1963.

Boenig, Robert, trans. *Anglo-Saxon Spirituality: Selected Writings.* Classics of Western Spirituality. New York: Paulist Press, 2000.

Borromeo, Carlo. *Instructiones pastorum ad concionandum.* Innsbruck: Wagner, 1846.

Bossuet, Jacques. *Oeuvres oratiores de Bossuet.* Edited by J. Lebarq. 7 vols. Paris: Desclee de Browuer et Cie, 1890–97.

Bouyer, Louis. *Newman: His Life and Spirituality.* New York: P. J. Kenedy & Sons, 1958.

Bright, John. *A History of Israel.* 2nd ed. Philadephia: Westminster Press, 1976.

———. *Jeremiah: A New Translation with Introduction and Commentary.* Vol. 21 of *The Anchor Bible.* Garden City, NY: Doubleday, 1965.

Brilioth, Yngve. *A Brief History of Preaching.* Translated by Karl F. Mattson. Philadelphia: Fortress, 1965.

———. *Landmarks in the History of Preaching.* London: SPCK, 1950.

Brodrick, James. *Robert Bellarmine: Saint and Scholar.* Westminster, MD: Newman Press, 1961.

Brown, Peter. *Augustine of Hippo: A Biography.* Berkeley: University of California Press, 1967.

Brown, Raymond E., Joseph A. Fitzmyer, and Roland E. Murphy, ed. *The Jerome Biblical Commentary.* Englewood, NJ: Prentice-Hills, Inc., 1968.

Brown, Raymond E. *The Gospel of John XIII-XXI*. Vol. 29A of *The Anchor Bible*. Edited by William F. Albright and David N. Freedman. Garden City, NY: Doubleday, 1966.

———. *An Introduction to the Gospel of John*. Edited by Francis J. Moloney. New Haven, CT: Yale University Press, 2003.

Bradshaw, Paul F. "The Liturgical Use and Abuse of Patristics." In *Liturgy Reshaped: A Festschrift for Geoffrey Cuming*. Edited by Kenneth Stevenson. 134–45. London: SPCK, 1982.

Bruce, F.F. *The Acts of the Apostles: The Greek Text with Introduction and Commentary*. 3rd rev. ed. Grand Rapids: Wm. B. Eerdmans, 1990.

Brueggeman, Walter. *Genesis*. Atlanta: John Knox Press, 1982.

Bullough, Donald A. *The Age of Charlemagne*, 2nd ed. London: Elek, 1973.

Bunson, Matthew, Margaret Bunson, and Stephen Bunson. *Our Sunday Visitor's Encyclopedia of Saints* Huntington, IN: Our Sunday Visitor Press, 1998.

Burghardt, Walter J. *Christ in Ten Thousand Places: Homilies Toward a New Millennium*. New York: Paulist Press, 1999.

———. *Dare to Be Christ: Homilies for the Nineties*. New York: Paulist Press, 1991.

———. *Grace on Crutches: Homilies for Fellow Travelers*. New York: Paulist Press, 1986.

———. *Hear the Just Word and Live It*. New York: Paulist Press, 2000.

———. *Justice: A Global Adventure*. Maryknoll, NY: Orbis Books, 2004.

———. *Let Jesus Easter In Us: More Homilies on Biblical Justice*. New York: Paulist Press, 2006.

———. *Let Justice Roll Down Like Waters: Biblical Justice Homilies Throughout the Year*. New York: Paulist Press, 1998.

———. *Long Have I Loved You: A Theologian Reflects on His Church*. Maryknoll, NY: Orbis Books Press, 2002.

———. *Love is a Flame of the Lord: More Homilies on the Just Word*. New York: Paulist Press, 1995.

———. *Lovely in Eyes Not His: Homilies for an Imaging Christ*. New York: Paulist Press, 1988.

———. *Preaching: the art & the craft*. New York: Paulist Press, 1987.

———. *Preaching the Just Word*. New Haven, CT: Yale University Press, 1996.

———. *Seasons That Laugh or Weep: Musings on the Human Journey*. Ramsey, NJ: Paulist Press, 1983.

———. *Sir, We Would Like to See Jesus: Homilies from a Hilltop*. New York: Paulist Press, 1982.

———. *Speak the Word With Boldness: Homilies for Risen Christians*. New York: Paulist Press, 1994.

———. *Still Proclaiming Your Wonders: Homilies for the Eighties*. New York: Paulist Press, 1984.

———. *Tell the Next Generation: Homilies and Near Homilies*. New York: Paulist Press, 1980.

———. *To Be Just Is To Love: Homilies for a Church Renewing*. New York: Paulist Press, 2001.

———. *To Christ I Look: Homilies At Twilight*. New York: Paulist Press, 1989.

———. *When Christ Meets Christ: Homilies on the Just Word*. New York: Paulist Press, 1993.

Burke, Peter. *The Historical Anthropology of early Modern Italy: Essays on Perception and Communication.* Cambridge: Cambridge University Press, 1987.

Callam, Daniel. *On Virginity by Ambrose, Bishop of Milan.* Toronto: Peregrina, 1980.

Canon Law Society of America. *Code of Canon Law: Latin-English Edition.* Washington, DC: Canon Law Society of America, 1999.

Carroll, Robert P. *Jeremiah.* Sheffield: JSOT Press, 1989.

Carroll, Mary Thomas Aquinas. *The Venerable Bede: His Spiritual Teachings.* Washington, DC: Catholic University of America Press, 1946.

Carroll, Thomas K. *Preaching the Word.* Vol. 11 of Message of the Fathers of the Church. Wilmington, DE: Michael Glazier, 1984.

Cassuto, Umberto. "The Arrangement of the Book of Ezekiel." Translated by Israel Abrahams. In *Biblical and Oriental Studies,* 1: 227–40. Jerusalem: Magnes Press, Hebrew University, 1973.

Catechism of the Catholic Church. 2nd ed. Vatican City: Libreria Editrice Vaticana, 1997.

Catechism of the Council of Trent for Parish Priests. Rockford, IL: Tan Books, 1982.

Chadwick, Henry. *The Early Church.* Vol. 1 of *The Pelican History of the Church.* London: Penguin Books, 1967.

Chadwick, Owen. *The Reformation.* Vol. 2 of *The Pelican History of the* Church. London: Penguin Books, 1964.

Childs, Brevard S. *Introduction to the Old Testament as Scripture.* Philadelphia: Fortress, 1979.

Chrysostom, John. *Homilies on Genesis.* Translated by J. Ashworth. Vol. 13 of *Nicene and Post-Nicene Fathers,* 1st ser. Grand Rapids: Wm. B. Eerdmans, 1956.

———. *On the Priesthood.* Translated by W. R. Stephens. Vol. 9 of *Nicene and Post-Nicene Fathers,* 1st ser. Grand Rapids: Wm. B. Eerdmans, 1956.

Clement of Rome. *Second Clement.* In vol. 1 of *The Apostolic Fathers.* Edited and translated by Kirsopp Lake. Loeb Classical Library no. 24. Cambridge, MA: Harvard University Press, 1965.

Colgrave, Bertram. *The Venerable Bede and his Times.* Durham: Jarrow, 1958.

Comay, Joan and Ronald Brownrigg. *Who's Who In the Bible.* New York: Wings Books, 1971.

Cox, James William. *A Guide to Biblical Preaching.* Nashville: Abingdon, 1976.

Craig, Gerald R. *The Church and the Age of Reason, 1648–1789.* Vol. 4 of *The Penguin History of the Church.* London: Penguin Books, 1960.

Craigie, Peter C. *Ezekiel.* Daily Study Bible Series. Philadelphia: Westminster, 1983.

———. *The Book of Deuteronomy.* New International Commentary on the Old Testament. Grand Rapids: William B. Eerdmans, 1976.

Crenshaw, James L. *Studies in Ancient Israelite Wisdom.* New York: KTAV, 1976.

Cross, F.L. and E. A. Livingstone, ed. *The Oxford Dictionary of the Christian Church.* Oxford: Oxford University Press, 1983.

Cullmann, Oscar. *The Christology of the New Testament.* Translated by Shirley Guthrie and Charles Hall. London: SCM Press, 1963.

D'Avray, D.L. *The Preaching of the Friars: Sermons Diffused From Paris Before 1300.* Oxford: Clarendon Press, 2002.

Daniel-Rops, Henri. *This is the Mass: New and Revised.* New York: Hawthorn Books, 1965.

Danielou, Jean. *From Shadow to Reality: Studies in the Biblical Typology of the Fathers.* Translated by W. Hibbard. Westminster, MD: Newman Press, 1961.

Davies, W.D. *The Setting of the Sermon on the Mount*. Cambridge: University Press, 1966.

Dawson, Christopher. *The Dividing of Christendom*. New York: Sheed & Ward, 1965.
_____. *The Formation of Christendom*. New York: Sheed & Ward, 1967.

Deferrari, Roy J. *Saint Ambrose: Theological and Dogmatic Works*. Vol. 44 of *The Fathers of The Church*. Washington DC: Catholic University of America Press, 1963.

De Guibert, Joseph. *The Jesuits: Their Spiritual Doctrine and Practice, A Historical Study*. Translated by William J. Young, edited by George E. Ganss. Chicago: Loyola University Press, 1964.

De Lubac, Henri. *History and Spirit: The Understanding of Scripture According to Origen*. San Francisco: Ignatius Press, 2007.
———. *Medieval Exegesis: The Four Senses of Scripture*. Translated by Mark Sebanc. Grand Rapids: William B. Eerdmans, 1998.

De Peyronnet, Philippe. *Index des Sermons de Saint Jean-Marie Vianney Cure d'Ars*. Paris, 1997.

De Vaux, Roland. *Ancient Israel: Its Life and Institutions*. Grand Rapids: Eerdmans, 1961.

Dix, Gregory. *The Shape of the Liturgy*. 2nd ed. Westminster: Dacre Press, 1949.

Dodd, C.H. *The Apostolic Preaching and its Development*. New York: Harper & Brothers, 1960.

Dudon, Paul. *St. Ignatius of Loyola*. Translated by W.J. Young. Milwaukee: Bruce, 1949.

Duffey, William R. *Preaching Well: The Rhetoric and Delivery of Sacred Discourse*. Ridgefield, CT: Roger A. McCaffrey, 1950.

Edwards, O.C., Jr. *A History of Preaching*. Nashville: Abingdon Press, 2004.

Ellis, E. Earle. *Pauline Theology: Ministry and Society*. Grand Rapids: Eerdmans, 1989.

Ephrem of Nisibis. *Hymns on Paradise*. Translated by Sebastian Brock. Crestwood, N.Y: St. Vladimir's Seminary Press, 1990.

Eusebius. *The History of the Church*. London: Penguin Classics, 1965.

Fee, Gordon D. *The First Epistle to the Corinthians*. New International Commentary on the New Testament. Grand Rapids: Wm. B. Eerdmans, 1993.

Fichtner, Joseph. *To Stand and Speak for Christ: A Theology of Preaching*. New York: Alba House, 1981.

Fitzmyer, Joseph A. *According to Paul: Studies in the Theology of the Apostle*. New York: Paulist Press, 1993.

Flannery, Austin. *Vatican Council II*. The Vatican Collection. 2 vols. Northport, NY: Costello Publishing Company, 1988.

Fortescue, Adrian. *The Mass: A Study of the Roman Liturgy*. Albany: Preserving Christian Publications, Inc., 1999.

Fretheim, Terence E. *The Message of Jonah: A Theological Commentary*. Eugene, OR: Wipf & Stock, 2000.

Friedl, Francis P. and Ed Macauley. *Homilies Alive: Creating Homilies that hit home*. Mystic, CT: Twenty-Third Publications, 1999.

Friedl, Francis P. and Rex Reynolds. *Extraordinary Lives: thirty-four priests tell their stories*. Notre Dame: Ave Maria Press, 1997.

Fuller, Reginald. *The Use of the Bible in Preaching*. Philadelphia: Fortress, 1981.

Fumaroli, Marc. *L'age de l'eloquence: Rhetorique et "res litararia" de la Renaissance Au seuil de l'epoque classique*. Geneva: Droz, 1980.

Gardiner, Spring. *The Power of the Pulpit*. New York: M.W. Dodd, 1848.

Gartner, Bertil. *The Areopagus Speech and Natural Revelation*. Lund: CWK Gleerup, 1955.

Gheon, Henri. *The Secret of the Curé d'Ars*. New York: Longmans, Green, 1929.

Gilson, Etienne. *History of Christian Philosophy in the Middle Ages*. New York: Random House, 1955.

Grafton, Anthony and Megan Williams. *Christianity and the Transformation of the Book: Origen, Eusebius,and the Library of Caesarea*. Cambridge, MA: Belknap Press of Harvard University Press, 2006.

Greenstock, David, ed. *The Preacher's Encyclopedia*. 4 vols. Westminster, MD: The Newman Press, 1965.

Grimm, Eugene. *The Complete Works of Saint Alphonsus Liguouri*. New York: Benziger Brothers, 1890.

Groeschel, Benedict J. *In the Presence of Our Lord: The History, Theology & Psychology of Eucharistic Devotion*. Huntington, IN: Our Sunday Visitor Publications, 1997.

Guardini, Romano. *Sacred Signs*. St. Louis: Pio Decimo Press, 1956.

Guelich, Robert. *Sermon on the Mount*. Grand Rapids: Wm. B. Eerdmans, 1972.

Hahn, Scott. *Understanding the Scriptures: A Complete Course On Bible Study*. Edited by James Socias. Woodbridge, IL: Midwest Theological Forum, 2004.

Hardick, Lothar. *He Came to You so that You Might Come to Him: The Life and Teaching of St. Anthony of Padua*. Chicago: Franciscan Herald Press, 1986.

Hardon, John A. *Modern Catholic Dictionary*. Bardstown, KY: Eternal Life, 1999.

Harmless, William. *Augustine and the Catechumenate*. New York: Pueblo, 1995.

Heschel, Abraham J. *The Prophets*. New York: Harper-Collins, 1962.

Hinnebusch, William A. *The History of the Dominican Order*. 2 vols. Staten Island, NY: Alba House, 1966.

Holladay, William. *Jeremiah: Spokesman Out of Time*. Philadelphia: Pilgrim Press, 1974.

Holland, DeWitte. *The Preaching Tradition*. Nashville: Abingdon Press, 1980.

Holy Bible: New Catholic Edition. New York: Catholic Book Publishing, 1957.

Huels, John M. *The Pastoral Companion: A Canon Law Handbook for Catholic Ministry*. Chicago: Franciscan Herald Press, 1986.

Huizinga, J. *The Waning of the Middle Ages*. Translated by F. Hopman. New York: Doubleday, n.d.

Hunter, David G., ed. *Preaching in the Patristic Age*. New York: Paulist Press, 1989.

Idelsohn, A.Z. *Jewish Liturgy and its Development*. New York: Shocken Books, 1975.

International Commission on English in the Liturgy. *Documents on the Liturgy: 1963–1979*. Collegeville, MN: Liturgical Press, 1982.

———. *The Liturgy of the Hours*. 4 vols. New York: Catholic Book Publishing, 1976.

———. *The Rites of the Catholic Church*. 2 vols. Collegeville, MN: Pueblo, 1979.

Jalland, Trevor. *The Life and Times of St. Leo the Great*. London: SPCK, 1941.

Jarret, Bede. *Life of Saint Dominic, 1170–1221*. London: Burns, Oats & Washburne, 1924. Reissued, 1964.

Jenkins, Philip. *The Cold War at Home: The Red Scare in Pennsylvania, 1945–1960*. Chapel Hill, N.C.: University of North Carolina Press, 1999.

John Paul II. *Crossing the Threshold of Hope*. New York: Alfred A. Knopf, 1994.

———. *Gift and Mystery: On the Fiftieth Anniversary of My Priestly Ordination*. New York: Doubleday, 1996.

———. *Go in Peace: A Gift of Enduring Love*. Chicago: Loyola Press, 2003.

———. *Memory and Identity: Conversations at the Dawn of a Millennium*. New York: Rizzoli, 2005.

————. *Rise, Let Us Be On Our Way*. New York: Warner Books, 2004.

Johnson, Haynes. *The Age of Anxiety: McCarthyism to Terrorism*. Orlando, FL: Harcourt, 2005.

Jungmann, Joseph A. *The Mass of the Roman Rite: Its Origins and Development*. 2 vols. Westminster, MD: Christian Classics, 1950.

Justin Martyr. *Apology*. In *The Ante-Nicene Fathers*, vol. 1. Grand Rapids, MI: Wm. B. Eerdmans, 1969.

Kaiser, Otto. *Isaiah 1–12*. The Old Testament Library. Philadelphia: Westminster, 1972.

Keel, Othmar. *The Symbolism of the Biblical World: Ancient Near Eastern Iconography and the Book of Psalms*. Translated by Timothy J. Hallet. New York: Eisenbrauns, 1997.

Killinger, John. *Fundamentals of Preaching*. Philadelphia: Fortress, 1985.

Kingsbury, J.D. *Parables of Jesus in Matthew 13*. London: SPCK, 1969.

Klein, Peter. *Catholic Source Book*. 3rd ed. Dubuque, IA: Brown-ROA, 1990.

Kleiser, Grenville. *Basil to Calvin*. Vol. 1 of *The World's Greatest Sermons*. London: General Books, 2010.

Ladd, Gregory Joseph. *Archbishop Fulton J. Sheen: A Man for All Media*. San Francisco: Ignatius Press, 2001.

Larsen, David L. *The Company of the Preachers*. Grand Rapids, MI: Kregel, 1998.

Latourette, Kenneth Scott. *History of the Expansion of Christianity*. 7 vols. New York: Harper & Brothers, 1944.

Lawler, Thomas Comerford, ed. *St. Augustine: Sermons for Christmas and Epiphany*. Westminster, MD: Newman Press, 1952.

Leclerq, Jean. *The Love of Learning and the Desire for God: A Study of Monastic Culture*. Translated by Catharine Misrahi. New York: Fordham University Press, 1982.

Leiva-Merikakis, Erasmo. *Fire of Mercy—Heart of the Word*. 2 vols. San Francisco: Ignatius Press, 2003.

Levy, Isaac. *The Synagogue: Its History and Function*. London: Vallentine Press, 1963.

Liguori, Alphonsus. *Sermons of St. Alphonsus Liguori*. Rockford, IL: Tan Books, 1982.

————. *The Glories of Mary*. 2 vols. Liguori, MO: Liguori, 2000.

Lohmeyer, Ernst. *Lord of the Temple*. Richmond, VA: John Knox Press, 1962.

Long, Thomas G. *Preaching the Literary Forms of the Gospels*. Philadelphia: Westminster, 1989.

————. *The Witness of Preaching*. Louisville, KY: Westminster John Knox, 1989.

Lyons, C.W. *The Catholic Bible Concordance*. Steubenville, OH: Emmaus Road, 2009.

Magonet, Jonathan. *Form and Meaning: Studies in Literary Techniques in the Book of Jonah*. Bible Literature Series. Sheffield: Almond Press, 1983.

Marcil, George, ed. *Sermones for the Easter Cycle*. St. Bonaventure, NY: Franciscan Institute, 1994.

Martin, J., ed. *Augustine, De Doctrina Christiana*. Vol. 32 of *Corpus Christianorum, Series Latina*. Turnholt, Belgium: Brepols, 1962.

Maxwell, Jaclyn L. *Christianization and Communication in Late Antiquity: John Chrysostom and his Congregation in Antioch*. Cambridge, MA: Cambridge University Press, 2006.

Mazza, Enrico. *Mystagogy: A Theology of Liturgy in the Patristic Age*. Translated by M. J. O'Connell. New York: Pueblo, 1989.

McGinness, Frederick J. *Rhetoric and Counter-Reformation Rome: Sacred Oratory and the Construction of the Catholic World-View, 1563–1621*. Ann Arbor, MI: University Microfilms, 1982.

————. *Right Thinking and Sacred Oratory in Counter-Reformation Rome.* Princeton, NJ: Princeton University Press, 1995.

McKitterick, Rosamond. *The Frankish Church and the Carolingian Reforms, 789–895.* London: Royal Historical Society, 1977.

McVey, Kathleen E., trans. *Ephrem the Syrian: Hymns.* Classics of Western Spirituality. New York: Paulist Press, 1989.

Migne, J.P., ed. *Patrologia Graeca.* Paris: Migne, 1857–66. Texts in the original Greek with a Latin translation on the facing page.

————. *Patrologia Latina.* Paris: Migne, 1844–55.

Miller, Charles E. *Ordained to Preach: A Theology and Practice of Preaching.* New York: Alba House, 1991.

Morrissy, Una. *The Sermons of the Cure of Ars.* Rockford, IL: Tan Books, 1959.

Murphy, Myles P. *The Life and Times of Archbishop Fulton J. Sheen.* Staten Island, NY: Alba House, 2000.

Navarre Bible: Readers Edition. Princeton, NJ: Scepter, 2002.

Neill, Stephen. A History of Christian Missions. Vol. 6 of The Penguin History of the Church. London: Penguin Books, 1986.

New American Bible: St. Joseph Edition. New York: Catholic Book Publishing, 1970.

Newman, John Henry. *John Henry Newman: Selected Sermons.* Edited by Ian Ker. New York: Paulist Press, 1994.

Newman, John Henry. *Parochial and Plain Sermons.* San Francisco: Ignatius Press, 1997.

————. *Sermons Preached on Various Occasions.* New York: Longmans, Green, 1913.

Nicholson, E.W. *Preaching to the Exiles.* Oxford: B. Blackwell, 1970.

Noth, Martin. *Exodus: A Commentary.* The Old Testament Library. Philadelphia: Westminster, 1962.

O'Brien, Bartholomew J. *The Curé of Ars, Patron Saint of Parish Priests.* Rockford, IL: Tan Books, 1987.

O'Connor, John Cardinal. *A Moment of Grace: John Cardinal O'Connor on the Catechism of the Catholic Church.* San Francisco: Ignatius Press, 1995.

O'Mahony, D., ed. *Great French Sermons from Bossuet, Bourdaloue, and Massillon.* London: Sands & Co., 1919. Reprint, St. Louis: B. Herder, n.d.

————. *Great French Sermons from Bossuet, Bourdaloue, and Massillon.* London: Sands & Co., 1919. Reprint, St. Louis: B. Herder, n.d.

O'Malley, John W. *Praise and Blame in Renaissance Rome: Rhetoric, Doctrine, and Reform in the Sacred Orators of the Papal Court, C. 1450–1521.* Texas: Duke University Press, 1979.

————. *Religious Culture in the Sixteenth Century.* Brookfield, VT: Ashgate, 1998.

O'Sullivan, John O., trans. *A Commentary on the Book of Psalms.* Albany, NY: Preserving Christian Publications, 1999.

Old, Hughes Oliphant. *The Reading and Preaching of the Scriptures in the Worship of the Christian Church.* 7 vols. Grand Rapids, MI: Eerdmans, 2010.

Origen. *Homilies on Joshua.* Translated by Barbara J. Bruce. Edited by Cynthia White. The Fathers of the Church. Washington, DC: Catholic University Press, 2002.

————. *On First Principles.* Gloucester: Peter Smith, 1973.

Paredi, Angelo. *St. Ambrose: His Life and Times.* Translated by M. Joseph Costelloe. Notre Dame, IN: University of Notre Dame Press, 1964.

Patte, Daniel. *Preaching Paul.* Philadelphia: Fortress, 1984.

Pelikan, Jaroslav. *The Christian Tradition: A History of the Development of Doctrine.* 5 vols. Chicago: University of Chicago Press, 1971–89.

———. *The Preaching of Chrysostom: Homilies on the Sermon on the Mount.* Philadelphia: Fortress, 1967.

Pennington, Basil. *The Last of the Fathers: The Cistercian Fathers of the Twelfth Century.* Still River, MA: St. Bede's Publications, 1983.

Pfeiffer, Rudolf. *History of Classical Scholarship from 1300 to 1850.* Oxford: University Press, 1976.

Pilch, John J. *The Triduum and Easter Sunday: Breaking Open the Scriptures.* Collegeville, MN: Liturgical Press, 2000.

Polman, A. D. R. *The Word of God According to St. Augustine.* London: Hodder & Stoughton, 1961.

Quasten, Johannes, *et al. Patrology.* 4 vols. Utrecht: Spectrum Publishers, 1966–94.

Ramsey, Boniface. *Beginning to Read the Fathers.* New York: Paulist Press, 1985.

Ramsey, P. A., ed. *Rome in the Renaissance: the City and the Myth.* Binghampton, NY: Center for Medieval and Early Renaissance Studies, 1982.

Ratzinger, Joseph Cardinal. *Called to Communion: Understanding the Church Today.* San Francisco: Ignatius Press, 1991.

———. *Jesus of Nazareth: From the Baptism in the Jordan to the Transfiguration.* New York: Doubleday, 2007.

———. *Jesus of Nazareth: Holy Week; From the Entrance into Jerusalem to the Resurrection,* San Francisco: Ignatius Press, 2011.

———. *The Spirit of the Liturgy.* San Francisco: Ignatius Press, 2000.

Ray, Stephen K. *Upon This Rock: St. Peter and the Primacy of Rome in Scripture and the Early Church.* Modern Apologetics Library. San Francisco: Ignatius Press, 1999.

Reeves, Thomas C. *America's Bishop: The Life and Times of Fulton J. Sheen.* San Francisco: Encounter Books, 2007.

Richardson, Cyril C., ed. *Early Christian Fathers.* New York: Macmillan, 1970.

Ruderman, David R., ed. *Preachers of the Italian Ghetto.* Berkeley: University of California Press, 1992.

Rutler, George William. *The Curé d'Ars Today: St. John Vianney.* San Francisco: Ignatius Press, 1988.

Satterlee, Craig Alan. *Ambrose of Milan's Method of Mystagogical Preaching.* Collegeville: Liturgical Press, 2002.

Schaff, Philip, ed. *Saint Chrysostom on the Priesthood, Ascetic Treatises, Select Homilies and Letters and Homilies on the Statues.* Vol. 9 of *Nicene and Post-Nicene Fathers of the Christian Church.* New York: Kessinger, 1889.

Schnackenburg, Rudolf. *Baptism in the Thought of St. Paul.* Translated by G. R. Beasley-Murray. Oxford: Blackwell, 1964.

Scott, Martin. *Medieval Europe.* New York: Dorset Press, 1964.

Sheen, Fulton J. *Characters of the Passion: Lessons on Faith and Trust.* Liguori, MO: Liguori, 1998. Originally published in 1947 by P.J. Kenedy and Sons.

———. *From the Angel's Blackboard: The Best of Fulton J. Sheen.* Liguori, MO: Liguori, 1996.

———. *Guide to Contentment.* New York: Maco, 1967. Reprint, Staten Island, NY: Alba House, 1996.

———. "Jesus Christ, Superstar—Superscar!" *Archbishop Fulton Sheen from the Hour of Power.* VHS. Garden Grove, CA: Crystal Cathedral Ministries, 1987. Sermon delivered on Sunday, March 5, 1972.

————. *Life is Worth Living.* 4 vols. New York: McGraw-Hill, 1953.

————. *Life of Christ.* New York: McGraw-Hill Book Company, 1958.

————. *Lift Up Your Heart: A Guide to Spiritual Peace.* Triumph Classic. Liguori, MO: Liguori Publications, 1997.

————. "The Marriage Feast of Cana," In *The Woman.* 8th ed. Huntington, IN: Our Sunday Visitor, 1957. Sermon delivered on Palm Sunday, March 18, 1951.

————. "Our Blessed Mother." In *The Rock Plunged into Eternity.* New York: Alba House, 2004. Sermon delivered on Palm Sunday, April 2, 1950.

————. *Peace of Soul: Timeless Wisdom on Finding Serenity and Joy by the Century's Most Acclaimed Catholic Bishop.* Triumph Classic. Liguori, MO: Liguori, 1996. First published 1949 by McGraw-Hill.

————. "Russia and Our Lady." In *Light Your Lamps.* 8th ed. Huntington, IN: Our Sunday Visitor, 1958. Sermon delivered on Palm Sunday, March 30, 1947.

————. *Seven Words of Jesus and Mary: Lessons on Cana and Calvary.* Liguori, MO: Liguori, 1996. First published 1945 by P.J. Kenedy & Sons.

————. *Simple Truths: Thinking Life Through With Fulton J. Sheen.* Liguori, MO: Liguori, 1998.

————. *The Cross and the Beatitudes.* Triumph Classic. Liguouri, MO: Liguouri, 2000. First published 1937 by P.J. Kenedy & Sons.

————. *The Mystical Body of Christ.* New York: Sheed & Ward, 1935.

————. "The Pulpit of the Cross." In *The Divine Romance.* New York: Alba House, 1996. Sermon delivered on Palm Sunday, April 13, 1930.

————. "The Purpose of Life." In *You.* New York: Alba House, 2003.

————. *The Priest is not his own.* San Francisco: Ignatius Press, 1963.

————. *The Seven Capital Sins.* Washington, DC: Alba House, 2000.

————. *The Seven Last Words:* New York: Century, 1933. Reprinted, Staten Island, NY: Alba House, 1996. Sermon delivered on Good Friday, April 19, 1935.

————. "The Seventh Word." In *The Prodigal World.* Reprinted, Staten Island: Alba House, 2003. Sermon delivered on Good Friday, April 10. 1936.

————. *The World's First Love: Mary, Mother of God.* San Francisco: Ignatius, 1996.

————. *Three to get married.* Princeton, NJ: Scepter, 1951.

————. *Treasure in Clay: The Autobiography of Fulton J. Sheen.* Garden City, NY: Doubleday, 1980.

————. *Victory Over Vice.* Manchester, NH: Sophia Institute Press, 2004.

Sherwood, Timothy H. *The Preaching of Archbishop Fulton J. Sheen: The Gospel meets the Cold War.* Lanham, MD: Lexington Books, 2010.

Sikes, Jeffrey Garrett. *Peter Abelard.* Cambridge: The University Press, 1932.

Smalley, Beryl. *The Study of the Bible in the Middle Ages.* 2nd ed. New York: Philosophical Library, 1952.

Smith, George Adam. *The Book of Isaiah.* 2 vols. New York: Harper & Brothers, 1927.

Smith, Hilary Davis. *Preaching in the Spanish Golden Age: A Study of Some Preachers of the Reign of Philip III.* Oxford: Oxford University Press, 1978.

Smith, Richard Travers. *St. Basil the Great.* Memphis, TN: General Books, 1879. Reprinted, 2010.

Southern, R.W. *Western Society and the Church in the Middle Ages.* Vol. 2 of *The Pelican History of the Church.* London: Penguin Books, 1970.

Stenton, Frank M. *Anglo-Saxon England.* Oxford: Oxford University Press, 1965.

Stott, John R. *Between Two Worlds: The Art of Preaching in the Twentieth Century.* Grand Rapids, MI: Eerdmans, 1982.

Strack, Hermann. *Introduction to the Talmud and Midrash*. New York: Harper & Row, 1965.

Thompson, William M., ed. *Berulle and the French School: Selected Writings*. Classics of Western Spirituality. New York: Paulist Press, 1989.

Thompson, Newton and Stock, Raymond. *Concordance to the Bible*. Fort Collins, CO: Roman Catholic Books, 1942.

Tisdale, Leonora T. *Preaching as Local Theology and Folk Art*. Minneapolis, MN: Fortress, 1997.

Toal, M.F., ed. *The Sunday Sermons of the Great Fathers*. 4 vols. Swedesboro, NJ: Preservation Press, 1996.

Tolkien, J.R.R. *Tree and Leaf*. Boston: Houghton Mifflin, 1964.

Trigg, Joseph Wilson. *Origen*. Atlanta: John Knox Press, 1983.

Trochu, Abbe Francis. *The Curé D'Ars: St. Jean-Marie-Baptiste Vianney, 1786–1859*. Rockford, IL: Tan Books, 1977.

Trouncer, Margaret. *Saint John-Marie Vianney: Curé of Ars*. New York: Sheed & Ward, 1959.

Tugwell, Simon, ed. *Early Dominicans: Selected Writings*. Classics of Western Spirituality. New York: Paulist Press, 1982.

Vianney, Joseph. *Saint John Vianney: Curé d'Ars, Patron of Parish Priests*. London: Burns, Oates & Washburne, 1929.

Vicaire, Marie-Humbert. *Saint Dominic and His Times*. London: Dartman, Longman & Todd, 1964.

Vickers, Brian. *In Defense of Rhetoric*. Oxford: Clarendon Press, 1988.

Vidler, Alec. R. *The Church in an Age of Revolution, 1789 to the present*. Vol. 5 of *The Pelican History of the Church*. London: Penguin Books, 1961.

Von Rad, Gerhard. *Genesis*. rev. ed. Old Testament Library. Philadelphia: Westminster John Knox, 1973.

———. *Old Testament Theology*. Translated by David Stalker. 2 vols. New York: Harper & Row, 1962–1965.

Warre Cornish, Francis. *The English Church in the Nineteenth Century*. 2 vols. London: Macmillan, 1910.

Weigel, George. *Witness to Hope: The Biography of Pope John Paul II*. New York: Cliff Street Books, 1999.

———. *The End and the Beginning: Pope John Paul II—The Victory of Freedom, the Last Years, the Legacy*. New York: Doubleday, 2010.

Williams, Michael E. *The Venerable English College Rome: A History, 1579–1979*. Dublin: Cahill, 1979.

Willimon, William H. "The Preacher as an Extension of the Preaching Moment." In *Preaching On the Brink: The Future of Homiletics*. Edited by Martha J. Simmons. Nashville: Abingdon Press, 1997.

Wilson, Paul Scott. *A Concise History of Preaching*. Nashville: Abingdon Press, 1992.

Wojtyla, Karol. (Pope John Paul II). *Sources of Renewal: The Implementation of the Second Vatican Council*. New York: Harper & Row, 1980.

Wolff, Hans Walter. *Jonah: Church in Revolt*. St. Louis: Clayton, 1978.

Zawart, Anscar. *The History of Franciscan Preaching and of Franciscan Preachers, 1209–1927*. Washington D.C: The Franciscan Education Conference, 1927.

Zimmerli, Walther. *Ezekiel*. Philadelphia: Westminster Press, 1979.

MAGISTERIAL DOCUMENTS

Benedict XV. Encyclical on St. Dominic *Fausto Appetente Die* (June 29, 1921). http://www.vatican.va/holy_father/benedict_xv/encyclicals/documents/hf_ben-xv_enc_29061921_fausto-appetente-die_en.html

——. Encyclical on Preaching the Word of God *Humani Generis Redemptionen* (June 17, 1917). http://www.vatican.va/holy_father/benedict_xv/encyclicals/documents/hf_ben-xv_enc_15061917_humani-generis-redemptionem_en.html

——. Encyclical on St. Boniface *In Hac Tanta* (May 14, 1919). http://www.vatican.va/holy_father/benedict_xv/encyclicals/documents/hf_ben-xv_enc_14051919_in-hac-tanta_en.html

——. Encyclical on St. Ephrem the Syrian *Principi Apostolorum Petro* (October 5, 1920). ttp://www.vatican.va/holy_father/benedict_xv/encyclicals/documents/hf_ben-xv_enc_05101920_principi-apostolorum-petro_en.html

Benedict XVI. Apostolic Exhortation on The Eucharist as the Source and Summit of the Church's Life and Mission *Sacramentum Caritatis* (February 22, 2007). http://www.vatican.va/holy_father/benedict_xvi/apost_exhortations/documents/hf_ben-xvi_exh_20070222_sacramentum-caritatis_en.html

Bishops' Committee on Priestly Life and Ministry—National Conference of Catholic Bishops. *Fulfilled In Your Hearing: The Homily in the Sunday Assembly.* Washington, DC: United States Catholic Conference, 1999.

Congregation for the Clergy. *Directory for the Life and Ministry of Priests.* Rome: Libreria Editrice Vaticana, 1994.

——. *The Priest and the Third Millennium: Teacher of the Word, Minister of the Sacraments, and Leader of the Community.* Rome: Libreria Editione Vaticana, 1999.

John XXIII. Encyclical on St. John Vianney *Sacerdotii Nostri Primordia* (August 1, 1959). http://www.vatican.va/holy_father/john_xxiii/encyclicals/documents/hf_j-xxiii_enc_19590801_sacerdotii_en.html

John Paul II. Address on the Occasion of the Eighth Centenary of St. Anthony of Padua's Birth (13 June 1994). http://www.ewtn.com/library/PAPALDOC/JP940613.HTM

——. Apostolic Letter on Augustine of Hippo *Augustinum Hipponensem* (August 28, 1986). http://www.vatican.va/holy_father/john_paul_ii/apost_letters/documents/hf_jp-ii_apl_26081986_augustinum-hipponensem_en.html

——. Apostolic Letter on Keeping the Lord's Day Holy *Dies Domini* (July 7, 1998). http://www.vatican.va/holy_father/john_paul_ii/apost_letters/documents/hf_jp-i_apl_05071998_dies-domini_en.html

——. Instruction on the Most Holy Eucharist *Redemptionis Sacramentum* (March 25, 2004). http://www.vatican.va/roman_curia/congregations/ccdds/documents/rc_con_ccdds_doc_20040423_redemptionis-sacramentum_en.html

——. Letter on the Mystery and Worship of the Eucharist *Dominicae Cenae* (February 24, 1980). http://www.vatican.va/holy_father/john_paul_ii/letters/documents/hf_jp-ii_let_24021980_dominicae-cenae_en.html

——. Letter to Priests on the Cure of Ars for Holy Thursday 1986 (March 16, 1986). http://www.ewtn.com/library/PAPALDOC/JP2CUR.htm

John Paul II and Eight Vatican Dicasteries. *Instruction on Certain Questions Regarding the Collaboration of the Non-Ordained Faithful in the Sacred Ministry of Priest* (November 13, 1997). http://www.vatican.va/roman_curia/pontifical_councils/laity/documents/rc_con_interdic_doc_15081997_en.html

Leo XIII. Encyclical on the Study of Holy Scripture *Providentissimus Deus* (November 18, 1893). *Acta Apostolicae Sedis* 23 (1931): 433–38.

Paul VI. Apostolic Exhortation on Evangelization in the Modern World *Evangelii Nuntiandi* (December 8, 1975). http://www.vatican.va/holy_father/paul_vi/apost _exhortations/documents/hf_p-vi_exh_19751208_evangelii-nuntiandi_en.html

Pius XI. Encyclical on the Catholic Priesthood *Ad Catholici Sacerdotii* (December 20, 1935). http://www.vatican.va/holy_father/pius_xi/encyclicals/documents/hf_p-i_enc _19351220_ad-catholici-sacerdotii_en.html

Pius XII. Encyclical on Promoting Biblical Studies *Divino Afflante Spiritu* (September 30, 1943). *Acta Apostolicae Sedis* 35 (1943): 290–345.

———. Encyclical on the Sacred Liturgy *Mediator Dei* (November 20, 1947). Boston, MA: St. Paul Books & Media, 1947.

Sacred Congregation for the Sacraments and Divine Worship. Instruction Concerning Worship of the Eucharistic Mystery *Inestimabile Donum* (April 17, 1980). Boston, MA: St. Paul Books & Media, 1980.

United States Conference of Catholic Bishops. *General Instruction of the Roman Missal.* Washington, DC: United States Conference of Catholic Bishops, 2011.

JOURNAL ARTICLES

Bossy, John. "The Counter-Reformation and the People of Catholic Europe." *Past and Present* 47 (1970): 51–70.

Buckley, James. "Contraception: A Challenge to Catholic preaching." *Homiletic & Pastoral Review* (January 1997): 22–25.

Burghardt, Walter. "Fire in the Belly: From Experience Through Imagination to Passion." *Seminary Journal* no. 3 (Winter 1997): 33–42.

Burke, John. "The gift of the priestly homilist." *Homiletic & Pastoral Review.* (November 1999): 12–20.

Connors, Joseph M. "Saint Charles Borromeo in the Homiletic Tradition." *The American Ecclesiastical Review* 138 (1958): 9–23.

Dailey, Thomas F. "The soulful homily." *Homiletic & Pastoral Review* (May 2000): 56–60.

Fantz, Donald. "Saint Robert Bellarmine." *Angelus* 1, no. 12 (December 1978): 1–3.

Filson, Floyd V. "The Christian Teacher in the First Century." *Journal of Biblical Literature* 60 (1941): 317–28.

Hardon, John A. "St. Robert Bellarmine—Preacher," *Homiletic & Pastoral Review* 47, no. 3 (December 1947): 186–92.

Hay, C. "Antiochene Exegesis and Christology." *Australian Biblical Review* 12 (1969): 10–23.

Heuser, Herman. J. "Saint Charles Borromeo as a Preacher." *The American Ecclesiastical Review* 7 (1892): 332–40.

Jones, A.H.M. "St. John Chrysostom's Parentage and Education." *Harvard Theological Review* 46: 171–73.

Kingsbury, J.D. "Form and Message in Matthew." *Interpretation* 29 (1975): 13–23.

Landes, G. M. "The 'Three Days and Three Nights' Motif in Jonah 2:1." *Journal of Biblical Literature* 86 (1967): 446–450.

Landini, Lawrence C. "St. Anthony of Padua: Portrait of the Ideal Preacher." *Josephinum Journal of Theology* 4, no. 2 (1997): 51–60.

MacMullen, Ramsey, "The Preacher's Audience." *The Journal of Theological Studies* 40 (1989): 503–11.

McManamon, John M. "The Ideal Renaissance Pope: Funeral Oratory from the Papal Court." *Archivum Historiae Pontificiae* 14 (1976): 9–70.

Marks, Frederick W. "Silence in the pulpit." *Homiletic & Pastoral Review.* (June 2000): 8–14.

McGinness, Frederick. "Preaching Ideals and Practice in Counter-Reformation Rome." *The Sixteenth Century Journal* 11, no. 2 (1980): 109–27.

McElvaney, William K. "Speaking Out From the Pulpit: No One Can Assume the Prophetic Mantle of Preaching for Long without Learning Some Lessons." *The Christian Ministry* 13 (May 1982): 5–8.

Melloh, John Allyn, "Preaching and Liturgy," *Worship* 65 (1991): 409–20.

Menoud, Philippe-H. "Revelation and Tradition: The Influence of Paul's Conversion on His Theology." *Interpretation* 7 (1953): 131–41.

Musurillo, Herbert. "The Problem of Ascetical Fasting in the Greek Patristic Writers." *Traditio* 12 (1956): 1–64.

Pavone, Frank A. "Preaching On Abortion From Scripture." *Priests for Life letter.* n.d.

Stasiak, Kurt. "Twelve Pleas from the pews." *Homiletic & Pastoral Review* (January 1999): 52–57.

———. "Five pleas from the pulpit." *Homiletic & Pastoral Review* (March 2000): 31–32, 44–48.

Tuck, William. "Preaching From Jeremiah." *Review & Expositor* 78 (Summer 1981): 381–94.

Unknown author. "Preaching in the Modern World." *Touchstone* 12, no. 3 (Spring 1997): 1, 4–5.

Wainwright, Geoffrey. "Preaching as Worship." *The Greek Orthodox Theological Review* 28 (Winter 1983): 325–36.

———. "The Sermon and the Liturgy." *The Greek Orthodox Theological Review* 28 (Winter 1983): 337–49.

Wilmart, A. "Easter Sermons of St. Augustine." *Journal of Theological Studies* 28 (1926): 113–34.

Young, John. "When homilies err by omission." *Homiletic & Pastoral Review* (February 2000): 19–23.

NEWSPAPER / NEWSMAGAZINE ARTICLES

Burghardt, Walter J. "Preaching: Twenty-Five Tips." *Church Magazine*, reprint 1996.

Craughwell, Thomas J. "Archbishop Sheen's Sainthood Cause Takes Next Step." *Our Sunday Visitor*, February 10, 2008.

Crowe, Marian E. "Don't Just Preach to Us About Safe Subjects! A Plea to the Clergy from the Pews." *New Oxford Review*, June 1996: 8–13.

Curran, Dolores. "And Then God Said, 'Lighten Up.'" *St. Anthony Messenger*, July 1997, 11–14.

Daly, Peter. "Homily Preparation in 10 steps." *The Witness,* April 19, 1988.

Dangel, Mary Jo. "Passionate." *St. Anthony Messenger*, May 1998, 36–40.

Gledhill, Ruth. "Liberal and weak clergy blamed for empty pews." The Times (UK), March 5, 2005. http://www.timesonline.co.uk/tol/news/uk/article419489.ece

Hemrick, Eugene. "A good homily?" *The Witness*, June 14, 1998.

Hughes, Lawrence M. "Bishop Sheen's Sponsor." *Catholic Digest*, May 1956, 17–21.

National Catholic Register. "Swedish Pastor's Conviction Overturned." February 11, 2005.

New York Times. "Thousands at St. Agnes Church Hear Sheen in Good Friday Rite." March 25, 1978.

O'Malley, William J. "Ten Commandments for Homilists." *America*, July 23–30, 1983.

Richburg, Keith B. and Alan Cooperman. "Swede's Sermon on Gays: Bigotry or Free Speech?" *Washington Post*, January 29, 2005, A1.

Roa, Gregory K. "Homilies from the Heart: The Life of John Chrysostom." *The Word Among us.* Lent 2007, 65–71.

Rodgers, Ann. "Claim of miracle studied for archbishop to be beatified." *Pittsburgh Post-Gazette*, August 27, 2006. http://www.post-gazette.com/pg/06239/716418-85 .stm

Rodriguez-Soto. "Priest offers tips for preparing better homilies." *The Witness*, June 21, 1998, 1.

Shan, Cardinal Paul. "To Be Converted in Order to Convert: A homily preached during the International Assembly of Priests in Mexico City, July 1998." *Sacerdos*, April 1999, 13–16.

Shaw, Russell. "Coping with Lousy Homilies." *Lay Witness*, November 1997, 10–12.

The Wanderer. "Possible Archbishop Sheen Miracle Sent to Rome." Sept. 14, 2006.

Willke, Dr. J.C. "Why Preach Against Abortion?" *Life Issues Today* Cincinnati, OH: 1997.

Wright, Gerald. "Thoughts on Preaching." *Soul Magazine*, February 1995, 10–11.

Index of Homilies

Index

About the Author

Reverend Ray E. Atwood is a Catholic priest serving in the Archdiocese of Dubuque, Iowa. He holds a Bachelor of Arts in Journalism/Mass Communications from Drake University in Des Moines, a Master of Divinity Degree and a Master of Arts Degree in Systematic Theology from the Josephinum Seminary in Columbus, Ohio. He is currently serving as pastor of Holy Rosary Cluster (consisting of Immaculate Conception Parish, Riceville; St. Peter's Parish, New Haven; St. Bernard's Parish, Alta Vista; Our Lady of Lourdes Parish, Lourdes; and Immaculate Conception Parish, Elma).

Printed in Great Britain
by Amazon